Intergenerational Justice

Intergenerational Justice

EDITED BY
Axel Gosseries and Lukas H. Meyer

OXFORD
UNIVERSITY PRESS

OXFORD
UNIVERSITY PRESS

Great Clarendon Street, Oxford OX2 6DP

Oxford University Press is a department of the University of Oxford.
It furthers the University's objective of excellence in research, scholarship,
and education by publishing worldwide in

Oxford New York

Auckland Cape Town Dar es Salaam Hong Kong Karachi
Kuala Lumpur Madrid Melbourne Mexico City Nairobi
New Delhi Shanghai Taipei Toronto

With offices in

Argentina Austria Brazil Chile Czech Republic France Greece
Guatemala Hungary Italy Japan Poland Portugal Singapore
South Korea Switzerland Thailand Turkey Ukraine Vietnam

Oxford is a registered trademark of Oxford University Press
in the UK and in certain other countries

Published in the United States
by Oxford University Press Inc., New York

British Library Cataloguing in Publication Data

Data available

Library of Congress Cataloging in Publication Data

Intergenerational justice/edited by Axel Gosseries and Lukas H. Meyer.
p. cm.
Includes bibliographical references and index.
ISBN 978-0-19-928295-1
1. Intergenerational relations. 2. Justice. I. Gosseries, Axel. II. Meyer, Lukas H.
HM726.I465 2009
320.01'1—dc22   2008053086

Typeset by Laserwords Private Limited, Chennai, India
Printed in Great Britain
on acid-free paper by
CPI Antony Rowe, Chippenham, Wiltshire

ISBN 978-0-19-928295-1

10 9 8 7 6 5 4 3 2 1

Contents

Notes on the Contributors

GUSTAF ARRHENIUS is Torgny Segerstedt Pro Futuris Fellow at the Swedish Collegium for Advanced Study and Reader (Docent) in Practical Philosophy at Department of Philosophy, Stockholm University. He is also an Affiliated Researcher at the Oxford Uehiro Centre for Practical Ethics and a Chercheur invite at CERSES, CNRS. Arrhenius has written extensively on our moral obligations to future generations, applying the methods of social choice and game theory. His papers have appeared in *Economics & Philosophy*, *Philosophical Studies*, *Utilitas*, and in many other journals and collections. He can be contacted at Gustaf.Arrhenius@philosophy.su.se

DANIEL ATTAS is senior lecturer in Philosophy and director of the Integrative Program: Philosophy, Economics, Political Science at the Hebrew University of Jerusalem. He is author of *Liberty, Property and Markets: a Critique of Libertarianism* (Ashgate, 2005).

CHRISTOPHER BERTRAM is Professor of Social and Political Philosophy at the University of Bristol and author of *Rousseau and The Social Contract* (Routledge, 2005) and various papers in political philosophy. He can be contacted at C.Bertram@bris.ac.uk

DIETER BIRNBACHER is Professor of Philosophy at the Heinrich-Heine-Universität Duesseldorf. He is the author of *Verantwortung für zukünftige Generationen* (Stuttgart, 1988), translated into French under the title *La responsabilité envers les générations futures* (Paris, 1994). He can be contacted at dieter.birnbacher@uni-duesseldorf.de

KRISTER BYKVIST is Tutor and Fellow in Philosophy at Jesus College, Oxford. He is the author of many papers on consequentialism, well-being and prudence, including 'The benefits of coming into existence' *Philosophical Studies* (2007) 135/3, 335–62, 'Prudence for changing selves' *Utilitas*, (2006) 18/3, and 'Violations of normative invariance: Some thoughts on shifty oughts' *Theoria* (2007) 73/2. He is now working on a book-length project on well-being for changing selves.

STEPHEN M. GARDINER is an Associate Professor in the Department of Philosophy and the Program on Values in Society at the University of Washington, Seattle. He is the editor of *Virtue Ethics: Old and New* (Cornell, 2005), and the author of *A Perfect Moral Storm* (Oxford, forthcoming). He can be contacted at smgard@u.washington.edu

AXEL GOSSERIES is a Permanent Research Fellow of the Fonds de la Recherche Scientifique (Belgium) and a professor at the Université catholique de Louvain. He holds an LL.M. (London, 2006) and a PhD in philosophy (Louvain, 2000). He is the author of *Penser la justice entre les générations* (Aubier-Flammarion, 2004) as well as contributing to books and journals such as *Economics and Philosophy*, *Journal of Political*

Philosophy, Canadian Journal of Philosophy, International Economics Review or *Politics, Philosophy and Economics.* He can be contacted at axel.gosseries@uclouvain.be

DAVID HEYD is Chaim Perelman Professor of Philosophy at the Hebrew University of Jerusalem. He is author of *Supererogation* (Cambridge University Press, 1982) and *Genethics* (California, 1992), and editor of *Toleration* (Princeton, 1996). His publications include articles on political and moral philosophy as well as bioethics. He can be contacted at david.heyd@huji.ac.il

RAHUL KUMAR is Associate Professor of Philosophy at Queen's University, Canada. His current research focuses on issues concerning the normative basis of intergenerational claims to reparations.

LUKAS H. MEYER is Professor of Practical Philosophy at the Karl-Franzens-University Graz, Austria. He is the author of Historische Gerechtigkeit (Berlin and New York: de Gruyter, 2005) and of articles on political and moral philosophy, especially intergenerational justice. He is also the editor of *Legitimacy, Justice and Public International Law* (Cambridge: CUP, forthcoming), *Justice in Time* (Baden-Baden: Nomos, 2004), the co-editor of *Rights, Culture and the Law* (Oxford: OUP, 2003) and of *Neukantianismus und Rechtsphilosophie* (Baden-Baden: Nomos, 2002).

VÍCTOR M. MUÑIZ-FRATICELLI is Assistant Professor of Law and Political Science at McGill University. He can be contacted at victor.muniz@mcgill.ca

DOMINIC ROSER is a doctoral student at the University of Zurich. He works on climate justice and on issues at the interface of ethics and economics. He can be contacted at roser@ethik.uzh.ch

HILLEL STEINER is Professor of Political Philosophy at the University of Manchester and a Fellow of the British Academy. He is the author of *An Essay on Rights* (1994) and co-author of *A Debate Over Rights: Philosophical Enquiries* (with Matthew Kramer and Nigel Simmonds, 1998). He is also co-editor of *The Origins of Left-Libertarianism: An Anthology of Historical Writings*, and *Left-Libertarianism and Its Critics: The Contemporary Debate* (with Peter Vallentyne, 2000), and of *Freedom: A Philosophical Anthology* (with Ian Carter and Matthew Kramer, 2007). He can be contacted at hillel.steiner@manchester.ac.uk

JANNA THOMPSON is an Associate Professor in philosophy at La Trobe University in Melbourne, Australia. She is the author of *Taking Responsibility for the Past: Reparation and Historic Injustice* (Cambridge: Polity Press, 2002).

PETER VALLENTYNE is Florence G. Kline Professor of Philosophy at the University of Missouri-Columbia. He writes on issues of liberty and equality-and left-libertarianism in particular. He is co-editor of the journal *Economics and Philosophy*. He edited *Equality and Justice* (Routledge, 2003, 6 volumes) and *Contractarianism and Rational Choice: Essays on David Gauthier's Morals by Agreement* (CUP, 1991), and he co-edited, with Hillel Steiner, *The Origins of Left Libertarianism: An Anthology of Historical Writings and Left Libertarianism and Its Critics: The Contemporary Debate* (Palgrave Publishers Ltd., 2000). He can be contacted at vallentynep@missouri.edu

CLARK WOLF is Director of Bioethics, and Associate Professor in the department of philosophy at Iowa State University. His papers have appeared in *Ethics, Philosophical Studies, Ethics and the Environment,* and in many other journals and collections. He can be contacted atjwcwolf@iastate.edu

Acknowledgements

We would like to thank the following colleagues for their invaluable critical support and, in many instances, for having contributed to the double- blind peer-review process undertaken for all the chapters of the book:

Richard J. Arneson, N. Scott Arnold, Bruce Auerbach, Brian Barry, Brian H. Bix, Alyssa R. Bernstein, Daniel Butt, Ann E. Cudd, Garrett Cullity, Geert Demuijnck, Avner De-Shalit, Marc-Antoine Dilhac, Speranta Dumitru, Katherine Eddy, Cécile Fabre, Christoph Fehige, Marc Fleurbaey, Andreas Føllesdal,, Roberto Gargarella, Olivier Godard, Stefan Gosepath, Rafaela Hillerbrand, John Horton, Richard B. Howarth, Sarah Kenehan, Kasper Lippert-Rasmussen, Christoph Lumer, Martin O'Neill, Michael Otsuka, Edward A. Page, Stanley L. Paulson, Grégory Ponthière, Per Sandin, Pranay Sanklecha, Daniel Statman, Christine Tappolet, Kimberly A. Wade-Benzoni, Peter Vallentyne, Will Waluchow, Andrew Williams, and Jonathan Wolff.

The editors we also wish to warmly thank; Peter Momtchiloff, Catherine Berry, Georgia Berry, Clare Hofmann, Michelle Thompson, Ceri Warner, and Janet Yarker at the Oxford University Press along with Keith Bustos at the University of Bern for their very fine work all along the way in the production of the volume.

Axel Gosseries and Lukas H. Meyer, Spring 2009

Introduction—Intergenerational Justice and Its Challenges

AXEL GOSSERIES AND LUKAS H. MEYER

Issues of intergenerational justice have long fascinated philosophers and political thinkers. Already at the end of the eighteenth century, Thomas Jefferson (1789) and Thomas Paine (1791) had a dispute with Edmund Burke (1790) on the intergenerational fairness of having a constitution, focusing on a concern for generational sovereignty. Although the reader will see traces of that old debate in this volume,[1] the current philosophical debate focuses less on generational sovereignty than on intergenerational justice. It is informed by a general context comprising concerns for e.g. the long-term consequences of climate change and for the survival of social security schemes as we know them. This debate draws on contributions from major authors in philosophy who seriously began to re-consider these issues in the second half of the last century, including most importantly Rawls (1971: esp. § 44), Barry (1978, 1989), and Gauthier (1986), as well as Jonas (1979), Parfit (1984, part IV), and Heyd (1992). Today there is a highly specialised and ongoing discussion in the journals along with a good number of monographs, including Birnbacher (1988), Weiss (1989), de-Shalit (1995), Auerbach (1995), Visser't Hooft (1999), Arrhenius (2000), Gosseries (2004), Meyer (2005), Mulgan (2006), and Page (2006). There are also a number of edited volumes specifically devoted to issues concerning intergenerational justice, including Sikora & Barry (1978), Partridge (1981), Laslett & Fishkin (1992), Fotion & Heller (1997), Dobson (1999), Meyer (2004), Ryberg & Tännsjö (2004), and Roemer and Suzumara (2007).

For invaluable support in preparing and polishing this Introduction we would like to thank Stanley L. Paulson, Brian H. Bix, Sarah Kenehan, and Pranay Sanklecha.

[1] See in this volume, the chapters by Thompson and by Muñiz-Fraticelli (Chapters 1 and 14).

The aim of the present volume is to offer a sustained discussion of intergen-erational justice as seen by practical philosophers. Our aim here is specific. First, we want to broaden the focus beyond the mere non–identity problem (to which we come back below). This is not meant to downplay the significance of and the difficulties that arise with this dilemma. Indeed, it is conspicuous in this volume, and the non–identity problem plays a significant role in a number of the arguments presented here. Still, we think that far too little attention has been paid to other issues that strike us as being at least as significant from a strictly philosophical point of view, as well as from a practical perspective. It is this deficiency that led us to structure the volume into two parts. The first part focuses on the way in which various schools of thought in moral and political philosophy approach the domain of intergenerational justice, while the second part focuses on more specific aspects, such as how these theories address the question of motivation, how they deal with demographic fluctuations, or how they can be applied to real-world issues such as climate change.

In addition, we have also taken great care to emphasize the extent to which intergenerational justice raises issues that are distinct from, for example, international justice, which is often seen as another significant 'extension' of standard domestic justice. Whether it follows that *sui generis* principles are required for the intergenerational domain remains an open question. Yet, what is clear is that this question cannot be answered unless and until we first determine what can be made in the intragenerational realm of standard theories of justice as they generally apply to domestic justice issues. To this end, the chapters in Part I of this volume take up and discuss what contribution standard theories can make to our understanding of intergenerational justice.

What's So Special About the Intergenerational Realm?

It is often claimed that issues of justice between generations are special. Still, there remains a lot of work to do, namely, in identifing these special features and their normative implications. This is particularly important with respect to the possibility of intergenerational obligations and the content of such obligations. In this Introduction, we will simply adumbrate some of these features, inviting attention to some of their implications. The various chapters will then develop several of these points in greater detail.

The unique features that distinguish issues of justice between generations from other issues of justice are often at the heart of key challenges. For example, some of these features potentially threaten the possibility of intergenerational obligations. Consider the fact, harmless enough at first glance, that future people do not exist today. The non-existence challenge implies that obligations can only make sense when they are owed to people who actually exist. People who did exist in the past or who could exist in the future would thus not qualify as rightful recipients of such obligations. Another distinctive and problematic feature is rooted in the fact that the composition of future generations (that is, whether it be Paul or John who comes into existence) depends in many cases on our own actions. This, of course, leads to the famous non-identity challenge. For those committed to a standard notion of harm necessarily involving a comparison between two alternative states of a single person (an actual state and a counterfactual one), the fact of non-identity can threaten the very possibility of harming future people. For those who claim that an obligation can only make sense if its violation can be associated with harming someone, then the fact of non-identity is a major challenge to the idea of obligations owed toward future people, as Meyer and Roser explain in Chapter 8.

Related to the non-identity challenge is the problem of optimal population, addressed by Arrhenius in Chapter 12. This problem is rooted in the idea that it is not only difficult to tell which of two options is better if different people are actually going to live under each of the two options, but it is equally difficult to pinpoint the optimal population size when the very answer to the first question will necessarily have an effect on the number of people coming into existence. This difficulty is obvious when we ask, 'For whom would it be better to have a larger or a smaller population?'. For someone whose very existence is contingent on the demographic decision at stake, how can we possibly say that a larger population or a smaller one would, *ceteris paribus*, be better?

Moreover, for some theories, the absence of *overlap* between generations, that is, the absence of physical co-existence between non-contemporaries, constitutes a further key challenge to the possibility of having obligations of justice to future people. This is especially so in the case of mutual advantage theories, a problem addressed in Gardiner's chapter. In deciding what to bequeath to our children, being in a position to engage in a dialogue with them may well be important. And for some, obligations are inconceivable unless mutual enforceability can be guaranteed. Still, we must be careful to distinguish the idea of an overlap (or its absence) from other closely related features, such as remoteness in time. The fact that one person was born one year after the death of another may be significant. Yet, if their respective existences were separated by a period of 300 years, for example, then the nature of the issues arising would probably differ due to more significant uncertainties.

Thus, in deciding what to bequeath to our great-grandchildren, additional uncertainties obtain, such as whether their own parents will fulfill their own obligations toward them, how many children our grand-children will have, and how technological evolutions will transform society. Complicating these issues is the fact that both overlap (or the lack thereof) and relative remoteness in time can have different sorts of consequences depending on the theory one adopts.

There are additional factors that will affect either the *possibility* of obligations of justice between generations or the *content* of such obligations, again with different impacts stemming from the application of different theories. Consider, for example, the ability of a theory to come to terms with an indefinite number of generations. Uncertainty regarding the number of generations is especially problematic for aggregative theories. If one cares about fairly dividing the intergenerational cake of well-being, it is important to know how many guests will be present at the table. Moreover, a non-ideal theory of justice needs to address the problem of non-compliance by both earlier generations and future generations. If earlier generations did not respect their own intergenerational obligations, should this affect the extent to which present generations ought to comply with these obligations? And should the likelihood of future non-compliance have an impact on the content or very existence of our own intergenerational obligations? Similarly, the sequentiality of generations not only generates dependence on the behaviour of earlier or later generations, but it also entails, for example, asymmetries of knowledge associated with variable time location (that is, someone tends to have more information about facts and events that are contemporaries to her than about those that would be remote in the future or in the past). Finally, as mentioned earlier, time distance (or remoteness) as such (in addition to time location and the absence of overlap per se) also has implications, not only in epistemic terms (greater uncertainty about what is remote), but also in motivational terms. This is exhibited by the fact that we may care more about our close relatives than about our distant ones.

As noted, these challenges do not affect the various theories in the same way, nor does each of these difficulties affect all types of intergenerational relations (with past or future generations, with overlap or without). For example, some theories depend less than others on the existence of an overlap. And we should not lose sight of the fact that justice between neighbouring generations is not, as such, a negligible field of investigation, as those insisting on justice between non-overlapping and remote generations may too quickly assume. Some theories are also less demo-sensitive than others, in the sense that they will render the content of our intergenerational obligations less dependent on the size of the next generations. And furthermore, some theories need to refer to obligations toward dead people in order to justify obligations toward future people, whereas others do not.

In short, in studying the normative implications of each of the specific features of intergenerational relations, it is crucial to understand that different theories of intergenerational justice will interpret each of the aforementioned characteristics differently. Moreover, what the particular implications are will also be important in assessing the relative consistency of various theories of justice. If a standard theory fares better than another in accounting for our intuitions of justice in the intergenerational realm, then this can be used as an argument in favour of this theory in general.

Before moving to a presentation of the chapters of this volume, let us also explain what areas of the ongoing debate in intergenerational justice we *do not* cover. To begin with, we will not be looking at our obligations toward dead people, nor will we address issues of historical injustice understood as determining what one community owes another today as a result of what their respective ancestors did to each other in the past. These issues are important when we consider the history of slavery in the United States, the various forms of dispossessesion forced upon the aboriginal peoples of several continents, the inflicting of countless atrocities on those of Jewish ancestry and on Gypsies during World War Two, and, more recently, the significance of historical emissions of carbon dioxide.[2] At the other end of the spectrum, we shall also leave aside the Jonassian issue of possible justifications for guaranteeing that future generations will continue to exist (as opposed to determining what we owe them *if* we can anticipate that they will exist).

Furthermore, issues of justice between age groups, in so far as they can be separated out from issues of justice between birth cohorts, will not be taken up either. Social sciences tend to use a distinction between cohort effects and age effects. For example, it may be strictly due to age effects that a group of people suffers from deficient audition or poor memory. Whatever the cohort, people at the age of 90 tend not to have auditive capacities or memory abilities which are as sharp as those of people aged 20. Yet, it may also be the case that in comparing people at the same age from different birth cohorts (for example, those in their 40s born in 1920 compared to those born in 2000), some proper cohort effects may occur, for instance due to the intensive use of headphones at a young age in recent times, or to lesser memorization habits. It is often assumed that the difference between cohort effects and age effects may be linked to two distinct realms of justice, though this is far from

---

[2] For more on historical injustice, see e.g. Meyer (2004) and Gosseries (2004a).

certain. Yet, at the very least, this age-group/birth-cohort distinction should certainly not be confused with the distinction between overlapping and non-overlapping generations. Cohorts (that is, groups of people born at the same time) can overlap or not. Issues of justice between cohorts do not necessarily need to involve non-overlapping generations only. Conversely, when facing overlapping generations, issues of justice do not necessarily need to be analysed in terms of justice between age groups. Here, we will limit ourselves to issues of justice between birth cohorts, be they overlapping or not.[3]

An additional omission is that among the general theories of justice discussed in this text, none of the chapters of this volume focuses on utilitarianism. Attas, Gardiner, and Heyd, however, discuss Rawls's view on intergenerational justice and his principle of just savings.[4] The latter aims at specifying when and to what extent savings are required. It asks whether we should be allowed, forced, or prevented from transferring less or more to our immediate descendants. This is important, for Rawls's account is constructed at least in part as a response to the difficulties encountered by utilitarians in proposing a plausible principle of generational savings. Which principle of savings utilitarians would be able to propose once we have taken into serious consideration issues such as descending altruism, diminishing marginal utility, and the like, remains an interesting topic of further investigation.[5]

Finally, at the conceptual level, those interested in issues of legal theory will find one chapter devoted to constitutionalism. They will not find here, however, any systematic treatment of the way in which specific challenges to the idea of rights of future people affect different theories of justice.[6] Likewise, an examination of the possible use of the legal concepts found in contract and property theories as a way of expressing intergenerational obligations has, regrettably, been left out. For example, there are likely to be very different implications for the content of our obligations depending upon whether we conceptualize such obligations as involving a loan from our children, a gift from our parents, a right of usufruct, or a trusteeship (to name but a few possibilities). At a level of greater application, essays connecting specific views of justice with debates over the funding of pension schemes and over questions of public debt, as well as chapters comparing various indicators to measure intergenerational

---

[3] Those interested in whether a separate realm of issues of justice between age-groups arises should read authors such as Daniels (1988) or McKerlie (1989). This involves e.g. a discussion of the complete-life view, i.e. whether the relevant units of normative assessment should be people's complete lives or shorter segments of their lives. This has implications e.g. for the assessment of age-based discriminatory practices. Connected to that are also issues of age-specific obligations, such as what parents owe their children in terms of education and what children owe their parents in terms of care at old age.

[4] See Chapters 7, 3, and 6.   [5] See Roemer & Suzumura (2007).

[6] On these challenges, see e.g. Gosseries (2008).

transfers, would of course have been more than welcome (and would, indeed, have been included if only space had allowed). Still, with the fourteen chapters included in this volume, the reader will come to appreciate how much food for thought is already at hand, even after aknowledging all that we have had to set aside. Let us now turn briefly to the content of each of the chapters.

Part I: Theories

The first chapters of this volume provide alternative interpretations of intergenerational justice from the perspective of some of the most influential accounts of what we owe to each other: communitarianism, libertarianism, contractualism, contractarianism, marxism, reciprocity-based views, and sufficientarianism.

In arguing for intergenerational obligations from a broadly communitarian perspective, we will want to take into account the interests of people as members of groups that have a past and a future. Indeed, as Thompson argues in Chapter 1, nations are best described as transgenerational polities, and consequently theories of justice, rights, and political responsibility ought to reflect the importance of transgenerational relationships. Thompson contends that liberal theories, in general, fail to do this for reasons related to the non-identity problem, or due to the impossibility of contracting with people who do not exist. In short, she argues that the communitarian perspective can more successfully incorporate intergenerational obligations than can contract theories. Still, this view also faces problems. A strong communitarian view runs into familiar and persuasive objections, including the idea that citizens in a modern multi-cultural nation state are unlikely to have a common identity of the sort she describes. In contrast, weak communitarianism allows that identities can be complex, and in this way it escapes such criticisms as are levelled against strong communitarianism. Nonetheless, weak communitarianism faces the challenge of explaining why present generations ought to accept obligations with respect to the future or the past.

Thompson argues that weak communitarianism can avoid the aforementioned problem by relying on the idea of lifetime-transcending interests. Lifetime-transcending interests are those interests that have as their subject matter events, objects, or states of affairs that either existed before the lifetime of the person who has that interest or that will exist after her lifetime (or, at any rate, could exist after her lifetime). This idea is probably best illustrated by considering the concerns we have regarding how our children or grandchildren will fare in the future, our posthumous reputations, the fate of projects we will leave behind upon our death, and the deeds of our ancestors. These special interests that Thompson describes play an important role in the lives of individuals and the formation of their identities for two reasons: they are essential for a meaningful life and required for making a rational plan for one's life. Furthermore, the existence of lifetime-transcending interests makes it likely that those who have such interests will be inclined to make demands on their successors. As a result, Thompson argues, one ought to meet certain morally legitimate demands created by other people's lifetime-transcendent interests. Moreover, members of communities have a moral interest in maintaining practices and institutions that enable legitimate lifetime-transcending demands to be made and fulfilled. This argument can be extended to include transgenerational obligations that people have as members of political societies. Trangenerational obligations arise in this context since members of political societies will have liftime-transcending interests. As such, they will also have a moral interest in the maintenance of practices and institutions that facilitate the making and fulfilling of lifetime-transcending interests and that provide for the conditions that make the flourishing of these practices possible.

Libertarianism offers a very different account of intergenerational justice. Self-ownership and the moral powers to appropriate unowned external resources are the main components of libertarianism, as explained by Steiner and Vallentyne in Chapter 2. Most important for a libertarian interpretation of intergenerational issues is the applicable account of the appropriation and use of external resources. Steiner and Vallentyne take as a starting point a Lockean type of libertarianism. They also stress the relevance of the 'choice-rights' versus 'interest-rights' debate for libertarians, since the possibility of recognizing rights to future people will depend crucially on whether an interest-protecting conception of rights is adopted. The authors also explore what a Lockean proviso—that requires to leave enough and as good to others—would require if applied in the intergenerational context. In doing this, they first distinguish between a mere 'decent share' proviso and an 'egalitarian' one, considering the former as possibly necessary but not sufficient, and defending the latter. Steiner and Vallentyne argue that one of the implications of the egalitarian proviso (understood as a requirement that no one be 'left with less than equally valuable initial [lifetime] opportunities to use natural/external/all resources') is that an accumulation phase (that is, a phase during which more is produced than is consumed, while, simultaneously, more is transferred to the next generation than was inherited from the previous one), such as the one argued for by Rawlsians, would be indefensible. Another implication of this proviso is that in cases in which a natural degradation of resources can be expected in the future, it would not be enough to merely make sure that the coming generations are no worse off than they would have otherwise been in our absence, as most libertarians may assume. Furthermore, it is not clear how practically to apply the proviso in the presence of generational overlap.

Steiner and Vallentyne conclude their chapter by discussing two intra-generational issues. First, since procreation is a (generally) voluntary act, who ought to have the responsibility for providing children with their fair share? Here, Steiner and Vallentyne argue that parents have a special responsibility while society at large acts at the same time as a default obligee. Second, what ought Lockean libertarians to think (and to do, if anything) about bequests and gifts? Respecting this second issue, the authors provide us with a fine-grained analysis, showing how an additional Lockean proviso on transfers (rather than on appropriation and use) is to be interpreted depending on whether the proviso applies to the transfer of natural goods, artefacts, and/or internal resources.

The problems of extending contract theories to issues of justice between generations is the subject of the Chapter 3. Gardiner first takes up challenges that both contractarians and contractualists (see also Chapter 9) face when they attempt to extend their approach to intergenerational relations, namely: Is cooperation beyond the overlap possible at all, and if so, will each generation have sufficiently strong reasons to engage in it? (Gardiner dubs this the 'rationale challenge'). Another challenge has to do with what Gardiner defines as the 'pure intergenerational problem' (the 'structural challenge'). The pure intergenerational problem differs in significant respects from a standard prisoner's dilemma. First, within the confines of the pure intergenerational problem, the obstacles to cooperation are not contingent as in the case of the standard prisoner's dilemma. Second, reducing, for example, current levels of pollution cannot be in everyone's interest, in contrast to what can happen in an intragenerational setting with a uniformly mixed pollutant. Gardiner then discusses how contractarians and contractualists can respond to these two challenges and explores whether their responses differ.

So, how are contract theorists to respond to such challenges? Gardiner takes up and assesses three possible strategies of extension. In the first two strategies, he attempts to bring the intergenerational problem closer to standard intra-generational settings by relying on the 'chain' idea, understood as a succession of interconnected generations (also discussed in this volume by Birnbacher[7]). The first of these strategies rests on the idea of 'local' cooperation at the overlap of and on the succession to such cooperation. Here, Gardiner discusses in detail the limitations of this approach, and to this end he employs the 'time bomb'

---

[7] See Chapter 10.

test case, which involves the hypothetical case of a generation setting up a time bomb that will only explode in the hands of a generation with which it does not overlap. The second approach that Gardiner explores consists of modifying the motivational assumption underlying contractarian approaches. And the third approach turns on introducing knowledge constraints on the reasoning of contractors, as per Rawls's veil of ignorance. Gardiner discusses these strategies in a specific way, focusing, among other things, on two issues: the problem of the initial generation and the problem of the generation of extinction. If we are unable to successfully defend any of these three approaches, all of them aiming at extending contract theories where the contractors are assumed to be contemporaries, then, Gardiner submits, we would have no choice but to consider the idea of a properly intergenerational contract involving all generations.

In Chapter 4, Gosseries discusses the idea of intergenerational reciprocity. Using a narrow definition of reciprocity, namely, one that precludes any of the parties in a reciprocal relationship from being either net contributors or net beneficiaries, Gosseries examines three reciprocity-based accounts of our intergenerational obligations. The first account, the descending model, holds that generation 2 (G2) owes something to generation 3 (G3) because generation 1 (G1) transferred something to G2, and so G2 owes at least as much to G3 as it received from G1. The second account, called the ascending model, holds that G3 owes something to G2 because G2 has transferred something to G1, with the proviso that this something is at least as much as what G2 transferred to G1. Finally, the double model holds that G2 owes something to G1 because G1 transferred something to G2, and G2 owes back at least as much as G1 transferred to it.

All these models, however, are confronted with a famous objection stemming from Barry: why does the mere fact of having received something justify an obligation falling on the receiver to give something back? To get around this objection, Gosseries argues that one strategy consists in extending the scope of the concept of free-riding and, further, that in the intergenerational context it could be claimed that by destroying (or failing to maintain) goods produced in the past, later generations are guilty of free-riding on the efforts of earlier generations. Understood as such, the obligation to reciprocate is grounded in the obligation to forbear from free-riding to the detriment of earlier generations. The objection from direction is also considered. That is, how is each model to justify the direction of reciprocity it upholds in each case? Gosseries dismisses this objection on the grounds that the alternatives for each model will force someone (person or generation) to be either a net contributor or net beneficiary, thereby violating the narrow reciprocity requirement.

Gosseries likewise considers the influence of the demographic variable (i.e. population fluctuations from one generation to the next) and asks whether the size of a population should affect the size and nature of changes in or the obligations that one generation has toward other generations. Gosseries argues that none of the three models can adequately deal with this question. If the models are insensitive to the relative size of populations (as the descending and ascending ones are), that leads either to counter-intuitive conclusions or to internal inconsistency. And while the double reciprocity model is indirectly sensitive to fluctuations in the relative size of populations, the incomplete nature of its material scope nonetheless gives rise to problems.

Bertram's aim, in Chapter 5, is to explore how the obligation to avoid exploitation, understood as a distinct type of injustice, can help us understand what we owe to future generations. The Marxian concept of exploitation turns on a discrepancy between the distribution of contributions requiring effort and the distribution of rewards in a co-operative scheme. This distinction is linked with discussions in other chapters, such as in the essays outlining the difficulties faced by contract theorists (Gardiner, Heyd, and Attas), and in the discussion exploring our understanding of intergenerational reciprocity-based requirements (Gosseries). Bertram invites the reader to envisage a temporally extended co-operative enterprise—a family-owned manufacturing business. With respect to such an enterprise he analyses three possible cases of exploitation. In the 'repair burden' case, maintenance work is not done. Instead, it is left for a later generation that, in some sense, can rightly be said to have been exploited by earlier generations. The same holds for the 'debts burden' case in which repayment obligations of credit are left at least in part to later generations, while the money from such credit is used for present consumption. The third case—the 'profligate generation'—is different from the first two. In this case, a generation acquires benefits from the hard work of its ancestors and decides not to do all that much itself. Bertram asks whether the conditions for exploitation are actually present in this situation. Specifically, he asks whether this generation, by failing 'to conform to the contribution/benefit pattern expected by its predecessors,' can be said to be exploiting earlier generations even though there is no 'experiential effect' on the now-dead contributors. He also points out the need to consider the fact that it can be reasonable to disagree with the work expectations of earlier generations. For these reasons, Bertram is skeptical about the appropriateness of characterizing the profligate generation case as a case of exploitation. Finally, he enquires into the broader implications of the three specific cases, in particular looking at the questions of when there can be said to be cooperation and when fair reciprocity can be said to have been violated.

Chapters 6 and 7 explore the viability of Rawls's contractualist account of intergenerational obligations. Rawls's short discussion of the 'savings principle' in *A Theory of Justice* and his later revisions have been highly influential in defining the problems of how we can and should relate to future people. In Chapter 6, Heyd focuses on Rawls's account of the design of the original position in an intergenerational setting (an aspect of Rawls's argument also examined by Gardiner and Attas in this volume). He contends that three main alternatives need to be considered: 'universal conference', 'present time of entry' (including a modified 'motivational assumption'), and 'strict compliance'. Each of these alternatives reflects an understanding of why we owe anything to other generations once we take seriously the unidirectionality of time since, for example, we cannot force dead people to have acted differently. As such, each of these three accounts of the contractualist position is likely to lead to different substantive principles.

Heyd shows that each of these attempts at redesigning the original position faces serious problems. He also argues that a contractarian reading of Rawls can only justify limited intergenerational obligations. Such a reading will interpret the duty of just savings as not being one of justice, but rather, as he puts it, 'as a statement about the value of justice and the duty to maintain or promote it.' Heyd further argues that the difference principle applies neither to the international sphere, nor to intergenerational one. In the end, if we consider the lack of mutual vulnerability and a similar lack of solidarity among remote generations, we are left—or so Heyd suggests—with two options: the first option relies on the natural duty to promote fair institutions for future generations, and the second points toward a shift away from contractarianism to impartialism. Just savings, to include more substantial obligations, would need to be interpreted as a moral principle, not as a political one.

In the second chapter dedicated to an analysis and evaluation of Rawls's understanding of intergenerational issues, Chapter 7, Attas elects a different starting point. Specifically, he submits an interpretation of the core intergenerational problem as a prisoner's dilemma in which there is a lack of mutuality; that is to say, earlier generations have nothing to gain from cooperating with future ones and future generations cannot benefit from earlier ones or threaten them in a credible manner. For Attas, the challenge consists of designing the original position in such a way that relations of mutuality obtain in that situation despite the lack of mutuality in the real world. In his analysis of the original position for the intergenerational context, Attas distinguishes six variations (usually tracking two variables, that is, 'what people know' and 'what motivates them'), showing in detail how each either attempts to introduce mutuality or attempts to compensate for the absence of mutuality. In doing so, he draws a distinction between two Rawlsian ways of incorporating universalization in the original position: full compliance and universality.

With respect to the status and content of the just savings principle, Attas provides an interpretation that constrasts with Heyd's. Attas argues that it should be read 'as a clause in the full formulation of the difference principle'. Still, he also makes a case for a two-stage interpretation of the principle. At stage one, savings is required up to the point where we have enough to establish and maintain institutions of justice. At stage two, Attas argues—contrary to others—that no further savings are required. He then focuses on two key issues. The first issue addresses the question of how such a principle is to be derived from the original position as designed. Here Attas argues that it is actually possible to derive a two-stage principle of intergenerational justice from the original position without having to rely on a special motivational assumption. The second issue addresses the problem of reconciling the conflict between the accumulation requirement that obtains during the first stage and the difference principle. According to Attas, the savings requirement does not actually conflict with the difference principle, properly understood. Interestingly enough, he even argues that rather than being justified, for example, by the priority of liberty over the difference principle, it is actually the difference principle itself that would justify the accumulation phase. As he puts it: 'at least with respect to the intra-generational aspect of the difference principle, maximizing the position of the least advantaged is obligatory until a threshold of adequacy is reached'. Beyond the point that is sufficient to cover 'everyone's basic and urgent needs', we enter the steady-state stage. At this time, further savings can be authorized but are neither compulsory nor prohibited. Furthermore, Attas adds an extra proviso to the savings principle such that 'inequality and saving at both stages are prohibited beyond the rates that would maximize the position of the trans-generational least advantaged'.

In Chapter 8, the last chapter of the first part of this volume, Meyer and Roser offer a specific defense of intergenerational sufficientarianism. Towards this end, they provide a detailed account of various 'broadly egalitarian' views. Strict egalitarianism (which focuses on the gap between more advantaged and less advantaged people) is contrasted with prioritarianism and maximin egalitarianism (which focus on the level of the badly off or least advantaged people in absolute terms). Two versions of sufficientarianism—weak and strong—are shown to be threshold-based views connected with prioritarianism and maximin, respectively. Next, Meyer and Roser identify specific reasons for adopting (strong) sufficientarianism in the intergenerational realm, even in those cases in which a sufficientarian conception of justice in the intragenerational context would not be adopted. These reasons are broadly of two types.

The first reasons concern the non-identity problem. As already mentioned, some rely on the non-identity problem to argue that we do not have obligations of justice to future generations. Others have relied on it to argue for the superiority of specific theories (for example, communitarianism in the case of Page). Here, the idea is of the latter type. Meyer and Roser argue that along with reliance on a standard conception of harm, we additionally ought to rely on the threshold conception of harm at least (but not exclusively) in contexts where the non-identity problem arises. The non-identity challenge would thus be circumvented by relying on a normative baseline to determine whether harm is taking place. The key step in their argument turns on an attempt to show that the idea of sufficiency, at the heart of sufficientarianism, actually provides us with the contents we need to specify this threshold of harm. If their argument succeeds, it shows that sufficientarianism makes it possible for us to defend obligations of justice in a non-identity context.

The second set of reasons for adopting a sufficientarian conception of justice in the intergenerational realm relies upon an interpretation of the normative significance of issues of various types, some of them also arising in the international realm. Here, Meyer and Roser discuss special features of intergenerational relations such as the asymmetry of power between generations, problems of measuring relative differences in well-being, uncertainties not only about the future effects of our present actions, but also about future people's way of life, and the impossibility of interacting beyond the overlap. Of course, some reasons for equalization (such as a concern for envy) do not plausibly arise in the intergenerational context, nor at any rate beyond the overlap. What is of special interest here is that since these reasons for adopting an intergenerational sufficientarianism reflect special features of intergenerational relations, they do not necessarily speak in favour of sufficientarianism outside the intergenerational context.

Part II: Specific Issues

The second part of this volume addresses important specific issues of intergenerational justice. It begins with Chapter 9, where Kumar suggests a way in which we can plausibly frame substantive questions concerning intergenerational obligations in interpersonal terms, a characterization that is at odds with an impersonal approach in this area. Kumar relies on and further develops a Scanlonian contractualist understanding of what it is for one person to have wronged another. Scanlonian contractualism offers an explanation of the interpersonal sense of 'morally wrong' in the following way: A wrongs B by culpably failing to regulate her practical deliberations in the way that B was legitimately entitled to demand of A. This account of wrongdoing allows one to claim that one person has wronged another, but without requiring that something has to have happened to a person in order for her to have been wronged. Furthermore, Kumar suggests that what we owe to others to whom we stand in a particular type of relationship (that is, how we ought to regulate our practical deliberations) is determined not by the specific token identity of the other, but rather by a relevant type description; mothers, for example, might be said to owe to their unborn children certain sorts of consideration quite apart from the token identity of that child.

This understanding, it is argued, diffuses the non-identity problem, for this account allows for the possibility of committing wrongs against future people without harming them. It also raises the issue, however, of how we ought to understand our relation to those who will live in the distant future. In the context of contractualism, valid principles for the regulation of behaviour must be justifiable to anyone on grounds that she cannot reasonably reject whether or not she currently exists. This means that even if we do not stand in any concretely characterisable relation toward future human beings, we do stand in a morally relevant relation to them, for those decisions that we make now, decisions that have implications for the quality of life likely to be available to them, must be justifiable to them by means of a principle that no one can reasonably reject. Finally, it is noted that the contractualist account developed here is identical to the one used in understanding interpersonal obligations that those living now owe one another. To the extent that this account is convincing, it implies that most of the interesting questions concerning obligations to future generations are not foundational in the sense that their justification is *sui generis*. Rather, the interesting questions are substantive. We need to enquire further into how best to specify our obligations to future people, given the special features of intergenerational relations.

In Chapter 10, Birnbacher addresses several of these special features in his discussion of the problem of the motivational force of considerations of intergenerational justice. He explores how best to articulate our theories of justice given the need to ensure that people will be motivated to act in a fair way toward future generations. Birnbacher argues that even for those who see in moral principles sources of the motivation to act morally, the problems associated with the intergenerational context remain serious. Admittedly, the moral reasons to act can remain unaffected by such a context.

As Birnbacher shows, this does not hold, however, for what he refers to as quasi-moral and non-moral reasons to act. Quasi-moral reasons to act (love, generosity, compassion, and the like) are rendered fragile by the anonymity and facelessness of future generations. Similarly, non-moral reasons to act (including self-centered ones) are weakened, not by the facelessness, but by the voicelessness of remote future generations and the near absence of possible backward benefits or sanctions. Still, Birnbacher shows that indirect sources of motivation can lead us—as a side-effect—to act in an intergenerationally fair way. These sources include the idea of a chain of love, the ability to value goods for their own sake, the concern for the well-being of the group to which one belongs, and the idea of seeking meaning in one's life. Birnbacher ends by offering a set of self-binding strategies.

Bykvist, in Chapter 11, discusses the significance of the indeterminacy of future preferences for desire-based theories of well-being in the intergenerational context. He suggests that future preferences are uncertain, but we can nonetheless influence their content. Assuming that the identity of future people is fixed (contrary to the non-identity problem), same-people choices are not always same-desire choices, since the desires of future people might be contingent on our present decisions. The influence of educational policies on preference formation is a clear illustration of this. This contingency means that which outcome people will prefer may well be indeterminate. However, one strategy for avoiding this indeterminacy is to take into account the preferences in each possible outcome and satisfy the strongest ones.

Bykvist argues, however, that while such moves eliminate indeterminacy, they do not save the theory from inconsistency, for such an account fails to take into consideration the fact that to prefer one's life is compatible with taking very different absolute attitudes in comparing this life and an alternative life of another person. Given this possibility, Bykvist argues that a strict preference-based theory implies that it is sometimes better to bring about an outcome in which all people would hate their lives than to bring about an outcome in which all people would love their lives, thereby generating the contradiction that a bad life can be better than a good life. Due to this potential inconsistency, Bykvist suggests that the strictly preference-based approach ought to be abandoned in favour of a polarity-based desire theory. This kind of theory takes the polarity or valence of absolute attitudes into account; it states, roughly, that an outcome A is better for a person than an outcome B just in case her A-self favours (in the sense of absolute attitudes, and not preferences) her life in A more than her B-self favours her life in B. This theory eliminates indeterminacy, for in order to decide what is better for each person we simply have to consider each outcome and see how she would feel about her life given that outcome. It also eliminates inconsistency, for according to the polarity-based theory, the fact that one prefers x does not mean that x is better for one. There is, however, a remaining challenge, namely that of desire adjustment. This challenge is general to all desire-based theories, not just the polarity-based theory, and it is grounded on the idea that if all that is important is desire satisfaction, then whether you change the world to match your desires or your desires to match the world is irrelevant. It is argued that the real problem is not determining the easiest way to satisfy desires, but rather that the desires do not seem to be about things that are worthy of concern. In response, the polarity-based theory is refined, so that what makes a person better off is not simply that she acquires what she would favour more, but also that her favourings are about things that merit concern.

Continuing, in Chapter 12, Arrhenius explores whether egalitarian concerns ought to be used to solve the paradoxes that bedevil the field of population ethics. To this end, he discusses the role of equality (referring to equality of welfare among people) in the evaluation of populations differing in size with respect to their goodness (in welfare terms). At the outset, Arrhenius considers Parfit's famous Mere Addition Paradox. Arrhenius argues that there is a *prima facie* case that illustrates how egalitarian concerns can solve this paradox. Generally speaking, a plausible egalitarian view might hold that the addition of a certain number of lives with very low positive welfare to a population with very high welfare will have negative contributive value, and the greater the number of added lives the greater the negative contributive value, understood as a function of the negative value of the increasing inequality. Another paradox constructed with weaker and intuitively appealing conditions, can, however, also be constructed. The initial condition here is the Weak Quality Addition Condition, which holds that for any population X, there is at least one perfectly equal population with very high positive welfare such that its addition to X is at least as good as an addition of any population with very low positive welfare to X, other things being equal. The second condition is the Weak Non-Sadism condition, which holds that there is a negative level of welfare and a number of lives at this level such that an addition of any number of people with positive welfare is at least as good as an addition of the lives with negative welfare, other things being equal. Arrhenius argues that this paradox cannot be resolved by appeal to egalitarian considerations, and, more generally, he suggests that the paradoxes of population ethics cannot be solved by an appeal to welfare egalitarianism.

A central moral and political issue of intergenerational justice concerns how we ought to respond to the long-term consequences of climate change. In Chapter 13, Wolf first develops a sufficientarian conception of intergenerational justice (similar to, but interestingly different in its justification from the versions of intergenerational sufficientarianism defended by Attas, Heyd, and Meyer and Roser). Next, Wolf applies his interpretation to the problem of climate change. His sufficientarian conception relies on an unusual interpretation of Rawls's theory of justice. On Wolf's interpretation, Rawls's two principles of justice are to be supplemented by a sufficientarian principle requiring the minimization of deprivation with respect to basic needs. He shows how such a basic needs-oriented view could be derived from the original position and fleshes out to the content of such a view, in particular, by specifying which needs ought to be regarded as basic. Wolf then extends the revised theory to the intergenerational sphere. He suggests that Rawls rejected the difference principle as a principle of justice between generations on the grounds that he believed it to be inconsistent with economic growth. Wolf argues that this was precipitous on Rawls's part, for there are contexts where capital accumulation will be fully consistent with the provision of maximal benefits for the worst off members of an intergenerational society. Instead of justifying an accumulation phase on, for example, the basis of the priority of equal liberty, Wolf does so on the basis of the priority of his needs principle. Moreover, since economic growth will sometimes be required by the priority of the needs principle included in this revised Rawlsian view, Wolf's view would in any case not be subject to the problems that led Rawls to reject the difference principle in the intergenerational case.

Wolf's account has interesting implications for the question of how to respond to climate change. He proposes a two-stage model for climate policy, echoing Rawls's own two-stage theory of savings. During the 'austerity' stage, in response to the unsustainable nature of our past and present anthropogenic greenhouse gas emissions, we would gradually have to accept net emissions targets below the sustainability level, gradually enabling us to reach a sustainable level of emissions. Once this point is reached, we would move to the 'sustainability' stage in which emissions levels would be held at the sustainable level.

In the last chapter of this volume, Chapter 14, Muñiz-Fraticelli addresses whether or not a perpetual constitution can be defended, an issue that gave rise at the end of the eighteenth century to the first serious philosophical debate about intergenerational justice. Constitutions are particularly rigid, imposing themselves to some degree on generations that were never asked to consent. Muñiz-Fraticelli critically assesses two approaches related to the idea of a perpetual constitution. The first is represented by Jefferson and the second by Otsuka. For Jefferson, constitutions automatically ought to expire after a given lapse of time, this in the name of a typically democratic concern for not subjecting people to a constitution that they have not been asked to consent to. Two responses to Jefferson are presented. First, Jefferson's proposal to pass and ratify a new constitution periodically would still leave the young people who are enfranchised between each of these enactments subject to laws to which they have not consented. Second, the price to pay for self-expiring constitutions is too great. The constant need to renegotiate the conditions of civil association would be paralyzing and might even lead to anarchy. The guarantees in a constitution that are offered to protect one against the power of the majority would constantly be called into question. Long-term projects, both at the collective and individual levels, would have little prospect of success in such a context.

Muñiz-Fraticelli also discusses the position of Otsuka, who relies on a thick idea of tacit consent in place of the Jeffersonian assumption of actual consent. Here the problem is that the conditions required by Otsuka for the sake of tacit consent are such that we are moved very closely to the idea of hypothetical consent. While sympathetic to the latter idea, Muñiz-Fraticelli, rather than merely focusing on actual, tacit, or hypothetical consent, proposes that the issue be approached on an ontological level as well. Drawing on the history of political thought, he argues along Rubenfeldian lines to the effect that it is constitutions themselves that bring about the existence of a collective self. In the end, Muñiz-Fraticelli claims that the idea of a constitution set for an indefinite period of time rather than being self-expiring can be defended by means of a combination of arguments that rely on the instrumental value of a constitution (for stability, enabling long-term projects, embodying anti-majoritarian guarantees, and the like), on the possibility of a justification through hypothetical consent, and on the ontological function of a constitution. This is not meant to preclude the possibility of a re-interpretation or amendment of a constitution. Muñiz-Fraticelli is even ready to accept, in certain extreme cases (such as Germany after World War II) that an entirely new constitution be passed, thereby re-constituting a political society.

References

ARRHENIUS, G. (2000), *Future Generations: A Challenge for Moral Theory*, FD-Diss. (Uppsala: University Printers).

AUERBACH, B. E. (1995), *Unto the Thousandth Generation. Conceptualizing Intergenerational Justice* (New York: Peter Lang).

BARRY, B. (1977), 'Justice between Generations', in P.M.S. Hacker and Joseph Raz (eds.), *Law, Morality and Society. Essays in Honor of H. L. A. Hart* (Oxford: Clarendon Press), 268–84.

BARRY, B. (1989), *Theories of Justice. A Treatise on Social Justice, Vol. I* (London: Harvester-Wheatsheaf).

—— (1995), *Justice as Impartiality. A Treatise on Social Justice, Vol. II* (Oxford: Clarendon Press).

—— (1999), 'Sustainability and Intergenerational Justice', in Dobson 1999, 93–117.

BIRNBACHER, D. (1988), *Verantwortung für zukünftige Generationen* (Stuttgart: Reclam).

BROOKS, R. L. (ed.) (1999), *When Sorry Isn't Enough. The Controversy over Apologies and Reparations for Human Injustice* (New York and London: New York University Press).

BROOME, J. (1994), 'Discounting the Future', *Philosophy & Public Affairs*, 23: 128–56.

BURKE, E. 1790 (1999), *Reflections on the Revolution in France* (Oxford: Oxford University Press).

DANIELS, N. (1988), *Am I My Parents' Keeper? An Essay on Justice between the Old and the Young* (New York/Oxford: Oxford University Press).

DE-SHALIT, A. (1995), *Why Posterity Matters. Environmental Policies and Future Generations* (London and New York: Routledge).

DOBSON, A. (ed.) (1999), *Fairness and Futurity. Essays on Environmental Sustainability* (Oxford: Oxford University Press).

FOTION, N., and HELLER, J. C. (eds.) (1997), *Contingent Future Persons. On the Ethics of Deciding Who Will Live, or Not, in the Future* (Dordrecht, Boston and London: Kluwer Academic Publishers).

GAUTHIER, D. (1986), *Morals by Agreement* (Oxford: Clarendon Press).

GOSSERIES, A. (2001), 'What Do We Owe the Next Generation(s)?', *Loyola of Los Angeles Law Review*, 35: 293–354.

—— (2004), *Penser la justice entre les generations. De l'Affaire Perruche a la reforme des retraites* (Paris: Aubier).

—— (2004a), 'Historical Emissions and Free-riding', *Ethical Perspectives*, 11/1: 36–60.

—— (2008), 'On Future Generations' Future Rights', *Journal of Political Philosophy* 16/4: 446–474.

HEYD, D. (1992), *Genethics. Moral Issues in the Creation of People* (Berkeley: University of California Press).

JEFFERSON, T., (1975), 'Letter to James Madison' (6 Sept. 1798), in M. D. Peterson (ed.), *The Portable Thomas Jefferson* (New York, Penguin Books), 444–51.

JONAS, H. (1979), *Das Prinzip Verantwortung. Versuch einer Ethik für die technologische Zivilisation* (Frankfurt: Insel Verlag).

LASLETT, P., and FISHKIN, J. S. (eds.) (1992), *Justice Between Age Groups and Generations* (New Haven and London: Yale University Press).

MCKERLIE, D. (1989), 'Equality and Time', *Ethics*, 99: 475–91.

MEYER, Lukas H. (ed.) (2004), *Justice in Time. Responding to Historical Injustice* (Baden-Baden: Nomos).

—— (2005), *Historische Gerechtigkeit* (Berlin and New York: de Gruyter, 2005).

MILLER, J., and KUMAR, R. (eds.) (2007), *Reparations. Interdisciplinary Inquiries* (Oxford: Oxford University Press).

MULGAN, T. (2006), *Future People. A Moderate Consequentialist Account of our Obligations to Future Generations* (Oxford: Clarendon Press).

NARVESON, J. (1967), 'Utilitarianism and New Generations', *Mind*, 76: 62–72.

—— (1973), 'Moral Problems of Population', *Monist*, 57: 62–86.

NOZICK, R. (1974), *Anarchy, State, and Utopia* (Oxford: Blackwell).

PAGE, E. (2006), *Climate Change, Justice and Future Generations* (Edward Elgar: Cheltenham).

PAINE, T. 1791–2 (1985), *Rights of Man* (Harmondsworth, Penguin).

PARFIT, D. (1976), 'On Doing the Best for Our Children', in Michael D. Bayles (ed.), *Ethics and Population*, (Cambridge: Schenkman), 100–15.

—— (1982), 'Future Generations: Further Problems', *Philosophy & Public Affairs*, 11: 113–72.

—— (1984), *Reasons and Persons* (Oxford: Clarendon Press).

—— (1986), 'Comments', *Ethics*, 96: 832–72.

—— (1997), 'Equality and Priority', *Ratio*, 10: 202–21.

PARTRIDGE, E. (ed.) (1981), *Responsibilities to Future Generations. Environmental Ethics* (New York: Prometheus Books).

—— (1990), 'On the Rights of Future People', in Donald Scherer (ed.), *Upstream/Downstream. Issues in Environmental Ethics* (Philadelphia: Temple University), 40–66.

RAWLS, J. (1971), *A Theory of Justice* (Oxford: Oxford University Press; second revised edition, Cambridge, MA: Harvard University Press, 1999).

—— (1993), *Political Liberalism* (New York: Columbia University Press).

—— (1999), *The Law of Peoples* (Cambridge, MA: Harvard University Press).

—— (2001), *Justice as Fairness* (Cambridge, Mass: Harvard University Press).

ROBERTS, M. A. (1998), *Child versus Childmaker. Future Persons and Present Duties in Ethics and the Law* (Lanham: Rowman & Littlefield).

ROEMER, J. E., and K. Suzumura (eds.) (2007), *Intergenerational Equity and Sustainability* (Palgrave Macmillan: Basingstoke).

RYBERG, J., and T. Tännsjö (eds.) (2004), *The Repugnant Conclusion. Essays on Population Ethics* (Dordrecht, Boston and London: Kluwer Academic Publishers).

SCANLON, T. M. (1998), *What We Owe To Each Other* (Cambridge, MA: Harvard University Press).

SIKORA, R.I., and BARRY, B. (eds.) (1978), *Obligations to Future Generations* (Philadelphia: Temple University Press).

TREMMEL, J. C. (ed.) (2006), *Handbook of Intergenerational Justice* (Cheltenham: Elgar).

THOMPSON, J. (2002), *Taking Responsibility for the Past. Reparation and Historical Injustice* (London: Polity).

VISSER 'T HOOFT, H. P. (1999), *Justice to Future Generations and the Environment* (Dordrecht: Kluwer).

WEISS, E. B. (1989), *In Fairness to Future Generations: International Law, Common Patrimony, and Intergenerational Equity* (Tokyo/Dobbsferry, N.Y.: United Nations University/Transnational Publishers).

PART I
Theories

1

Identity and Obligation in a Transgenerational Polity

JANNA THOMPSON

A political society is intergenerational. Citizens are born into a pre-existing polity that in most cases will continue to exist, perhaps for many generations, after they are dead. They obey laws and act in the framework of institutions that were brought into being by past generations, and their government makes laws that will affect the lives and relationships of future generations. 'We the people' consists of a procession of citizens through time. But most citizens do not merely conceive of themselves as people who happen to share a territory and institutions with people of the past and future. They regard themselves as inheritors of a history and a political tradition. They understand themselves and their political actions in a historical framework that connects the deeds of past generations to their own deeds and to aspirations for the future of their society. They see themselves as carrying on a tradition, maintaining a valued institution, righting a historical wrong, or continuing a struggle to achieve a national ideal. They honour their nation's dead, or the dead of other communities to which they belong, and make sacrifices for posterity. They preserve their heritage and pass it on to future generations. Their government makes agreements and incurs obligations which succeeding generations are supposed to honour. Intergenerational relationships, and the obligations and entitlements that go with them, are central to the moral fabric of a political society. A nation for them is, in essence, a transgenerational polity: a society in which the generations are bound together in relationships of obligation and entitlement.[1]

---

[1] I have taken the term, 'transgenerational', from de Shalit (1995). A transgenerational community, as I understand it, is one in which the generations share valued relationships of cooperation. A transgenerational obligation is justified by reference to these relationships. Intergenerational duties, on the other hand, are justified by reference to the interests of future (and past) people as individuals (as in theories of human rights). A 'polity' is generally a national state; but the term can also be applied to semi-independent political communities—for example, indigenous nations.

Theories of justice, right and political responsibility ought to reflect the importance to citizens, and to the nature and operation of their society, of transgenerational relationships. Liberal theories generally fail to do this. One problem with liberal theories is that their approaches, concepts and principles are not adapted to deal with intergenerational issues. For example, liberal theories of justice often aim to establish that individuals have certain rights as human beings or as members of a society. Though they give different accounts of why people have rights, most philosophers appeal to needs or interests that must be satisfied if individuals are to function adequately as human agents or as citizens. But those who are dead or unborn have no agency or interests.[2] The unborn *will* have interests but the idea that we can through our actions violate their future rights encounters the well-known problem of non-identity. How can future people claim that their interests have been set back if their coming into existence depended on our 'harmful' activities?[3]

Liberal social contract theory also has difficulty encompassing duties to other generations. If the obligations of citizens are determined by what self-interested or disinterested individuals would agree to if they had to make a contract with each other, then it is difficult to understand how the unborn or the dead can be objects of consideration.[4] In *A Theory of Justice* (1971, pp. 128–9) Rawls arrives at a 'just savings principle' by assuming that the contractors in the original position are representatives of families: agents who are likely to care about their descendants and thus are predisposed to accept that they have duties to them. But Rawls's critics rightly complain that his account of justice between the generations is *ad hoc*. How does the supposition that contractors are representatives of families fit together with the idea that dominates his contractual approach: that an agreement is supposed to be made between disinterested individuals who are prevented by a veil of ignorance from knowing information about themselves, including their ideas about the good?[5]

In *Political Liberalism*, Rawls (1993, pp. 271–5) reasons that contractors, who recognize the value of intergenerational cooperation and, in the framework of ideal theory, can assume perfect compliance with principles, do not need

---

[2] Wellman (1995, pp. 146–57) disqualifies the dead from having rights because they are no longer agents. De George (1981, p. 160) thinks, for similar reasons, that the unborn cannot have rights.

[3] The 'non-identity problem' has been discussed by many philosophers, most notably in Schwartz (1978), and Parfit (1984, Ch. 16).

[4] Gauthier (1986, Ch. 9) thinks that the fact that generations are overlapping makes it possible to 'bargain' with the unborn. For criticisms, see Arrhenius (1999); and de-Shalit (1990).

[5] English (1977, pp. 93 ff) points out other problems concerning Rawls's motivational assumption. See also Hubin (1976).

a special motivation in order to endorse a principle of intergenerational justice. But Rawls depends on the contractors believing that intergenerational cooperation exists. If contractors think it does not exist (and Brian Barry thinks that the environmental destruction caused by past generations makes it evident that it does not (1979, pp. 71–2)) then they have no reason to endorse the principle.[6] Why shouldn't each generation regard the products of their predecessors, good or bad, as simply a given—like the climate or soil of their country?

The particular difficulties that intergenerational issues pose for liberal theories may be solvable in one way or another. But the problem with liberal theories is not merely that their concepts and approaches do not work very well when applied to future or past generations. Problems also lie in the way that they are constructed: what they take as central and the assumptions that they make about individuals and their interests.

The first aspect of this problem is that liberal theories, classical and modern, focus on relations between contemporaries. Intergenerational relationships are treated as marginal concerns: as a problematic addendum to theories that focus on contemporaries. The second aspect of the problem has to do with the conception of the individual on which liberal theories of justice and right depend. Liberals tend to take as central the lifetime interests of individuals: the goals, needs and motivations that relate either to their present wants and circumstances, or to their ideas about what they want to achieve or enjoy during the course of their lives. However, the scope of individual interest is not confined to concerns of a lifetime. Individuals have ideas about the good, which are bound up with their hopes for their descendants and their regard for their forebears. They have views about how people should treat and regard them after their death. They have projects and things of value that they want to pass on to successors. They care about their heritage and what happens to it. They take pride in or feel shame concerning events of their nation's history. They want their ideals to flourish in future generations. Liberals do not deny that individuals often have such interests, but they tend to treat them as peripheral, or even as suspect to the extent that they threaten to get in the way of present and future individuals living their lives free from the impositions of the past. A theory of the transgenerational polity, I will argue below, ought to regard these interests as central to the lives of individuals and to an account of relationships between the generations.

In searching for a more adequate approach to justice, obligation and responsibility in a transgenerational polity, it seems appropriate to turn to

---

[6] See also see Barry (1989, Ch. 5).

those theories that are labelled 'communitarian'. There are two ways in which communitarians typically distinguish themselves from liberals. The first is that they insist that the self is essentially embedded in a community. Individuals identify with fellow members, and their self interests and communal interests are identical, or at least intersecting. This identity motivates their actions and creates their obligations.

> I am someone's son or daughter, someone else's cousin or uncle … I belong to this clan, that tribe, this nation. Hence what is good for me has to be the good for one who inhabits these roles. As such I inherit from the past of my family, my city, my tribe, my nation, a variety of debts, inheritances, rightful expectations and obligations. These constitute the given of my life, my moral starting point (MacIntyre: 1981, p. 220).[7]

The second idea typically advanced by communitarians is that members of a community share a common good, and that it is this good, above all, that defines their relationships and obligations. Since a community is transgenerational, individuals who are embedded in it, who take the communal good to be their good, will as a matter of course regard themselves as having obligations from the past that extend into the future. Communitarians are able to give relationships between generations a central place in their view of community, and thus are well placed to provide a more satisfactory understanding of obligations in a transgenerational polity. For them obligations arise out of relationships of cooperation in a community based on a common idea of the good, and are thus truly transgenerational.

My aim in this chapter is to provide a view of these obligations that exploits advantages associated with the communitarian position, while taking well-founded criticisms of communitarianism into account. The position I will present is communitarian in the sense that it takes ideas about obligation to be intrinsic to social relationships of certain kinds and shows how these moral ideas are grounded in the nature of the self. But it is not meant to be an alternative to liberalism. Communitarians have often identified themselves as opponents of liberal views of individuals and social relations. In the last decade, the debate between liberals and communitarians has become a rather tired affair. Most liberals allow that community and culture play a large role in the lives of individuals and in their moral thinking. Most philosophers with communitarian sympathies agree that individuals can, and sometimes should, be critical of their social traditions and roles; they acknowledge that modern individuals are embedded in a number of

---

[7] For other classical statements of the communitarian position see Sandel (1982) and Taylor (1989).

communities and have to find a way of dealing with different, and sometimes conflicting, requirements. Many social theorists now agree that an adequate theory about the identity of citizens and their entitlements and obligations is likely to bring together liberal and communitarian perspectives. My claim is that a perspective that can be described as communitarian is particularly important in formulating an adequate theory of entitlements and obligations in a transgenerational polity.

Varieties of Communitarianism

Those who hold communitarian views about identity, community and the common good do not all have the same relationship to liberalism. Communitarians can be regarded as 'strong' or 'weak' according to the degree of incompatibility between their positions and liberal views about individual freedom and the just society. Strong communitarians typically hold two views: that selves do not choose to be constituted in a particular way: their identity and resulting obligations are givens (as MacIntyre claims); and that the ethical consciousness that results from this constitution is strongly communal.

From the perspective of strong communitarianism, there is a sense in which ethical deliberators, present generations and future generations, have the same identity and the same interests. What is in the interests of one is in the interests of the other. Their very identities are shared because the values they share are constitutive of their identities (Marshall: 1993, p. 109).

Appeals to liberal rights or freedoms are likely to play little or no role in the ethical life of such deliberators.

Weaker communitarians combine liberal ideas about individual rights and freedom with an ethical perspective that results from identification with a community. Yael Tamir's 'liberal nationalism' (1993) and David Miller's defence of nationality (1995) are positions that combine liberal ideas with obligations that come from identity—including obligations in respect to history. Miller, for example, claims that the existence of a nation as a historical community is one of the features that make it 'a community of obligation'. 'Because our forebears have toiled and spilt their blood to build and defend the nation, we who are born into it inherit an obligation to continue their work…' (1995, p. 23). But he insists that we are free to choose what aspect of our inheritance we want to maintain by reference to our preferences and liberal ideas about justice and right (1997, p. 79).

Stronger versions of communitarianism have received extensive, and often justified, criticisms.[8] Not all ideas of obligation that arise from community identities are morally acceptable. To regard yourself as having inherited obligations is not desirable if this requires you to take revenge on the descendants of those who have harmed your ancestors or to carry on a feud. Members of communities need a standpoint from which to criticise traditional ideas about obligation, and in contemporary societies, at least in the Western world, liberal ideas about individual rights, human dignity and justice have often provided that standpoint. In particular, what it means to be a citizen of a modern national polity does not fit well alongside strong communitarian ideas about identity and duty. Citizens of these polities come from many different ethnic and religious backgrounds; they are likely to identify with a number of communities, and are subject to conflicting demands, which they have to resolve as best they can. They have different and conflicting ideas of the good. As polities become more multi-cultural, more cosmopolitan in the ways of life that they embrace, the idea that citizens have a common identity and pursue together a common good becomes more and more implausible.[9]

However, weaker forms of communitarianism are not so obviously subject to these familiar critiques. Weaker communitarians allow that identities can be complex and subject to criticism. Community identity in its best form, de-Shalit says (1995, p. 25), is something that individuals affirm as the result of moral reflection and by engaging together in a free and open debate aimed at defining a common good. They are bound together by their participation in this debate, but do not have to reach a consensus, either now or in the future. And the obligations of members of such a community are up for discussion; they are among the things that they debate.

Let us assume that citizens of a polity are oriented, as de-Shalit supposes, to debating, defining and achieving common goods. Future citizens are not direct participants in this enterprise, but he thinks that their inclusion follows from the fact that present individuals have interests that stretch beyond their lifetime. They want the things that they regard as good to flourish. They are future directed in their endeavours, but will inevitably be frustrated by their mortality. The solution to the problem is for them to immortalize themselves through creative activity: through work, thoughts and ideas (pp. 34–40). These thoughts and ideas will be available to future citizens who will continue the debate about the good. By putting forward

---

[8] Critics of stronger versions of communitarianism include Buchanan (1999) and Kymlicka (2002, Ch. 6).

[9] See Waldron (1996).

ideas that they will or could develop, present citizens, according to de-Shalit, are participating with future generations in a cultural interaction. They are obliged to regard these future people as participants in a community defined by its commitment to a pursuit of the good—and thus as people to whom they have obligations. De-Shalit can be understood to be providing what Rawls in his later account of intergenerational justice fails to provide: an explanation of why intergenerational cooperation exists.

De-Shalit takes it for granted that belonging to a constitutive community of the sort he describes means that we have obligations to future as well as present people, but says almost nothing about how these duties arise. The following account seems plausible. We have obligations to people with whom we share the cooperative aim of promoting something we have reason to regard as good. We owe duties to present people because we are now cooperating with them. We owe duties to future people because, according to de-Shalit, they too can be regarded as belonging to a tradition of interaction—to a discourse that spans the generations and unites us with them in a common community. These obligations exist because these future individuals will be members of our community: our descendants or successors. They do not depend on who these descendants or successors turn out to be, or on the course of events that will bring them into being. They do not depend on future people being able to establish that they would have been worse off if we had acted in a way contrary to what our duty requires.[10] The communitarian approach to intergenerational justice, so interpreted, is be able to circumvent the non-identity problem.

Does it provide an adequate account of transgenerational obligations? The main problem with de-Shalit's view of intergenerational cooperation is that it heavily depends on people's perception that they have enough in common, morally speaking, to be members of the same community. Whether they do so in a diverse, multi-cultural polity is questionable. Whether present citizens can suppose that the outlook of their successors will be sufficiently like their own is even more doubtful. Even generations near to each other in time can perceive of each other as irreconcilably different in moral outlook. In modern societies younger people are apt to think that they have very different moral ideals from their elders—to the extent that they sometimes resist the idea that they belong to the same moral community. There have, in fact, been significant moral changes within the history of many nations, and those people whose moral concerns are deeply affected are likely to regard them as a complete break with the past, for better or worse. A view of obligation that depends

---

[10] Kumar (2003) presents a similar idea of how to circumvent the non-identity problem, but in relation to Scanlon's contractualism.

on how people perceive their moral interests and their relation to others does not provide a firm basis for duties in a transgenerational polity. Nor is it an adequate one. Should our obligation to make recompense for the injustices of our predecessors have to depend on whether we regard ourselves as morally similar to them?

Is there a more substantial form of interaction that binds present, future (and, perhaps, past) generations together in relationships of obligation? The nation, says Jeff McMahan, has provided the language in which one thinks and speaks, an intellectual heritage, a way of thinking about the world. 'In short, the nation itself, as a transhistorical entity, is one's benefactor, and there are duties that one owes to it in consequence' (1997, p. 130). But the moral ties generated by gratitude to our nation or our predecessors seem too feeble and uncertain. We obtain the culture, language and intellectual life of our nation as a matter of course and it is difficult to explain why we ought to feel grateful to the nation or its people for providing these things, or what we ought to do to demonstrate our gratitude. It seems more plausible to insist that we ought to be grateful to our predecessors when they have taken the trouble to supply us with something of value: educational institutions, for example. But it is not clear to whom we owe gratitude or how we ought to express it. Added to this problem is the fact that citizens of a polity frequently disagree about the value of things supplied by their predecessors.

In summary, weak communitarians escape the criticisms levelled at strong versions of communitarians, but, like liberals, run into difficulties explaining why present generations ought to accept obligations in respect to the future (or the past). The accounts of intergenerational cooperation that they provide, whether based on common values or gratitude, do not seem sufficient to ground relationships of obligation and entitlement in a transgenerational polity. Nevertheless, by stressing the way in which common endeavours can create obligations, communitarians seem well placed to provide a more satisfactory account of transgenerational obligations. I will argue that the communitarian perspective can rise to the challenge by showing that there are practices of passing on obligations through the generations grounded in interests which, given the nature of the self, people of different generations have reason to share.

Basic to my approach are two ideas: that intergenerational obligations include obligations in respect to past people, their desires and deeds; and that obligations to future generations and obligations in respect to the past are in many cases grounded in a conception of what present generations of a society ought to do for their predecessors and successors. Presently existing people make moral demands on people of the future and in turn fulfil demands that were made of past people. Presently existing people take responsibility for transferring the inheritance that they received from their predecessors to their successors and for ensuring that these successors will be in the position to maintain this heritage and pass it on to future generations. The generations share responsibility for maintaining the institutions and practices that enable transgenerational demands to be satisfied and successors to receive their inheritance. The generational transactions of the transgenerational polity, and the obligations that surround them, constitute what Edmund Burke described as 'a partnership between the living, the dead and the not yet born' (1995, p. 110).

Lifetime-Transcending Interests

The scope of individual interest is not confined to concerns of a lifetime. Individuals have ideas about the good which are bound up with their hopes for their descendants and their regard for their forebears. They have views about how people should treat and regard them after their death. They have projects and things of value that they want to pass on to successors. They care about their community's heritage and what happens to it. They take pride in, or feel shame concerning, events of its history. That individuals often have such concerns is the starting point for de-Shalit's account of duties to future generations. I will argue that these interests, which I will call 'lifetime-transcending interests', are the proper basis for an account of obligations in a transgenerational polity—an account that encompasses duties in respect to the past as well as duties to the future. In this section I will concentrate on explaining what they are.

An interest, as I will understand it, is a valued object, activity or state of affairs around which clusters an interrelated set of desires, beliefs, hopes, predilections, motivations, attitudes and intentions. The interest gives these desires and predilections their point, and an interest, as an abiding state of a person, explains many of the things that she wants, does, demands or feels. Lifetime-transcending interests have as their subject matter events, objects or states of affairs that either existed before the lifetime of the person who has the interest or will, or could, exist in the future beyond his lifetime. People who are concerned about how their children and grandchildren will fare after their death clearly have lifetime-transcending interests. So do those who have an interest in what happens to their bodies or in their posthumous reputation, or the fate of their projects or the possessions that they will leave behind, or in the future of an ideal or a community. Such interests often motivate them to do certain things during their life: to make a will, to provide for their children, to agree to become an organ donor, to engage in projects that are likely to bear fruit in the future after their deaths. Some lifetime-transcending interests are necessarily post-mortem: for example, my interest in how my body is disposed of. Other interests—though directed toward a future in which I will probably no longer exist—are not necessarily associated with my death. I may live long enough to know how my children fare in their adult life; I may even outlive them. There is no definite line between lifetime-transcending interests and interests in states of affairs in the more distant future that I might live to experience. But my interest in the well-being of my children in their later lives is an interest in how they will fare in a future where I may well not exist, and for this reason can be called lifetime-transcending.

That people often have an interest of one kind or another in something that will or could exist or happen in the future beyond their lifetimes is a commonly acknowledged phenomenon. But lifetime-transcending interests, as I understand them, can also be interests in past events before a person's lifetime or in people of the past and their deeds. In this respect, my conception of these interests is wider than that of de-Shalit. An interest in our nation's history or in particular events in its history, an interest in the lives and deeds of our ancestors or predecessors count as lifetime-transcending interests. An interest in a heritage, in so far as its value to us has to do with its being passed on to us by preceding generations, is a lifetime-transcending interest. These 'past-directed' interests are also motivating. If we are interested in events in our nation's history, we may desire to learn more about them, to teach children about them, to be faithful to them, to demand rectification for wrongs that we believe were done to the people of our nation in the past, and to participate in projects that continue our history in a particular way. If we are interested in the deeds of our predecessors, we may want to honour them, to put up monuments that celebrate them, and so forth. If we are interested in the heritage that we received from our predecessors, then we are likely to want to preserve it and pass it on to future generations.

Other interests can be regarded as lifetime-transcending even though they are not interests in particular events or states of affairs in the past or the future. People who have ideals or value their nation or some other community are likely to want their successors to value these things too. They are likely to want their ideals to flourish or their community to prosper in the future beyond their lifetime.[11] Even if people who have these ideals do not express views about the

<hr/>

[11] As Partridge puts it (1981b, p. 207), 'the well-being and endurance of the significant object apart from, and beyond the lifetime of, the agent may become a concern *of* and a value *to* the agent—a part of his inventory of personal *interests or goods*'.

future or future people, it will almost always be the case that their reasons for valuing the ideal will *imply* beliefs and desires concerning the future.

An interest in an ideal or a concern for a community also tends to bring with it certain concerns relating to past events and past people. Those who subscribe to ideals are likely to think it important to remember things that have happened in the past, to preserve goods or a tradition that comes from the past, and to honour those who have made sacrifices for the ideal. Those who value a community are predisposed to regard themselves as part of a history of struggle and achievement. They find it natural to see themselves as interacting with people who upheld the ideal in the past and with those whom they expect to carry on the endeavour in the future (as de-Shalit claims).

Most interests are what people take note of; they feature in people's account of the values they adhere to, the goals that they strive for and the beliefs and intentions that they have about these values and goals. But it is reasonable to claim that people can have interests that they may not acknowledge. If, for example, a person has an interest in the future well-being of her children and grandchildren, and it is reasonable to believe that their well-being depends on the continued existence of an affluent democratic society, then she has an objective interest in the maintenance for future generations of an affluent and democratic society—whether she is aware of having this interest or not. That she has it follows logically from her acknowledged interest along with background information about what is required for the desires motivated by her interest to be fulfilled. In my discussion of lifetime-transcending interests I will be concerned not only with the interests that individuals profess but also with their objective interests, and thus with the conditions and states of affairs that must exist if the objectives associated with their professed interests are to be realised.

The lifetime-transcending interests of some people are altruistic. They care about the fate of future people; they want their predecessors to be properly honoured. Others are more concerned about what people will think of them or their works after their death. People do not all have the same lifetime-transcending interests. Some are concerned about how their body is treated after their death or what is done with their possessions, but others are not. Some people care about the past of their nation or family, but others do not. Like liberals, we have to allow that the interests of individuals are diverse and sometimes conflicting. Nevertheless, it seems plausible to suppose that most people have lifetime-transcending interests of one kind or another. But to establish that lifetime-transcending interests are the basis for obligations in a transgenerational polity it is not enough to point out that they are prevalent. We must also establish that they play an important role in the lives of individual and the formation of their identities. This is an especially important thing to do because their importance, even their rationality, has sometimes been denied. Why should people be concerned about things that will happen after they are dead? Why should they care about the past before their lifetime?

There are a number of ways of arguing for the importance to individuals and their identity of lifetime-transcending interests. The following concentrates on two ideas: that lifetime-transcending interests are essential for a meaningful life and that they are a pre-requisite for making a rational plan for one's life.

That living a meaningful live involves having lifetime-transcending interests is strongly supported by some philosophers. Charles Taylor thinks that individuals find a moral orientation and meaning for their activities by subscribing to a higher good—by establishing a connection with something universal and eternal, such as justice, God, aesthetic beauty or knowledge, that makes them part of something larger than their own lives (1989, p. 62 ff). An ideal makes individuals part of something larger than their own life not only because it encourages them to be become concerned with the good of others but also because it motivates them to work or hope for a result that will probably not be achieved in their own lifetimes, and it connects them with those who have worked to achieve the ideal in past generations. Partridge argues that those who have no concerns that transcend their lifetimes are living impoverished lives. 'Self-transcendence', as he calls it, gives meaning to our lives and projects, especially when we face the fact of our own mortality (1981b, p. 204).

Partridge fears that this argument is less than conclusive because it does not eliminate the possibility that people might live satisfactory lives that contain no objects of interest that do not relate to themselves and their lifetime experiences (1981b, p. 208). The miser cares about money for the sake of his experience of owning it, and not for what objective values it might serve. A millionaire art collector may buy a valued painting not because he cares about its continuing value as a work of art but because he gets pleasure from locking it away from the gaze of others and keeping it for himself.

However, Partridge assumes that lifetime-transcending interests have to be altruistic and that people must be conscious of what all of their interests are. The millionaire would not get satisfaction from owning great works of art and denying them to the public gaze if he did not believe in the value of these works as important contributions to an artistic heritage. Even if he gets satisfaction only from denying them to others, he is nevertheless riding piggyback on the lifetime-transcending interests of others. He has to care that people value and want to preserve their artistic heritage. If they ceased to value it then locking his treasures away would be a meaningless act. He has perverse lifetime-transcending interests of his own. Misers gloat over money and not, like magpies, over brightly coloured pieces of string. They seem, in other words, to have an objective interest in the people of their society using money as a traditional and persisting standard of value, now and into the future.

So it *is* difficult to imagine how someone can live a meaningful life without any kind of lifetime-transcending interests. The same conclusion follows from a reflection on the importance to individuals of their projects. Having projects, according to many philosophers, is intrinsic to a satisfactory life and the way that people identify themselves.[12] The project may be raising a family, doing artistic work, participating with others in running a business, amassing a fortune, or working for the realization of an ideal. Whatever the project, it will almost inevitably involve or presuppose lifetime-transcending interests. An artist may want his works to be appreciated by his successors. But even if he doesn't care what happens to his works in the future, his being able to find meaning in his life work is likely to depend on the ongoing existence of traditions and practices which encourage artistic work to be valued in his society. A person who builds up a business or amasses a fortune is likely to be concerned about what will happen to it. But even if this doesn't matter to her, she is likely to have an interest in the existence and persistence of social values and traditions that make amassing wealth a worthy or enviable activity in her society. She may care about her posthumous reputation—she would not want someone suggesting after her death that she got her wealth dishonestly, or that her boasts of great wealth were false.

Having lifetime-transcending interests is also a pre-requisite for an individual becoming and being an autonomous agent: that is, to formulate and live according to a rational life plan. A person who wants to live a meaningful life, one that she can continue to find meaningful when she becomes older and has to face the prospect of her own mortality, will choose a life plan that contains projects and goals involving lifetime-transcending interests and will be aware of how her projects are predicated on conditions and values that are lifetime-transcending. However such interests may be involved in a deeper, formative way in her development as an agent. Annette Baier argues that we are essentially second persons:

Persons are essentially successors, heirs to other persons who formed and cared for them, and their personality is revealed both in their relations to others and in their response to their own recognized genesis (1985, p. 85).

To develop as an autonomous agent, a person ought to be aware of his nature as a second person: to understand how his proclivities, ideas, attitudes and

---

[12] On the centrality of projects to living a satisfactory human life see Lomasky (1987, Ch. 2).

beliefs have been formed by his family, his community and culture. They are his inheritance, his cultural resources, the nature and value of which must be understood and critically assessed in order for him to rationally choose a satisfactory course for his life. He has an interest in appreciating their value, comprehending their drawbacks and appreciating their history and the way they have influenced the activities of his predecessors. And in so far as his pursuit of what he regards as good involves communication with others, including people of younger generations, and contributing to their lives or thoughts, he has an objective interest in the continued existence and survival into future generations of the heritage he has obtained from the past.

The above arguments do not prove that everyone *must* have lifetime-transcending interests. Not everyone wants to make a rational life plan; not everyone lives a meaningful life. But the fact that these interests are common and play an important role in human lives is sufficient reason for thinking that philosophers ought to regard them as central to their account of social relationships. The critical question is whether and how we can move from particular lifetime-transcendent interests, and the reasons why people possess them, to a view about obligations in a transgenerational polity.

Transgenerational Cooperation and Duties with Respect to the Dead

Lifetime-transcending interests can be motivating. Those who have them are predisposed to want certain things to happen after their death. In some cases they may be inclined to *demand* that their successors do something. Someone who cares about how her body or her goods are disposed of after her death is likely to think that her survivors ought to fulfil her requests. Those who labour to provide future generations with something of value are inclined to think that future generations ought to be grateful; at least they ought to try to appreciate their inheritance. From the fact that people sometimes make demands of their successors it does not follow that their successors are obliged to fulfil them. In a liberal society, people are likely to resist the idea that existing citizens can impose their wishes or values on their children or people of the future. Nevertheless, I will argue that we ought to accept the existence of obligations in respect to the deeds and wishes of our predecessors. I will argue, first, that lifetime-transcending interests of certain kinds can explain why we have duties in respect to the dead.[13]

Let us consider a duty to the dead that many people affirm: the duty to avoid harming someone's posthumous reputation through malicious slander. Most philosophers assume that the only way to justify the existence of such a duty is to establish that it is possible to harm the dead.[14] But this idea, though some have defended it, is extremely problematic. An appeal to lifetime-transcending interests that people had before their deaths provides another, less problematic way of explaining why survivors can have obligations in respect to their predecessors.

There are two principal reasons why people with such interests would care about their posthumous reputations. First of all, they are likely be concerned about the harm that could be done after their death to their objectives, projects, values, and the people they care about. Since slander can harm a person's family or community or cause her works or ideals to become objects of ridicule, she will be predisposed to demand that her survivors not allow this to happen. This is not the same as demanding that her survivors care about the same things that she does, or that they carry on her projects or uphold her ideals. It is a demand that they not undermine or destroy the objects of her lifetime-transcending interests by inventing or broadcasting malicious untruths.

The second reason is that people are likely to want their efforts, accomplishments, and objectives to be properly appreciated after their death by those whose opinion they respect and by the groups and institutions to which they have tried to make a contribution. Having the respect of others is for most people central to a meaningful existence, and slander to a person's posthumous reputation would frustrate her desire to have her projects and endeavours respected by making her labours or intentions objects of ridicule and disrespect.

Whether a person has one or both of these reasons for being concerned about her posthumous reputation she is justified in demanding that her survivors protect it from malicious lies and misrepresentations. If a person thought that her posthumous reputation would be vulnerable to those who would have no compunction against telling malicious lies for their own gratification or profit, she could not with confidence pursue lifetime-transcending interests or believe that what she did would make a contribution or have a chance of being appreciated. This lack of confidence would seriously interfere with

---

[13] For more detailed discussion of these obligations, see Thompson (2003, pp. 71–83).

[14] See Feinberg (1984, Ch. 2) and Pitcher (1984, p. 183). Why the view that we can harm the dead is problematic is well explained by Partridge (1981).

her ability and inclination to pursue projects or acquire ideals that involve lifetime-transcending interests. An important dimension of human activity and aspiration would be undermined or diminished, thus diminishing the ability of a person to live a meaningful life. A morality that centres on respect for individuals must also be respectful of their important interests, particularly those that are central to their ability to live good lives. Given that this is so, individuals have a good reason for demanding that their survivors *ought* to protect their posthumous reputation.

It might be objected that once people are dead they no longer have an interest in their reputation or anything else. Why, then, should their survivors regard themselves as obligated to protect posthumous reputations or fulfil any other lifetime-transcending demand? The answer is obvious. Though the dead no longer care about their lifetime-transcending interests, the living do, and if successors do not regard it as their duty to fulfil the demands made by their predecessors, then each generation faces the prospect that its reasonable demands will be ignored by its successors, with the resulting undermining consequences for activities and aspirations based on lifetime-transcendent interests. So there are moral reasons for members of each generation to value, and regard themselves as obliged to maintain, practices that require them to fulfil morally legitimate demands made by their predecessors.

These legitimate demands take other forms. Suppose Aunt Mabel is a fundamentalist Christian and wants her body to be buried with proper Christian ceremony with all of its organs intact. I, her only surviving relative, am an atheist who believes that bodies should be cremated without ceremony after all their useable organs have been donated to save the lives of others. It can be argued that when Aunt Mabel is dead she won't care what is done with her body. However, it is reasonable to insist that lifetime-transcending demands of such importance to an individual should be fulfilled. As an atheist, it is true that I have no lifetime-transcending interest in being given a Christian burial with all my bodily organs intact (quite the contrary). But I do have an interest in how my body is disposed of (being a strong supporter of organ donation), and think it reasonable to demand that my request be honoured by my successors. Even if I have no interest at all in the matter, I know that many people do and that this is something that they care about—that it is important to their lives and peace of mind. Aunt Mabel's confidence in being able to live and die according to her faith depends on her confidence that her survivors will fulfil her wishes. So I have reason to support and act according to a transgenerational practice which requires survivors in most circumstances to dispose of the bodies of the dead according to the wishes that they expressed before death.

Since reasoning about the legitimacy of lifetime-transcending demands requires judgment about their moral reasonableness, we also have a basis for refusing to fulfil some of the demands made by those now dead. Parents sometimes demand that their children adhere to certain values or live their lives in a particular way. But most of us believe that children should be able to determine their own values and way of life and thus would regard this demand as morally illegitimate—not something the children are obliged to obey. We think that people should be able to pass on to their heirs some of the things that they valued during their lives, but not to the extent that doing so would seriously undermine well-motivated ideas about distributive justice. Our views about what people are entitled to demand of their successors are going to be influenced by our values and our ideas about what members of successor generations should be free to decide and do. But the existence and importance of lifetime-transcending interests give us reason to put some limits on this freedom.

By appealing to lifetime-transcending interests we can justify duties that many people think that they have to dead: to fulfil their wishes concerning the disposal of their bodies and at least some of their possessions, to protect their posthumous reputations, and, in some cases, to fulfil their promises.[15] The importance of lifetime-transcending interests, the moral legitimacy of some of the demands that arise from these interests are sufficient to provide a justification even if we believe that the dead cannot be harmed. In addition, it is plausible to believe that members of enduring communities—families, towns, churches, nations—have duties in respect to past members. Suppose that the member of a town council has made it one of his life's projects to provide something of value to future generations of his community. It seems reasonable that he can demand, or have demanded on his behalf, that he be appropriately remembered for his service to the community and that his successors make an effort to appreciate their inheritance: to understand why he thought that it would be of value to them (an idea of duty that allows that they could decide that it is not of value).

Members of communities can also have an obligation to preserve and pass on a heritage to future generations. Suppose that Jean inherits a necklace from her mother—a family heirloom that has for a long time been passed from mother to daughter. It has been cherished by her forebears not because of its aesthetic or market value, but because of its association with the history of the

---

[15] The duties, as I have described them, are not duties *to* the dead, but duties *in respect to* them. In this respect, my account is similar to that offered by Partridge (1981, p. 259). But Partridge thinks that our duties in respect to the dead are the result of a social contract motivated by self-interest. I have stressed that the obligations to fulfil some of the demands made by those now dead are justified by reference to the moral legitimacy of the demand.

family. However Jean does not care about family history or tradition. She sells the necklace and uses the proceeds to buy a bicycle and some clothes for her own daughter.

Suppose that in our city past generations have put a lot of money and effort into preserving and maintaining buildings which are associated with our early history and have made it clear that they regard them as an inheritance for future generations. However, most people in our generation are not interested in this inheritance and would prefer to use the sites on which the buildings stand for other, more productive purposes: housing, shopping malls, etc. Our city council, with our overwhelming support, decides to knock the buildings down and put up the kind of structures we currently prefer. By the time that the next generation comes to maturity the historic buildings are all gone.

By selling the necklace and by destroying the historic buildings successors have been deprived of an opportunity to value and maintain a heritage. If heritage is of value to individuals—something that is supported by Baier's view of us as second persons—then these actions count as doing harm even if people do not suffer from their deprivation. But in destroying an inheritance Jean and our generation are also doing wrong in respect to the intentions and desires of past generations. Those who make an effort to provide an inheritance for their successors, or to preserve and pass on what they received as an inheritance from their predecessors, have a lifetime-transcending interest in their successors valuing their inheritance and maintaining and passing it on to *their* successors. They can reasonably demand that these successors make an effort to appreciate it. In the case of a community or familial inheritance that is intended for a line of successors, an effort to appreciate should bring with it an acknowledgement that it is not just meant for us, and that our failure to appreciate it should not necessarily determine its fate.[16] Jean should not have sold the necklace even though she did not care about the family tradition. Since it wouldn't have cost her much to maintain it, the lifetime-transcending interests of her predecessors, as well as the idea that it would be good for her daughter to have an opportunity to value the necklace and the family tradition, should have influenced her behaviour. For the same reason, we should have made an effort to preserve some of our city's historic buildings—at least if we could have done so without great sacrifice. We are entitled to express our own tastes and values but not to the extent of destroying everything that was meant to have been a heritage for future generations.[17]

---

[16] A similar position is taken by Baier (1980, p. 176).

[17] How much of a sacrifice should we be expected to make in order to preserve a heritage? What if we have to make choices about what heritage to preserve? I don't think that any formula will decide

By appealing to lifetime-transcending interests to justify obligations we accomplish a number of objectives. First of all, we establish that members of communities have obligations in respect to their predecessors and that there is a way of determining what these are. Second, we show that members of communities have a moral interest in maintaining practices and institutions which enable legitimate lifetime-transcending demands to be made and fulfilled. This moral interest does not exist merely because present people happen to think that their lifetime-transcending demands ought to be fulfilled. Because they have moral reasons for making the demands that they do, they are entitled to insist that practices and institutions supporting the fulfilment of morally important lifetime-transcending demands ought to be valued by future as well as present generations. Members of a community have moral reasons to regard their fellows, past, present and future, as sharing a common good—namely, practices of making and fulfilling lifetime-transcending demands and the institutions that support these practices. The existence of these goods, and the particular obligations that arise from them, provide a vindication of the communitarian point of view. By being committed to maintain practices that require each generation to fulfil the morally legitimate demands of its predecessors the generations of a community are bound together in relationships of cooperation and have the obligations that follow from these relationships.

Duties to the Past and Future in the Transgenerational Polity

Individuals may be members of many different transgenerational communities and will have transgenerational obligations as members of these communities. The question remains whether they have transgenerational obligations as members of political societies.

There are two senses in which a political society might be described as transgenerational. In a weak sense a polity is transgenerational if it supports, underwrites, or at least makes possible transgenerational relationships of the kind discussed in the last section and the fulfilling of responsibilities associated with these relationships. In a strong sense a polity is transgenerational if citizens have responsibilities in respect to their nation's past and future: if their being citizens gives them obligations in respect to their national predecessors and successors.

such issues. Aesthetic, as well as practical and moral, considerations will be important. My purpose here is simply to establish that the demands of predecessors have a moral weight in this as in other cases.

For patriots their polity is transgenerational in the strong sense. They take their polity to be their primary community and accept that they have duties to preserve its heritage, honour those who made a contribution to it in the past and to make an effort to appreciate the inheritance provided by those who laboured for its sake. Not all citizens are patriots. But even non-patriots ought to value their polity in so far as it underwrites through its institutions and laws the practices that make the fulfilment of transgenerational obligations possible. I will argue that this requires that citizens, whether patriotic or not, ought to accept some duties in respect to their polity's past and future.

A transgenerational polity must maintain over time the institutions and practices that make cooperation between the generations possible. It ought to pursue policies that underwrite, or are at least compatible with, the important lifetime-transcending interests of its citizens, the maintenance of transgenerational practices and fulfilment of obligations associated with them. Those who are concerned about the future well-being of their children and grandchildren, the future of projects or traditions, or the achievement of an ideal will have an objective interest in the continued existence of practices and institutions that make it more likely that their successors will be able to live well, continue projects, or achieve an ideal. They have an interest in their polity pursuing long-term policies for protecting social and environmental conditions that make this possible. But as a corollary to their particular lifetime-transcending interests, they also have a moral interest in the maintenance of practices that underwrite the making and fulfilling of lifetime-transcending interests and of the conditions that make it possible for these practices to flourish. If, for example, the members of communities are to maintain a practice of passing on an inheritance to their successors and think that their successors ought to make an effort to appreciate it, then they ought to ensure that their successors will be in the position to do so. This requires that their successors have sufficient means; at least they cannot be miserable, poor, or preoccupied by problems of survival. Institutions that underwrite the fulfilment of lifetime-transcending aims and obligations require the perpetuation of favourable social and political conditions, and citizens have an objective moral interest in these conditions being perpetuated.

These requirements have two implications for a theory about the trans-generational obligations of citizens. First of all, they imply that citizens have responsibilities for past actions and policies of their polity. The perpetuation of favourable conditions for the satisfaction of lifetime-transcending demands depends on the ability of polities to maintain institutions and pursue policies and objectives over a long period of time. This means that a polity must be able to act as a responsible agent in its relationships with other polities. For example, if maintaining environmental or social infrastructure or ensuring the security of institutions requires long term agreements with other polities, then our polity must be prepared to make and fulfil commitments and to make recompense for past failures to do so. Citizens must be prepared to fulfil agreements made by their predecessors; they must sometimes be prepared to make recompense for historical wrongs.[18]

The requirements associated with transgenerational demands and practices also mean that citizens have duties in respect to the future of their polity. Those citizens who have particular lifetime-transcending interests—for example, in the well-being of their descendants or in the achievement of an ideal—will obviously have reason for supporting policies and institutions that ensure that the desires associated with these interests can be fulfilled. But citizens also have obligations to people of the future simply because they are involved with them in cooperative relationships aimed at maintaining transgenerational practices and institutions and are members of a polity that supports these practices and institutions.

As members of a transgenerational polity, citizens present and future have an obligation to take responsibility for past commitments and actions of their polity—at least in so far as it is a political society that acts in the interests of its citizens. They have a duty to maintain practices and favourable conditions for future generations. Past members of the polity had similar obligations. In maintaining transgenerational institutions and practices, and maintaining conditions under which these institutions and practices can thrive, the generations in a transgenerational polity are embedded in relationships of mutual dependence. It is important to stress that this is so, because liberals often present intergenerational relationships as a one-way street on which present people do all the giving and future people all the taking; or on which present people are free to exercise their power to affect future people and future people have no recourse.[19] This is mistaken. We depend on future people to fulfil legitimate demands based on lifetime-transcending interests, to fulfil our commitments and to perpetuate institutions that ensure that practices of fulfilling such demands and commitments can be maintained. We play our role in these communal relations of cooperation by fulfilling the legitimate lifetime-transcending demands of our predecessors, honouring the commitments of our political predecessors, and pursuing policies that ensure that future citizens will be in the position to play their role.

[18] I argue for this in much more detail in (2003b, Ch. 2).

[19] Brian Barry (1978) argues that the powerlessness of future generations means that our relationship to them does not satisfy what Hume called the 'circumstances of justice'. Barry takes this as a reason for rejecting a view of duties to future generations which depends on cooperation.

Communitarianism and Distant Strangers

In the last sections I have assembled reminders for the purpose of revealing the ways in which political societies are transgenerational polities with institutions and practices that generate transgenerational obligations and encourage citizens to regard themselves as playing a role in transgenerational systems of cooperation. In doing so, I have been defending a position that can be described as communitarian. However, there are objections to such a position that need to be addressed. Many people who enter the debate about intergenerational duties have environmental concerns. They point out that our activities have the potential to do harm not just to our successors but also to people remote in time.[20] They insist that a concern for future generations must be a concern for all future people on the planet and not just the members of our community or polity. A communitarian approach, which focuses on obligations that arise from communal relationships, seems ill-equipped to tell us what we should do for the sake of distant strangers, geographic or temporal.

Communitarians, especially those who accept liberal ideas about the moral considerability of all individuals, have no great difficulty explaining how political societies and their citizens can acquire responsibilities to people of other communities. The people of such communities are also embedded in transgenerational relationships of cooperation that they have reason to value. A respect for their interests and their communities requires us to avoid doing them harm and not doing things that could harm their successors. It may also require, in the face of environmental and other global problems, that we cooperate with them to ensure that present and future generations will be able to live well and maintain the relationships that they value.

The problem posed by the possibility of harm to people remote in time seems more difficult to overcome. In fact, many accounts of duties to future generations which rely on people sharing a common good or being in relationships of corporation seem to give them duties only to their more immediate successors. The moral difference that we can expect will exist between us and more remote generations suggests that de-Shalit's account of obligations to future generations is not going to take us very far into the future. In Rawls's early account of justice between the generations, our duties extend no further than our goodwill, which, he suggests, stretches over not much more than two generations (1971, p. 128).

[20] See, for example, the Routleys (1980).

These severe limitations can be overstepped—at least to some extent. In the face of our present ability to affect conditions in the more remote future, the concern of family representatives for their children and grandchildren should surely include a concern about the ability of these descendants to ensure a good life for their descendants, and so on. Given that we do not know what moral ideals will be possessed by our more remote successors, it is, perhaps, morally preferable to assume that they will be sufficiently like ours so as to make them members of our community. But neither of these ways of extending the temporal scope of our duties seems entirely satisfactory. Good will and ability to assume a continuity of moral interaction are still going to have their limits.

The position that I have defended is more easily extended to encompass distant generations. We can reasonably assume that people of the more remote future will have lifetime-transcending interests and will make lifetime-transcending demands. Given the importance of these interests to human life, as we understand it, it is morally necessary to make this assumption. Even remote generations can be regarded as successors, as participants in a never-ending chain of relationships in which each generation fulfils moral requirements in respect to its predecessors and successors. The people of the remote future may have different moral ideas and different political institutions, but so long as they are in the above sense our successors, we have a duty not act in ways that might undermine the conditions that need to exist if they are to maintain their institutions and pursue their interests.

Conclusion

The position that I have been defending is communitarian in the sense that it holds that members of a polity, and other communities, share a common good and, in maintaining this good and fulfilling its requirements, are embedded in relationships which give them moral obligations. Communitarianism has the potential to do what liberal theories do not do: to make relationships between the generations central to an account of moral obligations in a political society. The theory I have defended shows how this promise can be fulfilled. Furthermore, it shows that these relationships give us obligations in respect to the past as well as to the future. On the other hand, the theory I have presented is not incompatible with liberalism. Indeed, it appeals to familiar liberal ideas about the importance of individuals being able to live good lives. It is incompatible only with the views of those liberals who deny that present people can make moral demands of their successors or are required to take responsibility for the deeds of their predecessors. But there are good reasons to reject these views. My account of transgenerational obligations does not claim that members of a nation or of other communities have a duty to maintain traditions or to carry on the projects of their forebears, but it insists on a respect for the efforts made by past generations; it requires that we fulfil their morally legitimate demands. Communitarianism, so understood, underwrites and justifies the conviction held by many citizens: that they belong to a historical community of obligation.

References

ARRHENIUS, G. (1999), 'Mutual advantage contractarianism and future generations', *Theoria*, 65/1: 25–35.

BAIER, A. (1985), 'Cartesian persons', in A. Baier, *Postures of the Mind* (Minneapolis: University of Minnesota Press).

—— (1980), 'The rights of past and future persons', in E. Partridge (ed.), *Responsibilities to Future Generations* (Buffalo, NY: Prometheus Books), 171–86.

BARRY, B. (1989), *Theories of Justice* (London: Harvester-Wheatsheaf).

—— (1979), 'Justice as reciprocity', in E. Kamenka and A. Erh-Soon Tay (eds.), *Justice* (London: Edward Arnold Press), 204–48.

—— (1978), 'Circumstances of justice and future generations', in R. I. Sikora and B. Barry (eds.), *Obligations to Future Generations* (Philadelphia: Temple University).

BUCHANAN, A. (1999), 'Assessing the communitarian critique of liberalism', *Ethics*, 89: 852–82.

BURKE, E. (1995), *Reflections on the Revolution in France* (New York: Bobbs-Merrill, 1995).

DE GEORGE, R. (1981), 'The environment, rights and future generations', in E. Partridge (ed.) *Responsibilities to Future Generations* (Buffalo, NY: Prometheus Books), 157–65.

DE-SHALIT, A. (1995), *Why Posterity Matters: Environmental Policies and Future Generations* (London and New York: Routledge).

—— (1990), 'Bargaining with the not-yet born?', *International Journal of Moral and Social Studies*, 5/3: 221–34.

ENGLISH, J. (1977), 'Justice between generations', *Philosophical Studies*, 31: 91–104.

FEINBERG, J. (1984), *Harm to Others*, vol 1 of *The Moral Limits of the Law* (Oxford, New York: Oxford University Press).

GAUTHIER, D. (1986), *Morals By Agreement* (Oxford: Clarendon Press).

HUBIN, D. C. (1976), 'Justice and future generations', *Philosophy and Public Affairs*, 6/1: 70–83.

KUMAR, R. (2003), 'Who can be wronged?', *Philosophy and Public Affairs*, 31/2: 99–120.

KYMLICKA, W. (2002), *Contemporary Political Philosophy* (2nd Edition, Oxford, New York: Oxford University Press).

LOMASKY, L. (1987), *Persons, Rights and the Moral Community* (Oxford, London: Oxford University Press, 1987).

MacINTYRE, A. (1981), *After Virtue: A Study in Moral Theory* (London: Duckworth).

MARSHALL, P. (1993) 'Thinking for the future: reflections on Avner de-Shalit', *Journal of Applied Philosophy*, 10/1: 105−13.

McMAHAN, J. (1997), 'The limits of national partiality', in R. McKim and J. McMahan (eds.), *The Morality of Nationalism* (New York, Oxford: Oxford University Press), 107−38.

MILLER, D. (1997), 'Nationality: some replies', *Journal of Applied Philosophy*, 14.

—— (1995), *On Nationality* (Oxford: Clarendon Press).

PARFIT, D. (1984), *Reasons and Persons* (Oxford: Oxford University Press).

PARTRIDGE, E. (1981), 'Posthumous interests and posthumous respect', *Ethics*, 91: 243−264.

—— (1981b), 'Why care about the future?', in E. Partridge (ed.), *Responsibilities to Future Generations* (Buffalo: Prometheus), 203−19.

PITCHER, G. (1984), 'The misfortunes of the dead', *American Philosophical Quarterly*, 21: 182−8.

RAWLS, J. (1993), *Political Liberalism* (New York: Columbia University Press).

—— (1971), *A Theory of Justice* (Cambridge: Harvard University Press).

ROUTLEY, V. and R. (1980), 'Nuclear energy and obligations to the future', in E. Partridge (ed.) *Responsibilities to Future Generations* (Buffalo, N.Y.: Prometheus Books).

SANDEL, M. (1982), *Liberalism and the Limits of Justice* (Cambridge, New York: Cambridge University Press).

SCHWARTZ, T. (1978), 'Obligations to posterity', in R. K. Sikora and B. Barry (eds.), *Obligations to Future Generations* (Philadelphia: Temple University Press).

TAMIR, Y. (1993), *Liberal Nationalism* (Princeton: Princeton University Press).

TAYLOR, C. (1989), *Sources of the Self: The Making of the Modern Identity* (Cambridge, New York: Cambridge University Press).

THOMPSON, J. (2003), 'Intergenerational responsibilities and the interests of the dead', in H. Dyke (ed.), *Time and Ethics: Essays at the Intersection* (Dordrecht: Kluwer), 71−83.

—— (2003b), *Taking Responsibility for the Past: Reparation and Historical Injustice* (Cambridge: Polity).

WALDRON, J. (1996), 'Multiculturalism and melange' in R. K. Fullinwider (ed.), *Public Education in a Multicultural Society: Policy, Theory, Critique* (Cambridge, New York: Cambridge University Press), 90−118.

WELLMAN, C. (1995), *Real Rights* (New York, Oxford: Oxford University Press).

2

Libertarian Theories
of Intergenerational Justice

HILLEL STEINER AND PETER VALLENTYNE

We here discuss and assess various libertarian positions on intergenerational justice. We do not attempt to defend libertarianism. Instead, we work out the most plausible version thereof and identify its implications for intergenerational justice.

1. Justice and Libertarianism

The term 'justice' is commonly used in several different ways. Sometimes it designates the moral permissibility *of political structures* (such as legal systems). Sometimes it designates moral *fairness* (as opposed to efficiency or other considerations that are relevant to moral permissibility). Sometimes it designates *legitimacy*, in the sense of it being morally impermissible for others to interfere forcibly with the act or omission (e.g., my failing to go to dinner with my mother may be wrong but nonetheless legitimate). Finally, sometimes it designates *what we owe each other* in the sense of respecting everyone's rights. Of course, these notions are closely related. What we owe each other may, but need not, be partly based on issues of fairness. Legitimacy and permissibility of political structures are largely, but perhaps not entirely, determined by what rights of non-interference individuals have. Nonetheless, these are distinct notions and we shall focus only on what we owe each other.

Justice as what we owe each other is not concerned with impersonal duties (duties owed to no one, i.e., that do not correspond to anyone's rights). If

For useful comments, we thank Dani Attas, Axel Gosseries, Eric Heidenreich, Jason Glahn, Lucas Meyer, Mike Otsuka, Eric Roark, Alan Tomhave, Jon Trerise, Andrew Williams, and an anonymous reviewer.

there are impersonal duties, then something can be just but nonetheless morally impermissible. For brevity, we shall often write of actions being permissible or agents having a moral liberty, but this should always be understood in the interpersonal sense of violating no one's rights.

Libertarianism is sometimes advocated as a derivative set of rules (e.g., derived from rule utilitarian or contractarian doctrines). Here, however, we reserve the term for the natural rights doctrine that agents initially *fully own themselves*. Agents are *full self-owners* just in case they own themselves in precisely the same way that they can fully own inanimate objects. Stated slightly differently, full self-owners own themselves in the same way that a full chattel-slave-owner owns a slave. Throughout, we are concerned with moral ownership and not legal ownership. We are concerned, that is, with moral rights to control the use of resources and related rights rather than the rights that some legal system creates.

Full self-ownership consists of full private ownership of one's person (e.g., body). Full private ownership of an object consists of a full set of the following ownership rights: (1) *control rights* over the use of the object (liberty-rights to use it and claim-rights against others using it), (2) *rights to transfer* any of these rights to others (powers of sale, rental, gift, or loan), (3) *rights to compensation* if someone uses the object without one's permission, (4) *enforcement rights* (rights to use force to prevent the violation of these rights or to extract compensation owed for past violation), and (5) *immunities against the non-consensual loss* of these rights.[1]

All forms of libertarianism endorse full self-ownership. They differ with respect to the liberties persons have to use, or the moral powers they have to acquire ownership of, *natural resources* (and perhaps other resources). In the narrow sense, natural resources are all the resources in the world, in their unimproved form, that were not created by any (non-divine) agent. Natural resources (land, air, water, space, etc.) are contrasted with *artifacts* (improvements to natural resources, such as improvement to soil or constructions of chairs) and with *beings with moral standing* (which we, for simplicity, assume to be agents). Libertarians assume that agents initially fully own themselves and that, when they own all the factors of production, they initially fully own the artifacts that they produce. The core issue for libertarianism concerns how unowned resources can come to be privately owned. More exactly, the core

---

[1] Although full ownership determinately includes full control rights and full rights to transfer, there is some indeterminacy concerning compensation rights, enforcement rights, and immunity to loss (since one person's compensation rights and enforcement rights conflict with another person's immunity to loss). This is not relevant for the present paper, but we address it fully in Vallentyne, Steiner, and Otsuka (2005).

issue concerns how natural resources *and abandoned artifacts* (artifacts over which no one claims ownership; e.g., the estate of a monk who renounces all rights to earthly possessions) can come to be privately owned. For brevity, in what follows, natural resources should be understood as including any abandoned artifacts.

The best-known versions of libertarianism are *right-libertarian* theories, which hold that natural resources are initially unowned and that agents have a robust moral power to acquire full private ownership of unowned things. *Left-libertarians*, by contrast, hold that natural resources (e.g., space, land, minerals, air, and water) belong to all individuals in some egalitarian manner and thus, for example, cannot be privately appropriated without their consent or significant compensatory payment to them.[2] On this view, natural resources are initially *unowned* in the sense that no one's permission is needed to use or appropriate them, but they 'belong' to all in some egalitarian manner in the sense that those who appropriate (and perhaps those who use) natural resources owe a compensatory payment to those who are left with less than their egalitarian share of the *value* of natural resources.[3]

We here assume that some form of libertarianism is correct and focus on identifying the most plausible version and its implications for intergenerational justice.

There is a version of left-libertarianism, *joint-ownership left-libertarianism*, which holds that natural resources belong to everyone *collectively* (rather than severally and equally) and thus that private appropriation—and perhaps, much more radically, even use—requires collective consent of some sort (e.g., majority or unanimity). Because it allows no appropriation without the consent of others, it is not a very plausible form of libertarianism: it is doubtful that self-ownership can have much meaning under conditions where each person's access to natural resources requires collective consent. This problem is particularly acute in the case of multiple generations, where it is strictly impossible to obtain the consent of non-concurrent individuals. For simplicity, we shall therefore set *joint-ownership left-libertarianism* aside. We shall thus focus on *unilateralist* versions of libertarianism, which hold that agents are permitted to use, and have a moral power to appropriate, unowned resources without

---

[2] For more on left-libertarianism generally, see Vallentyne and Steiner (2000a, 2000b). For a critical assessment of left-libertarianism, see Fried (2004) and Vallentyne, Steiner, and Otsuka (2005).

[3] That is, we here rely on the following distinction: *owned* means protected by a property rule (i.e., consent is required for others' use), whereas *belongs to* means protected by a property rule or by a liability rule (consent is not required for others' use, but compensation is owed by them for use or appropriation). Unowned resources are resources that are not protected by a property rule, but they initially belong to all because they are protected by a liability rule.

anyone else's consent—but perhaps conditional upon making a compensatory payment to others.

Almost all unilateralist libertarian theories are *Lockean* in that they allow unilateral appropriation only on the condition that 'enough and as good' be left for others.[4] As we shall see below, there are several ways of interpreting this proviso. There is, however, one unilateralist theory, *radical right-libertarianism* that imposes no proviso on appropriation. It holds that individuals have the power to appropriate unowned things unilaterally simply by claiming them (or mixing-labour with them, etc.). They deny that any further conditions are relevant.[5] Radical right-libertarianism is, we believe, implausible. It holds that there is no injustice in one person destroying the world prior to appropriation by others, nor in appropriating the entire world and leaving everyone else in a miserable situation. In any case, it is clear that, according to radical right-libertarianism, there are no issues of intergenerational justice in the distribution of opportunities to use resources—which is the focus of this paper—and we shall therefore set it aside.

In what follows, then, we shall focus on Lockean libertarianism, which, as we shall see, comes in both left- and right-libertarian versions. Traditionally, the distinction between the two has been drawn in terms of a difference in their respective limits on *powers to appropriate* unowned resources (i.e., acquire rights over previously unowned things). It has been generally assumed that everyone is initially free to *use* unowned resources as they please (as long, of course, as they do not violate the self-ownership, or other established property rights, of others). Under certain assumptions, to be detailed below, this now seems to us to be a mistake (although we have both endorsed this view until now). One can use a resource (e.g., stand on some land) without appropriating it and, we shall now suggest, a proviso is needed on *permissible use* in addition to one on powers of appropriation. Given that this will be relevant for our discussion of intergenerational justice, we shall address this point here.

Consider an agent in a densely populated world who claims no private property rights over any natural resources, but goes around systematically destroying or radically degrading them on a massive scale. Given that there is no appropriation, standard accounts of Lockean libertarianism would see no injustice here, but we believe that this is a mistake. The core issue of importance is not merely when agents may *appropriate* resources; it also concerns issues of permissible *use*. One person's use of natural resources—even without appropriation—must be compatible with some kind of fair opportunity for others to use.

---

[4] For superb analysis of Locke's own quasi-libertarian views, see Simmons (1992, 1993).
[5] See, for example, Narveson (1988) and Rothbard (1978, 1982).

The need for a proviso on permissible use—and not merely on powers of appropriation—has been recognized and defended by Eric Mack (1995).[6] For example, in one of his many insightful cases, a group of people, without engaging in appropriation, form a human circle around another without touching her. This encircling makes it impossible for that person to move without infringing the self-ownership of the encirclers. Thus, if the encirclers are using resources (e.g., the land they are standing on) permissibly—and thus forfeiting none of their self-ownership rights for wrongful action—the encircled person is not permitted to move about. This implausible result leads Mack to endorse a proviso on permissible use of external resources. Roughly, it prohibits actions that severely disable another person's 'world interactive powers'. We fully agree that some such proviso is needed (although, as will become apparent below, we would reject the particular proviso that he defends).[7]

Thus, although there are forms of libertarianism that invoke neither a proviso on appropriation (radical right-libertarianism) nor a proviso on use (almost all standard versions of libertarianism), we believe that a plausible version will invoke a proviso on both use and appropriation.[8] In what follows, we shall therefore assume that some such proviso is needed and focus on what form it should take.[9]

2. Necessary Conditions for Having Rights

Libertarianism holds that individuals of a certain sort have rights of self-ownership and also have certain rights (powers) to appropriate unowned

[6] It is also implicit in Tideman (2000).

[7] Although Mack calls this 'the self-ownership proviso' and takes it to be part of the theory of self-ownership, we believe that it is just a proviso on the use of external resources. It places restrictions on the use of resources even when it does not violate self-ownership strictly understood (i.e., are not what Mack calls 'invasive' violations).

[8] Strictly speaking, we deny that a proviso on appropriation (acquisition of ownership of previous unowned things) is needed. Instead, all *ownership* of natural resources (even that acquired by transfer) is *conditional* on continued satisfaction of a proviso. For simplicity, however, we shall formulate the proviso on ownership as a proviso on appropriation.

[9] Mack believes that once an adequate proviso on use is imposed, no further proviso on appropriation is needed. As indicated in the previous note, there is a sense in which we agree with this. Mack, however, denies that there is any proviso on ownership generally (and not merely appropriation), and we disagree with this. The issue is complex, but if use is understood (as we do) narrowly as physical use, then this seems mistaken. Suppose that I appropriate the entire world except for a small plot around each other person. Even if my use disadvantages no one (e.g., I use only a small plot of land that no one else would use in any case), my ownership does (since they are not permitted to use other plots of land that I own without my permission).

things. There is, however, room for differing views about what kinds of beings have these rights. All agree that agents who now exist now have rights. There is disagreement, however, about whether dead people and future people have rights.

This disagreement can be traced to the presence of two longstanding broad views of the nature of rights.[10] On the *choice-protecting* conception, rights protect choice-making capacities and, thus, only beings that are capable of making choices can have rights. Moreover, the relevant choice-making capacities are typically understood in a fairly robust manner. Thus, they are lacked—not only by rocks and plants, but also—by lower animals, and young children. On the *interest-protecting* conception, rights protect the interests of individuals, and thus only beings that have interests can have rights. Rocks do not have rights. Nor do plants on most views (since the relevant interests are restricted to those of sentient beings). Children and many animals, however, do have rights on this conception.

Historically, libertarianism has always been based on the choice-protecting conception. Moreover, this conception has almost always been understood as implying that, for any given time, only those who are capable of *then* making choices *then* have rights. Thus, normal young children who will eventually be able to make (rationally robust) choices as adults are deemed not to have rights when they are young. On this view, at a given time, neither the deceased nor future people have rights.

If future people have no rights now, then it seems that there are no duties of justice owed to them now. There may be impersonal duties with respect to future people, but, since these are not duties *owed to them*, they are not duties of justice. Admittedly, this view imposes some intuitive strain. Suppose, for example, that there is a fully determinate (specific) autonomous agent who will come into existence, as such (and thus with full rights), tomorrow. Suppose that I now set a time-bomb that, with certainty, will kill this agent tomorrow. My action today sets off a causal process that, with certainty, will kill her. It seems at least arguable that my action today wrongs her (violates her rights)—even if, at the time of my action, she has no rights (because she does not then exist). After all, when the bomb goes off, she has a right not to be killed and the bomb, which I set, kills her.[11]

This is a complex and controversial issue, and we shall not attempt to resolve it here. We simply note that, if rights are restricted to choice-protecting

---

[10] For an extensive account of this disagreement, see Kramer, Simmonds, and Steiner (1998).

[11] For further discussion of this issue, see Feinberg (1984: 97), Meyer (2003c, sec. II), and Gosseries (2004: ch. 1).

rights, then it may well be that there are no issues of intergenerational justice between members of generations that do not temporally overlap one another.

Consider now the interest-protecting conception of rights. It has typically allowed that, at a given time, t, those who will definitely exist with significant interests at later times have rights at t, since those interests can be affected by what is done at t. Thus, if rights are understood in interest-protecting terms, then there may well be duties of justice to sentient fetuses and future people. To the best of our knowledge, however, no libertarian has endorsed the interest-protecting conception of rights. One main problem is that rights, so understood, permit, and may even require, others to use force against an autonomous agent against his will, when it is for his own benefit (e.g., forcibly preventing someone from smoking, or forcing someone to participate in exercise programs). Few, if any, libertarians can endorse that. The resulting conception of self-ownership is far too weak.

There is, however, a hybrid view—articulated by Vallentyne (2007)—that is relevant to the subject of this essay. Let us call it the 'choice-prioritizing theory'. It holds that rights protect *both* choices and interests, but that the protection of choices is *lexically prior* to the protection of interests. More specifically, it asserts that an individual, Holder, has a right that another, Agent, not perform action X just in case each of the following is a sufficient condition for the wrongness of Agent X-ing: (1) Holder has validly (e.g., freely and informedly) *dissented* from the performance of this action (i.e., expressed his opposition thereto), or (2) Holder has not validly *consented* and Agent's X-ing is *against Holder's interests*. Like the choice-protecting theory of rights, the choice-prioritizing theory allows that, for autonomous beings, their valid consent and dissent trump all countervailing concerns for their interests, but it also allows that non-autonomous beings with interests (e.g., children and animals) can have rights. The choice-prioritizing view thereby implies that, if Holder has a right against Agent performing action X, and Holder has neither validly consented to, nor validly dissented from, Agent X-ing, then Holder's interests are relevant for determining whether his rights are violated by that action. Thus, it has the plausible implication that saving someone's life by pushing her out of the way of an on-coming truck (of which she is unaware) does not violate her rights, even though she did not consent to being subjected to such force.

If the choice-prioritizing conception of rights is adopted, then future people can have rights because they can have interests. Indeed, with respect to future people, the choice-prioritizing conception is equivalent to the interest-protecting conception (since they have no relevant choices).

We shall not attempt here to resolve the complex issue of what features are necessary to be a rights-holder. If future people do not have rights, then we owe them no duties of justice. We shall therefore simply assume for the sake of argument that future people have rights and discuss the implications for justice according to different versions of libertarianism.

There is, of course, an analogous issue about whether dead people have rights. The standard choice-protecting view denies that they have rights because they no longer have any capacity for choice.[12] The interest-protecting and choice-prioritizing views could also deny that they have rights on the ground that they not now have the potential for experience (whereas future people do now have that potential). Although this is a somewhat controversial issue, for simplicity, we shall assume (as we each believe) that dead people have no rights.[13] We shall thus focus our attention on intergenerational duties of the current generation to future generations.

3. Our Core Case

We are now ready to begin our examination of the implications of Lockean libertarianism for intergenerational justice. We shall focus on the justice of the distribution of rights over external (natural and artifactual) resources, and we shall set aside injustices that arise from the violation of self-ownership. All forms of libertarianism agree that a violation of self-ownership is unjust. Thus, if future people will have rights of self-ownership, and setting a time-bomb now will, at some later date, but with certainty, kill them (and thus violate their self-ownership), then this counts as a form of intergenerational injustice. In what follows, however, we focus solely on the distribution of rights over external resources.

Throughout, we shall assume that generations are defined in the very strict sense as maximal sets of individuals born exactly at the same time. Obviously, in practice, looser definitions may be useful, but for present purposes it will simplify matters if all members of a given generation can be assumed to be born at exactly the same time.

Throughout, for simplicity, we shall assume that the only beings that have rights are agents (i.e., psychologically autonomous beings) who pop into

---

[12] It is worth noting here that, while standard (i.e., right-) libertarianism has thus denied that future people have rights, it has typically affirmed that the deceased *do* have rights—most notably, the right of bequest (discussed below).

[13] For more discussion of this issue, see Feinberg (1984: ch. 2), Steiner (1994: ch. 7(C)) and Gosseries (2004: ch. 2).

existence without going through pre-agency childhood. Moreover, we assume that there is no uncertainty about what people will exist or how their interests will be affected, if a given action is performed. Obviously, these assumptions side-step very important issues relevant to a theory of intergenerational justice. Dealing with the core issues is sufficiently complex, however, even with these simplifying assumptions.

We shall start with an extremely simple case and then serially introduce additional complexities. More exactly, we shall start with *the core case*, which is one where:

(1) Agents take no interest in other agents and thus there are no gifts or bequests.
(2) There is no procreation: individuals come into existence by natural forces and thus no agent bears any causal responsibility for the existence of other agents.
(3) There is a fixed natural number—assumed, for simplicity, to be two or three (depending on the example)—of non-overlapping generations.
(4) All generations have the same number of agents.

What constraints might a Lockean libertarian place on use and/or appropriation of unowned resources? As indicated above, we believe that some constraints must be placed on use—and not merely on appropriation. Suppose, for example, that the members of the first generation appropriate no resources, but destroy or radically degrade almost all natural resources (e.g., through massive pollution and radical deforestation)—with the net effect that members of the second generation are left with miserable, and much worse, opportunities to use natural resources. Standard versions of Lockean libertarianism—even left-libertarian versions—see no injustice in this, since no one has appropriated more than her fair share. We believe that this is implausible. Some constraints on permissible use are needed.

A Lockean proviso on use and appropriation requires, in some loose sense, that 'enough and as good' be left for others. There are different ways of making this more precise, but the standard approach, followed here, is to require that the *value of the initial opportunities* to use resources that are left for others be high enough. There are three main ways of doing this. One focuses solely on the initial opportunities to use *natural* resources.[14] A second focuses, more inclusively, on the initial opportunities to use *external* (natural and artifactual) resources (i.e., all resources other than the internal resources of one's

---

[14] See, for example, Steiner (1994), although the idea is invoked for a proviso on appropriations (but not on use).

person).[15] The third focuses, still more inclusively, on the initial opportunities to use *all* (natural, artifactual, and internal) resources.[16] Although this third approach takes internal endowments (i.e., the resources that are constitutive of persons) into account when evaluating the relevant initial opportunities, it, like the first two, holds that agents fully own themselves. A person with malfunctioning kidneys has a greater entitlement to external resources, but she has no entitlement to anyone else's kidney. The exact significance of the differences between these three versions will become clearer below when we discuss gifts. For the sake of generality, we formulate the proviso so as to be compatible with any of the three versions. For simplicity, however, we shall tend to focus on the narrow natural resource interpretation.

Let us start by considering a weak version of the Lockean proviso. It appeals to the idea of a 'decent' share of opportunities to use natural resources. There are many possible criteria of decency that might be invoked, but the core idea is that a decent share enables individuals to have some *minimally adequate* or *sufficient* quality of life. For example, it might ensure that they can satisfy all their basic needs. Consider, then:

Decent Share Proviso: An agent has a presumptive moral liberty to use, and has the moral power to appropriate, an unowned resource if and only if this (1) gives her no more than decent initial (lifetime) opportunities to use natural resources, or (2) adversely affects no other agent who is left with less than decent initial (lifetime) opportunities to use natural/external/all resources.[17]

Here and throughout, an agent, A, has *presumptive* moral liberty to use an object just in case no one has a claim right *over the object* that A not use it. For example, others do not have a presumptive moral liberty to use the car that I own (because of my claim rights over it), but I have a presumptive moral liberty to use that car (because no one has a claim right that I not use it). A presumptive moral liberty to use an object merely establishes that using it without anyone's consent does not *necessarily* violate anyone's claim rights. Of

---

[15] As far we know, this position has not been defended by anyone. It seems, however, worthy of exploration.

[16] See, for example, the equal opportunity for well-being approach of Otsuka (2003), although the idea is invoked for a proviso on appropriations (but not on use). Related approaches (although not in the context of a proviso on appropriation or use) are developed by Ackerman (1980) and Van Parijs (1995).

[17] The focus on *decent* lifetime opportunities to use natural resources is similar in spirit to the focus on severely disabling another person's 'world interactive powers' in the self-ownership proviso of Mack (1995). For related discussion of provisos on use or appropriation in the context of libertarian theory, see Elliot (1985), Wolf (1995), Gosseries (2001), and Gosseries (2004: ch. 3). For doubts about there being a principled (non-arbitrary) way of setting the decency level, see Arneson (2000; e.g., 56).

course, many uses of the object will violate the claim rights of others (as when I violate your self-ownership by hitting you with my car).

The proviso above and those below should be understood as satisfied when a person uses (or appropriates) more than the specified share of the specified resources but offsets the consequent disadvantage to others by leaving enough other resources for them to use.

We believe that, at least if the threshold for decent opportunities is set low enough (e.g., at the level needed for a life worth living), the Decent Share Proviso is correct in the necessary condition that it imposes. We believe, however, that this condition is not a sufficient condition for permissible use or appropriation. Suppose, for example, that natural resources are bountiful enough to give everyone a wonderful life and one person radically devastates them but leaves enough for each person to have a decent life. We believe that such use is not permissible. Natural resources belong to all of us in some egalitarian manner, and such a person is using more than her fair share.

Consider, then:

Egalitarian Proviso: An agent has a presumptive moral liberty to use, and a moral power to appropriate, an unowned resource if and only if this adversely affects no one who is left with less than an equally valuable initial (lifetime) opportunities to use natural/external/all resources.[18,19]

We believe that something in the general area of this proviso is plausible, but we shall not attempt a full defence here.[20] The core point is simply that natural resources, by definition, were not created by any human agent, and

[18] For simplicity, we here ignore complexities that are needed to deal with cases where inevitably someone will be left with less than equally valuable share but there is more than one way of doing this (e.g., where 0-6-6 and 0-3-9 are the only two feasible distributions). We also here ignore a possible weaker version of the Egalitarian Proviso on use: one might allow agents to leave less than an equally valuable opportunity to use external resources where this is necessary for the agent to have a life-opportunity worth having. The idea is that where an equal opportunity would leave everyone with an opportunity worse than death, then agents are permitted to use resources to obtain a life-opportunity worth having—even if this leaves much less for others. For defence of this idea, see Roark (2006).

[19] We take the Egalitarian Proviso to be in the same spirit as the following: '[M]embers of each generation [must] ensure that, at their deaths, resources that are at least as valuable as those they have acquired lapse back into a state of non-ownership.' (Otsuka 1998: 89). '[E]ach entering citizen receives a share of material wealth that is *equal* to that of others who are roughly contemporary and *no less* than that received by his predecessors.' (Ackerman, 1980: 208). It is also roughly the view expressed in fn. 2 of Rakowski (1991: 150).

[20] We here leave open the important issue of whether the value an agent's initial opportunities to use natural resources is her *total* lifetime opportunity, her *average* opportunity per unit of time lived, or something else. We are inclined to believe that each agent should indeed have equally valuable (total lifetime) opportunities—independently of how long she lives, but this will play no role in the argument that follows.

thus it is plausible that everyone has some kind of equal claim to having an opportunity to use them. This also seems true of abandoned artifacts (e.g., from earlier generations). Thus, a plausible version of Lockean libertarianism will be egalitarian about initial opportunities to use natural resources. It will, that is, be left-libertarian.[21] Obviously, even this is not uncontroversial, but we shall assume it in what follows.

As noted earlier, 'natural resources' is being understood in an extended sense to include any abandoned artifacts (e.g., from previous generations). Thus, the narrow natural resource interpretation of the Egalitarian Proviso requires that one disadvantage no one by leaving her less than an equally valuable share of strict natural resources plus abandoned artifacts. It is not sufficient, that is, to leave others an equally valuable share of strict (unimproved) natural resources (and, for example, leave them none of the abandoned artifacts). One must pass on a fair share that includes abandoned artifacts as well.[22] (Below, we shall consider the exact status of bequests.)

Given the Egalitarian Proviso, we can draw the following conclusions about the core case. For simplicity, we shall focus on the narrow natural resources interpretation. Assuming, as we are, that there are only a finite number of generations (and thus of individuals), individuals may use up their per capita share of the value of the opportunities to use natural resources. Thus, oil may be used up, but, subject to one qualification, only up to the per capita share. The qualification is that more oil may be used up if enough other resources are left to compensate for the additional use. Thus, for example, if an individual uses up less than her share of water, she may use up more than her share of oil—as long as she uses up no more than her per capita share of the value of *totality* of natural resources. Moreover, any artifactual resources that an individual leaves can compensate towards any excess use of natural resources. Thus, for example, if an individual leaves improved land or factories, that may—to the extent that they can be used by others—partially compensate for an excess use (or appropriation) of oil.

---

[21] Left-libertarianism is a form of liberal egalitarianism: its distinguishing feature is that it holds that agents are full self-owners and that this can place limits on the permissible means of achieving the relevant equality.

[22] As Gosseries (2001: 306) notes, the need to include abandoned assets from previous generations is not taken into account adequately in the following passages (which may not reflect the authors' considered views): '[T]he continued legitimacy of private ownership from the standpoint of self-ownership depends on each person in each successive generation obtaining the equivalent of a per capita share of unimproved, undegraded land.' (Arneson 1991: 53). '[A]s I will argue, the egalitarian proviso, when fully spelled out, requires that the members of each succeeding generation have at least as great an opportunity to own worldly resources as did the first generation to acquire resources out of the state of nature.' (Otsuka, 1998: 88; he later qualifies this statement to avoid limiting attention to the first generation).

It's worth noting that the Egalitarian Proviso leaves no room for a 'just savings principle' of the sort suggested by Rawls (1971: section 44) and others. Such a principle requires that, until society reaches a certain minimal level of prosperity, individuals have an obligation to invest some of their wealth to improve the prosperity of later generations (who will have greater prosperity than the generation in question). Neither libertarianism in general, nor the egalitarian component of left-libertarianism, supports any duty to invest so as to make others better off than oneself. This seems eminently plausible to us.[23]

We shall now consider an implication of the Egalitarian Proviso (interpreted narrowly in terms of natural resources only) that has been questioned by Axel Gosseries. Consider a case where there are just two individuals whose existence is predetermined and who do not overlap. There are only two natural resources: 100 units of oil and environmental warmth. Due to natural forces, warmth is diminishing. Warmth is not affected by human activity (e.g., because of low population size and primitive technology). Both individuals regard the cooling as a reduction in the value of opportunities to use natural resources that would be exactly compensated by 100 units of oil. Thus, both individuals are indifferent between the warmer temperatures of the first person with no use of oil and the colder temperatures of the second person with the use of 100 units of oil. The Egalitarian Proviso holds that the first person must leave all the oil to the second person (since otherwise he would be disadvantaging her by leaving her with less than an equally valuable share).

Gosseries (2001: 307–11) has suggested that a plausible interpretation of the Lockean proviso will not require individuals to compensate later individuals for the negative effects of *naturally* caused degradations (such as the cooling of the planet in our example). Gosseries claims that the Lockean proviso only requires compensation for the negative effects of one's actions (or one's existence) *relative to inaction (or non-existence)*. Since, naturally caused degradations occur even if one does not exist, one owes no compensation for such effects. Thus, in our example, the first person may use 50 units of oil and leave 50 for the second person—even though this will mean that the second person's opportunities to use natural resources are less valuable. Glossaries' interpretation of the Lockean proviso is thus incompatible with the Egalitarian Proviso interpretation.

---

[23] It should be noted that Rawls emphasizes that: 'Justice does not require that early generations save so that later ones are simply wealthier. Savings is demanded as a condition of bringing about the full realization of just institutions and the fair value of liberty.' Nonetheless, we find it implausible that justice requires the worst of members of society (viewed intergenerationally) to make a sacrifice that benefits the better off. For discussion of savings requirements from several moral perspectives, see Gosseries (2001) and Gosseries (2004: ch. 4).

Gosseries assumes that an interpretation of the Lockean proviso must focus solely on the impact of one's actions (or existence) relative to inaction or non-existence. He is right that this is the standard way of interpreting Locke and of developing a Lockean position. He is also right that so understood, the effects of naturally caused degradation are irrelevant. Such a position, however, is (as Gosseries recognizes) implausible. Everyone has an equal claim to the benefits of natural resources. The first person thus violates the rights of the second person if he leaves her only 50 units of oil (given her colder temperatures). This case is no different from a case where two contemporaries live on different islands and know that the first island's natural resources are more valuable than those of the other. Suppose that the only non-island-based natural resource is fish and that the more valuable first island is 'upstream' from the second. Suppose that the stream provides a total of 100 fish and that both agree that 100 fish exactly compensates for the less valuable island-based natural resources on the second island. It is quite implausible to claim that the person on the first island may take 50 of the fish. This leaves the second person with a less valuable share of natural resources. It is the value of the overall bundle of natural resources that individuals have that matters and the mere fact that some differences in opportunities to use particular kinds of natural resources are *naturally* imposed is irrelevant.

If Lockeanism is committed to focusing solely on the effects of one's action (or existence) relative to inaction (or non-existence), it is thus implausible. Lockeanism need not, however, be construed so narrowly. As we construe it, it allows that the relevant test is whether a fair share is left for others and that can depend on the acts of nature (and perhaps on the acts of other agents). The Egalitarian Proviso is compatible with this broader conception of Lockeanism, and provides, we believe, a plausible interpretation. It does not fetishize natural resources. It allows that they may be degraded if this makes for a better life. No individual, however, may degrade or use up more than her per capita share of natural resources without suitable offsetting compensation.

4. Generations of Different Sizes

Let us now relax the assumption that each generation has the same number of agents—but continue, for simplicity, to focus on the case where there are just two generations. For concreteness, suppose that the first generation has 10 people and the second generation has 20. Suppose that the first generation uses up half of the value of natural resources and leaves no offsetting artifacts. Is this just?

One view—tentatively endorsed by Gosseries (2001: 311)—is that justice is a relation between generations as collectivities. In this example, since there are just two generations, the first generation is permitted to use up half of the value of natural resources. If there were three generations, then each generation would be permitted to use up one third of the value of natural resources. On this view, there is no injustice in the above example.

We believe that this view is mistaken. Justice—and libertarian justice in particular—is matter of relations between individuals, not relations between generations viewed as collectivities. Thus, the equal opportunity test should be applied to individuals, not to generations. In the example, there are 30 people. Each is thus permitted to use up one-thirtieth of the value of natural resources. In aggregate, the first generation (with 10 people) is thus permitted to use up one third of the value of natural resources. The Egalitarian Proviso, as we have formulated it, requires that an agent leave each other agent opportunities to use unowned natural resources that are at least as valuable as the ones that she has. Thus, it correctly applies the egalitarian test to individuals and not to generations.

5. Overlapping Generations

Let us now drop the assumption that there is no overlap between generations. Suppose, for example, that there are just two generations, that everyone lives for 100 years, and that the second generation comes into existence 50 years after the first. Does this change anything important?

One significant change is that, when there is overlap, the choice-protecting conception recognizes duties of intergenerational justice. When there is no overlap, it arguably does not recognize any such duties because the members of the subsequent generation do not exist at any time at which the members of the current generation perform actions. When there is overlap, however, then members of the subsequent generation exist, with rights, at the time of action of members of the first generation. Thus, the fact of overlap makes a very significant difference on the choice-protecting conception of rights.

The implications of the choice-prioritizing conception and the interest-protecting conception, however, are not affected, since they can recognize duties of intergenerational justice even when there is no overlap. For these conceptions, overlap requires no change in principles, but it does introduce two important changes in empirical implications.

The empirical implications concern ownership rights. When there was no overlap, the agents of the first generation could fully appropriate natural resources. They merely had to ensure that, at death, the value of the natural resources and artifacts that each left for each member of the next generation was at least as great as the per capita value of the natural resources that had been initially available to each of them. However, when generations overlap, the equal entitlements of the second-generation members take effect prior to the death of the members of the first generation. Thus, although there is no problem (as in the non-overlap case) with the first generation initially appropriating *all* natural resources, their ownership of these natural resources is not unconditional. When the second generation comes into existence, the members of the first generation may lose some of their rights over resources—if they are now disadvantaging someone by taking more than their per capita share. More specifically, if there are n members of the first generation and m members of the second generation, and the initial value of natural (and abandoned artifactual) resources was V, then each member of the first generation must relinquish rights over (natural or artifactual) resources to the extent that their rights over natural resources exceed the value $V/(n + m)$. Suppose, for example, that the initial value of natural resources was 90 units, that there were 10 members of the first generation, and that there are 20 members in the second generation. Prior to the arrival of the second generation, each member of the first generation could appropriate natural resources worth up to 9 (90/10) units without the need to compensate others (as long as they do not degrade those resources). Once the second generation arrives, however, compensation is then required from those who have appropriated natural resources in excess of 3 (90/30) units of value.

In short, when generations overlap, the fair shares for the purposes of appropriation are recalculated when new right-bearing individuals come into existence, and individuals with excess shares must relinquish them or provide compensation. The new fair share is no different from that which they would have to leave at their death in the case of non-overlap (on the assumption that future individuals have rights). The only difference is that it must be provided during the agents' lifetimes when new individuals come into existence.

The second important empirical implication that arises where generations overlap is that there is the opportunity for members of different generations to cooperate in mutually beneficial ways. Where the generations do not overlap, first generation individuals have no incentive to leave more than the required minimum share of natural resources for the later generation. With overlapping generations, however, agreements can be made that make both parties better off and have the effect of enhancing the likelihood that artifactual wealth is passed on to later generations. For example, it might be that, for a given generation, the costs of their limiting global warming outweigh the benefits, but that (given the positive externalities of such limitation), *for the totality of overlapping generations at a given time*, the benefits of their limiting global warming outweigh the costs. Each generation will therefore have an incentive to limit global warming if overlapping generations also do so. The net effect over time of such limitation is that later generations will benefit from the limitations of much earlier non-overlapping generations.

6. Procreation

So far, we have been assuming that there is no uncertainty about who will exist. Moreover, we have also been assuming that agents come into existence simply as the result of deterministic natural forces and without any role for the choices of other agents: agents are not procreated. Things become very complex when there is indeterminacy about who will exist, and it is beyond the scope of this paper to address this issue generally. Instead, we shall now introduce only an extremely limited—and highly artificial—form of indeterminism about who will exist. We shall assume that there is one person who has one opportunity to add one additional person to the world by making an appropriate procreative choice (as well as the opportunity not to do so).[24] For simplicity, we shall, however, continue to assume that agents pop into existence fully formed (without first going through non-autonomous phases). The question on which we focus is that of who is responsible for providing the offspring's fair share of opportunities to use natural/external/all resources: the procreator or the members of society in general? Although this does not raise issues of intergenerational justice in the collective sense, it does raise such issues in the individualist sense, since it is concerned with the issue of what duties individuals owe members of later generations.

---

[24] We do not here attempt to deal with the very important issues that arise from the non-identity problem in the context of person-affecting principles of justice. Some excellent books on this issue and population ethics generally include Roberts (1998), Arrhenius (2000), Broome (2004), and Blackorby, Bossert, and Donaldson (2005). For a view about how egalitarians should respond to the non-identity problem while endorsing a person-affecting view of morality, see Tungodden and Vallentyne (2006).

To start, we note that libertarianism—like many other views—denies that there is any general duty to procreate. First, no matter how wonderful a possible person's life might be, one owes her no duty (of justice) to bring her into existence. For, if she does not come into existence, she never acquires the features necessary for having rights (autonomy or interests), and hence her non-existence does not violate any of her rights (since she has none). Second, under normal conditions (e.g., absent any contractual obligation), one owes no duty of justice to others to procreate.[25]

The question that we shall address is this: Who has the duty to provide the fair share of opportunities for procreated individuals? No one? The parents? All members of society? Some combination of these? The issue, of course, is extremely complex. For simplicity, we shall consider only the easiest case—one where parents *intentionally* procreate offspring with no unexpected results. Other cases may require a more nuanced treatment and we shall not here attempt to address such cases.

The mere fact that an individual was procreated (as opposed to coming into existence merely by forces of nature) does not eliminate or reduce her right to an equal share of opportunities to use the relevant resources. Hence, some others have a duty to provide her fair share. The question is whether her parents have a special duty to provide this fair share or whether it falls to the members of society generally. We assume that, at a minimum, the members of society owe this duty to the offspring to the extent that it is not possible for the parents to provide the fair share (e.g., because they are dead or too poor). Individuals, that is, do not lose their right to their fair share of resources simply because their procreators fail to provide it. The core question, then, is whether the duty to provide the fair share falls *in the first instance* to the parents or to the members of society.

The argument in favour of the view that procreators—rather than members of society in general—have a duty to provide the fair share to their intentionally procreated beings is reasonably straightforward. For simplicity, assume that the only relevant resources are natural resources. Suppose that we have only a single generation consisting of two people. The total value of natural resources is 60 and thus each has a right to a share worth 30. Suppose that one agent, A, then intentionally uses up 20 of his units of value, and is left with 10 units. He cannot now plausibly claim that each person has a right to an equal share of the remaining 40 units—that is, that he, like his contemporary, is now entitled to 20 (40/2) units. The right to an equal share is not, after all, a right

---

[25] For discussion of non-libertarian reasons why one might owe a duty to others to procreate, see section 2 of Meyer (2003a).

to an *ongoing* equal share. It is a right to an equal *initial* share. The right of his contemporary to 30 units is not affected by A's decision to use up some of his units. The contemporary still has a right to 30 units and A has a right to only 10 units.

Suppose now that, instead of using up 20 units, A intentionally procreates an additional (adult) agent. Again, it would be implausible for A to claim that he, like the two others, is now entitled to 20 (60/3) units. The right of his contemporary is to a certain initial share and that is not affected (at least not in the first instance) by A's decision to procreate. Thus, A's contemporary still has a right to 30 units. The new third agent has the same rights as anyone else. In particular, he has the right to the same initial share as the other two. That right was a right to 30 units. Thus, the new third agent has a right to 30 units. The procreating first agent thus has no rights to any of the natural resources and, indeed, has an obligation to transfer his 30 units to his offspring.[26]

It's important to note that the above case is quite different from the case where the third person was destined (inevitably) to come into existence by natural forces (and not by procreation). In this case, each individual has a right to 20 (60/3) units of natural resources. Where an individual intentionally procreates, however, she is responsible for the existence of procreated being and is thus accountable for providing the same share to her as the share of other individuals.

We conclude that it is procreators who have the duty, in the first instance, to provide the fair share to their intentionally created offspring.[27] The rights of offspring to their fair share are, however, also held against all the pre-existing people. The latter have the duty to provide the fair share, if (but only if) procreators cannot be made to do so.

7. Gifts and Bequests

So far, we have assumed that agents take no interest in each other and thus make no gifts—whether they be bequests (gifts from dead people) or *inter vivos*

---

[26] Whether further transfers are warranted, from procreators who use higher-valued genetic inform-ation to procreate, may depend on whether such information counts as a natural resource; see Steiner (1994, chs. 7(B), 8), Steiner (1997) and (1999).

[27] We here leave open the more difficult issue of non-intentionally created offspring. The view that parents have the duty to provide the fair shares to their offspring is advocated by Ackerman (1980: 200), Rakowski (1991: 153), Casal and Williams (2004), and Tideman (2000). For a general discussion of the rights and duties of procreators from a quasi-libertarian perspective, see Vallentyne (2002a). For a discussion of the rights and duties of custodial parents, see Vallentyne (2003).

gifts. We shall now relax this assumption. The question is whether a plausible form of left-libertarianism will place restrictions on gift-giving in order to reduce its disruptive effects on initial equality of opportunity. Although this issue arises even within a given generation, it is particularly acute when there are gifts between generations.

As background, we note that no plausible version of left-libertarianism (or any theory of justice) will prohibit, as a matter of public policy, gift-giving outright. Gift-giving is something that most people find intrinsically valuable (e.g., distributing birthday gifts to children). Prohibiting gifts outright would not only deprive almost everyone of this benefit, it would also significantly reduce the incentive for individuals to accumulate wealth and leave it for the benefit for others. If legal restrictions are placed on gift-giving, they will take the form of a tax liability and not a prohibition. Moreover, the tax liability will be only for gifts that disrupt initial equality of opportunity. Thus, for example, gifts to a person who has less than average initial opportunity will not generate a tax liability. Finally, the enforced tax rate will typically be less than one hundred per cent, for it will be set at a rate that will maximally benefit those who have less than equal initial opportunities. It might be set, for example, at a rate that will maximize tax revenues from gift taxation. (This is normally not one hundred per cent, since such a rate provides no incentive to accumulate wealth and make gifts.)

Let us start by addressing bequests. Bequests in the strict sense are gifts from dead people. Because dead people have no rights, there is no right to make bequests. This is straightforward on a choice-protecting conception of rights, since dead people no longer have the capacity to exercise their wills. It is arguably also true on the choice-prioritizing and interest-protecting conceptions. Of course, there is a clear sense in which the interests that people had prior to death can be advanced or thwarted after their death, but the question is whether this sense is relevant for justice. We claim that it is not. The only relevant interests, we claim, are those that presuppose the potential for sentience. Since dead people have no such potential, they have, we claim, no interests in the relevant sense.[28]

Bequests in the strict sense need to be distinguished from quasi-bequests, where these are understood as transfers of rights that take place during the lifetime of the donor, but which are conditional and temporarily delayed. A quasi-bequest has roughly the following form: I now transfer to you the conditional right of ownership over my car that takes effect when and only

---

[28] For an argument that there are duties owed to someone that survive that person's death (and moral standing), see Meyer (2003b).

when I die and you are alive. Unlike genuine bequests, a quasi-bequest immediately deprives the bequeather of some of the ownership incidents they would otherwise continue to possess up to the moment of their deaths. Thus, for example, having quasi-bequeathed my car to you, I no longer have the power to sell it or the liberty to destroy it. Given that almost all real-life 'bequests' can be made to take the form of quasi-bequests, the absence of a right of bequest in the strict sense has little practical import in most cases. It does, however, have some import: any resources that agents own at the time of their death are abandoned assets and become part of the pool of natural resources (in the extended sense).

Of course, agents may still be able to transfer their assets by *inter vivos* gift. In the remainder of this section, then, we shall focus on *inter vivos* gifts. Such gifts can take place between members of the same generation, as well as between members of different, but overlapping, generations. (By definition, *inter vivos* gifts are not possible between members of non-overlapping generations.)

If an agent fully owns a given resource, he is morally free to destroy it if he wishes. Moreover, he has—as part of his full ownership of the resource—a full formal right to transfer his rights over the resource to someone else. In order for a right to be transferred to someone, however, the recipient must have the moral power to acquire the rights involved. (One cannot transfer property to a mosquito merely by so willing.) The crucial question here is what kinds of rights agents have to acquire property by gift.

From a libertarian perspective, there are two main kinds of right to acquire property: (1) rights of initial appropriation, which govern the conditions under which an agent can acquire rights over a previously unowned thing; and (2) rights of transfer, which govern the conditions under which an agent can acquire rights over a previously owned thing with the consent of the previous owner. (We here ignore, for simplicity, rights of rectification, which govern the conditions under which agents can acquire rights over a previously owned thing in virtue of the previous owner having violated their rights.) Neither of these rights follows from full self-ownership or from the full ownership of the thing transferred. Full self-ownership tells us nothing about the moral power to acquire other things. Full ownership of a particular thing includes the full right to transfer it to others if they consent *and have the moral power to acquire rights by transfer.* That leaves open, however, whether agents have such moral powers.

We assume—as do all libertarians—that agents have an unrestricted moral power to acquire rights by transfer in cases where there is an exchange of rights with equal competitive value (as in typical cases of market exchange).[29] The question here is whether agents also have an unrestricted moral power to acquire rights transferred *by gift* (e.g., where there is only a one-way transfer, or where there is an exchange of rights of unequal competitive value).[30] The standard libertarian assumption is that agents do have such a power, but this is required neither by the libertarian thesis of full self-ownership, nor by any particular view about the moral powers of appropriation (initial ownership). It is thus open to libertarians to adopt a restricted view of the power to acquire rights by gift. Right-libertarians, of course, will find such an adoption implausible, but left-libertarians need not.

Indeed, given that left-libertarians impose something like the Egalitarian Proviso on use and appropriation, it seems natural for them to impose comparable conditions on acquisition by transfer as well. For clarity, let us rename and restate the former condition:

Egalitarian Proviso on Use and Appropriation: An agent has a presumptive moral liberty to use, and a moral power to appropriate, an unowned resource if and only if this adversely affects no one who is left with less than an equally valuable initial (lifetime) opportunity to use natural/external/all resources.

As noted above, there are three versions of this proviso depending on what kinds of resources—natural, external (including artifacts), or all (also including the internal endowments of agents)—are relevant for the equally valuable initial opportunity to use test. For simplicity, we have tended to focus on the natural resources version. We shall now see these different versions of the proviso have different implications for the right to acquire gifts.

Consider, then a comparable proviso on acquisition of rights by transfer:

Egalitarian Proviso on Transfers: An agent has the moral power to acquire by transfer rights over an owned resource if and only if this adversely affects no one who is left with

---

[29] Of course, not all apparent market exchanges, or even all market exchanges, involve the exchange of rights with equal competitive value. When I buy the normal apple from my niece (or from a charity) for $100, I am making a gift of the amount by which the competitive value of the apple is less than $100.

[30] Gifts, which involve a transfer of rights, are distinct from *favours*, which involve the use of one's property to benefit others where recipient has no right to such use (e.g., my mowing your lawn or my granting you (revocable) permission to use my lawn mower). A person's full ownership of a thing (herself or some artifact) gives her the right to use it to perform favours for others, and since the beneficiary requires no special moral power to benefit from favours (since, unlike gifts, there is no transfer of rights), there is no room within libertarian theory to restrict favours. It should be noted, however, that one of us (Steiner) is uncertain whether the gift-favour distinction can invariably be drawn in such a way as to support *both* the claim that no special power is needed to acquire rights to benefits that have been bestowed by favours, *and* the claim that such a power is needed to acquire rights transferred by gift. Particularly problematic, in this regard, are bestowals of personal services, e.g., a dental treatment or a shoeshine.

less than an equally valuable initial (lifetime) opportunity to use natural/external/all resources.

No matter which kind of resources (natural, external, or all) are deemed relevant, this proviso imposes no restrictions on exchanges of equally valuable rights (as in many market exchanges)—since such exchanges do not adversely affect anyone else's share of opportunities.

Moreover, if only opportunities to use *natural* resources are deemed relevant, then the transfer proviso will also impose no restrictions on gifts. Gifts of internal endowments (e.g., kidneys) or of artifacts do not adversely affect anyone's initial opportunities to use *natural* resources. Moreover, gifts of natural resources do not either: If one person transfers her share of natural resources to another, this does not adversely affect anyone's initial opportunities to use natural resources (if they had a fair share before the transfer, they do after as well). Thus, the Egalitarian Proviso on Transfers imposes no restrictions on acquisition by gift—or any other kind of transfer—if the relevant resources are limited to natural resources.[31]

Consider now the version of the transfer proviso that considers initial opportunities to use natural resources *and artifacts* (i.e., all external resources). The transfer proviso does not restrict gifts of *internal* endowments (e.g., kidneys). Moreover, if individuals all have equally valuable initial opportunities to use external resources, it imposes no restrictions on gifts (since the initial opportunities remain equal). The transfer proviso does, however, restrict the moral power to acquire by gift, when this gives the recipient more than her per capita share of initial opportunities to use external resources (and adversely affects someone with less than her per capita share). For example, if everyone has her per capita share of natural resources and no one other than Silver Spoon starts life with any artifactual gifts, then Silver Spoon may acquire artifactual gifts only to the extent that others also do (e.g., a gift tax would tax away all but her per capita share of natural resources). In this respect, the transfer proviso functions exactly as the use and appropriation proviso (applied to external resources): one has the power to acquire up to one's per capita share, but no more (without compensating by giving up some of one's internal resources).

---

[31] We here rely on our assumption that individuals have a right to equally valuable *initial* opportunities to use natural resources. Although this is sensitive to initial chances of later brute luck events, it is not sensitive to whether these events occur. A different (but closely related) view is the requirement that individuals have a right to equally valuable *brute luck* opportunities to use natural resources. (See Vallentyne 2002b for more on the difference between these two views.) On this view, gifts of natural resource that are a matter of brute luck (and not all are) do upset the relevant equality.

Finally, consider the version of the egalitarian proviso that considers initial opportunities to use *all* resources (natural, artifactual, and internal). Unlike the previous version, this version can also restrict gifts of internal endowments (e.g., kidneys). The general logic, however, is much the same. If individuals all have equally valuable initial opportunities to use resources generally, it imposes no restrictions on gifts (since the initial opportunities remain equal). It does, however, restrict the moral power to acquire by gift when this gives the recipient more than her per capita share of initial opportunities to use resources (and adversely affects someone with less than her per capita share).[32]

With respect to *inter vivos* gifts, then, left-libertarian theory is indeterminate. A version that is concerned only with the distribution of initial opportunities to use *natural* resources will not impose any restrictions on gifts, but versions that are concerned with initial opportunities to use external or all resources will impose some restrictions on gift. We shall not attempt to resolve this issue here.

8. Conclusion

For simplicity, we have assumed that agents pop into existence fully formed and thus have not addressed any of the issues relevant for individuals who pass through a phase of childhood. We also assumed, for the sake of argument, that interests can ground rights—either by standard interest-protecting rights or by choice-prioritizing rights. If only the capacity for choice can ground rights, then it is arguable that future people have no rights and thus there are no issues of intergenerational justice between non-overlapping individuals. Finally, we have addressed only the highly artificial case where the existence and nature of each individual either: (1) is fully certain and unaffected by any human choice or by acts of nature; or (2) is fully determined by intentional procreative acts (and not by anything else). We have thus not attempted to address non-intentional procreation nor the deep and complex issues that arise when non-procreative acts affect who is later procreated (given the non-identity problem and the contingency of existence).

We have sketched the outlines of libertarian views on intergenerational justice. We have assumed (with motivation) that right-libertarianism and joint-ownership left-libertarianism are implausible and have explored versions of

---

[32] For discussion of related issues, see Ackerman (1980: 201–7) and Rakowski (1991: ch. 7).

left–libertarianism—which impose egalitarian requirements on the distribution of initial opportunities to use natural/external/all resources. Because left-libertarianism is individualist, it requires (roughly) that the use and appropriation of unowned resources leave other individuals with an equally valuable initial opportunity to use the relevant resources (natural, external, or all). It requires, that is, that one leave an appropriate *per capita* share for others. It does *not* require that the *total* value of the initial opportunities be the same for different generations (perhaps of different sizes). Moreover, those who intentionally procreate individuals owe others a duty to provide the fair share to their offspring—although others have a duty to provide a fair share should the procreators fail to do so. Finally, because left-libertarianism requires only that no one be disadvantaged by being left with less than her per capita share of the relevant resources, it does not require members of the current generation to make any sacrifices for the benefit of members of later generations, if the latter will, in any case, have better initial opportunities to use the relevant resources.

Let us close with a speculation about the real life applications of left-libertarianism to the issues of natural resources depletion (e.g., oil) and degradation (e.g., global warming). Let us assume, as seems plausible, that members of the current generation are, in aggregate, using far more than their per capita share of natural resources. Does left-libertarianism view this as an injustice? Not necessarily. First, the degradation and depletion of natural resources is an individual matter and some individuals may be using less than their fair share even if most use more. Second, even those whose are using more than their fair share of natural resources may leave adequate compensation for the members of future generations. The value of resources that they add to the world for all to use—technology, knowledge, and improvements to natural resources (e.g., trees or fish) in the commons, for example—may compensate for their excess degradation or depletion.

We don't know enough about the facts of the situation, but we speculate that *on average* the (expected) initial opportunities to use natural (or external, or all) resources available to members of future generations are at least as great as those had by members of the current generation. We speculate that this is so because we believe that the current generation will pass on significant benefits of knowledge, technology, and abandoned but valuable resources. If that is so, then, although there may be (as there surely are) *individual* cases of injustice towards members of future generations, such injustices are not *widespread and systematic*. This, however, is simply speculation about a very complex issue.

References

ACKERMAN, B. (1980), *Social Justice in the Liberal State* (New Haven: Yale University Press).

ARNESON, R. (1991), 'Lockean Self-Ownership: Towards a Demolition', *Political Studies*, XXXIX: 36–54. Reprinted in Vallentyne and Steiner (2000b).

—— (2000). 'Perfectionism and Politics', *Ethics*, 111: 37–63.

ARRHENIUS, G. (2000), *Future Generations: A Challenge for Moral Theories* (Ph.D Dissertation, Uppsala University).

BLACKORBY, C., BOSSERT, W., and DONALDSON, D. (2005), *Population Issues in Social-Choice Theory, Welfare Economics, and Ethics* (New York: Cambridge University Press).

BROOME, J. (2004), *Weighing Lives* (Oxford, Oxford University Press).

CASAL, P. and WILLIAMS, A. (2004), 'Equality of Resources and Procreative Justice', in J. Burley (ed.), *Dworkin and His Critics* (Oxford: Blackwell, 2004), 15–169.

ELLIOT, R. (1986), 'Future Generations, Locke's Proviso and Libertarian Justice', *Journal of Applied Philosophy*, 3: 217–27.

FEINBERG, J. (1984), *Harm to Others* (New York: Oxford University Press).

FRIED, B. (2004), 'Left-Libertarianism: A Review Essay', *Philosophy and Public Affairs*, 32: 66–92.

GOSSERIES, A. (2001), 'What Do We Owe the Next Generation(s)', *Loyola of Los Angeles Law Review*, 35: 293–355.

—— (2003), 'Intergenerational Justice', in H. LaFollette (ed.), *The Oxford Handbook of Practical Ethics* (Oxford: Oxford University Press), 459–84.

—— (2004), *Penser la justice entre les générations: De l'affaire Perruche à la reforme des retraites* (Paris: Alto Aubier).

KRAMER, M., SIMMONDS, N., and STEINER, H. (1998), *A Debate over Rights: Philosophical Enquiries* (Oxford: Oxford University Press).

MACK, E. (1995), 'The Self-Ownership Proviso: A New and Improved Lockean Proviso', *Social Philosophy and Policy*, 12: 186–218.

MEYER, L. (2003a), 'Intergenerational Justice', *The Stanford Encyclopedia of Philosophy (Summer 2003 Edition)*, Edward N. Zalta (ed.), <http://plato.stanford.edu/archives/sum2003/entries/justice-intergenerational/>.

—— (2003b), 'Obligations Persistantes et Réparation Symbolique', *Revue Philosophique de Louvain*, 101: 105–22.

—— (2003c), 'Past and Future. The Case for a Threshold Notion of Harm', in L. Meyer, S. L. Paulson, and T. W. Pogge (eds.), *Rights Culture, and the Law*, (Oxford: Oxford University Press), 143–60.

NARVESON, J. (1988), *The Libertarian Idea* (Philadelphia: Temple University Press).

NOZICK, R. (1974), *Anarchy, State, and Utopia* (New York: Basic Books).

OTSUKA, M. (2003), *Libertarianism without Inequality* (Oxford: Clarendon Press).

RAKOWSKI, E. (1991), *Equal Justice* (New York: Oxford University Press).

RAWLS, J. (1971), *A Theory of Justice* (Cambridge, Mass.: Harvard University Press).

ROBERTS, M. (1998), *Child versus Childmaker: Future Persons and Present Duties in Ethics and the Law* (New York: Rowman & Littlefield Publishers).

ROARK, E. (2006), 'A Defense of Left-Libertarianism That Will Satisfy a Real Egalitarian' (unpublished, University of Missouri).

ROTHBARD, M. (1978), *For a New Liberty: The Libertarian Manifesto*, revised edition (New York: Libertarian Review Foundation).

—— (1982), *The Ethics of Liberty* (Humanities Press).

SIMMONS, A. John (1992), *The Lockean Theory of Rights* (Princeton: Princeton University Press).

—— (1993), *On the Edge of Anarchy* (Princeton: Princeton University Press).

STEINER, H. (1994), *An Essay on Rights* (Cambridge, MA: Blackwell Publishing).

—— (1997), 'Choice and Circumstance', *Ratio*, X: 296–312.

—— (1999), 'Silver Spoons and Golden Genes: Talent Differentials and Distributive Justice', in J. Burley (ed.), *The Genetic Revolution and Human Rights: 1998 Oxford Amnesty Lectures*, (Oxford: Oxford University Press). Reprinted in D. Archard and C. MacLeod (eds.), *Children and Political Theory* (Oxford: Oxford University Press, 2003).

TIDEMAN, N. (2000), 'Global Economic Justice', *Geophilos*, 00: 134–46.

TUNGODDEN, B., AND VALLENTYNE, P. (2006), 'Paretian Egalitarianism with Variable Population Size', in J. Roemer and K. Suzumura (eds.), *Intergenerational Equity and Sustainability* (Palgrave Publishers), ch. 11.

VALLENTYNE, P. (2002a), 'Equality and the Duties of Procreators', in D. Archard and C. MacLeod (eds.) *Children and Political Theory* (Oxford: Oxford University Press).

—— (2002b), 'Brute Luck, Option Luck, and Equality of Initial Opportunities', *Ethics*, 112: 529–57.

—— (2003), 'The Rights and Duties of Childrearing', *William and Mary Bill of Rights Journal*, 11: 991–1010.

—— (2007), 'Libertarianism and the State', *Social Philosophy and Policy*, 24: 87–205.

——, and STEINER, H. (eds.) (2000a), *The Origins of Left Libertarianism: An Anthology of Historical Writings* (New York: Palgrave Publishers).

——, and STEINER, H. (eds.) (2000b), *Left Libertarianism and Its Critics: The Contemporary Debate* (New York: Palgrave Publishers).

——, STEINER, H., and OTSUKA, M. (2005), 'Why Left-Libertarianism Isn't Incoherent, Indeterminate, or Irrelevant: A Reply to Fried', *Philosophy and Public Affairs* 33: 201–15.

VAN PARIJS, P. (1995), *Real Freedom for All* (New York: Oxford University Press).

WOLF, C. (1995), 'Contemporary Property Rights, Lockean Provisos, and the Interests of Future Generations', *Ethics*, 105: 791–818.

3

A Contract on Future Generations?

STEPHEN M. GARDINER

Contract theories seek to justify (and sometimes to explain) moral and political ideals and principles through the notion of 'mutually agreeable reciprocity or cooperation between equals'.[1] Let us call this ambition 'the basic idea' of contract theory. The purpose of this chapter is to explore a fundamental difficulty facing the basic idea in the intergenerational setting.

The difficulty concerns the understanding of cooperation standardly employed by contract theorists. I will begin by identifying three central challenges facing this understanding in the intergenerational context, and then consider a range of possible solutions. My main claims will be as follows. First, the three challenges constitute a deep and serious problem for contract theory. Second, the most central reason for this is that the intergenerational setting appears to constitute a different kind of collective action problem than that facing contract theory in the traditional, single-generation context. Third, the standard approach contract theorists have adopted to address this challenge—that of attempting to extend the normal single-generation model to the intergenerational context—has thus far proven inadequate. Fourth, this suggests, at the very least, that the standard approach needs to be rethought. But it may also imply that a new kind of contract theory is needed, one that specifically addresses the intergenerational collective action problem. If so, this would be of wider theoretical interest. For such a move appears to have

An early draft of this paper was written while I was a Laurance S. Rockefeller Visiting Fellow at the Center for Human Values at Princeton University. I thank both the Center and the University of Washington for their support. For comments on various drafts, I am grateful to Sandy Askland, Richard Daggar, Nir Eyal, Dale Jamieson, John Meyer, Lukas Meyer, Adam Moore, James Nickel, Angela Smith, Bill Talbott, Michael White, two anonymous reviewers, and especially Axel Gosseries.

[1] Darwall 2002b, 1.

significant ramifications for how contract theory is understood in the usual settings as well.

Before we begin, let me emphasize two limitations of the present discussion. First, the chapter aims neither to bury contract theory, nor to save it. Instead, it presents an initial overview of one set of difficulties facing the theory in the intergenerational setting. The hope is that getting clearer on the nature of these difficulties serves as a useful preliminary to finding out whether they can be overcome.

Second, the basic idea of contract theory is employed in a variety of ways, and for different purposes. For some contract theorists, the aim of the approach is to offer a fully-fledged account of morality and political philosophy all by itself. But more often the contract device is employed as way of fleshing out other, independent accounts of the foundations of ethics and politics. This raises a problem. For the current discussion aims to assess the prospects of the contract device *as such* as an approach to questions involving future generations. But, since most actual contract theorists are not 'pure' contract theorists—they do not rely solely on the contract device—they have more resources at their disposal than those specific to their use of that device. Since assessing all the possibilities open to such 'mixed' theories would require much more than one chapter, and may well be impossible, at least at our present stage of theoretical development, here we must be content with something more restricted. Hence, the current discussion will concern itself only with those aspects of contemporary contract theories that appear to be tightly connected to their employment of the contract device, rather than those generated primarily out of other ethical or methodological commitments.[2]

The paper has four main parts. Part I briefly introduces the two standard approaches to contract theory. Part II sketches three challenges facing the application of such theories to the intergenerational setting. Part III considers four attempts to extend traditional contract theories and asks how well suited they are for dealing with the three challenges. Part IV briefly discusses an alternative strategy.

I. The Usual Suspects

The basic idea of contract theory draws on three main subsidiary concepts: cooperation, agreement, and equality. It is not surprising, then, that many of

---

[2] This restriction may mean that the main argument of the chapter fails to address some kinds of contractualist theories, especially, perhaps, that offered by T. M. Scanlon. See n. 10.

the disputes that arise within the theory concern how these three concepts are to be understood and employed. In the contemporary debate, there are two main strands of contract thought. The first is based in self-interest, and has come to be called 'contractarian'. It takes as its main inspiration the work of Thomas Hobbes, and its major contemporary proponent is David Gauthier.[3] The contractarian approach has been characterized thus:

Contractarianism … holds that persons are primarily self-interested, and that a rational assessment of the best strategy for attaining the maximization of their self-interest will lead them to act morally (where the moral norms are determined by the maximization of joint interest) and to consent to governmental authority.[4]

The second strand is grounded in the idea that we are rationally required to respect other persons, and that this implies that moral and political principles must be justifiable to them. This strand is inspired by Immanuel Kant, and its major contemporary proponents are John Rawls and T. M. Scanlon.[5] This strand has come to be called 'contractualist'.[6] It has been described thus:

Contractualism … holds that rationality requires that we respect persons, which in turn requires that moral principles be such that they can be justified to each person. Thus, individuals are not taken to be motivated by self-interest but rather by a commitment to publicly justify the standards of morality to which each will be held.[7]

Contractarianism and contractualism can be usefully compared in light of the three main components of the basic idea of contract theory. A paradigmatic contractarian theory would offer the following accounts of the three concepts. First, it would conceive of the equality of agents as a *de facto*, descriptive equality

---

[3] Hobbes 1994; Gauthier 1986.   [4] Cudd 2000.

[5] See Scanlon 1982, 1998; and Rawls 1971, 1999a. Rawls advocates the position for justice alone, but does say that it might be attempted for morality in general if the results are good for justice. Scanlon offers such a wider theory.

[6] This terminology is not yet universally employed. For example, in a recent standard collection, Gary Watson uses the term 'contractualism' to refer to both the Hobbesian and Kantian strands (and so as equivalent to my usage of the term 'contract theory'). See Watson 2002, 255. But in his introduction to the same volume, Stephen Darwall employs the terms in the way I report in the text. See Darwall 2002b, 1. Note that Watson does accept that a distinction can be made between the Hobbesian and Kantian strands, for he proposes 'consensualism' as a term for referring to the Kantian-style theories alone. See Watson 2002, 266, n. 26.

The confusion may have been facilitated (unintentionally) by Scanlon, who appears to have introduced the term. In his original classic paper, Scanlon refers to himself and Rawls as contractualists, and so may appear to imply the distinction in the text. But in his later book, he lists Gauthier as a fellow contractualist (1998, 190). It is unclear whether this is because he intends Watson's usage of the term, or because he regards Gauthier as more Kantian than Hobbesian. Some doubt is cast on the latter possibility by his claim that Gauthier 'expresses a quite different moral view' to himself and to Rawls, and that this view is sometimes called 'contractarian' (1998, 375, n. 2).

[7] Cudd 2000.

in some relevant respect.[8] Second, it would describe the basis for cooperation as the possibility of mutual advantage for the individual contractors. Third, it would envision the role of agreement to be that of securing the consent of actual agents as presently constituted, with the purpose of underwriting a stable system of cooperation.

By contrast, a paradigm contractualist theory would hold the following positions. First, it would understand the equality of the parties as primarily normative, and grounded in considerations of morality. Second, it would conceive of the cooperation to be achieved as characterized by fairness, usually as exemplified in reciprocal exchange under circumstances characterized through the notion of a reasonable agreement. Third, it would consider the primary role of agreement as being to guarantee the justifiability of moral and political principles to those affected by them through an account of what rational beings would consent to in a morally loaded hypothetical situation.

In summary:

Table 3.1

	Contractarianism (Paradigm Version)	Contractualism (Paradigm Version)
Equality of the Parties	Descriptive	Moral
Basis for Cooperation	Mutual advantage	Fairness
Role of Agreement	Underwrite stable system of social interaction between actual agents	Underwrite moral justifiability of Principles

It is important to note that the contractarian and contractualist strands are not rigidly defined types. Moreover—and this point deserves special emphasis—the two strands do not exhaust the possibilities for contract theory. For one thing, in their paradigm instantiations they differ along three dimensions, so there are clear possibilities for hybrid positions. For another, it is open to rival contract theories to endorse different accounts of the three concepts. Finally, as we shall see later, these are not the only dimensions on which contract theories may differ. In my view, such considerations point to important areas for future investigation. Still, for present purposes, we can sidestep such matters. This is because the preliminary characterizations are sufficient to illustrate an initial

---

[8] For the *de facto* characterization, see Darwall 2002b, 1. See also Hobbes on the equality of power in the state of nature.

set of difficulties faced by contract theories *as such* when dealing with future generations.

The need to deal with future generations creates serious presumptive problems for each component of the basic idea of contract theory. Put very briefly, given that many generations are temporally distant from each other, and can never meet, it seems impossible for them either to engage in genuinely *cooperative* activities, or to *agree* to contracts, with the current generation, at least as these notions are usually understood. Moreover, it is widely believed that there are important respects in which members of the current generation should not treat the interests of future people with equal, but instead with *greater*, concern than those of current people. (Hence, for example, it is sometimes said that the current generation must aim at making future people better off than present people.) In my view, these presumptive problems both exacerbate some standard difficulties faced by contract theory, and also introduce some new, potentially more serious ones. However, showing this for all of the components would require more than one chapter. Hence, here I will focus on cooperation alone.

II. Cooperation Problems

I will now consider three central challenges facing cooperation in the intergenerational setting.[9] In this section, I sketch these challenges in their starkest form, in order to get a clear grasp of their main characteristics. In section III, I explain why they re-arise even under less severe assumptions.

1. The Rationale Challenge

The first challenge concerns the applicability of the standard rationales for cooperation to the intergenerational setting. This challenge can be explained in terms of three key problems.

a. The Interaction Problem   The first problem emerges from the fact that the very notion of cooperation appears to require the possibility of interaction—of 'working together', or engaging in 'joint' or 'reciprocal' activity. Contract theorists typically understand this notion through the model of market exchange. That is, they see cooperation as essentially involving an explicit and agreed 'give-and-take': one party gives something to another and receives something back in return, on the basis of a mutual understanding that this

---

[9] I will leave aside the Non-Identity Problem, which is discussed elsewhere in this volume.

will be the character of the interaction.[10] (Call this, 'The Exchange Model of Cooperation' ('EMC').)

Unfortunately, on a strict interpretation of what this entails, the exchange model appears to create a serious difficulty for intergenerational ethics. Suppose that we adopt a very expansive understanding of what it is to be a future generation. Let us suppose, that is, that the current generation is constituted by those people currently alive and those whom they will live to meet, and that future generations involve those people yet to exist who are excluded by this definition.[11] (This assumption will be relaxed later.) Next, suppose that causation runs only in one direction—from the past and present to the future, and not from the future to the past and present. Then, it is not possible for future people to cause events in the present. Hence, it is impossible for them either to receive goods from and then give back to their predecessors in the paradigm sense, or to agree to do this. But this seems to rule out genuinely cooperative behaviour between generations, whether that is mutually advantageous (in the contractarian case) or reciprocal (in the contractualist) behaviour. (Call this, 'the Interaction Problem'.)

b. The 'Fruits of Common Labour' Problem   The second problem is brought on by the first. Traditionally, contract theories have taken as their primary subject matter the question of how to distribute goods produced by shared productive endeavours.[12] But understood in the stark form above, the

---

[10] One question that arises is whether T. M. Scanlon's theory, usually taken to be a core instance of contractualism, employs this or any other notion of cooperation. This question is too large to address properly here, but a couple of general remarks may be helpful. First, one option would be to deny that Scanlon's theory employs the notion of cooperation at all, and so concede that his view escapes the difficulties outlined in this chapter. The obvious cost of this move to my approach would be that Scanlon does not count as a contract theorist in the sense defined. But it is not clear if this is a significant worry. After all, it has already been acknowledged that many theorists who invoke contracts actually hold 'mixed theories' in which other moral notions play a significant role. Perhaps Scanlon simply belongs in this camp. The less obvious cost is to Scanlon himself. The notion of cooperation plays a number of important roles in conventional contract theory. In particular, the guiding thought of much of contract theory is that the account of cooperation (a) tells us a lot about what the relevant agreement is supposed to be about, and (b) that this tells us something about (i) how that agreement is supposed to arise, (ii) between whom, and (iii) what form it can be expected to take. In short, its account of cooperation is often what gives any given contract theory much of its shape. Given this, it is not so clear that Scanlon can simply reject it (at least if he wants to remain an interesting kind of contract theorist). Second, one might claim that Scanlon does employ a notion of cooperation, but that it is structurally different from the standard exchange model, and in such a way as to escape the problems raised by that model in the intergenerational context. The challenge here is to specify exactly what that notion of cooperation is, and how it avoids those problems. Although I have some sympathies with Scanlon, confronting and assessing that challenge is beyond the scope of this paper.

[11] See de-Shalit 1995. I discuss the issue of how one should go about individuating generations in Gardiner (2003).

[12] In economics, this is often called the 'cooperative surplus'.

Interaction Problem seems to imply that current and future generations can have no such endeavours: the relevant sense of 'shared' does not (and cannot) apply. This suggests a deep difficulty. If the notion of shared productive endeavour is essential to the contract rationale, then it seems that contract theories will be forced to say that questions of distribution simply *do not arise* in the intergenerational case.[13] (Call this, the 'Fruits of Common Labour Problem'.)[14]

c. The Problem of Parochialism   Now, no doubt it is too restrictive to limit use of the term 'cooperation' to cases of strict interaction. Surely, it will be said, there is an extended sense in which different generations can engage in cooperation. For one thing, future people can 'give something back' to their predecessors by honouring their memories, their wishes, and their ideals. For another, different generations can contribute to intergenerational projects, such as the development of a great university system, or the advance of contract theory.

Still, the existence of such possibilities only moderates the problem posed by future generations. There are two reasons. First, the scope for cooperation may not be large. For one thing, perhaps there are only a limited number of intergenerational projects; for another, perhaps the current generation cares little about the views of its successors and its place in history. Second, to the extent that there is a basis for cooperation, this may be overwhelmed by other

---

[13] At first glance, it may seem that this problem applies only to the contractarian paradigm (given its focus on mutual advantage) but not to the contractualist. But this is too hasty. First, the notion of fairness in productive endeavours is of central importance to many political contractualists. Moreover, even if this can be couched in terms of reciprocity, rather than mutual advantage, there are still difficulties in extending that account across generations. (More on this later.) Second, many contractualists believe that even if this *kind* of cooperation is not essential to political relations considered as such, its absence makes a great difference to the kind of relations that hold, and especially to the nature of the obligations that flow from those relations. For example, contractualists often believe that the obligations that hold within a political unit that creates fruits of common labour (such as a state) are much stronger than those that hold between such units. Third, this division faces a challenge from people's pre-theoretical beliefs. For one thing, many people seem to hold that the fruits of past and current production should be shared with future generations, *even though future people do not contribute to that production*. Moreover, they typically claim not only that the obligation is much stronger and more demanding than any similar obligations that may hold between contemporaneous political units that do not create a productive surplus, but also that they *are almost as strong, as strong, or even stronger* than those obligations towards contemporaries within the same unit who do contribute to production.

[14] If it is not the fruits of mutual endeavour that are being distributed, then there seem to be two main possibilities. First, resources passed on to future generations might appear to be pure transfers of goods. But then the challenge is to describe this transfer in terms of either mutual advantage or reciprocity. Second, the subject matter might be the basic circumstances under which future generations will come into existence. But then there are difficulties in regarding this as a matter for negotiation between present and future people, since the latter depend on a certain outcome for their existence.

considerations. Perhaps a given generation does care about what future people think of it, and would, other things being equal, prefer that it perpetuate its traditions and projects; but on balance, it cares much more about other things—for example, the prestige, social status and convenience of driving a big, but environmentally destructive, vehicle—and perhaps even sees this as an essential means of participating in its culture.

The general (and often neglected) point to be made here is that even if there are good reasons in favour of some kinds of intergenerational cooperation, it is not clear that these will be especially strong reasons, or that, all-things-considered, the relevant parties will (or should) be motivated to act on them. Merely suggesting that a given generation has some intergenerational concerns does not show that such concerns will hold sway when it comes to making decisions. Particular generations are likely to have diverse goals, many of which are purely intragenerational in nature; and to the extent that their inter- and intra-generational goals conflict, there is no guarantee that the intergenerational goals will win out. Indeed, given the nature of the various goods at stake, we have every reason to suspect the reverse.[15] (Call this, 'The Problem of Parochialism'.[16])

Each of the first three problems casts doubt on the applicability of the exchange model of cooperation employed by standard contract theories (whether this is based on mutual advantage or reciprocity) to the intergenerational setting. In summary, under the expansive definition of 'future generation', it is far from obvious either (a) that 'interaction' between generations is, in any meaningful sense, possible, or (b) that there are any reasons to engage in whatever kind of contact may be possible, or even (c), if such reasons exist, that these are especially strong reasons, or that the relevant parties will (or should) be sufficiently motivated to act on them. Given all this, it is far from clear that there is a rationale for intergenerational cooperation. This observation creates a serious *prima facie* challenge for contract theory. For it

---

[15] One way of responding to this problem would be to argue that different generations *should* be motivated to pursue intergenerational projects to a substantial extent. So, for example, one might try to defend a theory of value that gave serious weight to intergenerational goods. Such an approach would be worth investigating. Still, it faces some significant challenges. In particular, a contract theorist would want to be sure that it did not simply (a) presuppose a theory of intergenerational justice rather than inform it, and/or (b) replace rather than supplement the contract approach.

[16] Parochial means 'concerned with only narrow local concerns without any regard for more general or wider issues'. The problem of parochialism resonates with a traditional, more general, challenge to contractarianism that claims that it is misguided to attempt to derive morality from self-interest, both because it is empirically likely that the latter provides too minimal a grounding for the former, and because it is, ultimately, the wrong kind of grounding.

suggests that it is not enough for the contract theorist simply to *assert* that the intergenerational setting has, or can meaningfully seen *as if* it has, the form of a genuine *cooperation* problem. Instead, she must show how and why the notion of cooperation makes sense in that setting. If this cannot be done, then it will seem that the basic idea of contract theory does not even apply across generations; and such a result appears fatal to the project of employing the contract approach in the intergenerational setting. (Call this general problem, emerging from the other three, 'The Rationale Challenge'.)

2. The Structural Challenge

The Rationale Challenge is a serious one. But it is not the only difficulty facing standard contract theories in the intergenerational setting. For even if we assume for the moment that there is some kind of rationale for intergenerational cooperation, it is not clear that this will yield a problem with the same *structure* as those provided by intragenerational rationales. Consider the following. According to the traditional understanding of the contract approach, in the absence of society agents face a particular kind of collective action problem. The proper role of society is then to resolve this problem; and it does so by announcing and then enforcing a set of social rules by which people are to regulate their actions.[17] This, according to many contract theorists, is the birth of ethics. Much then depends on *how the relevant collective action problem is described*, since it embodies the reasons for social life in such a way as to determine not just the substance, but also the *shape* and *scope* of public rules of ethics.[18]

a. The Standard Problem of Fit In the intragenerational setting, contemporary writers typically assume that the structure of the relevant collective action problem is, or closely resembles, that of the infamous Prisoner's Dilemma ('PD'). Thus, for example, Gauthier says:

The natural condition of mankind is an irrational condition, because it condemns persons or nations to non-optimal outcomes that, in 'Prisoner's Dilemma-type' situations, may be little better than disastrous.[19]

---

[17] Society usually does this through a set of formal and informal sanctions. For example, one set of formal sanctions are those of the civil and criminal justice systems, and one set of informal sanctions are those of public opinion.

[18] Contract theorists differ on whether the collective action problem generates ethics, or only political philosophy, and on whether it captures all of the relevant domains.

[19] Gauthier 1986, 82–3.

And:

[In] contexts structured by the Prisoner's Dilemma ... we shall find a place for morality as a set of constraints on the pursuit of maximum utility that every rational person must acknowledge.[20]

A prisoner's dilemma is a situation with a certain shape.[21] For our purposes, the problem can be (roughly) characterized as follows:

(PD1) It is *collectively rational* to cooperate: each agent prefers the outcome produced by everyone cooperating over the outcome produced by no one cooperating.

(PD2) It is *individually rational* not to cooperate: when each individual has the power to decide whether or not she will cooperate, each person (rationally) prefers not to cooperate, whatever the others do.

Such a situation poses a problem when each individual has the power to decide whether or not she will cooperate. Then, given (PD2), if each person is individually rational, no one cooperates. But this results in an outcome that both parties disprefer over an alternative that is available. For, according to (PD1), each prefers the cooperative over the noncooperative outcome. In other words, the problem is that by acting as individuals, in the individually rational way, the parties end up in a place they'd both prefer to avoid.

The relevance of the prisoner's dilemma to the present discussion is as follows. First, suppose that we assume, with many contract theorists, that the purpose of ethics in the traditional (intragenerational) setting is to overcome some kind (or kinds) of prisoner's dilemma, and so that the task of moral and political philosophy is to specify some mechanism (usually a combination of rules and sanctions) that will do that job. Second, suppose then that we make the seemingly innocuous assumption that the form of the problem addressed influences the type of solution required. Then, third, it seems that the basic characteristics of the prisoner's dilemma model mandate that the task of moral and political philosophy has certain parameters. But, fourth, this creates a basic difficulty. For if there are other settings (such as the intergenerational setting) that are not prisoner's dilemmas, then it is not clear that traditional (contract) ethics will apply to them. In short, if, in the intergenerational setting, we depart from the prisoner's dilemma model, then the traditional contract approach seems to be undercut, and in a particularly deep way: *its basic analysis of the problem appears not to apply*. There is, we might say, a problem of fit.

---

[20] Gauthier 1986, 103−4. Similarly, Hobbes' state of nature is often said to be a Prisoner's Dilemma. See, for example, Rawls 1999a, 238.

[21] For a fuller discussion, see Gardiner 2001.

Now, the problem of fit can presumably arise in a number of different ways, corresponding to various possible sources of the failure of fit. One such failure is very general. As the Rationale Challenge has already revealed, given the expansive definition of 'future generation' and the standard exchange model of cooperation, it is not clear that the intergenerational setting has, or can seen as if it has, the form of a genuinely cooperative problem of *any sort*; and, at first glance, this seems to rule out the prisoner's dilemma analysis (as well as any other analysis of the problem based on cooperation). (Call this, 'The Standard Problem of Fit'.)

b. The Resolution Problem Interestingly, however, it turns out that the relevance of the prisoner's dilemma analysis does not stand or fall with the Rationale Challenge and the Standard Problem of Fit. This is because, considered simply as such, the basic Prisoner's Dilemma model is neither couched in the language of the exchange model of cooperation, nor takes a position on the more substantive issues of interaction, fruits of common labour, and parochialism. Indeed, it simply does not mention such notions.[22] Instead, it invokes a more abstract notion of cooperation, relying on the possibility of implicitly coordinated behaviour.[23]

Still, this is not to say that the Standard Problem of Fit is irrelevant to the application of the prisoner's dilemma model. For one thing, given the Rationale Challenge, anyone wanting to employ a prisoner's dilemma analysis must now specify exactly what their rationale for cooperation is, and why it

---

[22] Consider, for example, the classic story of the prisoners:

'Two prisoners must make a decision about whether or not to confess to a given crime. Each must do so knowing that the actual consequences of her own choice will depend on the decision made by the other. But each must make her decision in isolation. The problem then arises that each would prefer the outcome produced by coordinating their behaviour so that neither confesses over the outcome produced by both confessing. Yet, when each has to act in isolation, this outcome is unstable, since it is individually rational for each prisoner to confess, no matter what the other person does.'

Nothing in this story invokes interaction or fruits of common labour considered as such. Indeed, as stated, the story presupposes that there is no interaction, since the prisoners are isolated from one another. Moreover, though there would be gains for each if they could coordinate their behaviour, these do not take the usual form of interest to contract theorists of some *joint product* whose benefits must be shared. Instead, the important aspects of the cooperative gains (such as their magnitude and distribution) are set externally, and not influenced in any way by the prisoners.

[23] In the original Prisoner's Dilemma example, the 'cooperation' referred to in (PD1) and (PD2) refers simply to contribution to action that will bring about the mutually desirable outcome. (See Gardiner 2001.) This sense of cooperation can be (and indeed usually is) explained without reference to the exchange model. Unfortunately, it is not clear that the more abstract notion will help the contract theorist with the Rationale Challenge. After all, the basic point of the prisoner's dilemma scenario is that this cooperative solution is unstable within it; and contract theorists typically resolve the prisoner's dilemma by appealing to the richer form of cooperation put forward in the exchange model.

results in a situation with the structure of a prisoner's dilemma. For another, the Standard Problem remains indirectly relevant. For considered simply as such, pure prisoner's dilemmas are not resolvable. Given the structure of the situation, individual rationality trumps collective rationality, and the preferred outcomes picked out as collectively rational cannot be achieved.[24] By contrast, the circumstances under which prisoner's dilemmas can be resolved arise in the real world, where other factors are in play. For example, a situation that initially, and in isolation, appears to be a prisoner's dilemma can be transformed into a different kind of problem when put into a broader context, such as when the parties must repeatedly interact to address this or other kinds of problem.[25] In such circumstances, collectively rational strategies often become dominant. But, at this point, the Standard Problem manifests itself again. For if, as many contract theorists suggest, we can only understand how real world 'prisoner's dilemmas' can be resolved by appeal to the exchange model of cooperation, and if that model is unsustainable in the intergenerational setting, then the Standard Problem is back in play. More specifically, if standard contract theories rely on the exchange model when they develop their solutions to intragenerational 'prisoner's dilemmas', then we cannot infer that those solutions will transfer to the intergenerational setting. (Call this, 'The Resolution Problem'.)

We can conclude that, even though by itself the Standard Problem of Fit does not imply that the prisoner's dilemma analysis must be false, it leaves the proponent of that analysis having to explain its continued relevance. Moreover, given the dominance of the exchange model, and its importance in resolving real world prisoner's dilemmas, this challenge should not be taken lightly.

c. The Problem of the Paradigm   The Resolution Problem must be taken seriously. Still, it is not the issue on which I wish to focus. Rather, there is a third, more specific, failure of fit that deserves our attention.

---

[24] Shepski 2006.

[25] Another proposed solution to prisoner's dilemma situations is to appeal directly to moral considerations, such as a 'sense of fair play'. This solution does not require that a real world 'prisoner's dilemma' depart from the theoretical model, nor does it necessarily rely on the exchange model. Therefore, considered merely as such, it is not vulnerable to the present criticism. Still, contract theory requires more help than this observation provides. For the guiding ideal of contract theory is that the model of cooperation in a contract provides us with the way in which 'fair play' should be understood, and the standard accounts employ the exchange model in order to do that. Hence, simply to invoke 'a sense of fair play' here is to presuppose a solution rather than provide one.

The thought is this. Suppose that the intergenerational setting can be described as *some* kind of cooperation problem, and one with some affinities to the traditional prisoner's dilemma. But suppose also that, ultimately, there are important differences between this new kind of problem and the prisoner's dilemma, and this implies that different kinds of solutions may be needed.[26] If this is right, then there are reasons to worry about the prisoner's dilemma analysis that are independent of, and go beyond the Rationale Challenge considered simply as such.[27] The intergenerational setting may yet pose issues of cooperation, but these issues may take a different form to those captured by the prisoner's dilemma. Let us call this, 'The Problem of the Paradigm' ('PP').

We can make the Problem of the Paradigm perspicuous by sketching one such competing analysis of the intergenerational setting. Let us begin by considering a pure form of this analysis.[28] Imagine a world consisting of a sequence of groups of inhabitants over a length of time. Suppose that each group is temporally distinct, no group has any causal impact on any previous group, each is concerned solely with its own interests, and the interests of earlier groups are independent of the interests of later groups (but not *vice versa*).[29] Imagine then that each group has access to goods which are temporally diffuse in a particular way: they give modest benefits to the group which produces them, but impose high costs[30] on all later groups. (Consider, for example, a case where the current generation gains from some form of overpollution because this generation receives the benefits but the costs are deferred to later generations.) Under the stipulated conditions, we would expect each group to produce such goods. Hence, we would expect earlier groups to impose uncompensated costs on later groups. Moreover,

---

[26] Even if the intergenerational problem does have the form of a prisoner's dilemma, it may not be resolvable in the usual ways. For example, the intergenerational setting may constitute a purer form of the prisoner's dilemma than that typically found in single-generation cases.

[27] The basic issue has sometimes been discussed in the literature, but often in ways that are unhelpful for present purposes. For example, some writers refer to the problem as 'the Intergenerational Prisoner's Dilemma', while others cast the issue as one of the Humean circumstances of justice failing to apply. See, for example, Sauve 1995, Barry 1978 and Hubin 1979.

[28] The next few paragraphs are excerpted from Gardiner 2003.

[29] I assume that the groups are self-interested only for ease of exposition. The problem arises more generally if the group simply has concerns that are dominantly group-relative. Moreover, even the assumption that the *group* is self-interested does not imply that its individual members are.

[30] I intend 'costs' to function as an umbrella term here, to refer to negative impacts of various kinds, including strictly economic costs, but also non-economic effects, such as physical harms.

we might expect those further along in the sequence to receive escalating burdens, since the costs will be compounded over time. Intuitively, such a world raises an issue of fairness.[31] Let us call this 'the Pure Intergenerational Problem' (PIP).[32]

The pure intergenerational problem differs from the prisoner's dilemma analysis in several important ways.

The first difference is that the PIP model is more clearly applicable to the intergenerational setting than the Prisoner's Dilemma model. Like the PD, the PIP does not mention interaction or fruits of common labour, and so is not undercut by the observation that these notions do not seem pertinent in the intergenerational setting.[33] However, the relevance of the PD model to this setting has yet to be established; in order to employ the model, the contract theorist must invoke some notion of cooperation that yields this structure. By contrast, the idea that the PIP makes central—that of one generation's inflicting high costs on future generations for the sake of modest benefits for itself—clearly applies. This represents a major advantage of the PIP.

A second difference is that, in contrast to the Prisoner's Dilemma, which appears to make only nonmoral assumptions,[34] the PIP makes an overtly moral one: that the infliction of high costs on future generations raises issues of fairness. Still, this presupposition seems both minimal and basic. In making its claim, the PIP does not invoke a specific or controversial moral theory. For one thing, it relies on an intuition that there are at least some cases where infliction of high costs would be unfair, and such an intuition seems to be widely shared. For another, the assumption appeals to set of moral considerations that seem, at least at first glance, to be more fundamental than those at stake in normal

---

[31] I use the term 'fairness' in a broad sense here. For example, if the costs transmitted are severe physical harms, then some theorists may prefer to speak of direct violations of particular duties, reserving the term 'fairness' for cases where what is at stake is distributive justice more narrowly-construed. However, for simplicity, I intend 'fairness' to cover both kinds of cases, as well as others, such as those involving procedural justice.

[32] Elsewhere I apply the 'PIP' label more broadly to include other kinds of 'intergenerational buck passing'. Hence, strictly-speaking what I refer to here counts only as a paradigm instance of the PIP. For a fuller characterization of the problem, see Gardiner 2006.

[33] Similarly, the PIP analysis, like the PD analysis, assumes that generations have self-referential concerns, and that these are operative in the intergenerational setting. But then the PD analysis assumes that, given these concerns, cooperation is collectively rational for all parties, whereas the PIP analysis does not assume this. The PIP is thus compatible with the presence of the Problem of Parochialism, whereas the PD analysis must deny it.

[34] See, however, section II.3.a: 'The Idealization Dilemma'.

cooperative ventures.[35] This suggests that the PIP may have wider theoretical relevance than the Prisoner's Dilemma analysis.[36]

A third difference between the two problems concerns their shape. Suppose we assume that the PIP can be roughly characterized as follows[37]:

(PIP1) It is *collectively rational* for most generations to cooperate: (almost) every generation prefers the outcome produced by everyone cooperating over the outcome produced by no one cooperating.

(PIP2) It is *individually rational* for all generations not to cooperate: when each generation has the power to decide whether or not it will cooperate, each generation (rationally) prefers not to cooperate, whatever the others do.

These features are both very similar to, and yet distinct from, the parallel characteristics of the Prisoner's Dilemma.[38]

Consider first the claims about individual rationality (PD2 and PIP2). In both cases, these arise because parties lack effective means through which to ensure that the behaviour of others is cooperative so long as theirs is. But PIP2 is worse than PD2 because the underlying rationale for it is more intractable. PD2 typically arises because there are contingent obstacles to coooperation (e.g. the inability to come together to make a contract, the lack of a coercive power to enforce a contract); hence, it may be rendered false by removing such contingencies. But the reasons for PIP2 are not contingent. If a collective agreement is in the interest of a given generation, it is because it does not want to suffer the ill-effects of the activities of its predecessors. But at the point where each generation has the power not to cooperate, it is no longer subject to action by its predecessors—by definition, they no longer exist,[39] and have already either cooperated or not. (One might call this, 'The Problem of Non-Contingent Obstacles'.)

---

[35] For example, it is often thought that intentional failures to cooperate are not as bad as deliberate inflictions of harm (if indeed, they are seen as bad at all). This is reflected in the common view that at most the former violate a duty of beneficence, while the later violate a duty of non-malfeasance.

[36] Cf. the later discussion of the 'Close to the Bone Problem'.

[37] These claims do not follow directly from the above description of the problem. (For example, PIP1 may be an optimistic assumption. It might turn out that a significant number of generations are prepared to suffer the high costs inflicted by their predecessors so long as they retain the ability to pass on even higher costs to their successors.) So, other models are possible which compete both with the PD and this version of the PIP. Still, it is worth focusing on the most optimistic version of the PIP, since it contains the most concessions to contract theorists' claims about cooperation, and yet still creates major difficulties for the PD model.

[38] The next few paragraphs are drawn from Gardiner 2001.

[39] We have assumed that each group is temporally distinct.

Consider now the claims concerning collective rationality. Here we see that PIP1 is also much more problematic than PD1. In PD1, it is in everyone's interest not to cooperate. But in PIP1 this is not the case. First, cooperation is not in the interests of the first group in the sequence. It is being asked to refrain from non-cooperative activity which is beneficial to itself simply for the sake of future groups. If it is motivated simply by self-interest, therefore, it will not cooperate. Second, the problem of the first group is iterated. Cooperation is in the interests of any given group if and only if the groups which precede it also cooperate and do not overpollute. But then the asymmetrical position of the first group threatens to undermine the rationale for cooperation. If the first group does not cooperate, then it makes it the case that the second group has nothing to gain from cooperation, and so, under the egoistic assumption, will itself not cooperate. But this makes it the case that the third group has nothing to gain from cooperation, and so on, for all the other groups in the sequence. (One might call this, 'The Problem of the Initial Generation'.[40])

A fourth major difference between the Pure Intergenerational Problem and the Prisoner's Dilemma is that the former seems more difficult to resolve. Consider again the standard solutions to the Prisoner's Dilemma. Such solutions typically involve appeal to the broad self-interest of the parties, or to some notion of reciprocity.[41] But these solutions do not work for the PIP. For example, appeals to broad self-interest characteristically make reference to a wider context of interaction where mutual advantage is possible. But in the scenario envisioned by the PIP, there is no such wider context, and mutual benefit is ruled out by the causal circumstances. Similarly, the possibility of reciprocity is ruled out by the description of the scenario.

It is clear from this brief discussion that the Pure Intergenerational Problem is distinct from the Prisoner's Dilemma. Hence, if the PIP accurately characterizes the intergenerational setting,[42] this has significant implications for contract theory. The good news is that, since the PIP does constitute a collective action problem, and one with notable similarities to the prisoner's dilemma, the new analysis suggests that traditional contract theory may still have relevance in the intergenerational setting. But the bad news is that the extent of this relevance is unclear. The important differences between the PIP and the prisoner's dilemma

---

[40] For more on this problem, and the related problem of the last generation, see the second half of the paper.

[41] It is worth noting that in a formal sense, these are not solutions to pure prisoner's dilemmas, since technically, the pure form of the problem is defined so as to exclude them. (See Skepski 2006.) So, they should be understood as solutions to problems with relevant similarities to the pure prisoner's dilemma.

[42] Some will want to resist this claim. The main reason to do so is overlap between actual human generations. The Problem of Parochialism already complicates such a defence; but for further discussion, see the second half of this paper and Gardiner 2003.

suggest that a new approach may be required. In particular, we cannot assume that the usual solutions to the prisoner's dilemma will simply carry over; and this means that there is a presumption against traditional contract theory in the intergenerational setting.

We can conclude that there are significant obstacles to the employment of contract theory's usual structural model (the PD) in the intergenerational setting. Some of these obstacles follow from the Rationale Challenge; but others do not. In particular, the Problem of the Paradigm reveals that even if we assume that there is some rationale for intergenerational cooperation, this need not imply that the prisoner's dilemma model may not carry over to the intergenerational setting. The PIP analysis, for example, is a serious competitor. (Such problems constitute 'The Structural Challenge'.)

3. The Justification Challenge

The third central challenge for the application of contract theory to the intergenerational setting concerns people's reasons for being contract theorists. Here I will consider two general problems that fall under this heading.

a. The Idealization Dilemma The first problem involves the use of idealization in contract theories. Consider again the two canonical forms of contract theory. The Rationale and Structural Challenges impact these in different ways. The most obvious divergence concerns the *status* of the cooperation component, and at first glance, the difference here looks stark.

On the one hand, on a paradigm contractarian theory, the basic claims about cooperation are supposed to be matters of descriptive fact. Hence, on this view, if it were to turn out that the basic claims fail to carry over to the intergenerational setting—e.g. because in that setting there really is no interaction, no fruit of common labour, and no Prisoner's Dilemma—then it seems that one would be forced to conclude that the contractarian model fails to apply. In this case, the intergenerational problem would have to be of a fundamentally different kind that that addressed by mainstream contractarian theories. At a minimum, this would suggest that one needed a different kind of contract theory to resolve it, but it may also imply either that some other kind of moral theory altogether must be invoked, or even that matters of intergenerational distribution do not constitute genuine questions of justice or ethics, properly conceived. (More on this later.)

On the other hand, on a paradigm contractualist theory, the basic claims about cooperation need not describe matters of fact, but rather merely report how the situation arising between various parties *ought to be conceived*, as part of a morally-appropriate way of understanding the problem from a theoretical point of view. Hence, on this view, if it turned out, as a matter of descriptive fact, that the basic claims about cooperation made by contract theory did not hold true in the intergenerational setting, this may be irrelevant. On the face of it, a contractualist might continue to assert that it is still *morally appropriate* to conceive of the intergenerational setting *as if* the claims were true. The contractualist might, therefore, be untroubled by the first two challenges.

At first glance then, there appears to be a sharp difference between the two usual views, and one which gives the contractualist the upper hand. But these appearances may be deceptive. First, it turns out that the idealization strategy may be available to contractarians. Traditionally, the alleged 'descriptive facts' against which contractarians judge their theories are not the facts of the world that we live in, but the hypothetical world of the state of nature—the world as it would be with no state. But, clearly, this is not the actual world of descriptive fact. Moreover, even the state of nature is usually sanitized in some respects—for example, its residents are typically assumed to be fully rational and concerned to optimize the benefits they receive from society—so that it is debatable whether such a condition even *could be* a world of descriptive fact. These points imply that, typically, even contractarians are committed to some kind of idealization; but if this is so, then they may be able to argue, with the paradigm contractualist, that even if contract theory's basic claims about cooperation fail to hold in the *actual* intergenerational setting, this need not undermine the application of that theory.[43]

Second, and more importantly, on closer examination it is not so clear that the idealization strategy allows for the two challenges (i.e. the Rationale and Structural Challenges) to be simply assumed away. Much might be said about this. But here let me make just two points. The first is that contract theory seeks to understand moral and political issues in terms of some kind of cooperative agreement about something. But, for any particular issue, if this is to work, it must be both *possible and appropriate* to conceive of that issue in those terms. Those invoking idealization, then, must explain how the intergenerational setting *can* be understood in such a way that the basic claims about cooperation hold (even hypothetically), and why it is *appropriate* to view the setting in that way. This implies that they too must connect the normative to the descriptive. Thus, if the first two challenges do accurately describe the intergenerational setting, this creates a obstacle to such views. The second point is that this suggests that the

---

[43] Of course, this account leaves contractarians having to explain the special relevance of the 'state of nature' as they conceive it to current deliberation, and so in a similar predicament to the contractualists.

relationship between normative and descriptive claims within contract theory is more complex than it first appears. For some descriptive facts about the world are sufficiently deep that they play a role in *defining* the problem at hand: that is, they are essential to the normative definition of the problem *as the kind of problem it is*. This suggests that such facts cannot simply be assumed away.[44] Hence, if contract theory's basic claims about cooperation turn out to be false because they conflict with such facts in the intergenerational setting, it may not be possible simply to claim (as I suggested above that the contractualist might) that such conflict is irrelevant. Since this scenario seems plausible, even contractualism faces a considerable burden of proof.

Third, the intergenerational setting suggests a specific problem of this form. In the discussion of the Problem of the Paradigm, it was said that typical solutions to prisoner's dilemmas do not carry over to the pure intergenerational problem. Hence, if the intergenerational setting is a PIP, even if the contract theorist claims that it is still appropriate to model it as a prisoner's dilemma, there will be a concern that—'taking men as they are'—the usual solutions will turn out to be unstable in practice. And this is a concern for both contractualists and contractarians.[45]

b. The 'Close to the Bone' Problem   These observations lead us to the last of our basic problems for the cooperation component of contract theory in the intergenerational setting. It has already been suggested that, in light of the first two challenges, some contract theorists have been tempted by the radical view that questions of morality do not arise in the intergenerational setting. (Hence the infamous slogan, 'What has posterity ever done for us?'.) Gauthier, for example, says:

Relations among persons of different generations may seem to fall outside the scope allowed to rational morality by our theory. ... If this is indeed the position to which reason leads us, then we must accept it, admitting another, and very deep, difference between our intuitive morality and what conforms to rational choice.[46]

As it turns out, most contract theorists seem reluctant to endorse this view, and (as we shall see) Gauthier himself is optimistic that other avenues are open.

---

[44] See, for example, Rousseau's proposal to 'take men as they are and laws as they might be', and the gloss on that idea provided by Rawls's account of political philosophy as 'realistically utopian' (Rawls 1999b, 11–13).

[45] Rawls, for example, frequently claims that principles of justice must be stable and workable in practice.

[46] Gauthier 1986, 298.

Still, it is worth asking why more contract theorists are not tempted by the radical response.

One obvious reason is that these positions may seem just too embarrassing from the point of view of conventional morality. But there may also be another, more interesting explanation: a refusal to countenance intergenerational issues may *undermine the appeal of the contract approach even for many of its core supporters.* This is because the intergenerational context involves several of the features that some contract theorists will take to be of the utmost moral importance, and which motivate their interest in the contract approach. For example, in the intergenerational setting, (a) earlier groups have asymmetric power over later groups, including the ability to determine their basic life prospects, and (b) the situation involves some basic questions of distribution (since claims that later groups have over their predecessors are likely to affect the life prospects of those predecessors). But both of these features seem likely to trouble many contract theorists. For one thing, most will take it as a fundamental fact that asymmetric power can be—and as a matter of empirical fact usually is—abused, and so that its exercise involves important moral and political issues.[47] For another, many will conceive of the central role of political philosophy as being to offer an account of what constitutes abuse, and what moral and political systems are best placed to avoid it. Hence, they will be committed to arguing that contract theory best fulfills this role through offering an account of the appropriate distribution of rights and responsibilities.

Such considerations suggest two things. First, the intergenerational setting might raise issues very close to those that motivate many to be contract theorists in the first place. This suggests that a deep inability to overcome problems in these areas may undermine the appeal of the whole contract approach. Second, the situation arising between generations closely resembles those of central concern to contract theorists *even though the element of cooperation (as understood on the exchange model) appears to be absent.* Hence, the analogy introduces some doubt about whether the standard account of cooperation must or should play a central role in how we understand such situations. These points imply that what to say about the intergenerational setting ought not to be a minor issue to contract theorists. For the issues raised by that setting go right to the core of the contract approach. (Call this the 'Close to the Bone Problem'.)

---

[47] Initially, this point may seem to imply that only contractualists need be concerned, since it is common to suppose that only they moralize issues of asymmetric power. But the discussion of the Idealization Dilemma above suggests that this is too quick.

III. Extension Strategies

Taken together, the three challenges create a strong presumption against attempts to apply traditional contract theories across generations. So, how might a contract theorist respond? A range of strategies suggest themselves. At one extreme, one might try to argue that the differences between the intergenerational and single-generation settings are small enough that the usual solutions can be made to transfer with only minor adjustments to conventional theory; at another, one might claim that the differences are profound, and that a new kind of contract theory is needed: in particular, one based on addressing the Pure Intergenerational Problem, rather than the Prisoner's Dilemma. Between these extremes, there is much middle ground.

In what follows, I will sketch a few of the possibilities and identify some of their shortcomings.[48] My main reason for doing this is that I believe that the most influential writers have tended to run together very different strategies, and that this has obscured what is at stake. Hence, clarification is useful. But I will also suggest that once this occurs, those proposals most friendly to traditional contract theory seem to fail, and this tends to lend plausibility to more radical approaches.

1. Direct Transfer

Contemporary contract theorists have not spent much time on future generations.[49] Still, the ways in which they address intergenerational concerns suggest that they are typically closer to the first extreme mentioned above, in that they believe that their standard methods can be carried over to the intergenerational setting with relatively minor adjustments. It is not entirely clear what justifies this attitude. But I conjecture that the main intuition underlying it is that the single-society, single-generation case is in some sense the primary subject-matter of justice (and, hence, of political philosophy more generally) and that, being so, it provides a suitable model for other such realms.[50] This intuition would imply that how one solves the single-generation

---

[48] Since these are large questions, a full treatment will not be possible here. Relevant discussions of the literature can be found in Gosseries 2003, Wolf 2004.

[49] For example, Rawls and Gauthier devote only small sections of their main books to the question, and many others ignore it altogether.

[50] Obviously, much depends on how terms like 'primary' and 'model' are to be understood, and this will give rise to important differences in approach. For example, 'primary' might be a matter of justification or just methodological ease; and 'model' might mean that solutions are simply directly inferred from one context to the other, or it may mean that though the primary context is the ultimate reference point for other contexts, its solutions may be adjusted to fit in with the peculiarities of those

case provides a model for the intergenerational case also.[51] So, for example, in the present context, it might suggest that if the single-generation case is a prisoner's dilemma, and therefore requires a prisoner's dilemma-style solution, then the intergenerational case requires a solution of the same type.

The claim that the single-generation case provides a model for the intergenerational case might be interpreted in a number of ways. Let us begin with the simplest, where the idea is that the two settings are similar in all relevant respects, so that the same kind of solution should work in both. In this situation, one would simply be able to transfer the solution from the primary case to the secondary. So, let us call this, 'the Direct Transfer Account'.[52]

The Direct Transfer Account rests on an argument by analogy. Consider, for example, the issue of the shape of the collective action problem. There, the basic idea would be that if the single-generation setting has the structure of a prisoner's dilemma, then the intergenerational setting must too. Of course, in the present circumstance, this view faces an obvious objection. As we have seen (in the discussion of the Problem of the Paradigm), on the face of it, the intergenerational case does not seem to be a prisoner's dilemma, but rather a PIP. Hence, the argument by analogy appears to be undermined. How might such an argument be resurrected?

One strategy would be to argue that the differences between the prisoner's dilemma and the PIP are irrelevant, and so claim that the analogy still holds. However, as we have seen, this response faces a considerable burden of proof. For example, one difference between the prisoner's dilemma and the PIP is that normal solutions to the PD appear to be undermined in the PIP case. But this implies that solutions to the PD do not straightforwardly transfer to the PIP, which is the central point at issue on the Direct Transfer account.

A second strategy would be to accept the basic problem, but argue that in practice the analogy between the two settings continues to hold because other factors are in play which restore the usual conditions, for example,

---

contexts. Moreover, it is worth noting that the extension model may be used to limit the application of justice. For example, some may say that the intergenerational context is so remote from the primary context that it makes no sense to apply 'justice' to future generations.

[51] Rawls 1999a, 20; Nussbaum 2006, 23. Nussbaum rejects the extension account for disability, international justice, and animals, but appears to endorse it for future generations.

[52] Arguments of this general kind are familiar both in other realms of justice and in the intergenerational setting itself. For example, Charles Beitz suggests that the context of international justice is relevantly similar to that of domestic justice, and so argues that Rawls's domestic principle of justice, the Difference Principle, should be extended internationally. (Rawls, of course, disagrees.) Similarly, Axel Gosseries argues that Rawls's first principle of justice, that of equal liberty, can be straight-forwardly carried over from the single- to the multi-generational context. (See Beitz 1999, and Gosseries 2001.)

by converting the PIP back into a prisoner's dilemma. On this strategy, the dominant question becomes, how might such a conversion work?

Conventional contract theorists are much enamored of a particular form of the conversion strategy. Typically, they propose that the intergenerational setting can be made more friendly to contract theory if we can establish a 'chain connection' between different generations. Hence, for example, Rawls says:

> I believe that the whole chain of generations can be tied together and principles can be agreed to that suitably take into account the interests of each. If this is right, we will have succeeded in deriving duties to other generations from reasonable conditions.[53]

There are various ways in which different generations might be 'tied together', and contract theorists often run these together. In what follows, I shall consider three prominent strategies (local cooperation, motivational assumptions, and constraints on reasoning), beginning with the least revisionary.

2. Local cooperation

The first approach seeks to ground the chain in the fact of generational overlap. This approach is much favoured by contractarians.[54] Thus, Gauthier, for example, says:

> The generations of mankind do not march on and off the stage of life in a body, with but one generation on stage at a time. Each person interacts with others both older and younger than himself, and enters thereby into a continuous thread of interaction extending from the most remote human past to the farthest future of our kind. Mutually beneficial cooperation directly involves persons of different but overlapping generations, but this creates indirect cooperative links extending throughout history. (299)

Gauthier's basic idea is that local cooperation between adjacent generations that overlap gives rise to a chain of interaction that links all generations, including the nonoverlapping ones.

Initially, this conversion strategy seems very attractive. First, it calls on the facts of human life to solve the intergenerational problem. We dispense with the PIP's seemingly artificial focus on generations that have no direct dealings with one another, and replace it with the idea of a sequence of overlapping groups. Second, the facts that are called upon in this model seem to bring back the essential features of the contract approach. For one thing, there is actual interaction and cooperation between the overlapping groups; for another, this

---

[53] Rawls 1999a, 111.
[54] This is presumably because they typically try to ground their claims in matters of descriptive fact.

interaction is said to have the features of a prisoner's dilemma,[55] and hence the paradigm appears to be restored.

Still, it is not enough simply to assert that local cooperation solves the problem. Instead, one must say what makes cooperation desirable or necessary, what it consists in, and why this restores the traditional paradigm. Unfortunately, on these issues, the local cooperation account is either unclear or implausible.

a. Rationales for Cooperation   Consider first the desirability of cooperation. Immediately after the passage quoted above, Gauthier says:

Each person, in considering the terms on which he is to cooperate with those in an earlier generation than himself, must keep in mind his *need* to establish similar terms with those of a later generation, who in turn must keep in mind their *need* to cooperate with members of a yet later generation, and so on.[56]

There appear to be three basic ideas here. The first is that each generation prefers to cooperate with at least one later generation (presumably its immediate successor). The second is that because of this preference any given generation will find itself constrained in the terms of cooperation it proposes to at least one earlier generation (usually, presumably, its immediate predecessor). The third is that the initial preference has a certain status: in repeatedly using the word 'need', Gauthier appears to suggest that each generation will find it in some way *necessary* to cooperate with at least one later generation.[57]

Now, each of these claims requires further defence. So, let us begin by asking, why does each generation prefer to cooperate with its successor? One answer would be simply that undertaking cooperative ventures with future overlapping generations yields new goods, and earlier generations have a strong desire to secure such goods. So, for example, perhaps earlier generations can benefit from devoting resources to medium-term projects that do not mature until the next overlapping generation is on the scene to make an essential contribution. (For instance, perhaps they would enjoy watching their future grandchildren play Little League baseball, and so are willing to invest in public parks that will make this possible.)

Considered in isolation, this idea looks promising. However, it is not clear that it provides any *constraint* on the behaviour of earlier generations (as Gauthier suggests). First, its influence seems to be limited by the Problem of Parochialism. After all, for earlier generations, projects with overlapping generations face

---

[55] E.g., Heath 1997.   [56] Gauthier 1986, 299; emphasis added.
[57] A fourth idea lurking here is that it is necessary to establish 'similar' terms of cooperation between (at least) three different generations. Doubts that beset both rationales for the cooperation preference considered below also make it clear what justifies this claim.

competition from shorter-run projects. If each earlier generation has only generation-relative concerns, it will select only projects that are maximally beneficial to it, regardless of benefits to the later generation. So, for example, it will refuse intergenerational projects that have very large benefits for future people merely if they are slightly less beneficial for it than some alternative. (For instance, suppose that the prospective grandparents above refuse to fund soccer—rather than baseball—fields (a) even though they have good reason to believe that the children would prefer to play soccer and also get much larger health benefits from it, and (b) that they do so simply because they cannot be bothered to learn the basic rules of soccer.)[58] Given this, it is not clear that any cooperation that is produced by these means will answer to common intuitions about intergenerational *justice* (rather than simply the convenience of the earlier generation).

Second, earlier generations may simply not be interested in the kinds of rewards offered by overlapping projects. Suppose, for example, that on his deathbed Henry Ford prefers to destroy his automotive empire rather than hand it over to his successors for a large amount of money.[59] There is nothing in the overlap account to show that he is in any way irrational or unjust.

Third, and perhaps most importantly, the use of the notion of 'need' to describe the earlier generation's interest in such projects seems inappropriate. Though it may be true that cooperation is rationally necessary in the weak sense that it is required for maximization, it does not seem that it is 'needed' in the stronger, more familiar sense. Moreover, it is this sense that seems more clearly connected with notions of justice.

This last observation leads us to a second possible interpretation of Gauthier's claim about the preferability of cooperation. Perhaps the idea is that in order to ensure either *vital* new benefits, or the *security* of existing benefits through the period of overlap, any given generation will want to cooperate with its immediate successors. So, for example, earlier generations might want future overlapping generations to cooperate with them on issues such as maintaining social security, or providing assisted care to elders during the period of overlap. Such concerns do seem compelling enough to reach the level of needs, and they are also more likely to overwhelm the problem of parochialism.

---

[58] Medium-term investment is made more appealing by the productive power of investment. Presumably, this softens the impact of this issue. However, it seems to make the question of whether the impact of local cooperation is enough to satisfy basic intuitions about intergenerational justice primarily an empirical one. For a discussion of this and other specific arguments of Gauthier's, see Gauthier 1986, 303–4, and Sauve 1995, 168–9.

[59] Sauve 1995, 167.

There is much to be discussed in this area. However, here I will make just three general points. The first is that Gauthier's claim that *intergenerational* cooperation—involving both successors and predecessors—is necessary to secure such goods still seems too strong. The earlier generation may have other options than acquiescing to an intergenerational contract. For example, perhaps its members can appropriate sufficient resources during the period without overlap such that they can simply pay some members of the later generation to provide the services they need during the overlap;[60] or perhaps they can manipulate the characters or environments of their successors in such a way that the latter see no other option but to assist.

The second general point is that the local cooperation theorist must be careful not to beg the question here. Presumably, a central problem with such 'direct' proposals is that the later generation might think that the extent of the earlier generation's holdings is itself unfair (e.g. because it is the result of an earlier exertion of monopoly power); and that, given this, the later generation would be justified in depriving the earlier of these possessions. So, perhaps Gauthier's point is that this is the reason that the earlier generation must take steps to ensure that its holdings 'look fair' to its immediate successor. Unfortunately, this explanation appears to presuppose much of what is at stake. After all, why should an earlier generation now suppose that the next generation will be more influenced in its behaviour toward them by what they do to their predecessors than by more direct means? Is it just because the next generation will think them *immoral* if they don't look after their parents and grandparents in old age? But this is to assume the very attitude the existence of which the overlap account is supposed to justify. Some rationale for truly intergenerational cooperation is still needed.

The third general point is that the focus on needs casts the issue of 'cooperation' in the intergenerational case in a new light. Instead of the model of two generations getting together to produce new goods that can then be shared between them, what seems salient here is the *vulnerability* of any given generation to its immediate successor. It is the idea that each earlier generation will find itself under the power of the next generation that generates the *need* to cooperate.[61] Not only does this sequential vulnerability make the

---

[60] This might include paying some members of the next generation to defend their holdings against the later generation considered as a whole.

[61] One could, of course, describe this vulnerability in terms of the production of goods for which the earlier generation has very strong preferences. But this does not capture the asymmetric situation of the two generations. The younger generation can choose its projects, and looking after the elderly is one amongst many possibilities; but the older generation cannot substitute other projects, and can engage no other providers.

situation different from a prisoner's dilemma, but it also appears to invoke the asymmetry of the Pure Intergenerational Problem rather than resolve it. (More on this issue below.)

b. The Structure of Cooperation   Gauthier's rationale for local cooperation thus remains unclear. But what about its implications? Suppose we assume for a moment that each generation does desire some form of local intergenerational cooperation. How is this supposed to achieve Gauthier's larger aim of tying together *all* generations? One possibility is as follows. Imagine that the generations succeed each other in a way similar to successive crews of a vessel at sea. Suppose, for example, that earlier crews are required to hand over the ship to their immediate successors in good working order—for example, by not letting the planks in its wooden hull rot away. Then, Gauthier's idea may be that each generation passes on relevant goods to the next in such a way that those goods are literally or effectively preserved across all generations. In the terms of the example, since maintenance work must be done continuously—one cannot allow a plank to rot away and replace it later or the ship will sink—this local need ensures that even temporally distant crews receive the ship in good working order.

Once again, there is something to this model. However, it should be noticed that the model rests on some highly contingent assumptions, which suggest that it applies only in a very specific kind of case. Consider the following. On the one hand, strictly-speaking, the need for maintenance cannot be continuous. For, if the intergenerational 'ship' requires absolutely constant maintenance, then each generation will have purely intragenerational reasons to replace the planks—if it does not, it will go under. But this makes the appeal to overlap superfluous: the problems of intergenerational justice are taken care of automatically, by the interest of each current generation in self-preservation. On the other hand, the need for maintenance cannot be too diffuse. If the idea is that local cooperation takes care of all issues of intergenerational justice, then it must be the case that the only maintenance issues arise between adjacent generations. In other words, it must not be possible to cause degradation whose effects are delayed for three or more generations. (One cannot, for example, abuse the sails.) For if that is possible, each generation will feel free to cause such degradation, knowing that they will never need to cooperate with any generation that feels the effects.[62]

This last issue is sometimes called the problem of 'time bombs'—projects whose costs are deferred for several generations. This problem bedevils mutual

---

[62] See, for example, Derek Parfit's 'downward escalator' case (1984, 383).

advantage accounts of intergenerational cooperation in general, and the local cooperation strategy in particular. How might it be resolved? There seem to be two prominent suggestions in the literature.[63]

The first is that immediate successor generations can act as 'middlemen' in transactions whose ultimate logic really involves distant generations. Suppose, for example, that a member of generation 1 owns an old-growth forest and, coming to the end of her life, is considering clear-cutting it for an immediate profit that she can spend before she dies. Then a member of generation 2 might offer to buy the forest in order to preserve the aesthetic benefits provided by the forest for another generation. But in doing so, she can expect a similar offer in her own twilight years from a member of generation 3, and so on for succeeding generations. This means that the member of generation 2 can offer a price for the forest that reflects the expected valuations of future generations of tree lovers as well. In this way, she acts as a *conduit* for intergenerational concerns. (Call this, 'the Conduit Argument'.)

The basic idea of the Conduit Argument is that prospective interactions between earlier and later generations in the chain act as a carrot to entice cooperation in the present. The basic idea of the second argument is the reverse of this: that they act as a stick. In this vein, Joseph Heath suggests that unfairness to future generations will cause a chain of cooperation between generations to unravel. His thought is this. If generations 2 and 3 strike a bargain that will turn out to be unfair to generation 6, then generation 6 will lack sufficient reason to cooperate with generation 5. But, Heath argues, this will mean that generation 5 will lack sufficient reason to cooperate with generation 4, and this will imply that 4 will not cooperate with 3 either, and this will break the chain by removing 3's reason to comply in the original bargain with 2. Hence, the result of the original unfairness to 6 is that the whole sequence of cooperation unravels, making the attempt to strike an unfair bargain self-defeating. (Call this, 'the Backward Induction Argument' ('BIA').)[64]

Now there are several reasons for skepticism about both arguments. Here I will mention just two.[65] First, if these arguments are to succeed in their stated aim of tying together very distant generations, then they will have to be very demanding of agents in terms of information and rationality.

---

[63] In practice, Gauthier and Heath appear to solve the problem simply by assuming that the intergenerational contract must have constant terms across all generations, and that acceptance of this contract is then 'all-or-nothing'. But the reasons for these assumptions are unclear.

[64] Heath 1997.

[65] One further concern, pointed out by Arrenhius, is that the BIA bears a strong resemblance to some well-known paradoxes of rationality, so that we should be suspicious of it for that reason.

Succeeding generations are supposed to anticipate and register the preferences and behaviour of distant future generations in their own.[66] In practice, this seems deeply implausible; and so, insofar as the local cooperation account is supposed to rest on considerations of what the world is really like, this undercuts the argument.

Second, both arguments assume that the mediating chain of generations delivers distant concerns back to the present essentially untouched, as mere additions to closer concerns. But this also seems implausible. On the one hand, the Problem of Parochialism suggests both (a) that intermediate generations will be selective about which concerns of future generations they take seriously, and (b) that distant generations will weigh their gripes against their ancestors against the gains to be made from cooperating with their immediate forebears. Hence, both the Conduit and Backward Induction Arguments present far too clean a picture of the ramifications of the actual connections. (For example, are we really to suppose that generation 6 will refuse to look after its parents because its great- and great-great-grandparents decided to burden it with an excessive amount of nuclear waste?)[67] On the other hand, it is plausible to think that a successful transfer of all the interests of the future back to the present would result in an overwhelming burden on present generations, from which they might quite rightly demand protection.[68] Hence, if the arguments work, they seem likely to show too much.

The problem of time bombs thus suggests that local cooperation is unlikely to offer a complete solution to the Pure Intergenerational Problem. Moreover, since some of the most troubling intergenerational issues—e.g. nuclear waste disposal, catastrophic climate change—seem to be of this form, this seems to be a serious practical as well as theoretical concern. Still, it is worth pointing out that the local cooperation strategy also faces more fundamental problems. In particular, it is not clear that it achieves the aim of restoring the usual exchange model and the prisoner's dilemma analysis. Moreover, there are important competitors to its explanation of what justifies intergenerational cooperation.

Consider first the following. Gauthier proposes that we solve the intergenerational problem through a chain of cooperation—since each generation in the sequence is vulnerable to the behaviour of its successor, it behaves well towards its own predecessor in the hope of establishing a precedent that will be followed when it grows old. But we should note that, whatever its other merits, this is not cooperation in the usual sense employed by contract

---

[66] Arrenhius 1999.

[67] The BIA argument especially seems to consider cooperation an 'all-or-nothing' affair. See Arrhenius 1999.

[68] Koopmans 1965; Arrow 1999.

theorists. The model is not one of direct exchange between contemporaries, which rests on roughly contemporaneous mutual reward. Instead, it is one of indirect reciprocity: the second generation gives something to the first in the expectation that the third will eventually give something to it, and so on.

Let us make three quick points about this difference. First, indirect reciprocity has a different logic to contemporaneous mutual reward. The basic mechanism that is in play seems to be something like 'preemptive sacrifice to one group with the expectation of thereby eliciting a future reward from another'; and, on the surface at least, these two things seem very different.

Second, this raises questions about the connection between indirect reciprocity and the exchange model of cooperation. One question is whether the 'preemptive sacrifice' model really counts as *exchange* in the relevant sense. The answer to this question is unclear. On the one hand, it is true that any given generation is making its preemptive sacrifice *for the sake* of the later reward. Hence, it is hoping to induce something that it would perceive as an exchange. On the other hand, on Gauthier's account, if this generation receives the later reward from the next generation, this is not directly *because* of its own sacrifice, but rather because the next generation wants to secure a future reward from its own successor. So, it is not clear that the transfer from the younger to the older generation itself counts as an 'exchange'. (Perhaps it should be seen as something else, such as some kind of sacrificial offering—or perhaps different values are at stake here, and Gauthier's focus on necessary exchange is misleading.)[69]

Third, there is a question about whether indirect reciprocity, even if succeeds in other respects, actually restores the prisoner's dilemma paradigm. On the face of it, the idea of the indirect reciprocity model seems to be that the place of agent B in a temporal chain of connection ABC gives rise to a system of local interactions based on preemptive sacrifice that would precisely mirror those that would arise in a direct contemporaneous exchange between B and a single other party D. But, for reasons raised earlier in the article—including prominently the Problem of the Paradigm itself—this argument by analogy faces serious obstacles, and thus requires independent support.

c. Justifying Cooperation   Finally, even apart from these concerns, Gauthier's indirect reciprocity model is in competition with a number of other possibilities. One such possibility might be illustrated through the following

---

[69] Another question is, even if we assume that indirect reciprocity counts as genuine exchange, it is not clear that this is the same *kind* of exchange as in the contemporaneous mutual reward case. Indeed, given the differences just mentioned, there seems to be some presumption against this view.

example. Imagine a campsite by a remote beach that is seldom but regularly visited by different groups of travelers. Suppose that a given group of visitors finds the site in pristine condition, obviously carefully cleaned by the previous inhabitants. Would it not seem natural for them to feel a responsibility to do the same before they leave?

The answer to this question appears to be 'yes'. But the explanation is less clear. On the one hand, the case might be conceived of as one of indirect reciprocity. But if so, notice how the kind of reciprocity differs from Gauthier's. For one thing, there is no overlap. None of the groups ever meet. Hence, the basic explanation for their behaviour does not rest on overlap as such. For another, the newcomers do not *need* to cooperate. By the time they arrive, the benefit to them of being part of the chain has already been secured. Given this, they cannot plausibly be though of as trying to secure benefits for themselves through their behaviour.[70]

On the other hand, the case might be approached without reference to reciprocity considered as such at all. Suppose, for example, that the newcomers would feel some responsibility to clean up even if the beach site had not been prepared for them—for example, if they were the first visitors, or if the previous campers had left a mess.[71] Under such circumstances, it seems that a different language for accounting for their responsibility might be necessary, or simply more appropriate. For example, rather than seeing themselves as indirect reciprocators, perhaps the newcomers are best described as believing themselves to have obligations as 'stewards of the land'. If so, perhaps they would be angry with any messy campers who preceded them not because those campers did not confer benefits on them, but because they both failed to discharge their stewardship obligations, and in doing so foisted additional burdens onto other stewards.

The beach example is important for several reasons. First, the example resembles the intergenerational setting more closely than Gauthier's own scenario. Essentially, Gauthier tries to turn the Pure Intergenerational Problem on its head by claiming that it is earlier generations that need the cooperation of later generations, rather than *vice versa*. But the beach example does not do this; instead, it seems to preserve the basic circumstances of the PIP.

Second, the beach example suggests that problems of this kind can be, and indeed often are, resolved. This is very important. For one thing, it implies that there are settings within which the PIP can be addressed. For another, if

---

[70] At most, they would be aiming to secure benefits for the group following their successors; but even that account of their motives seems unlikely.

[71] The responsibility might be different in the three cases. In the last case, the cleanup would certainly be carried out in a different spirit.

this is compelling, dubious attempts to establish Gauthier's inversion may not be necessary.[72]

Third, and perhaps most importantly, the beach example suggests that the basic appeal of Gauthier's proposal that we should pay attention to the connections between generations may reside not in his invocation of overlap and reciprocity, but elsewhere. For example, perhaps it is the intergenerational connection to other members of humanity *itself* that matters, not what else we might get for ourselves from such connections; or perhaps there are wider duties associated with being a member of the species that thinking about local cooperation makes salient.

I conclude that despite its initial appeal the local cooperation model of chain connection does not successfully address the three central challenges. It remains seriously unclear how the contract approach can address worries about rationale, structure and justification.

3. Motivational Assumption

The contract theorists' second attempt to establish a chain connection rests on dropping the usual assumption of self-interest and allowing the parties 'more realistic'[73] concerns for their spouses and offspring. Here I will make just three general observations about such proposals.[74]

The first observation is that when appeal is made to 'realistic motivational assumptions', we should be careful to isolate exactly what claim is being assumed. First, in practice, discussions of such proposals often invoke a number of very different ideas, sometimes simultaneously. For example, Rawls's view is often described as incorporating a two-generational model, where the idea is that members of each generation care only about their immediate offspring. But he also refers to generational lines, and this suggests an ongoing and completely general concern. More extravagantly, Gauthier moves very quickly from the observation (a) that 'characteristically persons do take an interest in their immediate descendants' to (b) the idea that 'human beings are engaged in a partnership over time in creating and maintaining a society' to (c) the claim that this might lead us to apply contractarian theory to a fictional agreement rooted in 'a conception of society as based on a contract among past, present and future generations'.[75] Second, intergenerational concern varies

---

[72] It is worth noting that these observations threaten to bring on the 'Close to the Bone' problem in a striking way.

[73] Gauthier 1986, 300.

[74] Motivational assumptions are discussed in more detail in reference to other papers in the volume.

[75] Gauthier 1986 298–9.

along at least three dimensions: scope (e.g. two-generations, or a generational line stretching indefinitely into the future, or one that extends into the past); the subject of concern (e.g. a person's direct descendents, society as such); and the profile of concern (e.g. constant, or gradually reducing in some way, or with a sharp cut-off at some generation). Clearly, then, any attempt to resolve problems of intergenerational ethics by invoking intergenerational concern must specify and then justify its account of such concern, for the nature of that account is likely to make a great deal of difference to its results, and some extrapolations of this idea involve significant normative assumptions. In short, what counts as a 'realistic motivational assumption' bears much closer scrutiny.

The next observation is that the basic approach suffers from similar practical problems to those afflicting local cooperation. For one thing, the actual concern people show for their descendants varies in its extent (and some people do not have descendants); for another, actual concern is not well placed to deal with problems that skip generations.

The final observation is that motivational assumptions introduce a further theoretical problem, at least for contractualists. On the contractualist picture, the point of the contract approach is to model the *appropriate* concern to be shown to other people as a matter of justice. But special motivational assumptions might undercut this understanding of the contract approach. For now an independent account of the appropriate kind of concern for future people is required: we need to know how much parties to the contract *should* take their interests into account. But this is at least close to the question that contract theory itself was being asked to answer.

4. Rawls's Constraint

A third approach to chain connection is to introduce direct constraints on the reasoning of contractors with the intention of forcing them to take seriously the interests of future people. The most prominent example comes from Rawls.[76] In his later writings, Rawls subjects the parties to the original position to a pro-cedural constraint on their reasoning: they are required 'to agree to principles subject to the constraint that they wish all preceding generations to have fol-lowed the very same principles.'[77] (Call this, 'the Constraint Principle' ('CP').)

Initially, this approach looks promising, since it forces the current generation to internalize the concern of other generations in a way similar to that in which different members of the current generations are forced to internalize each

---

[76] The suggestion was initially made in print in English 1977. Rawls also cites Thomas Nagel and Derek Parfit; see Rawls 2001, 160, n. 39.

[77] Rawls 1999a, 111.

others concerns in the usual contract. However, it is doubtful whether this method of extending the traditional model really works.

a. The Problem of the Initial Generation   Consider first the Problem of the Initial Generation. As Rawls recognizes, and the PIP makes clear, the fact that an initial generation receives no benefits from cooperation undermines the normal contract procedure, both because there is one generation that has no self-interested reason to accept the contract, and because this problem is iterated—if the first generation does not comply with the contract, then the second has no reason to either.

How might Rawls's Constraint Principle overcome this difficulty?[78] One possibility is that it does so simply by ignoring the perspective of the first generation. Suppose that one adopted an uncharitable reading of what is meant by 'they wish all preceding generations to have followed the very same principles'. According to that reading, the Constraint Principle asks us to consider only what each *later generation* would demand *of its predecessors*, under the condition that we do not know which later generation we will be. (Call this, 'the Predecessor Principle'.)

Now the Predecessor Principle faces an obvious objection: the perspective of a first generation that has no predecessors is simply ignored. We ask only what the second generation would ask of it, and not what its legitimate expectations might be. But this seems wrong on both procedural and substantive grounds. As a matter of procedure, we expect the position of all generations to be represented; as a matter of substance, the rule leaves open the possibility that later generations will exploit the first: since it has no representation they can devise a rule which is unfairly prejudiced against its interests.

Now, as I suggested, this is an uncharitable reading of the Constraint Principle. Rawls presumably rules the Predecessor Principle out through a different assumption: that the parties do not know which of all of the generations they are to be. Given this assumption, the idea is that they must take seriously the possibility of occupying the position of any given generation, including the first. But now we must confront a further issue. If the parties to the original position are supposed to take seriously the possibility that they may be the first generation, then they must consider the possibility that they

---

[78] Rawls himself seems to suggest that the Problem of the Initial Generation is overcome by a *combination* of the Constraint Principle, a motivational assumption and the veil of ignorance. Hence, he is not committed to the view that the Constraint Principle overcomes the problem alone. Nonetheless, he does not really say how the three work in combination. So, it is worth examining the defects of each considered in isolation, and pointing out that we should not simply assume that their defects simply cancel each other out when they are combined.

might be asked to make sacrifices for future generations for which they would receive no compensation. But, intuitively, this suggests that they will require less in the way of savings than if all generations had been similarly situated and may ever gamble. (Call this, 'the Hedging Principle'.)

To illustrate, consider the following simple model.[79] Suppose that three generations will live on a given planet, and that there is no generational overlap. Suppose also that the last generation will not benefit from being the last, since it will need the resources it might have passed on (to a hypothetical fourth generation) in order to postpone for its lifetime the effects of an exogenously produced disaster that ultimately wipes out life on the planet. (Suppose, for example, that the third generation must build expensive domes in which to live because of worsening environmental conditions.) Imagine then that the planet initially provides the first generation with resources worth 10 units, and that each generation can produce an extra unit of resource for every one that it initially receives. Suppose also that any level of consumption above 4 units per generation is enough to allow that generation to create and maintain just institutions. Finally, suppose that the generations must choose between three proposals for intergenerational transfer, which give rise to three possible development scenarios. According to the first proposal, each generation must transfer 10 units to the next (call this 'Proposal A'); according to the second, 15 units ('Proposal B'); and according to the third, 8 units ('Proposal C'). These proposals give rise to the possible scenarios shown in Table 3.2.

Intuitively, Proposal A seems most likely to appeal to many contract theorists.[80] But this conclusion does not necessarily follow from either of the

---

[79] This model incorporates more information that Rawls would allow behind his veil of ignorance. I do not think that this alters the basic point. Rawls does allow the parties to choose different rates of saving above and below the threshold. So, they ought to consider possibilities such as the one I will consider in deciding which rate of saving to choose.

[80] Proposal A is appealing for a number of reasons. For example, it seems fair procedurally (e.g. since the first generation receives its initial endowment as a matter of brute good luck) and it also seems in accordance with equal concern and respect. Proposal B would be favoured on utilitarian grounds, as it maximizes expected utility. Proposal C is more difficult to justify, as A and B each have higher expected utility if one assumes risk neutrality. But I am not sure why a contract theorist should assume risk neutrality, given the stipulation that all three proposals put each generation above the Rawlsian threshold. Perhaps generations would be happy to gamble a little under these circumstances. (If this is unsatisfying, one might imagine an alternative version of Scenario C where the first generation has a one-off opportunity, available only to that generation, to boost its production to 15, but where this increase is not transferable and has the effect of restricting the maximum output of future generations to 8. In that case, the payoffs would be 15, 8, and 8, the demand to transfer 8 would be satisfied, and the expected utility for any given generation under Proposal C would be higher than under A, but less than under B.) In any case, my purpose here is merely to show that *the various interpretations of what is demanded by the Rawlsian constraint can diverge both from each other and from what might otherwise have been expected.* Hence, the plausibility of the particular proposals in the illustrative examples is not too important.

Table 3.2

	Generation 1				Generation 2				Generation 3			
	Inherit	Produce	Consume	Transfer	I	P	C	T	I	P	C	Expenses
Scenario A	10	10	**10**	10	10	10	**10**	10	10	10	**10**	10
Scenario B	10	10	5	15	15	15	**15**	15	15	15	**15**	15
Scenario C	10	10	**12**	8	8	8	**8**	8	8	8	**8**	8

interpretations I have offered of Rawls's Constraint Principle. On the one hand, according to the first interpretation (the Predecessor Principle), parties consider only the possibilities that they might be the second, or third generation. Hence, it seems likely that they would endorse Proposal B: each generation should pass on 15 units. This allows the second and third generations each to consume 15 units and pass the same amount along. But it leaves the first generation with only 5 units. On the other hand, according to the second interpretation (the Hedging Principle), the parties take into account the fact that they might occupy the advantageous position of the first generation. Presumably, this means that they will reject Proposal B. But it leaves it open whether they will favour Proposal A or Proposal C (that 8 units should be passed on), since the latter allows the second, and third generations to have 8, but the first to retain 12. I conclude then, that it is not clear that Rawls's Constraint Principle solves the problem of the first generation.[81]

b. The Problem of Extinction   The second reason to doubt whether the Constraint Principle really works is provided by the problem of extinction. Suppose we modify our previous example, and assume that the disaster that ultimately wipes out life on the planet under Proposals A, B, and C is endogenous to production at levels greater than 7 units per generation. (So, for example, imagine that the technology available to the three generations is such that they cannot produce at levels greater than 7 units per generation and also clean up the pollution their production causes.) Suppose then that there is an alternative proposal—Proposal D—according to which each generation limits its production and consumption to 7 units, and transfers 10 units to

---

[81] Bill Talbott suggests that a contract theorist such as Scanlon may well favour a proposal that involves modest sacrifice by the first generation for the sake of benefits to later generations. I agree. For example, if the choice where between A and A*, where A* involved 9 for the first generation and then 15 for each subsequent generation, it seems to me that some contract theorists may well favour A* over A. Nevertheless, I am interpreting the choice between A and B (and C) as more stark than this.

Table 3.3

	Generation 1				Generations 2 and 3				Generations 4 to 10			
	Inherit	Produce	Consume	Transfer	I	P	C	T/E	I	P	C	T/E
Scenario A	10	10	**10**	10	10	10	**10**	10	–	–	–	–
Scenario B	10	10	5	15	15	15	**15**	15	–	–	–	–
Scenario C	10	10	**12**	8	8	8	**8**	8	–	–	–	–
Scenario D	10	7	7	10	10	7	**7**	10	10	7	**7**	10

the next generation, and then that this enables life on the planet to persist for ten generations rather than three. (Assume again that the extra 10 units left to the last generation are needed for them to deal with their accumulated environmental costs.) This leads to the scenario shown in Table 3.3.

Intuitively, it seems that Proposal D has much to recommend it; but the Constraint Principle gives us no reason to favour Proposal D. Indeed, there is some reason to believe that if the situation is modelled as a single generation trying to decide on proposals, it will choose A, B, or C over D, since it expects to come into existence under any proposal, and D promises a lower level of resources than all of the others.

c. The Problem of Stipulation   This brings me to the final difficulty for the Constraint Principle. Rawls himself escapes the extinction problem by stipulation. For he defines society as 'a fair system of cooperation between generations over time',[82] and has a stringent interpretation of this claim:

> [P]olitical society is always regarded as a scheme of cooperation over time indefinitely; the idea of a future time when its affairs are to be wound up and society disbanded is foreign to our conception of society.[83]

Thus, he excludes the possibility of choosing extinction in setting out the very foundations of his project through his definition of society.

This seems objectionable, for several reasons. First, it implies that certain questions in intergenerational ethics cannot be raised. But it seems to me that sometimes it does make sense to raise such questions. Second, Rawls's stipulation deprives contract theory of resources that it might otherwise employ

---

[82] Rawls 2001, 160. This is not explicit in the initial definition of 'society' at Rawls 1999a, 4.
[83] Rawls 2001, 162.

with respect to these questions. If contract theory *must* assume that society is indefinitely extended in time, then it seems that it must remain silent on some important questions. But it is not clear why contract theory must assume this and remain silent. Third, the stipulation may be employed in a way that makes it give answers that seem intuitively implausible. Suppose, for example, that we revise our example one last time and stipulate that the 7 units per generation suggested in Proposal D is below the threshold necessary for the creation and maintenance of just institutions. (Call this, Proposal D*.) Then there seem grounds for preferring Proposal A over D* even though D* involves a greater number of generations. But Rawls's stipulation appears to suggest either that no choice can be made, or else that the correct proposal is D*.[84]

IV. Pure Solutions

The discussion so far suggests that the various strategies for extending the traditional single-generation model either fail, or else are considerably under-specified. I conjecture that this fact is usually obscured by the tendency of the principal writers to run different versions of the various strategies together. But if the extension strategies in general, and chain connection in particular, do not seem to work, what other options are there?

The obvious one is to consider a truly intergenerational contract, involving all generations at once. Moreover, there is some presumption in favour of this method in any case. If contract theory is to be applied to future generations, surely it is natural, at first glance, to expect the contract to be *between* generations in this most straightforward sense.

Traditional contract theorists, of course, typically resist this approach. They offer various reasons for doing so. Rawls, for example, considers the possibility of a 'general assembly' of all actual or possible people,[85] but dismisses it as 'stretch[ing] fantasy too far'.[86] His reason is that it 'would cease to be a natural guide to intuition and would lack a clear sense'. The problem here seems to be partly practical—Rawls thinks that the method is too indeterminate to yield definite conclusions—and partly theoretical—he thinks that we do not know how it should be understood. David Heyd suggests an additional and even more damning objection. The general assembly model is, he says, logically

---

[84] Rawls, of course, could invoke the duty to create and maintain just institutions in order to choose A over D*. This is an interesting proposal, and one that deserves discussion. Nevertheless, since it appears to require abandoning the stipulation, or modifying the way in which it is understood, it is not of central relevance here.

[85] Rawls 1999a, 119.   [86] Rawls 1971, 139.

incoherent: one cannot successfully conceive of a bargain between persons whose very existence is at stake in the negotiation.[87]

I remain unconvinced by these complaints. In particular, Rawls's worries seem premature, and Heyd's complaint appears to rest on the interesting, but unsubstantiated, claim that we can make no sense of the idea of a hypothetical person wishing not to come into existence. Still, whatever may be the truth about these issues, it is not clear that they are decisive, since it seems possible that an intergenerational contract could be modelled in ways that avoid them. Consider, for example, a contract made between *representatives* of all those who might exist during a certain period. Such representatives might have a fairly clear idea of which scenarios should be avoided; and they might also be willing to consider not having some (or perhaps all) of their constituents come into existence in order that those scenarios are avoided. Moreover, since the (theoretical) existence of such representatives would seem not to depend on how the contract turns out, there is no logical incoherence in envisioning their getting together to make a contract.

Now, obviously, the investigation of such alternatives must be left for another occasion. Here my point is simply that the realm of pure intergenerational contracts remains relatively underexplored, and there are whole classes of possibilities to be considered. That being said, I shall conclude with two more general thoughts about why such projects might prove to be important.

The first thought is that though producing a pure intergenerational contract theory may prove to be a good strategy for converting the Pure Intergenerational Problem into the Prisoner's Dilemma format so beloved of traditional contract theory, it also may not. Instead, it may be that contract theorists need to *model directly for the Pure Intergenerational Problem*. This suggestion is so underexplored that it is not even clear what it amounts to. But perhaps cases like the beach example are a useful starting point. In any case, modelling for the PIP directly is an important conceptual possibility that is worth considering.

The second thought is that such possibilities may have wider importance for contract theory more generally. One reason for saying this is that it is tempting to think that intergenerational ethics is prior to intragenerational ethics in at least some important respects. Rawls, for example, says that his intergenerational principle of just savings *constrains* his intragenerational difference principle.[88] This suggests that there are ways in which an intergenerational contract might frame and limit the intragenerational version; and it may even imply that traditional contract theory covers only a special case of justice nested within a wider framework. If either of these suggestions is correct, then one's

[87] Heyd 1992.   [88] Rawls 1999a, 258.

wider theory of intergenerational justice may have profound influence on the narrower theory of justice within a generation. The prevalence of the extension model has obscured this possibility; but the apparent weaknesses of the extension approach bring the issue to life.

V. Conclusion

In this chapter, I have argued for three claims. First, the intergenerational setting poses three serious challenges to conventional contract theory. These challenges involve the theory's basic accounts of the rationale for, structure of, and justification for cooperation. Second, the standard approach contract theorists have adopted to deal with intergenerational issues—that of trying to adapt the normal single-generation model to the intergenerational context through postulating some kind of chain of connection between generations—has thus far proven inadequate. Third, the inadequacies of the standard approaches may reflect the fact that the intergenerational setting constitutes a different kind of collective action problem than that facing contract theory in the traditional, single-generation setting.

In light of these problems, it may be that contract theory should be rejected, at least for intergenerational ethics. But I am not so sure. If the pure intergenerational problem is really a particular kind of collective action problem, then there is reason to think that the contract theory approach can be resurrected. How? One possibility, of course, is that all that is required is a better theory of chain connection. This should be investigated. But another possibility is that we should try to move beyond the single-generation model to see if a more universal kind of contract theory is possible. Contract theorists usually eschew this approach because they want to avoid the considerable conceptual difficulties involved in modelling a contract across generations. But my arguments in this chapter has suggested that it may not be possible to avoid such difficulties.

References

Arrhenius, G. (1999), 'Mutual Advantage Contractarianism and Future Generations', *Theoria*, 65: 25–35.

Arrow, K. J. (1999). 'Discounting, Morality and Gaming', in P. Portney and J. P. Weylant (eds.), *Discounting and Intergenerational Equity* (Washington, DC: Resources for the Future).

BARRY, B. (1978), 'Circumstances of Justice and Future Generations', in R. I. Sikora and B. Barry (eds.), *Obligations to Future Generations* (Temple), 204–48.

BEITZ, C. R. (1999), *Political Theory and International Relations* (2nd edition, Princeton).

CUDD, A. (2000), 'Contractarianism', *Stanford Encyclopedia of Philosophy*. Available online at <http://plato.stanford.edu/entries/contractarianism> (posted version dated 18 June 2000; accessed January 2005).

DARWALL, S. (ed.) (2002a), *Contractarianism/Contractualism* (Blackwell).

_____ (2002b), 'Introduction', in Darwall 2002a.

DE-SHALIT, A. (1995), *Why Posterity Matters: Environmental Policies and Future Generations* (Routledge).

ENGLISH, J. (1977), 'Justice Between Generations', *Philosophical Studies*, 31: 91–104.

GARDINER, S. (2001), 'The Real Tragedy of the Commons', *Philosophy and Public Affairs*.

_____ (2003), 'The Pure Intergenerational Problem', *Monist*.

_____ (2006), 'Why Do Future Generations Need Protection?' Available at <http://ceco.polytechnique.fr/CDD/PDF/DDX-06-16.pdf>.

GAUTHIER, D. (1986), *Morals By Agreement*. (Oxford).

GOSSERIES, A. (2001), 'What Do We Owe the Next Generation(s)?', *Loyola of Los Angeles Law Review*, 35: 293–355.

_____ (2003) 'Intergenerational Justice' in Hugh LaFollette (ed.), *Oxford Handbook of Applied Ethics*, Ch. 18.

HEATH, J. (1997), 'Intergenerational Cooperation and Distributive Justice', *Canadian Journal of Philosophy*, 27: 361–76.

HEYD, D. (1992), *Genethics* (California).

HOBBES, T. (1994), *Leviathan* (Hackett. Ed. Edwin Curley).

HUBIN, D. C. (1979), 'The Scope of Justice', *Philosophy and Public Affairs*, 9/6: 3–24.

KOOPMANS, T. C. (1965), 'On the concept of optimal economic growth', *Pontificae Academiae Scientiarum Scripta Varia*, 28, 225–300.

KUHN, S. (2007) 'The Prisoner's Dilemma', *Stanford Encyclopedia of Philosophy*. Available at <http://setis.library.usyd.edu.au/stanford/entries/prisoner-dilemma/#Bib>.

NUSSBAUM, M. (2006), *Frontiers of Justice: Disability, Nationality, Species Membership* (Harvard).

PARFIT, D. (1984), *Reasons and Persons* (Oxford).

RAWLS, J. (1971), *A Theory of Justice* (Harvard).

_____ (1996), *Political Liberalism* (Revised paperback edition, Columbia).

_____ (1999a), *A Theory of Justice* (Revised edition, Oxford).

_____ (1999b), *The Law of Peoples* (Harvard).

_____ (2001), *Justice As Fairness: A Restatement* (Harvard).

SAUVE, K. (1995), 'Gauthier, Property Rights and Future Generations', *Canadian Journal of Philosophy*, 25: 163–75.

SCANLON, T. M. (1982), 'Contractualism and Utilitarianism', in Amartya Sen and Bernard Williams (eds.), *Utilitarianism and Beyond* (Cambridge).

_____ (1998), *What We Owe to Each Other* (Harvard).

SHEPSKI, L. (2006), 'Prisoner's Dilemma: the Hard Problem'. Paper presented at the *American Philosophical Association* (Pacific Division) Annual Meeting, Portland, Oregon: March 2006.

WATSON, G. (1998), 'Some Considerations in Favor of Contractualism', in C. Morris and J. Coleman (eds.), *Rational Commitment and Morality* (Cambridge), 168–85. Reprinted in Darwall 2002a, 249–69.

WOLF, C. (2004), 'Intergenerational Justice' in R. G. Frey and C. H. Wellman (eds.), *A Companion to Applied Ethics* (Blackwell).

4

Three Models
of Intergenerational Reciprocity

AXEL GOSSERIES

Introduction

Any theory of intergenerational justice needs to deal with a twofold question: what do we owe to the next generation, and why? Various accounts are available to answer this question, ranging from communitarian, utilitarian, libertarian to luck egalitarian or sufficientarian ones. In this chapter, I wish to focus on one family of theories, i.e. those relying on the idea of reciprocity, both to justify and define our obligations towards the next generation.[1] Personally, I do not consider reciprocity-based theories as the most defensible account of our intergenerational obligations, because of misfit with my other well-considered judgements as they apply among others in the intragenerational realm. Yet, even as a non-defender of such views, I consider it essential to explore them, both because I believe that they are more robust than one may think—which says something about what exactly would be wrong with them—and because they point at specificities as well as difficulties that other views have left unnoticed. If we are to criticize reciprocity-based accounts, we need to do so for the right reasons. This also explains why I will examine three—rather than merely one—types of reciprocity-based accounts of our intergenerational obligations, with the aim of increasing the level of generality and precision of our analysis.

Drafts of this chapter were presented in Bremen (GSSS, March 11, 2005), at the Ecole normale supérieure (Ulm, Paris, March 21, 2005), at the Katholieke Universiteit Leuven (May 20, 2005), at University College (London, September 22, 2005) and at the IEP of Lille (September 24, 2005). I wish to warmly thank these audiences as well as A.-P. André-Dumont, A. Autenne, J. Bichot, D. Casassas, J.-M. Chaumont, D. Cosandey, M. Fleurbaey, A. Gheaus, S.-K. Kolm, V. Muniz Fraticelli, F. Peter, G. Ponthière, G.-F. Raneri, Chr. Vandeschrick, Ph. Van Parijs, K. Wade-Benzoni, and two anonymous referees for comments and suggestions on earlier drafts.

[1] For reference work on reciprocity in general: Kolm (1984), (2000) & (2006). On intergenerational reciprocity more specifically: Barry (1989), Masson (1999).

Before proceeding, let me emphasize two points. First, I will rely on a relatively *narrow* definition of reciprocity here, and on two corollaries resulting respectively from the *multilateral* and *open* nature of the intergenerational context.[2] Let me explain. The idea of reciprocity refers here to a notion of equivalence in respective contributions, in the context of an exchange. Of course, equivalence does not mean that we should give back the very same object, but rather something of equivalent 'value'.[3] Moreover, whether an object should be seen as equally valuable will depend on a set of variables, including e.g. price fluctuations or environmental changes. Yet, it follows from a strict understanding of the reciprocity requirement that no one would be allowed or forced to end up being a net beneficiary or a net recipient. In a bilateral context, this entails a prohibition on any net transfers. In an intergenerational context, the idea that no one should end up being a net contributor or a net recipient calls for two important clarifications.

On the one hand, in a context involving more than two individuals, the prohibition on net transfers should not be applied in a segmented way to successive generations (i.e. 'is it complied with between generation 1 and 2?', '... between generation 2 and 3?', etc.). In other words, rather than operating such *direct* comparisons, one needs to construe the rule prohibiting net transfers as involving a comparison between one individual (or one generation) on the one hand, and *all* the other people (or generations) taken together, on the other. Hence, if a net transfer obtains between two persons (e.g. x and y), it may well be the case that another net transfer would have taken place between one of these two persons and a third one (e.g. y and z), such that neither x, nor y would end up being net contributors or net beneficiaries. The problem is that z may then end up being a net beneficiary, even under such an extended (and yet, narrow) interpretation of reciprocity.

Yet, the intergenerational context is not only multilateral (rather than merely bilateral). It is also *open ended towards the future*. This is crucial as to the ability of

---

[2] There are at least two good reasons to adopt such a narrow definition of reciprocity. First, this allows to concentrate on what I take to be at the heart of the very idea of reciprocity, on what makes it different from other notions such as impartiality, mutual advantage or solidarity. Second, as a way of methodological minimalism, I wish to show that even such a narrow notion of reciprocity allows to propose a relatively robust theory in the intergenerational realm. Let us note as well that the notion of reciprocity is used here in a non-Ralwsian way. See Rawls (2001: 77).

[3] When we talk about reciprocating the equivalent, we need to wonder each time: 'equivalent in which terms?' (e.g. of monetary value at time t, of potential for well-being for the beneficiary, ...). While I leave the answer to this question open, it is clear that it may be of crucial importance, especially when people's preferences change with time, as we move from one generation to the next.

at least some of the reciprocity-based theories to propose an intergenerational model that would avoid any net transfer among generations. For in a *closed* context (involving a definite or finite number of people or generations), no matter how multilateral it may be, no one could be a net contributor without forcing at least some people into the position of net beneficiaries. This is not necessarily true in a context that is open towards the future, since each person (or generation) is able to pass on to the next person (or generation) her net benefit. This explains for example why a rule of reciprocity is not incompatible with the idea of transferring more to the next generation than what it received from the previous one. In short, it is possible for one generation, without violating the prohibition on net transfers, to be both a net beneficiary in relation with a given generation (admittedly not 'all generations considered'), and a net contributor with regard to the rest of all the other generations. It is thus worth noticing here that if the infinite/indefinite number of future people can be seen as a serious challenge for aggregative theories of intergenerational justice, and possibly as well to distributive ones,[4] it constitutes here—in contrast—the very feature which makes it possible to stick to a prohibition on net transfers while letting each generation free to transfer more to the next than it inherited itself.

Besides insisting both on the narrow interpretation of reciprocity that I will rely upon, as well as on the importance of the 'multilateral' and 'open-to-the-future' features of the intergenerational context, there is a second point I wish to make. It has to do with a rather sociological hypothesis: reciprocity-based intuitions of intergenerational justice would be especially popular among the general public,[5] even among those who, once dealing with intra-generational issues, would not be especially attracted towards such a theory. For, as stated above, it is to be expected that a theory prohibiting any net transfers among people would not necessarily be regarded as an extremely common account of what we owe each other. So, the sociological assumption is: reciprocity-based theories of justice are especially popular in the intergenerational realm, regardless of their level of popularity insofar as *intra*generational contexts are concerned. This hypothesis helps in justifying our focus on such theories. I do not provide empirical support for it here. I simply assume it.

Then, the question that arises is: if this were a sound sociological hypothesis, how would we explain the degree of attraction exerted by reciprocity-based accounts of intergenerational justice once compared with e.g. truly

---

[4] Lauwers & Vallentyne (2004).
[5] For one of the rare sources on this point: Wade-Benzoni (2002).

redistributive approaches of justice? Among possible answers, let me point at two of them. The first one underlines the mixed function of what we inherit from the previous generation. It serves as a source of obligation (as we shall see), explaining *why* we would owe something to other generations. It simultaneously serves as a source of inspiration as to *what* we owe other generations. We need such inspiration because we may owe something to the next generation, in some cases without having benefited from anything from this generation in the first place. This is what justifies the need for such a baseline.[6]

The second hypothesis as to the reasons why people may find intergenerational reciprocity views especially attractive has to do with a distinction among three sources of advantage or disadvantage: nature's action, the action of others, and one's own actions on oneself.[7] It may well be that when we envisage issues of intergenerational justice, we only consider two of these three sources. In other words, we would be considering that what we inherited would result either from what the previous generation transferred us, or from the activities from the members of our own generation. We would thus be overlooking the possibility of *exogenous* transfers, through the third source of advantages and disadvantages, i.e. nature. In the absence of such a third source of (dis)advantages, relying exclusively on a focus on the two other sources would make a commutative approach perfectly sufficient and a distributive approach redundant in most cases.[8] And yet, it makes perfect sense to consider the possibility of disadvantages resulting directly from natural events, even in an intergenerational context.[9] This being said, let me now move to a closer examination of intergenerational reciprocity as a theory of justice.

---

[6] See Wade-Benzoni (2002). Also Cigno (2005) ('family constitution') and Bichot (*in litt*, 9 Jan. 2006) ('imitation effect').

[7] As pointed out to me by one of the referees, in real life, these three sources of advantage/disadvantage do of course interact.

[8] In fact, this is not true for all distributive theories. Consider an egalitarian theory that is 'choice-sensitive', i.e. sensitive to responsibility, such as Dworkin's (2000). If a morally problematic disadvantage that affects me is a result from my choices, it is not society's job to compensate for it. And if it results from the action of identifiable third parties, it is these very people who are in charge of such compensation, as opposed to society as a whole. In contrast, let us imagine a distributive theory that would *not* deny a right to redistribution to a person who would be fully responsible for her extreme poverty, which is typically the case of a sufficientarian theory that would not be luck-sufficientarian. In such a society in which the disadvantages suffered by people would never result from causes different from free actions of its members (be it the very victim or a third party), such a distributive theory (sufficientarianism) would still operate in a way distinct from a commutative view, since the latter would be incapable of justifying redistributive transfers to the benefit of a very poor person who would be fully responsible for her situation. My thanks to G. Ponthière for having forced me to clarify this point.

[9] See Gosseries (2004).

1. Three Models

In order to focus on the core features of these theories, let us limit ourselves to four generations, defined as birth cohorts of 10 years each. G1 represents all those born during the first decade, G2, G3, and G4 all those born respectively during the second, the third, and the fourth decades. Among the different possible variants, let's single out three models of intergenerational reciprocity—not necessarily mutually exclusive if applied to different objects—each of them coming in two forms. One is the justificatory form, aiming at *justifying* the very *existence* of intergenerational obligations. The other form is substantive and it has to do with *defining* the *content* of such obligations.[10] Each of the three models that will now be presented comes in these two forms, i.e. substantive and justificatory.

Let us start with the first model, i.e. the *descending* one. According to its *justificatory* form, *G2 owes something to G3 because G1 transferred something to G2.* As to its *substantive* version, it states that *G2 owes at least as much to G3 as what it received itself from G1.* This descending model is the most standard of our three models. Its scope is the most *general* one, as it applies to all types of transfers from one generation to the next one. More importantly, together with the more limited ascending model described below, it relies on an idea of *indirect* reciprocity. By the latter, I refer to the fact that the 'final beneficiary'[11] (G3) is not identical to the initial benefactor (G1). And this has of course a connection with the *multilateral* character of the intergenerational context underlined above. In short, reciprocation is oriented towards an individual or a generation which is initially only a third party. And each of these reciprocation steps can be connected together to form a chain involving the successive generations. This may allow for a transitive approach to intergenerational justice.

As to the second model, it differs from the descending one by the direction of the transfers it involves. It goes in the opposite direction, which explains why I call it the *ascending* model. In its justificatory form, it states that G3 owes something to G2 because G2 has transferred something to G1. The substantive form adds that *G3 owes to G2 at least as much as what G1 transferred earlier to G1.* Such a model, especially in its justificatory form, is relevant for example to account for the logic of pay-as-you go pension schemes. The fact that an active generation owes something to another generation that is just reaching

---

[10] Note the connection between this (i.e. 'justifying the existence' and 'defining the content') and the distinction we drew above between source of obligation and source of inspiration.

[11] This is of course too rough since as soon as we abandon the model, such a four-generations world is itself anchored to an indefinite number of past and future generations.

retirement age is justified here by the fact that the latter cohort did the same for its own parents during its own active life.

However, the relevance of this ascending model in accounting for our intergenerational obligations in pay-as-you-go pension schemes is challenged by advocates of the idea of *double* reciprocity.[12] This is the only one of our three models that involves *direct* rather than indirect reciprocity. In other words, the initial contributor is also the final beneficiary in the context of a bi-directional relationship (whereas the two other models are mono-directional). Those who defend this model claim that our children's obligation to pay for our retirement benefits should not at all be conceived as a reciprocation of the fact that we would have done the same for our own parents in the past (ascending model). Instead, as Cosandey states:

> ... the only true contribution to retirement benefits is the money invested to the benefit of the next generation. Contributions paid to the benefit of the previous generation represent a duty for any citizen and should not give rise to new rights. They reimburse a debt that each of us has towards the previous generation, for having been taken care of during our own childhood.[13]

In short, paying the pension of our parents is not in reply to what they did themselves to the benefit of their own parents. It is rather in reply to what they did to us in terms of investing in our own education.

Before proceeding with an examination of three key objections to these models, let us add two points, one of a conceptual nature and the other of a rather practical one. The conceptual point is that we should not confuse the 'descending/ascending' distinction with the 'prospective/retrospective' one.[14] It is one thing to decide whether we transfer something *forward* (to the next generation) or *backward* (to the previous one). It is another to decide about whether *past* (actual) or *future* (expected) transfers should serve as a reference point in defining how much we owe to the generation to which we are making the transfer. To put things differently, it is one thing to ask 'in which direction should I reciprocate?'. It is another to ask 'when I reciprocate, which transfer should I take as a baseline to assess what I owe back?'. The 'descending/ascending' distinction has to do with the direction of transfers whereas the 'prospective/retrospective' distinction has to do with the temporal location of the reference transfer. In retrospective models, the reference transfer

---

[12] These are Cosandey's (2003) words. Bichot (1999) developed earlier arguments going in the same direction. However, he considers the notion of 'double reciprocity' as inappropriate (*in litt.*). We use it here to preserve a reference to Cosandey's view, even if the idea of 'direct reciprocity' is probably more appropriate. See as well Bichot (1980) and (1982).

[13] Cosandey (2003: 21) (our translation).   [14] See Kolm (2000: 30).

precedes the transfer that we are trying to define in terms of content. And in prospective models, we are taking as a reference transfer one that did not yet take place.

To illustrate this, let me take a substantive ascending model. It is presented in Table 4.1 in its retrospective form: G3 can find out what it owes to G2 by looking at what G2 did to G1. When it comes to the justificatory form of the ascending model, we will tend to use indifferently the retrospective and the prospective form. Moreover, the prospective form of the justificatory ascending model may have at least two advantages. First, when it comes to justifying the obligations of G3 towards G2 in specific cases in which G2 is a 'free lunch' generation (e.g. the very first generation to have benefitted from the establishment of a pay-as-you-go pension scheme), there is by definition no relevant G2-to-G1 transfer that could serve as a reference transfer. In theory at least, the only available strategy in such cases is to refer to the promise of a future transfer from G4 to G3. Second, leaving aside the free lunch generation(s) hypothesis, mutually disinterested people may be motivationally more concerned about securing their future pension through ascending transfers by the next generation than about making sure that promises made by others in the past be kept. For the promise we may be referring to could be one made by G1 to G2 claiming that G3 would do the same to G2. This being said, when it comes to the *substantive* form of an ascending model, the retrospective version is much more helpful since it provides us with a transfer that is certain because it already took place and that can serve as a secure reference point to define what the pivotal generation will now owe to the previous one. This equally holds for the descending model. This is why in the rest of this chapter, I shall assume that the retrospective versions are the standard

Table 4.1. **The three models of intergenerational reciprocity and their two forms**

	Justificatory	Substantive
Descending	G2 owes something to G3 because G1 transferred something to G2	G2 owes G3 at least as much as what G1 transferred to G2
Ascending	G3 owes something to G2 because G2 transferred something to G1	G3 owes G2 at least as much as what G2 transferred to G1
Double	G2 owes something to G1 because G1 transferred something to G2	G2 owes G1 at least as much as what G1 transferred to G2

ones, which is not always the case in practice, e.g. when it comes to the pension debate.

As to the more practical point, it has to do with the comparison between the ascending and the double models and their relative plausibility. I shall return to this point below (section 4). At this stage, it is worth emphasizing that despite the claim of defenders of double reciprocity—notably regarding the demo-insensitivity of the ascending model—the ability of the former model to serve as a normative guideline for intergenerational transfers will depend on factors such as the importance of education or people's life expectancy. Imagine for example a society in which children study normally but in which most people die before reaching the age of pension (if any). In such a society, the educational transfers will necessarily be much larger than those regarding pension benefits. In a double reciprocity model, if the two types of transfers are not equivalent, it will not be possible to end up with a plausible account.

2. Barry's challenge

Having presented the three central models of intergenerational reciprocity, let us consider a first challenge, faced more specifically by their *justificatory form*. The challenge is well expressed by Brian Barry:

If someone offers me a toffee apple, out of the blue, and I accept it, does my enjoyment of the toffee apple create even the tiniest obligation to distribute toffee apples to others? I do not see that it does.[15]

What we are asked to answer is why the mere fact of receiving something from someone would justify an *obligation* falling on me to give something back—regardless of whether empirical social sciences would actually show that people do (or not) *feel obliged* to reciprocate, of *feel bad* if they don't reciprocate. And we may indeed be willing to conclude that there is no way

---

[15] Barry (1989: 232). Nozick has the same kind of objection: 'So the fact that we partially are "social products" in that we benefit from current patterns and forms created by the multitudinous actions of a long string of long-forgotten people (...) does not create in us a general floating debt which the current society can collect and use as it will' (1974: 95). We do not examine here a more specific form of this objection that has to do more with the justification of the obligations of end-of-chain generations (first generation in the descending model, last generation in the ascending model). Note here that the first generation problem is relevant both to reciprocity-based views (as a generation having received nothing from an earlier one) and for contractarian theories (as a generation allegedly unable to benefit from the cooperation with later generations). See also Gardiner (Chapter 3 of this volume)) and Attas (Chapter 7 of this volume).

to justify an obligation of justice to give back. This may take several forms. We may of course conclude that we have no intergenerational obligations. We may also want to claim that what is at stake is not justice but mere gratitude. This could be Hobbes's position:

As Justice dependeth on Antecedent Covenant; so does GRATITUDE depend on Antecedent Grace; that is to say, Antecedent Free-gift: and is the fourth Law of Nature; which may be conceived in this Forme, *That a man which receiveth Benefit from another of meer Grace, Endeavour that he which giveth it, have no reasonable cause to repent him of his good will.*[16]

A third way would consist instead in claiming that there is an obligation of justice, but that our obligation to give back does not originate in the fact of having received something. For example, a theory of justice such as maximin (luck) egalitarianism would claim that it is not what we received, but rather the concern that members of the next generation do not end up with circumstances worse than ours that justifies the need for descending transfers. In the absence of such transfers, members of other generations may end up with circumstances worse than ours, due to no fault of their own. So, the reasons underlying intergenerational transfers for an egalitarian clearly differ from those that may be invoked by a reciprocity defender, notwithstanding the fact that both rest with concerns of justice.

How to address Barry's challenge while remaining faithful to the idea that our intergenerational obligations are real obligations and that they constitute obligations of justice? An attempt at saving the reciprocity-based approach would need to come up with an account that would add a reason to the mere fact of having benefited from a transfer, such that the obligation to give back would amount to an obligation of justice. Let us consider for a moment the view that mere insistence on the idea of reciprocity is not enough to properly address Barry's challenge. We would therefore want to explore two approaches that are *prima facie* compatible with the reciprocity approach and which may help to support it. One is phrased in terms of collective intergenerational property and oriented towards the idea of an obligation towards future people. The other rests on a notion of free-riding and focuses directly on the (ascending) idea of obligations towards dead people. Both approaches can actually complement each other.

---

[16] Hobbes (1651: 209). For another example, in the realm of intellectual property: 'as we enjoy great advantages from the inventions of others, we should be glad of an opportunity to serve others by any inventions of ours; and this we should do freely and generously' (Benjamin Franklin, quoted in Boyle, 2003: n. 98).

Proprietarian metaphors

According to the proprietarian family of approaches, we do not fully and exclusively own as a generation what we inherited from the previous generation. This lack of full property is what will justify the existence of an obligation to give back to its owner what we are simply not entitled to freely dispose of. Such proprietarian approach comes in various forms. According to one possible metaphor, following the famous native American proverb,[17] what the current generation detains is actually supposed to have been lent to it by the next generations, which presupposes that the full collective ownership of our heritage (broadly taken) is constantly slipping into the hands of non yet existing, *future* generations. The same happens when we use the *usufruct* metaphor rather than the one of a loan. Again, the existing generations are either usufructuaries or borrowers and their entitlement ceases as soon as they die. As to future generations, the metaphor suggests that they would only keep the full property (in both cases) as long as they do not come into existence. The difficulty, present in both metaphors, is that in order to justify an obligation to keep (and transfer) something to future people, we need to ascribe ownership rights to people who don't exist yet, on objects that do currently exist. The same difficulty also arises when we rely on the co-ownership metaphor, rather than the loan or the usufruct one.

This calls for a set of four remarks, two of a more technical nature, followed by two more serious difficulties. First, while these analogies may be relevant to support the descending model, they are far less so for the ascending or double models. This suggests that it is unlikely that a single proprietarian analogy could automatically serve to support the three models altogether. Second, once we examine their legal regime in detail, each of these proprietarian metaphors have their specific limitations.[18] For instance, in case of a loan, in principle it is the very same good that we borrowed that should be restituted, which is not possible whenever we are dealing with non-renewable resources. Similarly, usufruct only applies to what are called fruits rather than products. Fossils fuels clearly belong to the latter category, not to the former. As to co-ownership models, they would in principle require the agreement of each and every co-owner, including future generations.

Third, and more importantly, suppose that we manage to characterize the nature of our intergenerational reciprocity obligations through the prism of

---

[17] 'Treat the earth well: it was not given to you by your parents, it was loaned to you by your children. We do not inherit the earth from our ancestors, we borrow it from our children' (various sources).

[18] Thanks to A.-P. André-Dumont and G.-F. Raneri for discussions on this point.

ownership-related ideas. The problem is that the existence of such ownership rights may need to be justified in turn. This is an uneasy task. One may want to refer to the will of God, as Locke did.[19] Another, more original strategy, consists in relying on the will of (some of) the earlier generations. This approach can be found in the work of Léon Bourgeois.[20] His strategy consists in producing a historical argument involving the following claim. Let us start with a minimalistic (normative) assumption such that the first generation was the exclusive owner of the Earth. This means that we could have had a scenario such that each generation would bequeath to the next what it owned as an exclusive owner, without any further condition. Let us now introduce a second (factual) assumption: we can plausibly claim that at least some of the generations that preceded us bequeathed what they had inherited from the previous generations with the view that it would belong to *all* future generations. If this is true for at least some of the generations that preceded us, it means that even assuming that the first generation was the exclusive owner of what it had, our heritage will be progressively collectivized (intergenerationally speaking) through the action of possibly just a few generations. And of course, the more such a collectivist intention can be found among recent generations just preceding ours, the more it will restrict our own freedom regarding what we inherited.

It is thus possible to justify the existence of an entitlement of all coming generations on what we inherited from the previous generations. This can be done through reference to an actual intention, either of God (Locke) or of some of the preceding generations (Bourgeois). And this can of course be done independently, by providing and defending a full theory of justice in line with our well-considered intuitions. But there is a fourth and quite decisive point to be made here. The logic of reciprocity insists on the contribution of each of us and on the idea that the reason why I owe something back is due to the fact that I received something in the first place. The ownership-based logic works differently since the reason why I owe something back has nothing to do with the fact that I received something. It has to do with the fact that

---

[19] Locke (1690, First treatise, §88). See as well in the same vein, referring to religion, Grégoire (1787: 132, our translation): 'Children of the Gospel, the religion that you are professing encompasses, through the links of love, all the mortals not only from all countries, but even from all centuries. Is it religion's fault if you ignore your duties towards posterity? It requires that, moved by the very fate of future generations, you would prepare the happiness of those who are still sleeping in nothingness, and who will only come to existence when you will be sleeping in dust'. My thanks to J.-M. Chaumont for pointing me to this.

[20] For further developments: Gosseries (2004: 161s). Compare: 'The improvements made by the dead form a debt against the living, who take the benefit of them. This debt cannot be otherwise discharged than by a proportionate obedience to the will of the authors of the improvements' (Madison, 1790).

what I possess is not (fully) mine. Hence, even if entitlement-based accounts of our obligation to transfer may coincide on their substantive claims with the reciprocity-based models, they would still misrepresent the very logic at work in the latter models. Can we do better than that?

Reciprocity and free-riding

In order to answer this question, let us look at a second possible option, consisting this time in turning more directly to the idea of obligation towards dead people and in relying on a revisited notion of free-riding. The idea consists here in accounting for our obligation to reciprocate, not on the ground of an obligation to give back a good that would not be (exclusively) ours, but rather on the basis of an obligation not to end up being a free-rider to the detriment of earlier generations. At first sight, one could think that the idea of free-riding should not be relied upon whenever the goods transferred from one generation to the next are of a rival type, i.e. whose enjoyment by one individual necessarily entails a reduction in the possibilities of enjoyment by others of the very same good (e.g. a car or a house). Yet, in the case of descending reciprocity (not under the two other models), a notion of free-riding could be usefully relied upon, even in the presence of rival goods, which is clearly the case for all non-renewable resources for example. Here is an account, in two steps. First, I discuss issues of scope of free-riding. Then I focus more specifically on the idea of free-riding with respect to dead people.

Let me begin with the assumption that free-riding obtains whenever a person derives a net benefit from the fruits of someone else's labour, the latter being fully voluntary, without diminishing in any sense the enjoyment that this other person derives from this good. Let us then define in general terms the scope of free-riding, considering on the one hand a non-rival good and a rival one on the other. First, if a good is both non-rival and of a strictly natural origin (e.g. sunlight, as opposed to public lighting with electricity), we clearly fall *outside* the scope of a notion of free-riding since we do not free-ride on anyone's contribution (given the natural origin of the good). In contrast, if this good is both non-rival as well as a product of human activity, we find ourselves in the *standard* scope of the concept of free-riding. We will then be concerned about whether, given the extent to which a person consumes this good, she has contributed enough or in excess to its production. *Ex hypothesi*, again, this good is assumed to result from the activity of third parties that voluntarily engaged in such a productive effort. It is because the concept of free-riding has to do with the production-consumption relationship (rather than focusing merely on consumption) that it is still capable of identifying injustices even if the good is non-rival.

Second—remaining within the realm of this free-riding-oriented analysis—suppose this time a *rival* good, and one that is man-made rather than of natural origin. In such a case, we could be tempted to consider this situation as laying outside the material scope of the concept of free-riding. Our claim is that this would be an incorrect analysis. The hypothesis here is that any rival good whose beneficiary would not be its producer belongs to the potential scope of the concept of free-riding, understood as referring to a contribution insufficient once we consider the voluntary production effort by others regarding this good. We generally tend *not* to analyse rival goods through the prism of free-riding. This is probably due to the fact that—contrary to what happens with non-rival goods—free-riding is not in this case the only concept available to account for our intuitions of injustice. For whenever a good exhibits rivalry, we can perfectly analyse the possible injustice of its consumer's behaviour, not only under the free-riding framework, but through the angle of a concept of deprivation (total or partial). In other words, we are able to check whether my consumption of this good unfairly deprives others from something. And we will tend to translate this with concepts such as theft or possibly exploitation (in the neo-marxian sense).

To put things differently, the key point here—of a psychologico-moral nature—is that accounts resting on the notion of deprivation tend to produce a sense of injustice much stronger than those flowing from an idea of insufficient contribution. Whenever both types of analysis (deprivation-based or free-riding oriented) are simultaneously available (which is the case for non-natural rival goods, not for non-rival ones), the first type (deprivation-based) will tend to outshine, to *dominate* the second type (insufficient contribution). This may nourish the mistaken impression that the latter would simply not be applicable to such cases. My view is that the concept of free-riding remains an available resource for the analysis of fair consumption of rival goods. A consumer could be *both* a thief and a free-rider. This is my first key hypothesis, having to do with the proper definition of free-riding's material scope. Let us call it the *coexistence hypothesis*, by reference to the two possible analysis in terms of justice of the consumption of a rival good. One refers to the impact of my consumption on the possibility for others to consume the same good (deprivation). The other focuses on the relationship between my consumption and the share that should have been mine in the production of this good (free-riding).

Coming now more specifically to the intergenerational realm, there are various ways of articulating generations and free-riding.[21] The one that is of interest to us here requires that we focus on a set of producers who became

---

[21] For another illustration: Gosseries (2006).

unable to consume the good they produced. Let us consider a good with objective features such that it could be rival. It would be man-made but its actual producers would now be *dead*. Think for example about a castle, inherited from your ancestors, and resulting from the hard work of seven generations of family members, all of them dead by now. It is clearly a rival good, not only towards the other members of my own generation (some would definitely enjoy living in such a castle), but also towards the coming generations (hoping that my own enjoyment of the castle will not reduce the enjoyment they could derive from it, had I not existed). In contrast, this good is *not* rival towards past generations. In other words, it is not rival towards all. Its degradation through my fault would not deprive earlier generations from any degree of enjoyment of this good that they could have had in my absence. And this is so even for those who believe that the dead do exist in a certain sense, since the latter sense would not in all plausibility entail their ability to enjoy material goods. However, it could be meaningful to claim that by destroying the castle or even by letting it fall apart,[22] the present generation would be free-riding on earlier generations. For it would take advantage, without adding anything itself, of the efforts they would voluntarily have put in this castle. The hypothesis would thus be: for this kind of good, the analysis in terms of free-riding could remain relevant, notwithstanding the fact that those on whom we are free-riding are now dead. At the same time, the idea of deprivation would not be available here for, when it comes to our relationship with dead people, the good we are dealing with exhibits the characteristics of a non-rival good. The obligation to reciprocate to the next generation would thus result from an obligation not to free-ride to the detriment of earlier generations.

Let me clarify this a bit further through a set of remarks. *First*, the idea is that for a certain number of goods, the death of one of the producers also leads to his death as a consumer. It then renders the good *non-rival towards that person*, since the latter is not a potential consumer anymore. My own consumption of this good is not at all able to deprive her from the enjoyment of the good. This presupposes the acceptance of the idea that someone may *exist* without being able to (fully) consume a given good. This is the case whenever a product's life

---

[22] There is a difference between degrading a good (i.e. worsening its situation as compared to a world in which I would not exist) and letting it fall apart (i.e. not doing anything to protect it from the effects of time). If we take as a reference point 'the world as it would be in my absence', we are unable to account for any obligations to actively care for degradable goods. Of course, from a free-riding perspective, the degree of my obligation to actively care for the good will have to be adjusted to the extent to which I derive any benefits from this good. If I merely inherited it without deriving any enjoyment from it, a free-riding-based account would be unable to criticize an inactive castle owner. See also *infra*.

expectancy extends beyond the death of its producer(s). However, the situation of dead people does not constitute the only possible illustration. Let us think about a vegetarian producer of cow meat (whose vegetarianism would rest on reasons that do not require from all of us not to consume meat). These cows are objectively rival 'goods'. Yet, they are not rival towards all. This being said, it is worth insisting on the fact that for those who consider that dead people do exist, some of the goods we inherited may remain rival *even towards the dead*. For example, if the paternity of a discovery can be recognized as a good, the fact that someone else would abusively claim the paternity of one of Einstein's inventions for example, could be seen as a potential source of deprivation (recognition deprivation) to the detriment of Einstein himself. For this type of goods, and provided that we accept the idea that the dead do exist in a given sense, Einstein's death will not entail that this good would become non-rival.

This leads us to a second remark. Deprivation-focused theories of justice, but also those that rest on a notion of free-riding (be it broadened) towards the dead *necessarily* presuppose that the dead do exist in at least a weak sense and that they could be affected by the consequences of actions taking place after their death. This is an important limitation of such a type of approach, as we indicated elsewhere.[23] A proprietarian approach à la Bourgeois would also be vulnerable to such a difficulty, as it rests on the idea of respecting the will of the dead. An egalitarian theory would in contrast escape this kind of difficulty.

Our third remark consists in underlining that whenever we use a notion of 'free-riding to the detriment of', we still rely on a notion of cost. It does not have to do with an opportunity cost that my consumption would impose on someone else's potential consumption. The cost rather has to do with the additional production cost resulting from my non-contribution to the production effort by others, bearing in mind that we are talking about voluntary production efforts by others. The question we need to ask ourselves is then the following: would the notion of free-riding not be also vulnerable to death's consequences, as is the case with the problem of deprivation? Death would remove the possibility of deprivation. But it would also remove the possibility of compensating people for costs that they would have incurred, be it voluntarily. This move should be resisted, for a reason illustrated by the following progression.

Suppose a closed world with two generations. Jo and Jack are contemporaries and we know that Jack will not have children. Jo produces a good alone but Jack would have been perfectly able to help him at the time of production.

---

[23] Gosseries (2004: ch. 2).

Jack then consumes part of that good without having contributed at all to its production, but also without having at all imposed such a production. Yet, there is a sense in which Jack imposed (by abstention) on Jo production costs that were higher than if the former had helped the latter. Let us now consider a slightly different situation in which Jack was born on exactly the same day as Jo's death. This means that Jack was absolutely unable to help Jo to produce this good. It would thus be inappropriate to consider him as a free-rider, at least in a sense that would have a minimally normative dimension.[24]

We could of course stop here. This would disregard the fact that the intergenerational space is an open one. It is open to the future. Jack will himself be followed by Jerry, who will himself be followed by Jim, etc. If the goods that have been produced are durable to a relatively significant extent (which is often the case), the non-contemporaneity of the potential producers does not mean that the 'production' effort of this good could not be pursued as time goes, a maintenance stage following the production stage. If this is so, we can re-consider the situation as follows. If Jack does not prolong to the benefit of Jerry the effort launched by Jo, he will be a free-rider towards Jo, not because the production costs (strictly understood) could have been lessened by Jack's contribution (although even that could be challenged), but rather because the production costs will have been incurred partly in vain if Jack simply does not care about preserving the good resulting from Jo's effort. When it comes to dealing with dead people, the nature of free-riding would thus be slightly different than in more common cases. Yet, it would still make some sense to claim that while not depriving the dead of the enjoyment of a good, the fact that his efforts have been allowed to become vain (by not caring about what he produced or by consuming alone a good that was aimed at the whole succession of coming generations) may affect this dead person.

It is thus clear that under such an analysis, free-riding towards the dead brings us back to the proprietarian approach defining our obligations towards coming generations. The proprietarian and the free-riding approach can thus overlap significantly, even if the former does not necessarily imply the latter. Rejecting the proprietarian approach when it comes to our relationship with the dead (because of the unavailability of deprivation-based accounts in such cases) does not entail that it should be rejected when it comes to our relationships with coming generations. Nor does it entail that we could not bring together the idea of free-riding towards dead people with a proprietarian definition of our obligations towards the next generations, considering or not the former as a foundation for the latter. Doing so however would certainly mean that the

---

[24] See however above n. 22.

apparent elegance of the descending reciprocity model would as a matter of fact hide the dual nature of its underlying justifications.

Let me add as well that the notion of free-riding will only be relevant for the fraction of our generational bequest that can be regarded as the fruit of earlier generation's labour. In contrast, the notion of e.g. collective property for example extends to the whole of our heritage, be it man-made or not, including untouched natural goods. Unless we ascribe an over-extensive scope to the notion of man-made goods, it follows that the idea of free-riding can only offer an *incomplete* account of the idea of descending reciprocity.[25]

Let me thus conclude on Barry's objection. It is not easy to dig underneath the three models of reciprocity in search of further justifications. And it is not certain at all that reformulations of the logic of reciprocity in terms of collective property or free-riding do full justice to the idea, do account for it, and really bring added value to the debate. At the same time, this does not need to be read as a sign of the weakness of reciprocity-based views. Any theory of justice will as some point hit a level at which it becomes too hard to dig deeper in order to identify even more fundamental intuitions at work.

3. The Problem of Direction

The objection we have just dealt with had to do with the justificatory versions of our three reciprocity-based models. Another objection has to do with whether reciprocity-based views are able to justify the *direction* of reciprocation in each case, i.e. why it should be ascending or descending.[26] This challenge potentially affects both justificatory and substantive forms. For, as a matter of theory, the 'initial transfer' to the current generation could in fact always be reciprocated in one of three possible directions: in an ascending manner (from the current to the previous generation), in a descending one (from the current to the next one), or through self-reciprocation (towards some members within the current generation).[27] A reciprocity-based model will thus only be robust if it is able to tell us why reciprocation should only follow one of these three directions, rather than the two other ones. From this perspective, how do our three models behave?

Let us envisage first the exclusion of self-reprociation, i.e. reciprocation of what was transferred by another generation to the members of one's own

---

[25] See also *infra*, n. 33.   [26] See e.g. de-Shalit (1995: 99).

[27] Note that this distinction among three possible *directions* does not fully overlap with the three general models. Self-reciprocation is not the equivalent of the double reciprocity model.

generation. A relevant intuition here could be that it is at least as fair to transfer part of the basket of goods inherited from the previous generation to the least well-off members of our own generation, rather than to the next generation. From the perspective of a theory of reciprocity, this may lead to the fact that those least well-off members of our own generation would end up having benefitted from net transfers, to the extent that they would not have reciprocated as much as what they received from the previous generation. Self-reciprocation is thus incompatible, both at the individual and at the generational level with the prohibition on net transfers, and more specifically with the prohibition on people ending up being net beneficiaries. All three reciprocity-based models are quite robust when it comes to the rejection of self-reciprocation.

Are they equally so when it comes to the two other options excluded by the models, i.e. ascending reciprocation in the case of the descending model, and descending reciprocation when it comes to the ascending and double models? From this perspective, the descending model is equally robust once we consider it carefully. For, suppose a world involving a stationary population (the size of each generation remaining constant) and let us assume that G1 transferred 10 units to G2 who would have transferred 10 units to G3. Imagine now that G3 decides to transfer only 8 units to G4 and 2 units back to G2. G3 would certainly not end up being a net beneficiary since it would clearly have emptied its debt. Moreover, such an option involving partial ascending reciprocation is a perfectly possible one in practice. For example, we can easily reciprocate something to our own parents in terms of health care or other non-durable goods. The problem, however, is that in this hypothesis, G2 will end up being a net beneficiary, which is problematic from the perspective of a reciprocity-based view as defined narrowly above. In a sense, by not following the descending direction, G3 will *force* G2 to end up having violated the reciprocity rule, for example if the latter is unable, because of her age, to reciprocate back to G3 the equivalent of what gives her the status of a net beneficiary. The descending model is thus especially robust insofar as the objection from direction is concerned, since the reciprocity-based logic allows us to exclude the two alternative options, namely, self-reciprocation and ascending reciprocation.

We still need to address the challenge when it comes to understanding why the ascending and the double reciprocity models would be able to exclude the option of descending reciprocation. The answer here is that if G2 decides to reciprocate to G3 rather than to G1 part of what had been transferred to it by G1, the latter will actually find itself in the position of a net contributor. The possibility of a descending transfer in this case will lead to a situation in which the previous generation will be forced to end up, not in the position of a net beneficiary, but rather of a net contributor, which is at least as problematic from the perspective of a reciprocity-based theory. To conclude, it turns out that our three reciprocity-based models are quite robust against the objection from direction.

4. Demographic Change

Let us finally consider a third difficulty. It is the most serious one. It becomes apparent when we take seriously the fact that a population will fluctuate from one generation to another. Are such fluctuations irrelevant when it comes to defining the nature of our obligations towards our neighbouring generations? Admittedly, this problem will not affect each and every type of intergenerational transfers.[28] And yet, the general public is right to be concerned with such population issues in connection with intergenerational transfers. An obvious illustration is the funding of our pension schemes as well as of health care for the elderly, which leads to special concerns when the reduction in birth rates is associated with an increase in life expectancy. Similarly, some of us are concerned with the ability of the planet to stand the agressions of a growing world population. As to the philosophical literature, it is rich in developments at the meta-ethical level,[29] but far less at the level of our substantive obligations of justice, probably in part because meta-ethical difficulties are often conceived as obstacles to advances at the substantive level. To put things differently, the philosophical litterature raises the question as to the conditions under which it is meaningful to claim that bringing to the world a larger population is more desirable than bringing about a smaller one. For example, if the number of people surrounding us, the size of our individual resources and the length of our lives affect in various ways our well-being, it is important to ask ourselves—*ex ante*—if it would not be fairer to bring to the world fewer children who would on average be happier, rather than more children whose average well-being would be lower. However, we are interested here in the *ex post* question: once this new generation has been brought to the world, its size should then be taken as given. Taking this for granted, we need to ask ourselves if the size of this population should affect

---

[28] The importance of transferring to the next generation democratic institutions, a culture of trust among people, etc is of course crucial as well. Such expectations of transfer should not be affected by the relative size of the generations at stake.

[29] See e.g. Arrhenius (2000), and also Chapter 12 in this volume.

the size and nature of the obligations of its surrounding generations towards it, as well as the size and nature of its own obligations towards the generations that surround it.

Under this *ex post* angle, there are two families of theories of intergenerational justice. The theories belonging to the first set tend to adjust what one generation owes to the other to the relative size of these populations, as opposed to merely to the size of the transfers that have or will take place, or to other factors. We refer to these theories as 'demo-sensitive' (or 'demo-reactive'). In theory, such demo-sensitivity could vary both in terms of degree and sign. In contrast, other theories will define what is owed to another generation exclusively by looking at the basket of goods that was or will be transferred to a generation, and perhaps as well on the basis of other factors, but certainly *regardless* of the relative size of the various neighbouring generations. We refer to the latter as 'demo-insensitive'.

A distributivist theory of the maximin egalitarian type for instance will certainly be demo-sensitive. It will probably require from one generation having decided to reproduce itself at a rate higher than the replacement rate, to transfer more—on aggregate—than it inherited from the previous generation. The goal is to make sure that the current generation and the next one will turn out having benefited, per capita, from an equivalent bequest. The demo-sensitive nature of such a theory results directly from the underlying logic according to which intergenerational transfers should aim at making sure that one generation does not end up having been disadvantaged by her cohortal circumstances.

The basic hypothesis that I wish to test here is the following : the very logic of reciprocity would exclude that our three theories be demo-sensitive. We have seen, while responding to the objection from direction, that the prohibition on forcing a person (or a generation) to end up being either a net beneficiary (in the case of descending reciprocity) or a net contributor (in the case of ascending and double reciprocity) played a key role in accounting for the robustness of such models. In the present case, the central idea would be the latter, i.e. the one according to which one should not force a person (or a generation) to end up being a net contributor. As was already said, the logic of reciprocity consists in getting rid of one's debts, regardless of *how many* people will be led to benefit from it. If I give back as much as what I received, this will suffice to exhaust or cancel out my obligations, even if it means that, in case of population growth, a larger number of people will have to share the same amount of resources. The latter conclusion is problematic, for it would allow, in full compliance with this definition of justice, in the context of a model of descending reciprocity, for a gradual impoverishment per head, as new generations come on board. This problem is often overlooked by those who consider reciprocity-based theories of intergenerational justice as intuitively attractive.

Our question is therefore the following: is it correct to consider that the reciprocity-based models are demo-insensitive? We will answer it in two steps, looking successively at theories of *indirect* reciprocity, and then at the double reciprocity model. Among the various possible demographic scenarios (e.g. non-linear decline or growth, baby-boom followed by a baby-bust, and conversely), we will focus each time on one single demographic scenario that leads to a requirement of justice that is either inconsistent or counter-intuitive.

The descending and ascending models

The simplest case involves a population increase with a *descending* model. Here, the difficulty is obvious since reciprocity allows us to leave the next generation in a situation less favourable per capita than ours. Because of the absence of an obligation to be a net contributor and the prohibition on imposing on other people to be net contributors, if the population doubles, there is no obligation on us to double the size of the basket of goods transferred to the next generation. This does not constitute a source of internal inconsistency. However, as it is compatible with the gradual impoverishment of humankind, generation after generation, it may be counter-intuitive, especially for opportunity/luck egalitarians. This is so because in such a case the members of a later generation may end up with having inherited an average productive potential (hence *circumstances*) worse than the one of earlier generations, due to demographic *choices* made by earlier generations.

Consider then the way in which the *ascending* model reacts in case of population decrease. Let me refer more specifically to the retrospective version of the ascending model, in which what G3 owes G2 corresponds to what G2 transferred in the past to G1, rather than to what G4 will transfer to G3 in the future. Imagine for a moment that our population decreases by 50 per cent at each generational step, and let us look at two sub-cases that have some connection with Musgravian pension models of 'fixed replacement rate' and 'fixed contribution rate'.[30] First case: if each member of G2 has invested 10 units in funding the pensions of G1, each member of G3 will in turn have to invest 20 units in funding the pensions of G2, and so on. This allows us to prevent the members of G2 from ending up being net contributors. Moreover, at first sight, the generational chain being open, it is possible, provided that

---

[30] See Musgrave (1981).

each generation progressively increases its contribution, to still comply with the idea that no member of generations ulterior to G2 would be constrained to end up being a net contributor. However, it will soon become clear that such an increase in contribution rate, allowing—*ceteris paribus*—the level of pension benefits to be kept constant *and* avoiding the violation, at least at the beginning, of the rule prohibiting the imposition of net contribution, will soon lead to a situation that is not economically sustainable. And it will necessarily lead at the end of the day to a violation of this very same principle.

Alternatively, one could consider that if each member of G2 has invested 10 units in funding G1's pensions, each member of G3 should in fact do the same towards G2. In such a case, the contribution rate could remain sustainable in the long-term. However, the level of pension benefits of the members of each generation would gradually decrease because of our scenario of demographic decrease. Each of us will then end up having contributed more (to the benefit of the earlier generation) than we will have received in return (from the next generation). The challenge that an ascending model needs to address in case of population decline is not only that this model would lead to counter-intuitive conclusions for those who defend approaches that differ from the reciprocity-based one. Rather, it is a problem *internal* to the theory, since it consists in its inability to propose in such a case a plausible transfer rule that does not violate in one way or another the principle according to which one should not be forced to end up as a net contributor in the intergenerational chain. The ascending model thus looks unable, in case of demographic decline, to propose a rule that would not end up violating this principle.[31]

---

[31] One possible way out of the difficulties faced by the descending and—more importantly—by the ascending one could consist in trying to include the demographic variable in the assessment of the size of our intergenerational transfers. Let us first look at what this would lead to in the case of a *descending* model. The idea would consist in arguing that 'making children' is as much a contribution as 'inventing new technologies', or 'setting up new types of institutions with long-term effects'. Children would therefore no longer be seen as future end beneficiaries of transfers, but rather as part of the very basket of goods being transferred from one generation to the next. Such an approach turns out, however, not to be very promising. For if a reproduction rate superior to the replacement rate were to be considered as a positive and higher transfer than the one done by the previous generation, it would then allow for a proportional reduction in other transfers (e.g. in terms of natural resources). This would just further worsen the problem identified above, in case of a growing population. In contrast, if this reproduction rate were perceived as adding an extra burden on the next generation, and would then have to be substracted when it comes to assessing the size of the basket transferred, the problem identified above would of course be lessened. But this would amount to denying completely the fact that, *ceteris paribus*, raising more children generates for a particular generation more costs than raising fewer children, and would in principle correspond to the idea of a more important transfer than the reverse. The strategy thus finally ends up being *ad hoc*, and not at all embedded in the very logic of reciprocity. Hence, it turns out that integrating the reproduction rate as a variable of the transfer itself rather than as a characteristic of the generational groups at stake looks quite inappropriate in the context of a descending model. What about an ascending one? It seems more difficult for the latter

The indirect demo-sensitivity of double reciprocity

Is double reciprocity more prone to integrate the demographic dimension, than the two indirect and unidirectional models? One reason for suspecting this is that defenders of double reciprocity are themselves motivated by a demographic concern. Bichot (1989) or Cosandey (2003) defend this view out of concern for an alleged anti-natalist incentive that would be built-in in some of the pension funding regimes. They consider as a misrepresentation the idea of viewing our contribution to pension benefits as a reciprocation by those who are now active, of the equivalent of what we paid ourselves to our own parents *in terms of contribution to pension benefits* (which is what the ascending model implies). As a matter of fact, for these authors, we should see such ascending transfers as in return for descending transfers, hence as an instance of *direct* reciprocity. More precisely, such ascending transfers would in fact reciprocate the education spendings that we made to the benefit of those who are now constituting the active population. Following such a line of argument, it becomes perfectly meaningful, *intragenerationnally*, to consider that those who did not (or less) make such descending transfers (typically through raising their children) would not be entitled (or less so) to ascending transfers on the part of the next generation. In other words, it would be unfair for non-parents not to compensate the fact that parents are contributing twice (intergenerationnally speaking), i.e. on the one hand, through part of the income of their labour, by funding the retirement benefits of their own parents, and on the other, this time through their parental activities, by raising future active people without whom future pensions would simply have no future, even in the case of funded pension schemes.

It follows that the double reciprocity model *is* demo-sensitive since if we have fewer children, we are contributing less to the future of pensions and we are therefore less entitled to an ascending transfer in return. Add to this the fact that defenders of double reciprocity consider that pension schemes that do not adjust their benefits or contributions to the number of children are not only unjust towards parents, but contribute by themselves by not providing the right incentives, to the demographic problem that they are facing. What matters even more to us here is that *mutatis mutandis*, we could shift from the intraganerational level (parents v. non-parents) to the intergenerational one ('rabbit' v. 'non-rabbit' generations), defending the view that a generation

---

to integrate such a dimension because of a problem of direction. For reproducing ourselves at a given rate, be it analysed as a benefit or as a burden, will constitute at best a *descending* transfer. So, whatever its sign, its direction will be a descending one. Since the descending model only involves descending transfers, it is unable to be modified in that way.

reprocuding itself at a rate lower than the rate of another one would only be entitled to lesser ascending transfers.[32] Hence, the double reciprocity model is demo-sensitive since it entails at the intergenerational level that 'rabbit' generations would be entitled to larger ascending transfers, simply because their descending transfers, i.e. their spending, would be larger.

To go a little bit further into this, if G2 doubles its population while its own parents (G1) had been reproducing strictly at the replacement rate, G2 would be entitled to a pension twice as large as the one of G1 (both in terms of aggregate size and per head), because it transferred twice as much to the benefit of its own children (i.e. G3). Conversely, if G2 decides to reproduce itself at a rate leading to a division in two of the next generation's population, as compared to its own population, it should be ready to accept a related reduction in ascending transfers (from G3 to G2) equivalent to the reduction in descending transfers (from G2 to G1) that could follow. It is clear that a person having two times fewer children does not necessarily divide up her education expenses by two when compared to those of her neighbour. Yet, the double reciprocity model exhibits a certain consistency in the demographic fluctuation scenarios envisaged here. It illustrates the possibility of a demo-sensitive model that would not necessarily violate the prohibition on imposing net transfers.

This being said, the double reciprocity model exhibits both a specificity as well as an important difficulty from the perspective of demographic fluctuations. Let us consider its specificity first. Its nature can easily be understood once we compare the demo-sensitivity of the double reciprocity model and the one of an egalitarian model. There are differences at two levels. First, the reason why an egalitarian theory is demo-sensitive, even when dealing with transfers taking place in only *one* direction (e.g. descending ones) has to do with the fact that such a theory is not indifferent to the nature and the number of beneficiaries of such transfers. In contrast, it is the very *bi-directionality* of the double reciprocity model that renders it demo-sensitive.

Second, still at the level of specificities, the egalitarian approach is demo-sensitive in a *direct* way, even if it will tend to treat differently descending and ascending transfers in a context of demographic fluctuations. For it is problematic for an egalitarian to reduce descending transfers per head if a generation *chooses* to reproduce above the replacement rate. In contrast, reducing ascending transfers because a generation *happens to be* smaller than the previous one is not necessarily problematic if the gap from the replacement rate can be ascribed to the choices of the generation assumed to benefit

---

[32] We would then come closer to Musgrave's 'fixed contribution rate' than to his 'fixed replacement rate' model. See Musgrave (1981).

from such ascending transfers. This would be the case at least with a luck egalitarianism relying on the choice/circumstance distinction. In contrast, the bi-directionality of the double reciprocity model only renders it demo-sensitive in an *indirect* and *not necessarily proportional* way, because the adjustment focuses on the relative size of the respective transfers rather than on the number of children as such. Indeed, what plays a key role in the case of double reciprocity is not so much the fact of 'producing' children as such in the physical sense. It is rather the fact that we invest in educating them, which means that we invested (which leads to the need for transfers in return) and that this educational investment allowed for the emergence of future active people (which allows for such a transfer in return). However, it is possible that the marginal rate of investment per child be a decreasing one. In the same line, it is not always true that having no children at all entails less investment in the education of the next generation. It follows that the adjustment of ascending transfers would not follow linearly the fluctuations in reproduction rate, for it is on the size of descending transfers (based on the number of contributors, not of beneficiaries) that it needs to be adjusted. This is not illogical from a reciprocity-based perspective. And it is also not counter-intuitive, even if it can become so once the egalitarian perspective is taken seriously.

Besides such a specificity of the double reciprocity model, there is also a problem, resulting this time from the *incomplete* nature of the double reciprocity model's material scope.[33] For if having fewer children may (but needs not always) mean that less will be invested in terms of education, it

---

[33] Such incompleteness/incomprehensiveness has to do with the model's (in)ability to cover by itself the whole material domain of intergenerational transfers. The key difficulty raised by the notion of incompleteness has to do with whether one of the three models can be considered more complete than the two others. The challenge to the ascending and double models is to integrate descending transfers of natural resources as well as those resulting from the use of the human capital of all the previous generations. The ascending model is clearly incapable to do so since such descending transfers are not even considered. As to the double reciprocity model, it could only take descending transfers into account if it were possible to reciprocate in an ascending manner the equivalent of what was transferred in a descending way. Since what is transferred in a descending way not only covers the natural heritage but also the fruit of part of the investment of *all* the previous generations (taken together), it seems absurd to require an ascending reciprocation from *each* generation of the equivalent of the fruit of the effort of *all* past generations as well as of nature. This would be far too demanding. This problem results in part from the fact that the double reciprocity model is not open towards the future in a way that would allow for net transfers without violating the requirement of reciprocity, as we saw above. Moreover, an accumulation compatible with a prohibition on net transfers is also jeopardized. Yet, it remains true that the descending model is not strictly more complete than the two other ones, as it ignores ascending transfers. However, perhaps the idea of completeness would refer rather to the idea of net transfers. A model would then be complete/comprehensive if it would leave room to more net transfers. The problem is that if descending transfers tend systematically to be of a larger magnitude than ascending transfers, it is then likely that the descending model is more adequate from this point of view, and to that extent less incomplete. See also above, text attached to n. 25.

could then justify lesser ascending transfers in return than in case of a 'rabbit' generation. Yet, we should bear in mind that we are dealing with a two-sided coin. Admittedly, if having fewer children may in many cases entail a lesser investment in educational terms, the consecutive reduction of ascending transfer will make sense. However, such a reproductive choice simultaneously entails that from the point of view of a set of rare goods such as space, natural resources, etc., each member of G3 will as a matter of fact inherit a basket per head much larger than what is inherited per head by G2. As a result, having fewer children also leads to transfering such types of resources in a *higher* proportion per head. Once we consider this, the reduction in ascending transfers appears less intuitively plausible. As we can see, even if it is indirectly or contingently demo-sensitive, the double reciprocity model is not necessarily devoid of difficulties in case of demographic fluctuations.

Conclusion

How should we conclude on our three models of intergenerational reciprocity, with regard to the three objections we just examined? We have shown first that Barry's objection is not decisive. As a matter of fact, it rather translates a difference in basic intuition compared to other approaches to intergenerational justice, such as Rawlsian egalitarianism. And it may be possible to reformulate in other languages, such as the one of property (and its derivates) or the one of rejection of free-riding, part of the intuitions at work in the reciprocity-based models.

We also indicated that the objection from direction revealed in fact an unexpected robustness of the reciprocity-based models. In contrast, it is probably the case of demographic fluctuations that constitute one of the most serious difficulties of such models comes to the front. Either the models are not demo-sensitive, which will lead to outcomes that are either counter-intuitive (when dealing with descending reciprocity), or inconsistent (in the case of ascending reciprocity). Or, as in the case of the double-reciprocity model, we have to face an approach that is indirectly demo-sensitive, but that, because of the incomplete nature of its material scope, also leads to trouble.

On top of having identified such difficulties, let us also emphasize the fact that in a context of demographic fluctuations, the possibility to transfer more to the next generation does not necessarily lead to a violation of the rule (key to the narrow notion of reciprocity relied upon here) according to which we should not impose on others the status of net beneficiaries.

This compatibility results from the fact that one of these reciprocity-based models—the descending one—is open towards the future. This may in turn lead to counter-intuitive results e.g. for egalitarians who would consider it potentially unjust to transfer more to the next generation (per head) than what we inherited from the previous generation.[34] But this is another story …

References

ARRHENIUS, G. (2000), *Future Generations. A Challenge for Moral Theory* (Uppsala: University Printers) (PhD Thesis).

BARRY, B. (1989), 'Justice as Reciprocity', in *Liberty and Justice* (Oxford: Oxford University Press), 211–41.

BICHOT, J. (1980), 'Le rôle du capital humain en matière de retraites et de prestations familiales', *Population*, 837–47.

—— (1982), 'Fonder un autre système de sécurité sociale sur un nouveau principe de justice commutative', *Droit social*, 9–10, 657–65.

—— (1999), *Retraites en péril* (Paris: Presses de Sciences-Po), 141.

BOURGEOIS, L. (1902), *Solidarité* (Paris: Armand Colin).

BOYLE, J. (2003), 'The Second Enclosure Movement and the Construction of the Public Domain', *Law and Contemporary Problems*, 66: 33–74.

CIGNO, A. (2005), 'A Constitutional Theory of the Family', IZA DP N° 1797 (Bonn), 26.

COSANDEY, D. (2003), *La faillite coupable des retraites. Comment nos assurances vieillesse font chuter la natalité*, (Paris: L'Harmattan), 164.

DE-SHALIT, A. (1995), *Why posterity matters. Environmental policies and future generations* (London/New York: Routledge).

DWORKIN, R. (2000), *Sovereign Virtue. The Theory and Practice of Equality* (Cambridge: Harvard University Press), 511.

GASPART, F., and GOSSERIES, A. (2007), 'Are Generational Savings Unjust?', *Politics, Philosophy and Economics*, 6/2: 193–217.

GOSSERIES, A. (2004), *Penser la justice entre les générations. De l'affaire Perruche à la réforme des retraites* (Paris: Aubier-Flammarion), 320.

—— (2006), 'Egalitarisme cosmopolite et effet de serre', *Les séminaires de l'IDDRI (Paris)*

GRÉGOIRE, H. (1787/1988), *Essai sur la régénération physique, morale et politique des juifs* (Paris: Flammarion) ('Champs' series), 219.

HOBBES, T., 1651 (1968), *Leviathan* (London: Penguin), 729.

---

[34] See Gosseries (2004: section 4). We have not been able to make here a detailed presentation of the egalitarian intergenerational theory. Those who are interested in this should refer themselves to Gosseries (2004: section 4) as well as to Gaspart & Gosseries (2007).

JEFFERSON, T. (1975), 'Letter to James Madison' (6 Sept. 1798), in M. D. Peterson (ed.), *The Portable Thomas Jefferson* (New York, Penguin Books), 444–51.

KOLM, S. (1984), *La bonne économie. La réciprocité générale* (Paris: PUF), 472.

——(2000), 'Introduction', in L. -A. Gérard-valet, S. Kolm, and J. Mercier Ythier (eds.), *The Economics of Reciprocity, Giving and Altruism* (Basingstoke: MacMillan), 1–44.

——(2006), 'Reciprocity: its scope, rationales and consequences', in S. Kolm and J. Mercier Ythier, *Handbook of the Economics of Giving, Altruism and Reciprocity* (vol. 1, Elsevier).

LAUWERS, L., and VALLENTYNE, P. (2004), 'Infinite Utilitarianism: More is Always Better', *Economics & Philosophy*, 20/2: 307–30.

LOCKE, J. 1690 (2003), *Two Treatises of Government* and *A Letter Concerning Toleration* (I. Shapiro, ed.) (New Haven/Londres: Yale University Press).

MADISON, J. (1790), Letter to Thomas Jefferson (Feb. 4). Available at: <http://www.familytales.org/dbDisplay.php?id=ltr_mad1668>

MASSON, A. (1999), 'Quelle solidarité intergénérationnelle?', *Notes de la Fondation Saint Simon* (Paris), n° 103.

MUSGRAVE, R. (1981), 'A Reappraisal of Financing Social Security', in (1986) *Public Finance in a Democratic Society. Vol. II: Fiscal Doctrine, Growth and Institutions* (New York, NYU Press).

NOZICK, R. (1974), *Anarchy, State and Utopia* (Oxford: Blackwell), 367.

RAWLS, J. (2001), *Justice as Fairness: A Restatement* (E. Kelly, ed.) (Cambridge (Mass): Harvard University Press), 214.

WADE-BENZONI, K. A. (2002), 'A Golden Rule Over Time: Reciprocity in Intergenerational Allocation Decisions', *Academy of Management Journal*, 45/5: 1011–28.

5

Exploitation and Intergenerational Justice

CHRISTOPHER BERTRAM

1. Introduction

Intergenerational justice is now an important part of the theory of justice. This is because we now have an awareness of problems concerning savings, pensions, and environmental issues such as global warming, and the way in which these problems have differential effects on the well-being of people born at different times. But justice and injustice are complex ideas and there are, consequently, many ways in which particular arrangements can be unjust. This paper concentrates on just one of these ways—exploitation—and asks whether it is possible for a generation at one time to exploit a generation at another. If there can be exploitation at all, then people who live at the same time as one another can stand in relations of exploitation to one another. So where generations overlap, it is clear that individual members of a later generation can exploit members of an earlier one, and *vice versa*. This paper will also discuss the tougher question of whether people at one time can exploit people at a later time even though they do not overlap with those people.

People who live at a later time than others with whom they are never contemporaries have one property that makes them promising candidates for exploitation: they are vulnerable. That is just to say that they can easily be harmed by the action of others, and that they can threaten nothing in return. But the feature of their circumstances that makes them vulnerable—their

Many thanks to Patti Lenard, Dean Machin and to the referees and editors of this volume for written comments on drafts of this paper and to Hugh Ward for comments on a very much earlier version. Discussion with Jimmy Doyle and Andrew Williams and with audiences at Bristol and at Nuffield College, Oxford, has also been helpful. Much work on this paper was done during my tenure of a British Academy/Leverhulme Senior Research Fellowship and I should like to acknowledge the support of the Academy and the Leverhulme Trust.

futurity—also appears to undercut the possibility that they might be exploited. This is because exploitation is usually thought to be about one person (or group) making use of another person (or group) for the benefit of the first and to the disbenefit of the second. And though their vulnerability makes it possible for an earlier generation to affect a later one adversely, it does not seem possible for the later one to act in ways that could benefit their precursors.

In the opening part of this paper I shall try to clarify the concept of exploitation as a form of injustice and I shall explore some conceptions of exploitation, including the Marxian one, before suggesting a working provisional definition of exploitation as a mode of failure of fair reciprocity. In the light of this, I shall then confront the central difficulty—that future persons cannot affect earlier ones—head on. I shall suggest that we ought to amend our provisional understanding of exploitation to cover cases where co-operative schemes and institutions extend across non-overlapping generations. In such cases, even though members of earlier generations cannot arrange matters so that members of later ones act so as to benefit them, the precursor generation can set things up so that their own lack of contribution effectively precommits the labour of their successors. Sometimes it is appropriate to think of such arrangements as giving rise to exploitation.

In one sense, the aim of this paper is modest. It is merely to make plausible the idea that people at one time can exploit people at another, including those with whom they do not overlap. It does not make the case that exploitation is the only way that present people can be unjust to future ones, and it leaves rather indeterminate how pervasive the phenomenon is. This is in part because our judgements about pervasiveness will depend on answers to other questions, some of which I shall suggest answers to but which could, plausibly, admit of different ones. These other questions concern how we judge whether or not people at different times are linked in co-operation, whether it is important for a charge of exploitation that making use of others is intended, and how we assess the relative contribution of people living at different times to a co-operative enterprise.

2. The Importance of Exploitation

Thinking about distributive justice may focus on at least two different aspects of a distribution. It can focus on the distributive pattern (the shape of the distribution of some good among persons) and it can focus on process (how the distribution came about). Clearly, these are not mutually exclusive concerns—we can be interested in both at the same time—but each raises a different set of questions about justice and injustice. Derek Parfit, in his paper 'Equality or Priority?' asks his readers to consider their intuitions about divided-world cases:[1] cases where one group of people have more than another group of people but where there is no history of interaction between the groups. Some people are inclined to judge that there is something bad about this inequality. But others are likely to follow Robert Nozick in his belief that to judge whether a pattern is unjust we need to know more than just its shape, but also how it came about.[2] These different axes for the evaluation of a distribution as just or unjust remain important even though we might try to elide the difference between them (perhaps by defining unjust processes as processes leading to unjust outcomes). Exploitation essentially involves a charge of injustice in process: it involves not just a judgement about the relative benefits and burdens endured by persons, but also about how the pattern of differential benefit arose from the interaction of producers and beneficiaries.

As a form of the charge that there is injustice in the way in which a distribution arose, exploitation has a special place for at least two reasons. The first of these is partly historical and has to do with the role which the idea plays in critiques of capitalist society by Karl Marx and others. Whether or not Marx himself thought of capitalism as unjust, many of his followers have thought of the exploitative relationship between worker and capitalist depicted in *Capital* as underpinning a charge of injustice.[3] The second reason is that exploitation is a form of injustice-in-process that may exist even where public rules concerning property are scrupulously observed. So, for example, whereas for David Hume justice was centrally concerned with compliance with property rights and injustice with their violation through theft,[4] a charge of exploitation can involve the thought that injustice-in-process is taking place despite such compliance. Indeed it can often be said that exploitation is going on not merely despite, but even because of, public rules of property. In Marx's classic discussion in *Capital*, the exploitation of the worker by the capitalist takes place even though they have freely contracted with one another in conformity with established legal rules and even though entering into the contract improves the situation of each party compared to their not doing so.[5]

The mid-1980s brought a flurry of books and papers which engaged with the notion of exploitation either by trying to clarify Marx's own use of the

---

[1] For Parfit on the divided world, see Parfit (2000).   [2] See Nozick (1974), pp. 153–5.

[3] See Geras (1985) for discussion of these claims.

[4] See, for example, his characterization of justice as 'a regard to the property of others' in 'Of the Original Contract' in Hume (1994), p. 196.

[5] Marx (1976), pp. 279–80.

term and its relation to justice, or by attempting to go beyond Marx's sense in order to develop a more general account.[6] Since that time, interest in Marxism among both philosophers and economists has waned in the light of world events, and this has led to an unfortunate diminution in theoretical interest in exploitation. This decline in interest is regrettable because it leaves an important dimension of justice neglected. We care not only about how things turn out for people, but also about how they came to turn out in the way that they did. And there are sometimes ways in which outcomes eventuate that are morally objectionable, even where people behave in ways that do not offend legal rights and procedures. Exploitation, which need involve neither theft nor cheating but is yet a form of injustice, is central to such cases.

3. A Conception of Exploitation

In order to make some progress with the question of whether earlier generations can exploit later ones we shall need to get some more clarity about what exploitation means. There are clearly uses of the term 'exploitation' that do not carry with them a charge of moral condemnation. So, for example, we can make use of natural resources or take advantage of an opportunity without there being, merely *ipso facto*, a implication or suggestion of wrongdoing. Even when human subjects are involved, use of the term does not have to carry any negative connotation. So, for example, if a chess player exploits a mistake by her opponent, there is no suggestion (rather the contrary!) that she is doing something other than she should have. This non-moral sense of the term does, however, share with its moral cognate the notion that the person who is doing the exploiting is thereby deriving some benefit or advantage—though not necessarily a material one—from whatever is exploited.

In contrast to this non-moral sense of exploitation we sometimes also encounter an idea of roughly Kantian provenance that forbids treating people as mere means to our ends. Rather, in our dealing with other persons we should pay due regard to those features they possess that give them dignity and value. There is much scope for argument about what the relevant features of human beings might be and how one might take account of them, but this moralized sense of 'exploitation' can condemn a very broad range of treatings of others. So, for example, creating a photographic depiction of a person, or using a person's body to display advertising, or conceiving a child with the

---

[6] See, e.g., Roemer (1982) and the essays included in Reeve (1987) Recent work which again explores the issue of exploitation includes Warren (1994), Wertheimer (1996) and Sample (2003).

aim of providing bone marrow for another child, might all be characterized as exploitative. There is no special connection with labour, effort, or even fairness involved with this sense of the term.[7]

Sitting somewhere between these two senses is the conception of exploitation employed within the Marxian tradition. The central Marxian thought is that one group of people (an exploiting class) is able to live off the labour of another group of people (an exploited class). The exploited class does not simply perform enough work to produce the goods that they themselves consume, they also contribute additional time and effort which goes to producing a surplus that is appropriated by the exploiting class.[8] That this happens is explained for Marxists by structural features of society. In capitalist societies, for example, it is explained by the fact that the exploiting class has effective control over material productive resources to which the exploited class does not have independent access: the direct producers, in order to acquire the means of life for themselves, must sell their labour power to the owners of the means of production.

At the centre of the Marxian picture, we can discern a key normative claim. This is that exploitation in class societies amounts to a violation of a principle of fair reciprocity. Many people are enjoying the benefits of a co-operative arrangement for the production of wealth. But the burdens of that co-operation are not distributed in a manner that corresponds, even roughly, to the distribution of those benefits. Instead, there are some people, the capitalist owners of the means of production—or, in earlier societies, feudal lords or slaveowners—who enjoy benefits greatly in excess of whatever productive contribution they make whilst others (the direct producers) engage in long hours of burdensome labour.

Now the principle of fair reciprocity that Marx tacitly appeals to here does not amount to a complete theory of distributive justice and it is unclear how fundamental a commitment it ought to be for him. The text where he gives us the most clues about his view is probably the *Critique of the Gotha Programme* where two further considerations complicate the picture. The first of these is that Marx recognizes that in any society workers will not receive the full fruits of their labour, and, indeed, he attacks this Lassalean slogan.[9] They will not receive the full fruits of their labour because there needs to be reinvestment to replace worn-out plant and machinery but also, and most relevantly for our

---

[7] We might term this generalized Kantian form of exploitation instrumentalization to distinguish it from the senses involving labour and effort.

[8] For a good account of the fundamental Marxian claims together with a cogent argument that they can be stated independently of the labour theory of value see Cohen (1988).

[9] See Marx (1974), p. 345.

purposes, there needs to be provision for those unable to work, such as the old, the sick and the very young.[10] The second complicating factor concerns Marx's attitude to justice in a fully-fledged communist society. Whilst Marx appears to endorse the idea that reward should be proportional to labour contribution as the guiding principle for the lower phase of communism, it is clear that this is a symptom of imperfection which will be transcended once society has conquered scarcity and thereby escaped the Humean circumstances of justice. With these qualifications, however, we can draw from Marx a broad principle of wide application according to which participants in co-operation should enjoy rewards that are roughly proportional to their contribution, a principle that Marx believes is systematically violated in class societies. It is important to note that this basic principle of fair reciprocity here is not a specifically Marxian one. Indeed we can find it clearly expressed in other writers. C. D. Broad, for example, himself a long way from Marxism, wrote:

... the appeal to 'fairness' seems to rest on the principle that the best possible state of affairs is reached when the group of producers and that of enjoyers is as nearly identical as possible. In fact common sense would probably go further than this and say that the best possible result was reached when (a) producers and enjoyers are identical and (b) the share in the good produced that falls to each producer is proportional to his sacrifice in producing them.[11]

Wide endorsement of such a principle raises the question of whether Marx can actually make stick the charge that class relations under capitalism violate it. It might be argued, for instance, that the rewards that accrue to capitalists represent their proportional fair share, and those that fall to workers theirs. We might reply on Marx's behalf that much labour is burdensome and demands a sacrifice from workers who would much prefer to enjoy leisure. Contributions by capitalists are principally of two kinds: first there is the supply of capital, and second there is the activity involved in making investment decisions and, generally, in organizing the production process. Only the second of these activities typically involves the burdensome sacrifice of leisure to work and, insofar as it represents a genuine effort, is worthy of reward. But on any reasonable assessment of the relative labour burdens that fall to capitalists and workers in a capitalist society and the wealth and income enjoyed by each, it is clear that the principle of fair reciprocity is violated.

[10] Alan Carling attributes to Marx what he calls 'a disjoint needs/contribution principle' stating that among 'equally able, equally needy adult individuals' there should be an distribution proportionate to productive contribution, but that those who 'cannot be expected to make a contribution to production' should receive in recognition of their group membership. See Carling (1991), pp. 142–3.

[11] Broad (1916), p. 388.

A full implementation of the principle of fair reciprocity would require us to differentiate between forms of work depending on how unpleasant they are and would require a more sophisticated measure of benefit than wealth and income. The philosophical and practical obstacles to both these tasks are formidable (and possibly insurmountable) but those difficulties are not a barrier to the judgement that the principle is being violated in the most egregious instances—and, for Marx, capitalism is, on a very large scale, a most egregious instance.[12]

We have the material at hand for a clear statement of a principle of exploitation. Where people are linked together in co-operation either as contributors to that co-operation or as beneficiaries of it, and where those people are able to make a contribution requiring effort, there is exploitation if and when the distribution of rewards from that co-operation fails to be roughly proportional to the distribution of effortful contribution. The ability-to-contribute clause corresponds to Marx's reminder of the need to provide for those unable to work and tells us that the exploitation principle can only be a part of a wider scheme of justice. One thing that remains problematic, however, is the notion of people being 'linked together in co-operation' as a condition for exploitation. There may simply be some irreducible vagueness here, but some normatively adjusted notion of mutual expectation is involved. To insist that it be necessary for people to count as 'linked together in co-operation' for them actually to have formed expectations about one-another's behaviour is too strong, since it excludes people who are simply ignorant or unreflective. However not all cases where people benefit from the action of others will count as them being linked in co-operation. If I dig up some valuable ancient artefact in my garden then I benefit from the actions of its producers without thereby being linked with them in co-operation.

It may be a mistake, though, to want to insist on a bright line dividing those who are part of a co-operative arrangement and those who are not. In some cases a person will clearly be a member of a well-defined co-operative arrangement with others where the principle of fair reciprocity is fully engaged. Examples might be group of friends who are engaged in clearing a piece of waste ground or a group of colleagues dividing up some burdensome administrative chore. At the other end of the spectrum are debates around global justice concerning whether the international economy constitutes a Rawlsian 'basic structure' or whether duties of justice only hold between people subject to

---

[12] The account of reciprocity and exploitation here draws heavily on Warren (1994). Warren's text is a critique of Cohen (1990) but his positive account of reciprocity is independent of his disagreement with Cohen on self-ownership.

common legal authority. If the principle of fair reciprocity has greater force where networks of co-operation are well-established and patterns of mutual expectation are entrenched than it does where co-operation is distant, fragile and episodic, we may have a criterion that we can employ in judgements about whether this or that actual relation is exploitative.[13] Knowingly to impose disproportionate burdens or benefits on those with whom one is clearly engaged in co-operation is exploitative, but the mere fact of disproportion between parties who are distantly connected may not be.

4. Exploiting Future Generations and Temporally Extended Co-operation

The principal difficulty with extending the notion of exploitation to future generations is this: that exploitation seems necessarily to involve someone (the exploiter) deriving some benefit from the labour of another (the exploitee) and in the case where generations do not overlap it is hard to see that benefiting from the actions of future generations is even possible. If such direct benefit from the actions of others is indeed a necessary condition for exploitation to occur, then it is impossible to exploit future generations with which one does not overlap. The reason why such future generations cannot benefit us is clear: they live in the future. There may be unconventional views about the direction of time, causality, and the possibility of time travel, but I do not intend to pursue their plausibility as a route out of this particular difficulty. Instead I propose merely to accept as a fact that no action performed by a person in the future can affect my enjoyment of life now, and nor can it affect such matters as the quantity of resources available to me to pursue that life.

There may, of course, be understandings of 'benefit' or of what it is for a life to go well, according to which actions performed in the future, and even after my death, can be of benefit to me.[14] So, for example, we might think that the successful completion of some project, to which I have devoted my life but which extends beyond my lifespan, counts as a benefit to me and that, conversely, the failure of that project would count as a disbenefit. An objective assessment of whether my life went well or whether it was wasted,

---

[13] On the question of whether or not there is a global basic structure see, e.g. Beitz (1979). Thomas Nagel has argued for a limitation of duties of justice to those subject to a common legal authority as has Michael Blake (see Nagel (2005) and Blake (2002)). For the idea that we might vary the application of a principle of distributive justice as a continuous function of interconnectedness see Julius (2006).

[14] See Griffin (1986), ch. 2 for some discussion.

as made posthumously by a biographer, might well involve such factors. But I do not intend to rely upon such extended notions of benefit or life evaluation to counter the commonsensical view that what future generations do cannot benefit us, simply because they can exercise no causal influence over us. To be clear: the issue here is methodological and not substantive. If I can make the case for future generations being exploited without relying on an extension of 'benefit' which may be justified but is nevertheless controversial, my argument will be stronger as a consequence of that restriction.

The key to extending the notion of exploitation to future generations lies in the idea that a co-operative arrangement may be extended in time. Clearly, there is a trivial sense in which this is so. If people co-operate at all, they do so in time, and, given the nature of human beings, there could be no co-operation over a mere instant. But I have in mind now the sort of continuity that may endure over many generations, and which, indeed may endure so as to bridge generations that do not overlap. Liverpool Football Club, established in 1892, and the most successful club in the history of English football, would be an example of such a temporally extended co-operative scheme. The Chatsworth estate, handed on through the generations by the Dukes of Devonshire, would be another. On a larger scale, we could mention the sort of entity picked out by Rawls when he discusses 'peoples' or even supranational institutions like the European Union. Not all instances of co-operation will take place in the framework of institutions. We can imagine two people co-operating quite informally with no framework of rules, even tacit ones, governing their working together. But institutions and other more or less formal co-operative schemes do play a massive role in mediating and structuring co-operation, and those institutions may extend over many years with behaviour within them regulated both by explicit rules and by patterns of mutual understanding. If there is work that is necessary to an enterprise and must be carried out at some point or other, then questions will arise about its temporal distribution. And it is not just a matter of a fixed number of tasks that must be carried out earlier or later: rather, the performance or non-performance of work at a one time change both the amount and the nature of the work that has to be done at a later one. The best way to make this idea clear, I believe, is to proceed by way of example.

5. A Temporally Extended Co-operative Enterprise

In what follows I discuss the example of a family-owned manufacturing business, a factory, that continues to operate over a number of generations. I discuss three possibilities for exploitation: the repair burden, the debt burden, and the profligate generation. In the first two, earlier generations impose burdens on later ones in various ways. In the third, a later generation fails to bear a similar level of burden to its predecessors, preferring to live off their efforts. All three of these cases will involve exploitation as conceived in section 3 above, namely, as a failure of reciprocity where the distribution of rewards from co-operation fails to be roughly proportional to the distribution of effortful contribution, though I shall express doubt about whether 'exploitation' is really the right expression in the third case. This example of a temporally extended co-operative enterprise is a somewhat artificial and circumscribed one in a similar way to the manner in which philosophical examples involving small numbers of producers on desert islands are. But as with those examples, discussion of a restricted case may help us to get a fix on what the normative possibilities are so that we can later look at their applicability to the real world.

5.1 The repair burden

In our factory all the workers are equally strong and equally skilled, all work hard for equal lengths of time, and all have identical utility functions. We also need to assume, implausibly, that there is no technological change either within the business or in any wider economy of which the business forms a part.[15] In such a business fair reciprocity would appear to demand that the burdens of production be equally shared and that the same level of benefits be distributed to all the co-operators. But not all of the activities in which our workers engage and which are essential to continued production over time need to be done with the same regularity. Some activities—switching on machines in the morning and sweeping the floors—need to be done daily. With others, involving the replacement of worn-out plant and equipment, an interval of many years may pass with nothing being done. For many cases of investment—as regular users of the British railways system know well—there is a choice between maintaining an infrastructure through regular payments, and letting it deteriorate gradually whilst risking future catastrophe.[16] If one generation neglects to invest in routine maintenance, their ability to make use of their equipment may be practically undiminished for their period of employment and this will allow them either to consume the resources that they might otherwise have invested or to economize on effort.

---

[15] These assumptions are implausible and unrealistic, but they are methodologically necessary if we are to focus our attention on the purely temporal aspect of the distribution of benefits and burdens.

[16] See, e.g. Wolff (2002).

For ease of exposition, we can imagine a series of generations of co-operators: G_1, G_2 ..., G_n. We can stipulate that each generations overlaps with its immediate predecessor and its successor: so G_6 overlaps with G_5 and G_7 but not with G_4 or G_8. A generation, say G_4, faces a choice. They can invest regularly in maintaining something essential to the production process—the building, for example—or they can choose not to do so despite knowing that a future generation, G_6, will be forced to invest urgently if production is to continue. Let us suppose that G_4 decides not to make that investment and that, in consequence, maintenance is not done until the costs of neglect approach the cost of fixing things. These costs will have all been pushed onto G_6. Even though maintaining the building is as much a part of the total process of production as, say, oiling and cleaning the machines, the cost of that aspect of the production process is imposed on G_6. G_6 will have to compensate for the G_4's lack of contribution if production is to continue at all.

In a group of co-operators living contemporaneously with one another, a co-operator who persistently worked at a lower intensity that the rest, despite having the capacity to put in the same effort as her fellows, would rightly be described as exploiting them. It seems odd and arbitrary to allow the fact that activities take place non-contemporaneously to affect that judgement. Perhaps it is true that people who are non-contemporaries will not have the same immediate psychological stimuli to just behaviour that contemporaries will have, since the human experience of people at a distant time will be less vivid to them that that of their contemporaries is. But such psychological factors, though doubtless important in explaining why people act justly when they do, are surely not determinative of what our obligations are.

5.2 The debt burden

In the example of the neglected building above, the imposition of burdens by G_4 on G_6 took place because G_4 manipulated the physical circumstances under which G_6 would operate. But there are many other ways in which human beings constrain one another's choices. As well as changing the physical environment in which others operate they can also change their social circumstances. Our factory is a corporate entity with a legal personality that may extend beyond one generation. It may therefore be possible for G_4 obtain credit on a long-term basis, with the repayments falling on subsequent generations such as G_5 and G_6.[17] Incurring a debt with a long-term repayment

---

[17] This sort of practice is, unfortunately, a fairly common one. Third World dictators are notorious for borrowing money from international institutions and then using that money to finance current luxury expenditure.

might be justified as a way of spreading the cost of an investment across all those who are likely to benefit from it. In the example above, if G4 had taken out a loan to pay for building maintenance and had spread the repayments to fall on G5 and G6 as well as on themselves, that would not be objectionable. But if G4 simply use the money they borrow for present consumption and thereby impose a heavier labour burden or diminished net income on their successors their actions are exploitative: they enjoy additional benefits whilst imposing extra labour burdens on their descendants in G6.[18]

5.3 The profligate generation

In the two cases I have looked at so far, members of a future generation are placed in a position where, if they are to continue as co-operators in the business, they have to do more work or enjoy fewer benefits because of the unwillingness of members of an earlier one to bear their fair share. But what of past generations? Can they be exploited by their successors? In many temporally extended co-operative schemes there is an customary expectation on each generation to do its part, an expectation which typically involves handing on the core assets of the scheme intact (or enhanced) from one generation to the next. Where that expectation is not met, because a particular generation contributes less or consumes more than it should, they may be thought to have taken unfair advantage of the labour of others.[19] We can apply this idea to the factory. The founding generation (G1) worked very hard to establish the business and passed it on to their children (G2) who bequeathed it in turn to their descendants (G3), and so on. Perhaps G4 decides to neglect and even consume part of the business (maybe selling off some of the land on which the business is sited to a property developer). If they do this may have placed an additional burden of restoration on their heirs (G5, G6) unless those successor generations reconcile themselves to the diminishing of the business. Additionally, they will have taken unfair advantage of their ancestor generations by enjoying consumption benefits on the basis of assets built up by those predecessors, without being willing to endure similar labour burdens to those predecessors.

---

[18] What of the intervening generation G5, that overlaps with both G4 and G6? Their situation looks ambiguous unless we know a great deal of further detail since they may benefit directly from the additional income of their parents but will also have to worker harder or for less in their turn.

[19] A familiar example of a real-world scheme involving expectations like this is that of English aristocratic families with their houses and estates. The shared understanding of the family is that each generation is expected to do its part for the upkeep of the property and should pass on the estate that it has inherited from its predecessors.

There is a difficulty here that does not arise in the earlier cases. Here as there it appears that there is a breach of the principle of fair reciprocity so that some people are getting more than they should out of the collective enterprise given their relative contribution, and, by implication, some are also getting less given theirs. But in those earlier cases members of an earlier generation had arranged matters so that later participants in the enterprise would work harder or accept lower benefits than they did. With the earlier examples there is therefore a similarity with the standard case of contemporaneous capitalist exploitations: one group of people (the net beneficiaries) can be said to have arranged things so that another group of people (the net contributors) work harder and enjoy less than they would do under fair reciprocity. Whilst it may not be exact to say of capitalist beneficiaries that they arrange things so that proletarian contributors have to do more for less, since those capitalists may not be personally responsible for deliberately putting the relevant structures in place, we can say of them that they play their part in making things worse for others. But in the case where a later generation fails to conform to the contribution/benefit pattern expected by its predecessors this is not so. Since past generations are dead and gone, there is nothing that past generations can do to harm them. The key point here may be semantic rather than substantive. In this example, as in the earlier ones, through their actions one set of persons makes it the case that the principle of fair reciprocity is violated. But in just some of those cases is the actual life-experience of net contributors worsened as a consequence of the actions of the net beneficiaries. We may want to use some term other than exploitation, such as 'parasitism' to refer to cases involving the violation of fair reciprocity where there is no experiential effect on the net contributors, but little hangs on this.

A further problem remains with this last example. We need, at least implicitly, to make use of some notion of 'reasonable contribution'. This is for the following reason: the first generations (say G1 and G2) may be Stakhanovites or people in the grip of the Protestant work ethic and we probably do not want to say that later generations who fail to labour to the same degree and extent as G1 and G2 must therefore be 'parasites' or exploiters. There may be room for a good deal of disagreement about what a 'reasonable contribution' amounts to, and I cannot resolve such possible disagreement here. The case seems analagous to cases of contemporaneous inequalities in labour contribution. So, for example, if we find that one member of a couple does 75 per cent of the housework we might be inclined to make the provisional judgement that there is a failure of fair reciprocity. But if we later learn that the person who does most housework has unusual and neurotic standards of tidiness and cleanliness, to which it would be unreasonable to expect the other partner to conform, we may revise that judgement.

6. From Local Examples to Global Application

Consideration of our three examples—the neglected building, the debt burden, and the profligate generation—has highlighted a number of pertinent issues. Some of these will become all the more pertinent if we try to move beyond the highly artificial example I used in order to ask about real-world cases of intergenerational justice where, for instance, people do not clearly belong to a common enterprise, or where there is technological change. In this section I look at two groups of issues: scope and collective identity and evaluation. These represent only a small subset of the matters that arise, and my answers are intended to be mainly provisional and suggestive for further discussion rather than definitive.

6.1 Scope and collective identity

What should lead us to judge that two or more non-contemporaneous people are linked together in co-operation? How closely connected do they have to be by common norms and institutions? And how far are later generations morally bound by the actions and decisions of their predecessors? It is, after all, one thing to be put in a situation by physical facts inherited from precursors (such as is the position of the workers in the imaginary factory), it is another to be subject to moral or legal obligations that are not self-incurred. Here we need to remain open to a number of different answers compatible with different degrees of interconnection.

As mentioned at the end of section 3 above, there are some parallels here with issues around global justice. There we may have people who lack a common legal and coercive framework but who nevertheless interact with one another in various ways, who in some sense form part of the same global web of co-operation. Whilst some theorists want to limit our obligations in justice to those with whom we share the same state framework, most have found this move implausible. If mere spatial distance should make no difference to our obligations it is hard to see that temporal distance should make a difference either. In the case of interaction with contemporaries, then, we can see how the terms under which we commission people in distant countries to make cheap goods for us might violate a principle of fair reciprocity. People at a temporal distance from us cannot do things directly for us, but the repair burden and debt burden examples show how we might possibly act so as to offload burdens onto them and how such offloading might violate fair reciprocity in a similar manner.

With debt burden cases especially, issues of legal and corporate identity become important. Entities like countries and firms can incur legal debts and obligations and such entities can persist far beyond the natural life of the individuals who constitute them at a particular time. If we think that members of such collectives really can impose obligations on their successors then we have one method by which intergenerational exploitation can take place. Of course we have the example of Third World dictators who incur debts on behalf of their countries in order to boost their present personal consumption, where repayment of this debt is then imposed on future generations of their compatriots who have not themselves benefited. Whilst in such cases it is tempting to say that the dictator's future compatriots are not under a genuine obligation and ought to repudiate or be forgiven the debt, other cases may be less clear cut. So, for example, members of one generation in an impeccably democratic nation may use that nation's collective decision-making mechanisms to derive benefits for themselves (favourable pension terms, for example) in ways that will impose repayment burdens on generations to come.

At least two possibilities arise here. One, which will appeal to communitarians and collectivists of various kinds, is that members of one generation can impose genuine moral obligations on their successors because the collective to which they and their successors belong can itself acquire temporally persistent obligations. Such a possibility will not commend itself to liberal individualists and voluntarists. The second is where, although no genuine moral obligation can be imposed on members of successor generations, the legal and institutional facts are such that they will in fact have to honour the commitments of their predecessors. The future citizens of countries indebted by dictators are often in just this position: morally they may be entitled to refuse payment, but practically they cannot.

6.2 The assessment question

How are we to judge that fair reciprocity has in fact been breached? We can call this the assessment question. This has at least three components: what should count as a breach of fair reciprocity rather than a mere failure of it; whom we should assess as contributor/beneficiary; and what metric should we use to assess burden and contribution.

Clearly not all failures of fair reciprocity will amount to breaches of it. So there will be cases where the benefits and burdens of co-operation fail to reflect the contribution of the various participants in co-operation but where no exploitation, or similar breach of fair reciprocity, is going on. The deliberately artificial examples above made no mention of technological change; they abstracted from it. But if there is technological development then later generations may have a life that is, on the whole, much easier than that of their ancestors: they have more leisure and greater material benefits. Yet we would not want to say that there is something morally reprehensible about this fact, even though their ancestors shouldered greater burdens and enjoyed fewer benefits despite being members of a common co-operative scheme. In the profligate generation case I stipulated that there was a clear expectation on each generation to maintain the business intact and if one generation failed in that duty and thereby benefited from the contributions of its ancestors whilst increasing a burden on its successors, it was reasonable to accuse them of being parasites with respect to the former and exploiters of the latter. But often there will be no such clearly defined expectation of duty with respect to some particular asset.

We might want to suggest some general duty of sustainability though. Whilst one generation does not inherit from another a set of assets as easily identifiable as an aristocratic family's estate, it does inherit a stock of natural resources as well as various cultural and social assets. Since some of these assets are non-renewable, each generation may well consume some of them and thereby deplete the stock of a particular asset in ways that lessen the opportunities available to its descendants. But they may also improve the opportunities available to succeeding generations in other ways: through technological development and discovery, for example. If the human race lives long enough, perhaps all assets will be depleted below a level where a tolerable condition of life can be supported. But these speculative possibilities are beyond my scope here. What we may reasonably condemn is the depletion of resources for current consumption where that depletion is uncompensated for by any bequeathed technological improvement and where a future generation is therefore condemned to choose between harder work and lower consumption because of the actions of its predecessor. There may be a question, though, of where such labour-imposing actions really count as exploitative. Certainly we do not want to extend the notion of exploitation to encompass all cases which involve the unfair appropriation of natural resources, but that is not what is being suggested. It is not the appropriation of natural resources by one generation that is exploitative but rather their knowing or careless appropriation in a way that will predictably impose higher labour burden (or lower benefits) on their successors in the light of the available technology.

Questions may also arise concerning the identity of the putative exploiters and exploitees and how we allocate burdens and contributions. Here again, there may be a disagreement between individualists and collectivists: that is, between people who think that only individuals can properly be held responsible for actions or benefit from policies, and so forth, and those who think that collectives can also be the bearers of agency and responsibility. If we take a purely individualistic line then the principle of fair reciprocity as applied to co-operation over time dictates a rough balance of benefits and contributions over all individuals who work together. In the case where population is stable there will be no difference between this case and a collectivist case. But where population in one generation is substantially larger or smaller than population in another the question will arise as to whether fair reciprocity imposes moral duties on individuals or on whole generations. In our debt repayment case this may matter a great deal. A successor generation that has to bear the cost of its ancestors' profligate consumption may be greatly burdened if considered as a unit, but if their population is ten times larger than that of their precursors, this may not impose any great imbalance on individuals.[20] My own instinct is to say that we should favour an individualist resolution of this problem, on the grounds that, ultimately, it is individuals who bear the burden of contribution and enjoy the benefits arising from co-operation. But no doubt a reasonable case could be made on the other side.[21]

Finally, we shall need to have some kind of metric in place to assess the intergenerational balance of benefits and burdens. This is, perhaps, a special case of the 'currency of egalitarian justice' problem: should we use welfare, or resources, or capabilities for our measure of interpersonal comparisons of well-being?[22] The intergenerational case is especially difficult. Welfare comparisons are hard enough to make between contemporaneous individuals, let alone between generations that live at different times. And even where individuals live at the same time, it can be very tricky to compute the value of the resources available to them. So, for example, even if money income is taken as a rough proxy for resources, purchasing-power-parity calculations governing the resources available to different people in different countries are both difficult and controversial. Perhaps a better measure for the intergenerational case is something like Amartya Sen's capability metric.[23] Even those who believe that,

---

[20] Although on the other side of the ledger will be the fact that their per capita share of natural resources will be halved!

[21] The other identity-related question I have left out here is that arising from Derek Parfit's so-called non-identity problem (see Parfit (1984), ch. 16. Readers may wish to reflect on how this impacts on the issue of intergenerational exploitation.

[22] For this discussion see, e.g. Cohen (1989).

[23] For discussion of the capability metric see many works by Sen, such as Sen (1992), but, also especially Nussbaum (2000). For the claim that a sophisticated resourcism can will take account of what people are able to do with their resources see Pogge (2002) and Dworkin (2000), ch. 7.

at a fundamental level, welfare or resources are what ought to count, may find the capability metric useful for making judgements about cross-generational well-being. The capability metric will at least enable us to ask what typical members of each generation can do with the resources available to them and thereby enable us to form a judgement about whether one generation is better off than another. We can now do many things that previous generations could not. Access to cheap air travel, for example, means that we do much better in terms of access to mobility than they did. At the same time, our capability for interaction with the natural environment may have been diminished. It may be that our current consumption choices will reduce access of future generations to both of these dimensions of capability: the first because access to air travel will have to be restricted due to the need to reduce carbon emissions; the second because of general damage to the environment. If this transpires it would seem that—other things being equal—an exploitative breach of fair reciprocity has taken place. At least this is so just so long as our current consumption choices impose an invidious choice between decreased consumption and increased contribution on successors with whom we are linked in co-operation. Not all harms we inflict on our descendants will be clear cases on injustice, and not all cases of injustice will be cases of exploitation. Where there is no common co-operative scheme and where we simply impose a harm on a future generation then this is an unjust thing to do, but it is not a case of exploitation.

7. Conclusion

I have canvassed the following idea: that at the heart of charges of exploitation such as the one Marx makes about capitalist society is the claim that exploitation essentially consists in the breach of a principle of fair reciprocity. That principle is very far from being all there is to distributive justice since it must compete with other claims, most importantly with claims of need. A breach of fair reciprocity occurs where people who are engaged in co-operation together, often, but not necessarily, in a common institutional scheme, act so as to derive a benefit that is greatly out of proportion to their contribution. Whilst it may be impossible to make fine-grained judgements about such benefit and contribution, we can do so in the most egregious cases. The possibility of intergenerational exploitation arises because co-operative schemes may endure over time, and, indeed, over periods that span a number of generations. It seems arbitrary to insist that whereas breaches of fair reciprocity among contemporaries are exploitative, even where those contemporaries are physically remote from one another, breaches among non-contemporaries are not. This being said though, there are many difficulties in applying the idea of exploitation over long time periods since judgements of relative benefit and contribution will be extremely difficult to make. Nevertheless, since exploiting people is wrong, we should take care not to act in ways that are likely to worsen the contribution-benefit position of those who succeed us. Consumption choices that we make today that have the effect of imposing debt burdens on our successors or of degrading the environment may well have such an exploitative character.

References

BEITZ, C. R. (1979), *Political Theory and International Relations* (New Haven: Princeton University Press).

BLAKE, M. (2002), 'Distributive justice, state coercion, and autonomy', *Philosophy and Public Affairs*, 30/2: 257–96.

BROAD, C. D. (1916), 'On the function of false hypotheses in ethics', *International Journal of Ethics*, 26/3: 377–97.

CARLING, A. (1991), *Social Division* (London: Verso).

COHEN, G. (1988), 'The labour theory of value and the concept of exploitation' in *History, Labour, and Freedom* (Oxford: Oxford University Press), 209–38.

—— (1989), 'On the currency of egalitarian justice', *Ethics*, 99: 906–44.

—— (1990), 'Marxism and contemporary political philosophy, or why Nozick exercises some Marxists more than he does any egalitarian liberals', *Canadian Journal of Philosophy*, Sup Vol 16: 363–86.

DWORKIN, R. (2000), *Sovereign Virtue: The Theory and Practice of Equality* (Cambridge, Mass.: Harvard University Press).

GERAS, N. (1985), 'The controversy about Marx and justice', *New Left Review*, 150: 47–85.

GRIFFIN, J. (1986), *Well-Being: Its Meaning, Measurement and Moral Importance* (Oxford: Oxford University Press).

HUME, D. (1994), *Political Essays* (Cambridge: Cambridge University Press).

JULIUS, A. (2006), 'Nagel's atlas', *Philosophy and Public Affairs*, 34: 176–92.

MARX, K. (1974), *The First International and After* (Harmondsworth: Penguin).

—— (1976), *Capital*, vol. 1. (Harmondsworth: Penguin).

NAGEL, T. (2005), 'The problem of global justice', *Philosophy and Public Affairs*, 33: 113–47.

NOZICK, R. (1974), *Anarchy, State and Utopia* (New York: Basic Books).

NUSSBAUM, M. (2000), *Women and Human Development* (Cambridge: Cambridge University Press).

PARFIT, D. (1984), *Reasons and Persons* (Oxford: Oxford University Press).

PARFIT, D. (2000), 'Equality or priority?', in M. Clayton and A. Williams (eds.), *The Ideal of Equality* (Macmillan), 81–125.

POGGE, T. (2002), 'Can the capability approach be justified?' *Philosophical Topics*, 30/2: 167–228.

REEVE, A. (ed.) (1987), *Modern Theories of Exploitation*, Sage Modern Politics Series, vol. 14 (London: Sage).

ROEMER, J. E. (1982), *A General Theory of Exploitation and Class* (Cambridge, Mass.: Harvard).

SAMPLE, R. (2003), *Exploitation* (Lanham: Rowman Littlefield).

SEN, A. (1992), *Inequality Reexamined* (Oxford: Clarendon Press).

WARREN, P. (1994), 'Self-ownership, reciprocity, and exploitation, or why Marxists shouldn't be afraid of Robert Nozick', *Canadian Journal of Philosophy*, 24/1: 33–56.

WERTHEIMER, A. (1996), *Exploitation* (Princeton: Princeton University Press).

WOLFF, J. (2002), *Railway safety and the ethics of the tolerability of risk*, Tech. rep. (WCA Consulting, London).

6

A Value or an Obligation? Rawls on Justice to Future Generations

DAVID HEYD

The Scope of Justice and its Circumstances

Every moral and political theory must define the scope of the subjects falling under its judgement. Kant thought that moral principles apply to all rational beings. Bentham held that they apply to all sentient beings. Plato and Aristotle restricted the scope of political morality to the free citizens of the *polis*. Christian theology referred to human souls created in the image of God. Every moral and political theory fixes the group of subjects with which it is concerned according to its fundamental normative principles: rationality in Kant; the maximization of pleasure in Bentham; the cultivation of virtue in the Greek case; or the salvation of the soul in Christianity. However, modern theories of justice, at least those belonging to the contractarian tradition, determine the scope of their subjects on the basis of formal rather than metaphysical, normative, or naturalistic constraints. Distributive justice, since Hume, is characterized in terms of a set of principles that regulate the relationship of cooperation between human beings. The formal constraints on the application of justice involve, accordingly, the description of the conditions under which human cooperation is, in Rawls' phrasing, 'possible and necessary'.[1]

Following Hume, Rawls refers to these conditions of just cooperation as 'the circumstances of justice'. On the one hand, human beings have a common interest in cooperation, since it promotes their welfare. On the other, they find themselves in an inherent conflict, since every individual seeks for him or herself a larger share in the product of the cooperative effort. Hence the need for agreed upon principles of distributive justice. But human cooperation is possible and necessary only when human beings who

---

[1] John Rawls (1971), *A Theory of Justice* (Cambridge: Harvard University Press), 126.

live side by side on the same territory are concerned;[2] only when they have roughly equal power (such power that prevents anyone from unilaterally gaining control over all resources); and only when there is moderate scarcity in resources (for an inexhaustible abundance makes cooperation superfluous, while extreme scarcity makes it impossible). These objective conditions of just cooperation are supplemented in Rawls' theory by subjective conditions, such as the pursuit of individual life plans and mutual disinterest (or limited altruism).

The circumstances of justice are thus essentially associated with the condition of *mutuality* or reciprocity. Kantian respect for persons, Humean sympathy for suffering fellow creatures, the Christian duty of care for the salvation of other people's souls, or, as we shall see, a principle of impartiality or a doctrine of an ideal observer—are all moral principles which are not conditioned by reciprocity, at least not in their actual exercise. However, just cooperation takes place only where human beings are mutually vulnerable as well as capable of benefiting each other. We can envisage an abstract or cosmic concept of justice, as in Plato, according to which everybody gets 'his or her share' in a way that is not dependent on the condition of reciprocity, but any concept of justice based on cooperation or agreement presupposes mutual relations. Since Rawls' conception of justice is, in my view, essentially contractual, it must satisfy the 'circumstances of justice'. The question is whether these circumstances hold in the intergenerational sphere.

Cooperation typically takes place only between people living in the same *time* and on the same *territory*. This explains why theories of justice have traditionally referred to individuals in a particular society and of a particular generation. In pre-modern times this double restriction (temporal and territorial) of the application of justice seemed very natural. For in the world preceding globalization the degree of influence of one society on another was quite limited. So was the impact of one generation on its descendants, particularly on distant future generations, and a given generation usually enjoyed a standard of living roughly similar to that of its parents, conducted its life by similar technologies and means of production, and received an education similar in quality and scope. Today, the third world is dependent on the first (and also, although to a lesser extent, the developed world is dependent on the developing world). And of course the welfare of future generations has become tremendously dependent on the actions and policies of the present

---

[2] 'Same territory' could have various references, depending on the state of communication and technology. It could mean anything from the same small island to the whole planet (especially if it becomes threatened by external powers of an alien planet).

generation: in long-term investment, the preservation of natural resources, pollution, and genetic practices—to name just a few dimensions of that dependence. Rawls has been the major pioneer in facing the theoretical and moral need to expand the theory of justice to both the inter-national and the inter-generational spheres.

However, it should be immediately pointed out that the extension of justice on the intergenerational axis raises a further problem that does not apply to the international realm: the dependence of various societies in the 'global village' of our age is mutual. Poor societies make claims on rich societies for economic assistance and immigration rights. They also pose a threat to the rich world if the latter should ignore their distress. But on the intergenerational dimension dependence seems to be in principle *unidirectional*, i.e. involves relations which are not and will never be based on reciprocity. We are dependent on the behaviour of our ancestors but they are in no way dependent on ours.[3] The conditions of justice seem, therefore, not to obtain in relations with past or future generations. John Rawls was the first philosopher to consider this problem systematically. Until 1971 the subject was dealt with mainly by economic theorists interested in the principles of savings, but Rawls' discussion has transformed it into an intriguing philosophical topic.[4]

Three alternatives seem then to suggest themselves regarding the extension of justice to future people: either modify the conception of the circumstances of justice, or establish intergenerational justice on non-contractarian grounds, or, finally, admit that intergenerational relations are in their nature not subject to judgements of justice at all (but rather to moral principles or duties of another kind). The first alternative is adopted by Rawls who invests much philosophical effort in redesigning the circumstances of justice so that they can capture the particular nature of justice to future people. My argument will be that this project fails. Some interpreters of Rawls' theory believe that he can establish principles of intergenerational justice on a non-contractual basis and hence that the second alternative is not incompatible with his general theory of justice and even serves as a better reading of it. I will try to show that these interpretations (or even self-interpretations) of Rawls do not

---

[3] 'Either earlier generations have saved or they have not; there is nothing the parties can do to affect it.' *A Theory of Justice*, 292 (and see a very similar statement at 140). Later in the paper I will qualify this thesis of unidirectionality by pointing both to a certain sort of dependence of a given generation on its descendants and to the problem of individuating generations due to their partial overlap.

[4] Rawls' discussion of justice between generations is concentrated in two main sections in *A Theory of Justice*, 44 and 45. But it is no coincidence that the beginning of the discussion is found in section 22 which deals with the circumstances of justice and in section 24 which is concerned with 'the veil of ignorance.'

do justice to his fundamental idea of justice as fairness and hence that the non-contractarian option (particularly that of impartiality) cannot serve as part of his general theory of justice. If that is the case, the third (sceptical) alternative becomes persuasive. And indeed, I will argue at the end of the article that what remains of the duty of 'just saving' is not a principle *of* justice but only a statement about the *value* of justice and the duty to maintain or promote it. The problem of accommodating intergenerational justice within Rawls' general theory of justice is an enlightening test to the general methodological issue whether Rawls is committed to a genuine *contractarian* method or whether his views can be understood in more impersonal (Kantian) terms of *impartiality*. Accordingly, my argument in this paper is partly interpretive, partly critical and partly constructive in ways which cannot always be easily separated.

Rawls is not prepared to renounce completely the application of judgements of justice in the intergenerational sphere, and understandably so. In a society that operates on the lines of capitalist economy the issue of savings for future generations is of much significance. Should we pass on to the next generation the capital which we have inherited from the previous generation? Should we promote the welfare of our descendants (in material goods, in the quality of education and health) as a token of gratitude to our ancestors for what we have inherited from them, or should we rather give to our children independently of what we have received from our parents? May we incur debts which our children and grandchildren will have to pay? Should we accept responsibility for covering the debts accumulated in the past so as to relieve the next generations from that burden? To what extent may we use natural resources for our advantage, on the assumption that future people will probably have access to other resources and to unpredictable technologies that will provide them with a similar level of welfare? Since Rawls wishes to maintain the applicability of justice to the intergenerational dimension, and to do so on a contractual basis, his theoretical task is to revise the conception of the circumstances of justice and interpret the condition of reciprocity as applying also to human beings who do not live at the same time.

Two Models for a Cross-generational Contract

Rawls discusses the just savings principle in the context of his analysis of the concept of the 'social minimum'—that minimal standard of living of the worst off group in society that is required by the difference principle. He makes clear that the difference principle does not require improvement of the condition of the worst off all the way up to making them equal to the rest of society.[5] There are two reasons for this.[6] The first relates to the danger of undermining economic efficiency, which would ultimately lead to a decrease in everybody's standard of welfare, including the weaker members of society; the second, which is our concern here, concerns the possible harm to future generations. In other words, the difference principle obliges us to take into consideration not only the situation of the worst off in our society but also the kind of society we are leaving for future generations. The just savings principle demands that we leave enough capital and resources for future generations while making transfers to our contemporary poor (as required by the difference principle). But the question is *how much* is enough?

Rawls would not accept utilitarian responses to this question. One may think of conditions under which a very high rate of savings, a huge investment exclusively aimed at the future, could have an economic justification in terms of the overall welfare of all human beings across time. However, such utilitarian logic is contrary to the principle of justice which prohibits sacrificing the welfare of one person in order to maximize the general utility, or in our case the welfare of our contemporary poor for the sake of the overall welfare of our descendants. Rather than the utilitarian principle, Rawls appeals to the device of the social contract as the way to determine the right savings principle. The goal of the Rawlsian social contract is not the maximization of welfare but an agreement on principles of justice which would determine the basic structure of society. Similarly, the aim of intergenerational justice is not to advance the wealth of future people but to secure the necessary conditions and stability of just institutions and the fair value of liberty.[7] The preservation and inculcation of just institutions is in Rawls' terms 'a natural duty' of individuals, and the device of the original position (in its intergenerational application) is designed only to fix the proper savings rate which is necessary for the maintenance of

---

[5] *A Theory of Justice*, 285. Rawls refers to the egalitarian understanding of his idea of a social minimum (according to which 'everyone has nearly the same income') as 'a misconception'.

[6] *A Theory of Justice*, 286. There is still a debate about the right interpretation of the idea of a social minimum in Rawls (especially, as Rawls himself notes, regarding its scope), but I shall not go into it here since it does not bear directly on the issue of justice to future generations. Rawls himself, as we shall see, explicitly sets apart the intra-generational and the inter-generational conditions of justice when he distinguishes between the difference principle and the just saving principle, implying that the former does not apply to the intergenerational sphere. Rawls (2001), *Justice as Fairness: A Restatement* (Cambridge, MA.: Harvard University Press), 159.

[7] 'Saving is demanded as a condition of bringing about the full realization of just institutions and the fair value of liberty' (*A Theory of Justice*, 290). Or in even stronger terms, 'Real saving is required only for reasons of justice: that is, to make possible the conditions needed to establish and preserve a just basic structure over time' (*Justice as Fairness*, 159).

just institutions. All we owe future people are life conditions which would secure liberty, just cooperation, meaningful work, and basic welfare. Wealth as such is not a value which creates a duty of saving for the future. Therefore, Rawls explicitly says that having achieved the level of welfare required for the preservation of the institutions of justice, society is permitted to stop saving for future generations, except for the necessary means to maintain this level of welfare.[8]

In order to decide the principle of just savings in terms of a fair contract Rawls has to re-draw the conditions of the original position so as to include the intergenerational axis. Rawls considers two alternatives. According to the first, the 'general assembly' version, *all* human beings of all generations, or at least representatives of all generations, take part in the original contract. According to the second, the so-called 'present time of entry' version, the contractors in the original position all belong to *one* generation. According to the first version, every representative of a particular generation knows that his fellow contractors belong to different generations but no one knows to which particular one. Similarly, the contractors in the second version know that they all belong to the same generation but due to the veil of ignorance do not know which one it is.

Both versions raise problems. Rawls himself admits that imagining a general assembly of representatives of all generations, actual or possible, is 'to stretch fantasy too far'.[9] Rawls does not explain why this is so, but his reasons are most probably psychological and epistemological. Thus, although we can in principle—given the necessary historical information—envisage ourselves as living in any particular generation of the *past*, we cannot imagine ourselves as belonging to any *future* generation about which we know nothing. Consequently,

---

[8] And any further saving could be considered supererogatory from the point of view of justice. See *A Theory of Justice*, 288 and *Justice as Fairness*, 159: 'If society wants to save for reasons other than justice, it may of course do so; but this is another matter'. Rawls suggests, for instance, that although bequests and gifts to future people may be taxed in a progressive manner, such a tax should be applied only for the sake of preventing the creation of wealth accumulation that would be 'inimical to background justice', i.e. hinder fair equality of opportunity or increase inequality in political liberties. See *Justice as Fairness*, 161. Axel Gosseries has pointed out to me the ambiguity in Rawls' view here. He could be read as either requiring only the maintenance of the institutions of justice, or as requiring also that the same level of welfare enjoyed by the current generation (which might be higher than that required for preserving the institutions of justice) be bequeathed to the succeeding generation. The second reading is in line with Rawls' claim that once justice is guaranteed, net savings may fall 'to zero' (but not *below* zero, as Gosseries adds); but the first reading makes more sense if we believe that Rawls is literally serious in making the duty to maintain future just institutions the *exclusive* concern of his savings theory. I am inclined to the first reading. There is nothing wrong from the point of view of justice if the current baby-boom generation in America leaves to its children a society which is constitutionally just and stable even though enjoying a slightly lower standard of living.

[9] *A Theory of Justice*, 139.

Rawls concludes that the model of a trans-generational assembly is an unhelpful tool in forming our intuitions about the principles of justice. I propose to add another consideration which Rawls does not mention.[10] A general assembly of representatives of all generations, which is expected to decide intergenerational principles of justice, is logically problematic, even absurd, since it presupposes the existence and size of all generations as *given*. But this presupposition ignores the connection between demographic policies and savings policies in modern society. Schematically, one may say that in order to secure and advance the level of welfare necessary for the existence of a just future society one can *either* increase the rate of savings and leave more capital and resources to the next generation, *or* reduce the rate of population growth and the size of the next generation, thus avoiding the duty to provide it with more resources.

Once a link is made between the just savings principle and policies of procreation it is easy to see why the general assembly idea is logically absurd. For how can an assembly of all *possible* people decide who is to be born? An assembly of individuals cannot decide on its own size. Even if we can imagine ourselves belonging to another sex or another social status, we cannot imagine ourselves unborn or assess the risks of such a situation. Hence, the number of represented generations must be fixed and so must the number of people in each generation if we wish to engage in the thought experiment of a contract. And although an assembly of all *actual* people (i.e. those who lived, are living and are actually going to live) is logically coherent, it is implausible. For we (at least since the invention of effective means of birth control) exercise control over the size of future populations, i.e. the number of people in the future is not given but subject to our choice (on the basis, among other things, of considerations of justice!).[11]

The failure of the version of the general assembly leads Rawls to its alternative, the 'present time of entry'.[12] Its advantage lies in that it does not call upon us to imagine a hypothetical agreement between people of distant generations but rather an agreement between contemporaneous individuals,

---

[10] This, in my opinion, is the reason why Rawls' two versions of intergenerational justice can *not* be conflated, as suggested by Hubin, one of the earliest commentators on Rawls on that subject. D. Clayton Hubin (1976), 'Justice and Future Generations', *Philosophy and Public Affairs*, 6: 70–83. Hubin, however, draws attention to the paradox involved in the dependence of the existence of the circumstances of justice on the intergenerational axis on the present generation's chosen savings policy (74).

[11] Cf. David Heyd (1992), *Genethics: Moral Issues in the Creation of People* (Berkeley: University of California Press), 41–51.

[12] Rawls explicitly, though concisely, expresses his preference for this second model in *Justice as Fairness*, 86: 'Can we enter it [the original position], so to speak, and if so when? We can enter it at any time. How? Simply by reasoning in accordance with the modeled constraints, citing only reasons those constraints allow.'

our own generation, as is the case in any actual agreement. We are asked to
think of a chain of generations in which our own is located, without knowing
where. Thus, we must take into account the possibility that we find ourselves
closer to the beginning of the chain (and hence enjoying less of the fruits
of intergenerational savings) or to the end of the chain (benefiting from the
savings of our predecessors). This ignorance forces us to consider in a balanced
and fair way the just savings rate: a low rate of savings would have negative
consequences for later generations; a high rate would impose an unreasonable
burden on the earlier generations; and with no duty of savings, all humanity
(excluding the first generation) would lose. It seems that the veil of ignorance
guarantees consent on a fair savings principle, as it does regarding the two
intra-generational principles of justice.

However, in contrast to agreement on the intra-generational level, there
remains on the intergenerational level a problem associated with the circumstances of justice mentioned above. In the present time of entry version, it
would make sense for us to avoid savings, irrespective of our actual location in
the chain of generations. For regardless of whether our ancestors have saved
or not (thereby benefiting us or avoiding to do so), we have no reason to
save for future generations. Unlike intra-generational relations, in which if
we do not contribute our share to the common social project we will not
benefit from the effort of others, on the temporal axis we do not have control
over what our predecessors did or did not do for us and we have no reason
to fear our successors' response to our indifference to their needs. Due to
the unidirectionality of time, the reciprocity condition does not apply in the
intergenerational context. Cooperation, and thus also the applicability of the
principles of justice, is possible when there are relations of give and take, and
these are precluded across time, in which we can give only to those from
whom we cannot receive and receive from those to whom we cannot give.

Rawls is well aware of this basic problem and tries to solve it by adding
an assumption of the kind he tried to avoid when he initially formulated the
conditions of the original position. He calls it 'the motivational assumption'.[13]
Rawls cannot assume an *obligation* of human beings to care for their progeny,
since it is exactly this obligation which he wishes to derive from the theory
of justice, but he can assume that human beings have a natural *motive* of
care for their children and maybe grandchildren. The motivational assumption
simply extends the theoretical construct of 'the contractor' in the original
position: it is not merely an individual concerned with his or her own
welfare but also a 'head of a family' concerned with the welfare of his or

---

[13] *Justice as Fairness*, 128–9, 292.

her offspring. Indeed, this concern does not extend beyond one or two generations, but since the children's generation is endowed with the same caring attitude towards their children, this family connection becomes, due to its transitive nature, a unified intergenerational chain. Thus, the social contract, according to the added motivational assumption, is an agreement between heads of families who represent trans-generational 'dynasties'. Take, for instance, a typical bourgeois family like Thomas Mann's Buddenbrooks, in which the prominent economic and emotional concern of the head of the family is trans-generational: his primary interest is always tested in terms of his success to transfer the family business to his children in a prosperous condition and to raise them up on the ideal of intergenerational commitment to the (ever-expanding) family firm.

However, the motivational assumption is problematic and consequently the 'present time of entry' version as a whole is cast in doubt.[14] Rawls himself feels uneasy about having to add, almost ad hoc, an assumption whose only role is to solve the problem of the intergenerational extension of his theory of justice. After all, he conceives the contractors in the original position as abstract individuals motivated exclusively by rational considerations. Furthermore, Rawls emphasizes that they are 'mutually disinterested'. We should add that although Rawls is correct in noting that human beings usually feel that the satisfaction of their children's interests is part of their own interest, this feeling does not depend on what they have received from their parents. Relations of justice are mutual, but on the intergenerational plane reciprocity is impossible and it would be artificial to consider the natural feeling towards our children in terms of gratitude to our parents for what they have given us.

But even if Rawls can show that direct parental concern for the welfare of the next generation is absolutely natural and guarantees a principle of beneficence *within* family chains, the issue of *social* justice to future generations remains unresolved. For the duty to save for the next generation (whether in the world at large or for one's own society) cannot be conceived as an aggregation of the natural concern of individual citizens for their own respective offspring.[15] Similarly, the duty cannot be based on the transitivity of the natural concern for one's progeny, since, as we have seen, human beings worry about their children and grandchildren, but not about their grandchildren's grandchildren.

---

[14] Jane English (1977), 'Justice Between Generations', *Philosophical Studies*, 31: 91–104.

[15] Barry criticizes the motivational assumption noting that the assumption makes the rate of intergenerational savings dependent on the degree of the *actual* concern of parents for their children. The just savings principle, according to Barry, is a normative principle which fixes the just savings rate regardless of natural parental inclination. Brian Barry (1989), *Theories of Justice* (London: Harvester-Wheatsheaf), 192.

And although they know that their grandchildren will have a natural interest in *their* grandchildren, this fact does not establish commitments of justice.[16] Take for example a long-term policy of storage of nuclear waste.[17] We know that such waste may cause harm to future people living in one hundred years' time. Due to the time distance, these are people for whom we have no natural feeling or personal interest. Although we know that our grandchildren would probably have a natural concern for those people, this knowledge cannot serve as a moral reason for avoiding the uncareful storage of this waste. The moral ground in this case lies in an abstract principle of justice which does not presuppose any personal relations, either direct or mediated by the transitivity of family relations.

From the discussion so far we can conclude that both interpretations of the conditions of the original position fail in their attempt to solve the problem of agreement on a just savings principle and other aspects of justice to future generations. The idea of a universal conference of all generations or their representatives faces logical and epistemological obstacles; and the idea of contemporary individuals deciding the principles of justice without knowing their identity in the chain of generations requires the addition of a motivational assumption which can guarantee intergenerational saving but only on a contingent rather than principled basis. Should Rawls give up the idea of extending the application of the principles of justice to the future?

Justice to the Future as an Intra-generational Commitment

We should remind ourselves that the whole idea of justice as fairness is based on the notion of a hypothetical or virtual consent. In reality, time is unidirectional and hence there is no reciprocity in the impact of human action across time: the earlier shapes the later, but not vice versa. But, as Rawls insists, from an abstract *external* point of view, which considers the chain of generations as a whole, fairness demands ignoring the temporal location of particular generations. There is no place for pure time preferences, that is to say, for giving a greater weight to the present or the near future only because they are closer to us.[18] In the same way, as rational choice theory prohibits giving a greater weight to my present welfare than to my future welfare, so does

---

[16] For a persuasive critique of the transitive application of the motivational assumption, see Hubin, 82–3.

[17] Barry, *Theories of Justice*, 193–4.   [18] *A Theory of Justice*, section 45.

fairness require impartiality towards all generations. However, Rawls does not deny the basic fact that humanity develops and makes progress across history and hence it would be absurd to interpret equal concern for all generations literally. That is to say, it is only natural and by no means contrary to justice as such that future generations should enjoy a higher standard of living, health, education, technological level, etc. than past generations. This inequality is no less legitimate than that between the better and the worse off in a given society, albeit for different reasons: in the former case, a natural parental wish that our descendants have better lives than us; in the latter, the safeguarding of incentives to produce for the benefit of all. All that Rawls requires is that this intergenerational inequality achieve at least the implementation of the principles of justice in future society.[19]

From this external viewpoint in which location in time plays no role, there is then no need for a motivational assumption but only for a universal rational commitment to the promotion of justice. Can such a commitment be derived from the virtual contract between contemporary individuals who see themselves as cooperating in the shaping of the future? Such a point of view is natural since we can look at human civilisation as an ongoing historical enterprise. Without the trans-generational perspective much of the present cooperation between ourselves and our *contemporaries* will be futile, since most of our deep social goals lie beyond our personal life expectancy.[20] Accordingly, seeing ourselves as part of a larger, intergenerational scheme of cooperation is not conditioned by a motivational (family) assumption but is a rational complement to the very possibility of *intra*-generational cooperation. Rather than 'heads of families', we should think of 'heads of societies' motivated by concern for the future of their political communities. And once we think about the realisation of deep human projects in trans-generational terms,

---

[19] This formulation is certainly too simple and open to objections. See Axel Gosseries' sophisticated argument developed in (2001) 'What Do We Owe the Next Generation(s)?', *Loyola Los Angeles Law Review*, 35: 293–355. Gosseries claims that not only should we not leave the next generation with too little, but equally we should not leave it with too much, once the steady state of a just society is achieved. His reason is that such over-bequest would come at the expense of care for our contemporary worst-off. I believe that this argument is compelling when we consider collective social savings policies, but we should think also of the (common) case in which the next generation is wealthier than ours due to numerous individual choices of parents to bequeath their (post-taxation) wealth to their children. Are we not allowed by Rawls to make intra-generational gifts to our friends (even if these could improve the condition of our contemporary poor)? Why would it be different on the intergenerational axis?

[20] Barry puts this point somewhat differently: I owe you, my contemporary, concern for the future of your children (and vice versa) since they form an important part of *your* interests (and mine). *Theories of Justice*, 192. As suggested to me by Axel Gosseries, marriage is probably the best example for such mutual obligation.

it seems that we have to qualify even the apparently trivial statement that people (and societies) are not vulnerable to harm by future people. They are vulnerable, at least in the sense that their long-term interests (like their posthumous reputation) can be frustrated after their death by the violation of the hopes, intentions and wishes which gave meaning to their lives and guided them in the way they invested their resources and brought up their children.

It seems then that a further way to ground our duties of justice towards future people lies either in our long-term rational self-interest or in the mutual obligations we have towards our contemporaries to respect everybody's long-term projects. It is ultimately *we* (in the present) who are the subject of the contract. Hence, the problems of justice to future generations under the two interpretations discussed in the last section are circumvented. However, such 'genero-centric' solution to the issue of justice to the future seems to be too easy. It may be effective regarding the short-term future of a society, but it hardly solves such issues as global warming, nuclear waste, or eugenic research.

But there is one lesson we can learn from focusing on the intra-generational perspective on the problem of justice to future people. It is not the case, as one might think, that the extension of Rawls' theory of justice on the temporal dimension is more problematic than that on the global dimension. Indeed, all contemporary people in the world are actual, while those in the future are merely possible, which creates an intractable logical obstacle to the formation of intergenerational principles of just distribution. But on the other hand, our *motivation* to cooperate with geographically distant contemporaries is much weaker than the motivation to cooperate with our close contemporaries regarding our own offspring, on whom we are much more dependent for the success of our fundamental life plans and with whose welfare we are far more concerned. The extension of society to its own projected future is more natural than to some global social entity. Most cultures see themselves as extending far into the future and have concrete stakes in the conditions of their self-perpetuation.

Rawls' Reconsideration of the Issue: Strict Compliance

We come back to the circumstances of justice which stand at the foundation of the issue of justice to future people: what does the condition of reciprocity mean? If we understand reciprocity only as mutual impact, the potential of benefit or harm to each other, then our relations to future people cannot be subjected to the principles of justice. But even in the intra-generational sphere we understand the principles of justice as applying to relations between people who *as a matter of fact* cannot harm one another (for instance, slaves and masters, or the third-world and first-world countries in the colonial period). The very idea of the veil of ignorance is to drop the condition of actual mutual influence and imagine a human community in which cooperation is based on the abstraction of all the contingent properties of its members, including their place on the temporal axis. Accordingly, based on considerations outlined in the previous section, we may speak of cooperation between generations despite the unidirectionality of time. Under the veil of ignorance it would be rational to choose a moderate savings principle for the sake of advancing the chances of some increase in welfare as well as for the sake of the realisation of just institutions for all across time. Opposing savings only because we happen to be located in the earlier links of the generational chain is a manifestation of envy of future generations, and as is well known Rawls does not allow envy as a legitimate consideration in the original position.[21] Furthermore, even from the psychological point of view envy is confined to the intra-generational level. We do not envy either past generations or future ones simply because we do not compete with them.

In the years after the publication of *A Theory of Justice* Rawls reached the conclusion that his theory of justice to future generations can determine the rate of just savings *without* recourse to the problematic assumption about people's concern for their close descendants. Rawls was remarkably attentive and open to criticism and willing to change his views when convinced that the objections were justified. In his later *Political Liberalism* he devotes to the subject of intergenerational justice one paragraph accompanied by a footnote, in which he accepts his critics' reservations about the motivational assumption and admits (following Tom Nagel, Derek Parfit, and Jane English) that it can be omitted without having to relinquish the virtual contract in the 'present time of entry' version. Rather than being concerned with their children, Rawls characterizes the contractors as required to comply strictly with the savings principle agreed upon in the original position. The contractors agree only to principles of savings that they want all previous generations to have followed. This agrees with the general condition of full compliance demanded by Rawls

---

[21] If the saving principle agreed in a trans-generational contract guarantees care (i.e. saving) for the worse-off generations, then the very fact that later generations enjoy a happier life does not create a legitimate claim of justice and the earlier generation should not feel envious towards them.

in his ideal theory of justice and without which no fair social arrangement is conceivable even on the intra-generational context.[22]

One may raise the question, however, about the connection between the condition of strict compliance and the condition of the enforcement of compliance. Indeed, the whole point of strict compliance is that it belongs to the 'ideal' part of the theory,[23] while enforcement is called for only in the non-ideal world. But a complete theory of justice must address not only the ideal, but also the non-ideal circumstances of its implementation, and hence complement the abstract principles to which individuals are expected to adhere by principles of enforcement. But while in the intra-generational contract we *can* always include ways of enforcing the principles to which individuals agreed under the veil of ignorance, such threat of sanction or 'corrective justice' cannot be *in principle* applied on the inter-generational level. The way a just society responds to violations of justice exposes the conditions of cooperation and reciprocity which are essential to the very idea of justice. For instance, blocking the possibility of 'free riding' is part and parcel of the conditions for the implementation of justice in the human world. Part of my agreement in the original position to adhere to the principles of justice is grounded in the understanding that others, who might be tempted to 'defect' from the agreement would be deterred by rational considerations from doing so. But though this is a reasonable assumption in contracts between contemporaries, it is impossible in the relations between present and future people.[24] It is difficult to avoid Rawls' above-mentioned earlier concern that in deciding the just rate of saving for the future, a representative of any given generation, under the veil of ignorance, would rationally opt for a policy of non-saving on the ground that previous generations have either saved for his generation or not, and 'there is nothing the parties can now do to affect that' (i.e. to enforce saving or retaliate for not doing so).[25]

Take as an example Norway's savings policy. After having discovered large amounts of oil in its waters, Norway made a decision to pump it slowly

---

[22] (1993), *Political Liberalism* (New York: Columbia University Press), 273–4. For a very similar formulation, see *Justice as Fairness*, 160.

[23] For instance, Hubin, 74–5.

[24] Roger Paden argues that the problem of justice between generations should not be discussed from the perspective of the ideal theory since we do not know whether future people will feel committed to the principles of intergenerational justice. Roger Paden (1997), 'Rawls's Just Savings Principle and the Sense of Justice', *Social Theory and Practice*, 23: 27–51. Paden is right in advocating the framework of the non-ideal theory, but the reason is not the lack of knowledge but the absence of the ability to redress the violations of justice, i.e. to punish those who do not give their fair share to the common enterprise.

[25] *A Theory of Justice*, 140.

both in order not to overheat the economy and to save much of the oil for future Norwegian generations. Now, imagine that the next generation decides to waste all the oil reserves for the sake of an extravagant way of life, leaving nothing for their descendants. Would that be considered a violation of intergenerational justice? It would *seem* to be an act of free riding, taking advantage of the generous bequest of the past generation in contradiction to the original virtual understanding that the resource serve further generations. But then again, free riding can take place only in contexts of cooperation and contracts, and the current Norwegians cannot cooperate or make an enforceable contract with future people. If that is the case, infringing the will of past generations cannot be strictly viewed as *injustice* in strictly contractarian terms, but only as an act of disrespect.

The Scope of Saving

Yet we have still said nothing about the way the level of savings is to be decided. Rawls says that we cannot formulate exact criteria but only lay out the constraints that determine the minimum and maximum limits. Thus, a theory of justice rules out complete avoidance of savings but equally an excessive rate of savings which would come at the expense of the worst off in the present society. The correct rate of savings is determined, among other things, on the basis of the standard of living of the generation in question.[26] A society which fell victim to a natural catastrophe or to an economic recession is expected to save less than a society or a generation that was lucky to live in prosperity. Similarly, in fixing the rate of savings we might have a reason to return to a family model in which there is a connection between what we received from our parents and what we leave to our children: since concern for offspring usually extends over *two* generations, part of what our parents gave us was meant to promote our children's welfare. In that respect, we owe our parents some savings for the sake of their grandchildren. Even though this is not, as we have just shown, a contract-based justification for the duty of savings as such, it could help determine the proper rate of savings.

In any case, we should remember that ultimately Rawls holds that the duty of just savings is limited and all it aims at is the establishment and perpetuation

---

[26] 'Presumably this rate changes depending upon the state of society. When people are poor and saving is difficult, a lower rate of saving should be required; whereas in a wealthier society greater savings may reasonably be expected since the real burden is less.' *A Theory of Justice*, 287.

of just institutions in society and the realisation of the liberty of its members.[27] Wealth and material welfare are not in themselves the goals of obligatory saving, and in that respect Rawls' principle is different from the Buddenbrook bourgeois ideal according to which the transfer of the family capital and its enlargement from one generation to the next is a value or even a duty. But if protecting the conditions of justice for the future is a natural duty, an impersonal commitment, then it cannot be justified by the motivational assumption which focuses on the emotional concern we have for our own children or future family.[28] Thus, the principles of intergenerational justice are meant to be only constraints on the implementation of the difference principle: the worst off in contemporary society have a right to have their welfare promoted as long as this does not mean undermining the ability of future generations to maintain just social institutions. Society may not distribute all its resources among its members on the basis of time preference without leaving enough for future people to be able to live in a just society.

But the question of scope does not refer exclusively to the maximal and minimal limits of the amount of resources that are left aside for the future. It also concerns the limit of the duty of saving itself in terms of the nature of future society. As already mentioned, a contractual agreement must assume knowledge of the kind of people with whom we are making the deal. There are people with whom we do not wish to create relations of justice. Consider, for example, a future generation that does not share the commitment to the very idea of justice as fairness—a generation of anti-liberal fundamentalists (unfortunately this is not a very far-fetched fantasy). How can we regard such a generation as a partner in a virtual negotiation on principles of intergenerational justice? Rawls admits that the idea of a social contract is appropriate as a principle of justification only in a generally liberal society and hence a trans-generational contract can take place only on the assumption of the priority of the right over the good or of justice over any ideology or a comprehensive moral conception. In the intra-generational context we are permitted to make the same assumption since we know the society in which we live and whose principles of justice we wish to formulate and justify. In the intergenerational context we cannot make this assumption since we know so little about future people. Although Rawls does not explicitly mention

---

[27] The duty to guarantee the conditions for the existence of a future *just* society implies a fairly extensive measure of savings: securing minimal conditions of subsistence for all individuals, the preservation of some natural resources, the fight against crime, defence of the borders with potentially hostile countries, and obviously the education of the young to the value of just institutions and the rule of law. See Roger Paden, 'Rawls's Just Savings Principle and the Sense of Justice'.

[28] Paden, 39.

this possible constraint on intergenerational obligations of justice, it may be implied by the analogy to the limits he draws for international justice. One of the main tenets of the 'law of peoples' is that it applies only among liberal and 'decent' societies. The so-called outlaw states, which do not maintain any respect for human rights or for international agreements, are beyond the pale of the relations of justice.[29] Although the use of force against such outlaw states, which is justified in international law, is impossible in the intergenerational case, present people should take into consideration the possibility that some future generations will abandon the commitment to justice and to the just savings principle altogether. If that were the case, the duty of saving, based on the commitment to the preservation of just institutions, would become vacuous. If we know that the resources we are now saving are going to be used to promote a racist dictatorship in the next generation, maybe it is our duty to consume them all rather than leave them for the future!

The Duty to Uphold Future Justice is Not a Duty of Justice

Having followed Rawls' developing reflections on the issue of intergenerational justice and various possible responses to criticism against its coherence, we are left with a sceptical conclusion. Renouncing the ambitious attempt to formulate principles of just savings which would include a trans-generational original position, Rawls reaches a modest conclusion. The requirement of saving consists merely of the duty to contribute to the next generation's ability to achieve just institutions, to secure a just scheme of cooperation, to maintain the basic conditions for leading an autonomously chosen way of life. Unlike the Buddenbrook family principle or the enterprise of scientific research, which are cumulative in nature, the project of justice is not open-ended but well-defined and limited. The philosophically crucial point is that as in the case of international justice, the theory is based on a two-tier model: there are strong obligations within a society, or within a given generation, most typically summarized by the difference principle; and there are much weaker duties to other peoples or societies and to future generations. In both cases, the difference principle does not apply beyond contemporaneous domestic society. What we owe distant societies, in space and in time, are the more limited duties of assistance (in the former) and the preservation of justice (in

[29] (1999) *The Law of Peoples* (Cambridge, MA.: Harvard University Press), 80–1.

the latter). We, contemporaneous members of a particular society ('people') may claim not only territorial sovereignty, but also 'temporal' or generational sovereignty. That is to say, we are entitled to choose our way of life and a particular scheme of distribution and re-distribution (within the constraints of the difference principle) with no regard to remote or future people (once we have secured the future of the institutions of justice).

What can be the ultimate justification of such a two-tier model of justice? Why resist the attempt to extend both globally and intergenerationally the principles of justice and particularly the difference principle and advocate weaker requirements on the extended level? The answer I wish to propose takes us back to the interpretation of the circumstances of justice. One of them consisted of the potential threat or harm to human beings at the hands of their fellow beings. However, the more meaningful reverse side of that condition is the *positive* motive we have to cooperate with particular people rather than with others, our wish to produce and consume together material goods and create for our society a fair scheme of cooperation and a common way of life. I refer to this motive as *solidarity*. Obviously, solidarity cannot be a requirement of justice, since it is a condition for its operation. It not only makes justice possible or imperative, but also serves to fix the scope of its application, namely it defines the group within which just cooperation is sought. Solidarity can be based on common cultural heritage, shared aspirations, economic interests and even on unchosen historical contingencies. But it is necessarily 'domestic' or partial, i.e. not extending indefinitely to all human beings, present or future. Unlike respect for human dignity, the protection of human rights, the natural duty to assist a person in distress—which are all universal in some Kantian sense—distributive justice and the principles of fair cooperation are 'local' in their nature, i.e. they apply only within a given society, a particular social practice, institution, etc.[30]

This particularistic aspect of justice is manifest in Rawls' opposition to the globalization of the difference principle in *The Law of Peoples*, but I believe it should also serve as the basis for the rejection of a sweeping attempt to implement relations of justice between generations, a move which Rawls is reluctant to take. I concede that the solidarity we feel towards the coming future generations of our society is much stronger than that we feel towards distant peoples currently living on the globe. But this future-oriented solidarity is of a fairly limited scope. First, it does not extend beyond two or at most three generations; and secondly, we feel solidarity with previous generations of

---

[30] For a detailed elaboration of this view of solidarity, see my (2007) 'Justice and Solidarity: The Contractarian Case against Global Justice', *Journal of Social Philosophy*, 38: 112–30.

our society only in the sense that it has to do with our identity rather than with a commitment to carry out their plans and respect their long-term intentions.

If the principles of justice are the product of a hypothetical contract under ideal conditions, the very requirement to establish just institutions and the scope of application of the principles cannot themselves be a matter of justice.[31] A sense of solidarity may serve as the natural motive for entering into the original position, but what could the normative grounds for the creation and perpetuation of just institutions be? Two options are left open for Rawls. According to the first, there is a *natural duty* to inculcate just institutions for future generations, a duty which precedes contractual relations and is similar to the duty to assist human beings in serious need or to respect human beings as ends. According to the second, just distributions of resources between generations are not a matter of contract-based commitments but of *impartiality*. From an external point of view (e.g. of an omniscient morally neutral divine power, an 'ideal observer', or Hare's Archangel), each generation is entitled to a fair share of world resources across time, regardless of conditions of cooperation (which do not obtain trans-temporally). The point of view of impartiality, in contradistinction to contract-based justice, characterizes, for example, the (*pre*-contract) Lockean proviso, the idea that since the world was created by God for the benefit of all, everyone should leave 'enough and as good' for others. Unlike a contract, which is based on a negotiated agreement between individuals seeking their best interests, impartial judgement is aimed at independently based entitlements or deserts.

Amartya Sen has rightly argued that the model of impartial arbitration is more promising than that of consent in solving the problem of justice between societies and justice between generations.[32] But there is a price to this shift from contractual agreement to neutral judgement, which Rawls, in my view, should consistently avoid, viz., the introduction of some external, impersonal, perspective. Impartiality is a point of view which is not necessarily adopted by everyone, while a contract is the product of the free exercise of everybody's will. By being willing to consider the thought experiment

---

[31] For a sharp way of putting it, see Robert P. Wolff (1977), *Understanding Rawls* (Princeton: Princeton University Press), 96: 'Remember that, in Rawls's model, their [the contractors'] task is not to select a *just* rate of savings, but to *select* a rate of savings that is, under the peculiar knowledge constraints of their situation, rationally self-interested.' Thus, my claim that in the inter- (unlike the intra-) generational sphere, rational choice cannot serve as a sufficient guide for establishing a just distribution of the burdens and benefits of savings.

[32] Amartya Sen, 'Justice across Borders', in Pablo De Greiff and Ciaran Cronin (eds.), (2002), *Global Justice and Transnational Politics* (Cambridge: Cambridge University Press), 45–6. Cf. Barry, *Theories of Justice*, chap. 5. Barry also notices the tension between these two models, leading to different results in the case of justice to future people.

of the original position as an exercise *within* the mind of one person Rawls risks conflating the contract model with the impartiality model, thereby losing the gist of the former and abandoning the social contract tradition which is based on a bargaining between actual individuals (even though admittedly under a veil of ignorance).[33] Impartiality is a much more controversial and value-dependent principle than the fair conditions of cooperation or agreed upon rules of a game. Maybe, above all, the argument against the impartiality interpretation of Rawls' theory of justice is that it undermines the very idea of 'justice as fairness', which is the hallmark of his entire theory. The whole point of grounding justice on fairness is that there is no external, impersonal, impartial, ideal observer's point of view which is independent of the terms of a fair agreement between cooperating individuals. Finally, we should note that despite appearances, impartiality does not take us much further than the idea of a contract in defining the *scope* of the group of the individuals concerned. For impartial judgement must also fix in advance the kind and identity of individuals about whom judgement is made.[34] Between *whom* should we be impartial?

Both alternatives, natural duty and impartiality, ground the requirements of intergenerational justice independently of the exercise of individual wills in the context of social cooperation. They both transcend the idea of justice as fairness in its original sense of an agreement on the fair rules of social cooperation. It seems, therefore, that Rawls must ultimately articulate principles of justice to future generations through the device of a hypothetical contract, or some extension of it, which we have shown to be highly problematic.[35] This does

---

[33] *A Theory of Justice*, 139–40. Rawls believes that the bargaining model of the original position can be disposed with and that the thought experiment can be undertaken by a single individual. This is true only in the sense that an individual can perform the mental experiment on her own, but I believe that the experiment still involves a *virtual* bargain with others, i.e., considering what others would claim. The impartiality model is, in contradistinction, devoid of any bargaining element. Like a Platonic ideal observer (e.g. the philosopher-king) it distributes welfare and deserts according to impersonal principles, regardless of individual wills.

[34] Tim Mulgan has raised the objection that contrary to his methodological requirement of metaphysical neutrality, Rawls adopts as the foundation of his theory a particular Western, individualistic conception of the human person. A Buddhist view of the rebirth of the human soul after the death of the individual could much more easily solve the problem of duties we owe 'future people' since these people are essentially 'us'. Mulgan's point may be valid, but the principle of neutrality which is the object of his criticism is a straw man since *some* basic assumptions about the nature of the 'entities' to which any theory applies must be independently determined. For example, Rawls also assumes that animals are not partners to the original position (or, alternatively, to impartial concern). Is that a violation of the principle of neutrality? Tim Mulgan (2002), 'Neutrality, Rebirth and Intergenerational Justice', *Journal of Applied Philosophy*, 19: 13–15.

[35] My sceptical approach varies from Barry's belief in the possibility of the extension of Rawls' principles of justice to the future. Barry rejects the claim that relations of justice assume reciprocity and interdependence. After criticising both the 'present time of entry' model and the attempt to defend it

not mean that there is no moral justification for saving for future generations. Justice as fairness is itself a primary *value* in the political life of liberal democratic societies, and hence correctly considered to be worthy of dissemination across all societies in the world and of bequest to future generations. Upholding justice might also be deemed a duty. But this duty cannot be a duty *of* justice, or—following the standard distinction between duty and obligation—an obligation.[36] Maintaining a system of justice is arguably a desirable goal for human beings, a social good, even an intrinsic value. But it is not a matter of fairness. Accordingly, we should understand Rawls' term 'the *just* saving principle' as referring to the principle *securing* justice rather than a principle *of* justice.

This conclusion casts light on the widely discussed problems in Rawls' persistent effort to circumvent comprehensive moral views in justifying the principles of justice. Even if justice is 'political, not metaphysical', the commitment to its perpetuation into the future must be 'moral, not political'. The philosophical attempt to extend the scope of justice to future generations exposes the limits of the justification of the idea of justice itself. The conditions of justice include some sense of solidarity, on which all cooperation is based. In that sense, I wish to argue that some weakened version of the 'motivational assumption', which drew much criticism and which Rawls consequently abandoned, is not only necessary for intergenerational justice but is an essential condition for intra-generational, domestic justice as well! But solidarity is a given (or ungiven) fact, and cannot be treated as a duty, or at least not as a duty of justice or an obligation. Thanks to our natural parental feelings towards our progeny and the interest we have in cooperating with the next generation or two due to the so-called generational overlap and to our expectation that they carry on our projects, we usually feel solidarity with the next two generations (of our society). And maybe that is the limit we can expect in the scope of our duties to future people. This may demonstrate that the principles of a moral theory are bounded by the psychological structure of human beings and that

by introducing the motivational assumption, Barry is left with the idea of a universal conference. But he is aware of the difficulties in maintaining the metaphysical assumptions that are necessary for this idea, primarily that of the moral value of the perpetuation of the human species. Brian Barry, 'Justice Between Generations', in P. M. S. Hacker and J. Raz (eds.) (1977), *Law, Morality and Society* (Oxford: Clarendon Press), 276 ff. See also his, 'Circumstances of Justice and Future Generations', in R. I. Sikora and B. Barry (eds.) (1978), *Obligations to Future Generations* (Philadelphia: Temple University Press), 239, where Barry argues that intergenerational justice can apply even when the Humean circumstances of justice do not obtain.

[36] Duty, according to this distinction, is a requirement derived out of a certain position or status (e.g. parent to child, human being as a human being, etc.); obligation is the product of a previous undertaking between people (e.g. a promise, an agreement, etc.).

in the end the relations of justice and fairness which we wish to establish in theory cannot lie beyond the scope of a group of human beings who have either mutual interests or some emotional ties.[37]

References

BARRY, B. (1977), 'Justice Between Generations', in P. M. S. Hacker and J. Raz (eds.), *Law, Morality and Society* (Oxford: Clarendon Press).

—— (1978), 'Circumstances of Justice and Future Generations', in R. I. Sikora and B. Barry (eds.), *Obligations to Future Generations* (Philadelphia: Temple University Press).

—— (1989), *Theories of Justice* (London: Harvester-Wheatsheaf).

ENGLISH, J. (1977), 'Justice Between Generations', *Philosophical Studies*, 31: 91–104.

GOSSERIES, A. (2001), 'What Do We Owe the Next Generation(s)?', *Loyola Los Angeles Law Review*, 35: 293–355.

HEYD, D. (1992), *Genethics: Moral Issues in the Creation of People* (Berkeley: University of California Press).

—— (2007), 'Justice and Solidarity: The Contractarian Case against Global Justice', *Journal of Social Philosophy*, 38: 112–30.

HUBIN, D. Clayton (1976), 'Justice and Future Generations', *Philosophy and Public Affairs*, 6: 70–83.

MULGAN, T. (2002), 'Neutrality, Rebirth and Intergenerational Justice', *Journal of Applied Philosophy*, 19: 3–15.

PADEN, R. (1997), 'Rawls's Just Savings Principle and the Sense of Justice', *Social Theory and Practice*, 23: 27–51.

RAWLS, J. (1971), *A Theory of Justice* (Cambridge: Harvard University Press).

—— (1993), *Political Liberalism* (New York: Columbia University Press).

—— (1999), *The Law of Peoples* (Cambridge, MA.: Harvard University Press).

—— (2001), *Justice as Fairness: A Restatement* (Cambridge, MA.: Harvard University Press).

SEN, A. (2002), 'Justice across Borders', in P. De Greiff and C. Cronin (eds.), *Global Justice and Transnational Politics* (Cambridge: Cambridge University Press).

WOLFF, R. P. (1977), Understanding Rawls (Princeton: Princeton University Press).

---

[37] Consider, as an illustrative thought-experiment, that human beings reproduced like bees: at the moment a new generation is born, the old one dies. Not only do we, present people, not raise our descendants; we do not know what kind of people they are going to be (or, alternatively, we know that they will be exactly like us). Would such a condition be considered as displaying the 'circumstances of justice'? Could we seriously believe that there are relations of (distributive) justice between generations? And even if we want to extend the notion of justice so as to apply even to such a 'fragmented' idea of human existence across time, could this notion of justice be contractual in its nature, as Rawls seeks to establish?

7

A Transgenerational Difference Principle

DANIEL ATTAS

1. The Mutuality Problem

No more than two sections of *A Theory of Justice* are devoted to the important issue of intergenerational justice, and Rawls returns to it in later works only in passing. Nevertheless, one might perceive (perhaps expect) Rawls's theory to be a promising framework for assessing obligations to future generations.

The core of Rawls's method of justification is the original position and its most definitive constraint—the veil of ignorance. While lacking any knowledge about themselves, the participants in the original position choose from a menu of distributive principles according to self-interest alone. That is to say, the motivational assumption in the original position is one of mutual disinterestedness. The veil of ignorance guarantees that the participant in the original position is unaware of her social position, and thus the principle she will choose will be fair towards all social positions. In this sense all social positions are represented in the original position. Since any person in such circumstances will choose the same principles, a sort of 'hypothetical contract' emerges among all persons in society, binding them all. These are the principles of justice that any person will agree to under fair conditions of freedom and equality.

A natural way to broaden Rawls's theory so that it might encompass the intergenerational dimension too, is to extend the veil of ignorance so that participants in the original position shall lack knowledge, not only concerning their social position, but also about the generation to which they belong. Rawls opts for such representation of all generations but insists that participants

For helpful comments I would like to thank Dror Arad-Ayalon, Avner de-Shalit, Axel Gosseries, David Heyd, Lukas Meyer, and an anonymous referee.

$$G_{n-1}$$

	S	¬S
S	2	4
¬S	1	3

G_n (row label)

Figure 7.1

know that they all belong to the same generation. Accordingly, he dubs this decision the 'present time of entry interpretation'. Under this interpretation of the original position, Rawls believes, the participants have no reason to agree on any rate of saving. As long as self-interest is what motivates them, and since their decision to save or not obviously has no bearing on the facts about previous generations' savings, they will prefer not to save.[1]

The neat intragenerational set up hardly applies to the intergenerational situation. The latter can be described as a transitive Prisoner's Dilemma. Generation G_n face previous generation G_{n-1} and deliberate whether to save (S) or not to save (¬S). Since G_n are later in time than G_{n-1}, they know that their choice cannot possibly affect G_{n-1}'s decision to save or to refrain from saving. Assuming G_n is not the first generation to save (an assumption I shall scrutinize later on), their preference matrix is as shown in Figure 7.1.

G_n's first preference is that the previous generation has saved and that they themselves do not; the second preference is that they both save; the third that neither save; and fourth, that the previous generation has not saved but they themselves do. Consequently, not to save is G_n's dominant strategy: since whether G_{n-1} have saved or have not, they would prefer not to save.

But G_{n-1} meet the same kind of situation with respect to the generation preceding them (G_{n-2}); and G_{n+1} face similar circumstances with respect to G_n. The dominant strategy for each and every generation rationally guides them not to save. Such a choice will leave all generations in box 3 which is, for everyone, worse than box 2. In terms of utilities the difference between 2 and 3 is greater as n gets later in time, that is to say as savings are accumulated for a greater number of generations.

Circumstances between two parties exhibit mutuality when each requires the other's cooperation to improve her situation. In such circumstances it makes sense to agree on the terms of cooperation and on the division of

[1] Rawls (1971: 292).

the fruits of cooperation. The intergenerational situation lacks this kind of mutuality. Earlier generations cannot improve their situation by 'cooperating' with later generations. Nothing done in the future can affect their situation in the present. Conversely, future generations depend to an enormous extent on the goodwill of past generations even for their sheer existence. This is not a matter of the mutual unenforceability of obligations. Nor is it merely the fact that generations cannot affect backwards in time the situation of previous generations, though this is a crucial aspect of lack of mutuality. It is primarily due to the fact that generations can neither offer anything to previous generations nor threaten them since they cannot affect them, and they cannot conditionally offer or credibly threaten future generations since they cannot postpone their action until the condition is fulfilled, and anyhow future generations cannot offer them anything in exchange.

Such circumstances, lacking as they do any form of mutuality, leave no room for an agreement or contract. Unless earlier generations want, for whatever reason, to benefit their descendants, no appeal to their own advantage can lead to a commitment that considers their posterity's interest too. This state of things strikes at the foundations of a contract, the only justification of which is the mutual advantage of the parties. The subject of justice in Rawls's theory, and each person's *prima facie* claim to a fair share, are based on the cooperation that generated the social product.[2] Earlier generations can improve the position of later generations, but no degree of effort by the latter could improve the situation of the former. Hence, such 'cooperation' does not work to the mutual advantage of all parties and, as Rawls asserts, the self-interest of each generation is not to save. The absence of mutuality makes the idea of contract extraneous to the intergenerational dimension.

Still, this is a feature of the real world, but it need not be the situation in the original position. If it is required to extend the scope of justice so that it covers relations between generations, then the original position can be reconstructed so as to model relations of mutuality between generations even if these are absent from the real world. The methodological problem we are facing is how to embed mutuality in the original position while avoiding theoretical difficulties or unintuitive implications. We can either directly incorporate mutuality into the original position through the conditions under which choice is made and agreement reached, or introduce some other features that might compensate for this lack of mutuality.

This kind of tinkering with the details of the original position is in line with Rawls's general methodological approach of constructivism. Constructivism is

---

[2] Rawls (1971: 4).

a theory to the effect that a principle, rule, or outcome that emerges from a particular kind of situation, specified by conditions legitimizing moves from such a situation, is to count as just.[3] An *impartiality* constructivist argument is one that characterizes the initial situation and the constraints it imposes in such a way as to ensure that the results of the process will take an equal account of the interests of all.[4] Much of Rawls's discussion on justice between generations in *Theory* and the critical literature that addressed it can be seen as an exercise in constructivism: a way of modifying the initial situation so that principles generated will take adequate account of future generations' interests too.

In what follows I shall trace this exercise—its failures, as well as its more promising avenues (section 2). I shall argue that the initial situation without any further qualifications in favour of future generations already gives their interests sufficient weight to generate a just saving principle. Moreover, the principle that ensues is analogous to the difference principle in its justification and rationale. In fact the just saving rate should be viewed as a clause in the full formulation of the difference principle, extending the intra-generational rationale of the principle to consider and make use of the trans-generational aspect in order to better reflect the interests of the least advantaged (section 3).

2. Reconstructing the Original Position

Taking the present time of entry as the basis, I shall go through the series of proposed modifications to the original position. Each of these is designed to introduce mutuality or a feature that would compensate for the lack of mutuality so that the original position would generate a plausible principle of intergenerational justice.

Features introduced into the original position must meet the following criteria: (1) *coherence*—they must be conceptually coherent; (2) *fairness*—they must be justifiable as a reasonable model of fairness, that is, parties must relate to each other on a free and equal basis; (3) *minimalism*—on the surface they must lack any particular conception of justice or of the good, and they must be minimal in terms of what they assume; (4) *efficacy*—together with a complete specification of the original position, they must be effective in generating a plausible conception of justice.

---

[3] Rawls calls this 'political constructivism' (1996: 89–130). For a lucid and more general discussion of constructivism along similar lines see: Barry (1989: 264–82). For critical discussions of Rawlsian constructivism see: Brink (1989: 303–21), Hill (1992), O'Neill (1989: 206–18).

[4] See Barry (1989: 269).

Table 7.1 summarizes the proposed amendments to the original position according to whether they apply to the knowledge available to the participants, to their motivation, or to some other feature of the full specification of the original position. I shall argue that all but the last of these amendments fail at least one of the criteria spelled out above.

A. Actual representation

The first and most obvious way to introduce mutuality into the original position is by bringing in, as parties to the agreement, all generations and not merely the present generation. I shall follow Hubin in calling this actual representation, taking our cue from Rawls who asks us to 'imagine that the original position contains representatives from all actual generations'.[5] Actual representation is a consequence of the veil of ignorance: constraints on the knowledge accessible to the participant in the original position determine who will be present in the original position. Although Rawls seems to believe that the presence of all generations might solve the problem, he rejects it on the grounds that such a notion is beyond the boundaries of the imagination. Here are the only few sentences he writes opposing such an interpretation:

The original position is not to be thought of as a general assembly which includes at one moment every one who will live at some time; or, much less, as an assembly of every one who could live at some time. It is not a gathering of all actual or possible persons. To conceive of the original position in either of these ways is to stretch fantasy too far; the conception will cease to be a natural guide to intuition.[6]

To take Rawls's argument seriously we should not view it as an appeal to a deficiency of his own personal imaginative powers but as a reference to a conceptual limitation. That is to say, something in the interpretation of the original position as an assembly of either all possible or actual generations is conceptually flawed or incoherent.

Strictly speaking, attendance of all generations isn't a requirement of the theory. Let me explain. The veil of ignorance serves to guarantee two independent goals. The first of these is impartiality. Since they know nothing about their own identity, the participants to the original position cannot take advantage of their superior position in real life to compel others to accept their favoured principle of justice, and they cannot give preference to their

---

[5] Rawls (1971: 291).

[6] Rawls (1971: 139). One might be tempted to say that even an assembly of all living people at one moment is way beyond the power of one's imagination. Indeed it has been claimed that, for a book that is based by and large on fantasy, this is an odd and weak argument. Hare (1973: 242). See also Gosseries (2001: 312).

Table 7.1

	Knowledge/ignorance in original position	Motivation in original position and other constraints	
Present time of entry	Participants know they all belong to the same generation; they don't know to which generation they belong	Mutual disinterest	Rawls in *TJ* thinks there's no solution based on this interpretation. In later works (*PL* and *JAF*) he thinks there is (see below).
a. Actual representation	Participants know that all generations are present; they don't know to which generation they belong	Mutual disinterest	Rawls considers this a bad interpretation of the original position, though it might provide a solution.
b. Amending motivation	Present time of entry	Care for close descendants	Rawls's proposed solution in *TJ*.
c. Supple-menting motiva-tion	Present time of entry + participants know that some people care for their children and grandchildren; they don't know if they are that kind of people	Mutual disinterest	Hubin's proposed solution
d. Assuming the best	Present time of entry + participants know that all generations comply with chosen principle (full compliance)	Mutual disinterest	Solution suggested and discarded by Hubin and English. Endorsed by Rawls in *PL* and *JAF*.
e. Narrowing choice	Present time of entry	Mutual disinterest Formal constraints on principles: uni-versality	My proposed solution.

own interests or that of their relatives in choosing the principles of justice.[7] The goal of impartiality can be described as *representation of interests*, and it is attained in the present time of entry interpretation for both intra-generational and inter-generational dimensions. That is to say, the participant's lack of knowledge regarding his own social position as well as the generation to which he belongs guarantees the representation of interests of all social positions and generations.

The second goal of the veil of ignorance is bindingness. The hypothetical consent in the original position grounds a duty to realise the institutions of justice and to comply with their directives. The veil of ignorance insures that any person taking part in the original position will agree to the same principles of justice and will therefore be bound by them. Within a generation, obliging all members of society to conform to the principles of justice is a vital condition for their realization. The establishment and maintenance of the institutions of justice depend on the cooperation of all people within a society and is therefore conditional on them being bound by the chosen principles. Between generations, however, for the realization of an intergenerational principle of justice (a principle of saving) it is enough to bind the current, saving, generation. Conservation and saving at a just rate depends on the cooperation of all contemporaries, and does not rely on the collaboration of either previous or subsequent generations. This goal can be described as *attendance* at the event of the agreement, or actual representation. In the present time of entry interpretation only the current generation is actually represented. Though they do not know to which generation they belong, those attending and giving their hypothetical agreement know that they are all members of the same generation. This attendance, that is to say this hypothetical agreement, binds them to comply with the principles of justice (the principle of saving included) that will be chosen in the original position.

This distinction helps explain why there is no theoretical need for actual representation of all generations. Since the interests of all generations are represented without it and since only the binding of the current generation is needed for the realisation of a saving principle and therefore only *their* attendance is required. Nevertheless, the attendance of all generations might accomplish the mutuality that the present time of entry interpretation fails to realize. Rawls seems to believe so.[8] In that case, why not make attendance of all generations a feature of the original position? Rawls's answer is phrased in terms of difficulties of the imagination but we should understand it as pointing out a conceptual limitation. Two such problems may be noted.

---

[7] Rawls (1971: 136–7).   [8] Rawls (1971: 291f).

First, from the point of view of the *individual* participant in the original position—she must assume or imagine that she might no longer exist (if she is a member of a past generation) or that she does not exist as yet (if she is a member of a future generation). In other words, actual representation of all generations means that the participant does not know if she exists at all. Such lack of knowledge seems conceptually impossible.

A second difficulty is with the notion of an *assembly* of all generations. Actual representation of all generations is open to two interpretations: an assembly of all actual persons, that is to say of all persons who have ever existed or who will exist in the future; and an assembly of all possible persons, that is to say all those who could exist under alternative scenarios including all actual persons. The former interpretation produces a paradox: the number of people that will actually exist and their identity depends on the principles of justice that will be chosen and agreed upon at the assembly.[9] It is therefore impossible to form a clear idea of an assembly of all actual persons independently of the principles of justice that are chosen and agreed to by such an assembly. Though we might be able to form a clearer idea of an assembly of all possible persons, presumably a function of all possible principles of justice, this makes an agreement at such an assembly highly improbable. Given that the principles chosen will determine the issue of existence of those attending, at least some will have to agree to their non-existence.

Actual representation of all generations in the original position is theoretically superfluous and conceptually strained. Yet Rawls and others believe that such representation could generate a just saving principle from the original position. Some of his commentators simply could not figure out why Rawls might insist on the present time of entry interpretation.[10]

All the same, even if we ignore the theoretical difficulties spelled out above and allow actual representation of all generations, a plausible principle of saving cannot be deduced from the original position. Whatever form an assembly in which all generations attend or are actually represented takes,[11] participants in the assembly know that, though negotiation is possible, the past is fixed and

---

[9]   This is known as 'the non-identity problem' Parfit (1984: 351−79). See also Hubin (1976/7: 74).

[10]   Barry (1977: 278), Hare (1973: 243), English (1977: 99).

[11]   Such an assembly could be thought of as super-temporal, a-temporal, or temporal: In the super-temporal assembly each participant remains fixed in his own time. Somehow the parties manage to overcome the time barrier and to bargain with past and future generations. The a-temporal assembly takes place off time. To attend the assembly the participants must leave their own time and negotiate with members of all generations at a rendezvous outside of any time. The temporal assembly takes place at a particular point in time—the present. The spirits of past and future generations are summoned to participate in the assembly that takes the form of a mass-séance. Everyone knows that the year is 2005, but no one knows if they are living, not yet, or no longer alive.

unchangeable. In particular the rate of saving at which previous generations have already saved cannot be altered at this assembly. Hence the rational choice for each generation in the multi-generational assembly interpretation is not to save.

The attempt to endow the intergenerational situation the mutuality that it lacks by widening the basis of participation in the 'constitutional assembly' has led to a cul-de-sac. This is hardly surprising since the notion of an assembly or contract is no more than a rhetorical device, a metaphor that serves to bring to life, to graphically represent, the idea of consent. In a sense, the didactic apparatus has taken a life of its own, displacing the idea it was meant to represent.[12] Reconstructing the original position by assuming the attendance of all generations fails two of the criteria that features of the original position must meet: coherence and efficacy. The idea of an assembly of all actual or possible generations is conceptually incoherent and fails to establish any kind of plausible principle of intergenerational justice.

B. Amending the motivational assumption

The absence of mutuality between generations poses an insurmountable problem to any contractarian theory that aims to ground obligations on the idea of mutual advantage. The earlier generation, not vulnerable to choices and activities of the later generation, might be tempted to consume the entire social product—no rate of saving would be to its advantage. Rawls attempts to remedy the situation by endowing the earlier generation with a feature that would reduce the effect of its invulnerability. He proposes to modify the motivational assumption.

In the original position, as initially constructed, the participants' motivation is characterized as mutual disinterest. That is pure self-interest, lacking envy, jealousy or spite; empathy, care or other concern for others. The parties to the original position want to improve only their own situation, and they choose the principles of justice most likely to promote it.[13]

In the intergenerational dimension Rawls changes the motivational assumption so that the participants' motivation includes not only the advancement of their own interests but also that of their immediate descendants (children and grandchildren). This, Rawls says, is a natural assumption.[14] If the earlier generation is motivated not only by their own interests, but also by that of

---

[12] Brian Barry (1978: 234) has forcefully criticized Rawls for conflating two kinds of theory: contractarianism as a theory of rational cooperation based on mutual vulnerability, and a theory of hypothetical consent designed to achieve impartiality.
[13] Rawls (1971: 146).   [14] Ibid.

later generations, the effect of their invulnerability is successfully defused, and they would presumably adopt a principle of positive saving.

The modification proposed by Rawls to the motivational assumption in the intergenerational context was the target of much criticism. Jane English, for example, raises against the new motivational assumption the same arguments that Rawls himself put against assuming benevolence.[15] Rawls prefers the motivational assumption of mutual disinterest to benevolence and to achieve the required impartiality with the assistance of the veil of ignorance. He gives two reasons for this choice: the concept of benevolence is too complex and thus ineffective as a component of a theory; and more important, postulating benevolence will weaken the general argument for the principles of justice by grounding them on such a strong condition.[16]

These arguments hold just as well when they are brought up against the motivational modification in the intergenerational dimension. Firstly, one must specify the degree of generosity, or benevolence, that the current generation feels towards its descendants. Do the descendants' interests carry the same weight in their motivation as does the current generation's own interest? If not, what is the relative strength of each in the motivation? Any answer to these questions is likely to be complicated and open to objections. Secondly, the power of Rawls's argument lies in the weakness of the conditions stipulated in the original position—not benevolence, but mutual disinterest. Similarly, if Rawls wants to ground principles of justice between generations, the argument for whatever principles he would espouse will be stronger the less it assumes in terms of concern the parties have for each other—for those with whom they will be required to share the benefits. Just as he would not assume in the intra-generational sphere that people are altruistic and are concerned with the interests of their contemporaries, so he should not assume that one generation is concerned about the interests of another when seeking to ground an intergenerational principle of justice.

A second crucial point is made by Brian Barry. He claims that the modification proposed by Rawls to the motivational assumption is ad hoc: the change is circularly justified by the result that follows from it. Indeed, this is taking the methodology of reflective equilibrium somewhat too far.

The only justification offered for the 'motivational assumption' is that it enables Rawls to derive obligations to future generations. But surely this is a little too easy, like a conjurer putting a rabbit in a hat, taking it out again and expecting a round of applause.[17]

---

[15] English (1977: 92–3).   [16] Rawls (1971: 148–9).   [17] Barry (1977: 279).

As he proceeds to explain, the idea inherent in 'justice as fairness' is to take people motivated solely by self interest and to place them in the original position, thus compelling them to choose impartial and universal principles of justice. In the intergenerational dimension, the affection we naturally feel toward our descendants is tossed into the justice-as-fairness processing machine, and it emerges stamped and approved as an obligation of justice.

Thirdly, Rawls aims to present a theory of justice that is neutral with respect to conceptions of the good. But here he inadvertently introduces into the theory an idea about the good. That is the concept of the family—if the natural care and concern for one's immediate descendants is a legitimate assumption of the theory, why not include also the care for one's tribe, nation, class, religion, and so on and so forth?

Amending the motivational assumption in the way proposed by Rawls fails the criterion of minimalism: it is not neutral with respect to the good, it already supposes some conception of justice, and it makes a more demanding assumption about human beings.

C. *Supplementing a psychological assumption*

In light of objections such as these, Clayton Hubin proposes to dismiss the modified motivational assumption and argues instead for the adoption of, what he calls, the psychological assumption. The motivation of the participants in the original position continues to be self-interest, but among the general knowledge they have, there is an assumption about the psychology of human beings: according to this assumption, the real interests of people generally include, in addition to their own welfare, also the welfare of their close descendants—children and grandchildren.[18]

With this psychological truth and with the thought that, once unveiled of their ignorance, they might discover themselves to be parents to children, the parties to the original position will agree to a principle of saving that establishes obligations with respect to future generations. The representative person does not know if he cares about his children and theirs, indeed he doesn't even know if he has children at all, but assuming the 'worst case' scenario (he has children, and he cares for their welfare), he is guided by the maximin principle of choice to choose a principle of just saving. The ensuing principle of justice is in fact an intra-generational principle—it grounds an obligation towards members of the current generation (parents who care) with respect to future generations.

---

[18] Hubin (1976/7: 81).

The parties to the original position, according to Hubin, are still motivated by self-interest alone. Thus, as far as the motivation is concerned, the condition upon which the saving principle is grounded remains weak. Moreover, the psychological assumption is not a stipulation on universal human nature—it does not assert that all people care for the welfare of their descendants. It is the much weaker claim that most persons in the society in which we live care for their children and grandchildren. The role of this assumption within the theory is not as a constraint on the emotional makeup of mankind, but a component of the general knowledge the participants in the original position have of the society in which they live.

In response to the question 'ought there be saving?' there is no direct reliance on the *desire* to save. Rawls's modification of the motivational assumption made a claim about every person (in the original position)—the assertion that he is motivated *inter alia* by the interests of the next generation—and on the basis of this desire an obligation towards future generation was inferred. Conversely, Hubin's psychological assumption highlights an empirical fact about some people; a fact that need not apply even to most people. The mechanism of the original position is responsible for the transformation of a psychological truth about some people—that the welfare of their children forms part of their interests—to an obligation that binds every person and hence society as a whole. In this sense, the psychological assumption is a weaker condition, making more modest claims than Rawls's amended motivational assumption (thus making a sounder argument for a principle of saving). In contrast to Rawls, Hubin seems to take more out of the hat than he put in.

We might hold a different view if we examine how the answer to the question 'how much to save?' is determined. The answer ultimately depends on the degree to which we identify the welfare of our descendants with our own interests. How much to save on Rawls's formulation depends on the relative weight the succeeding generation's interests has in our motivation; how much to save on Hubin's formulation depends on the relative weight the succeeding generation's welfare might have in our interests. In other words: how much to save? As much as we might want! No morally constrained procedure—such as agreement among free and equals, impartiality, and so on—sets the just rate of saving. Nothing more than the desire that some of the least advantaged happen to have to benefit their own children determines the quantitative aspect of the obligation to save. Thus Hubin's proposal to assume a certain common motivation fails to meet the efficacy criterion: the principle of saving it can generate is implausible as a conception of intergenerational justice.

D. *Assuming the best*

A moral solution to prisoner's dilemma situations is the Kantian solution of universalization—the agent must choose as if he is choosing for everyone. A decision according to such a rule reduces the preference matrix to just two boxes: 2—all generations save, and 3—all generations do not save. When these are the circumstances the rational choice is to save.

However, the rationality of the participants in the original position is the simple economic conception of maximizing self-interest. In circumstances such as the intergenerational situation, lacking mutuality, they would not choose to universalize. Modifying the conception of rationality to achieve the required mutuality would be to base the argument on too strong a premise violating the minimalism criterion. Instead two other options for incorporating universalization in the original position may be found within Rawls's theory.

The first of these is the condition of full or strict compliance. This is a constraint on the knowledge about the world available to the participants in the original position.

> The parties can rely on each other to understand and to act in accordance with whatever principles are finally agreed to. Once principles are acknowledged the parties can depend on one another to conform to them. In reaching an agreement, then, they know that their undertaking is not in vain: their capacity for a sense of justice insures that the principles chosen will be respected … Thus in assessing conceptions of justice *the persons in the original position are to assume that the one they adopt will be strictly complied with.* The consequences of their agreement are to be worked out on this basis.[19]

The parties 'know', that is to say they should assume, that the principle of distribution they will choose in the imaginary original position will be strictly complied with in the real world. They should consider the consequences of full compliance when they choose the just principle of distribution (or principle of saving). In the intergenerational sphere this may be thus interpreted: the current generation—the one that participates in the original position under the present time of entry interpretation—know that previous generations have either saved or have not. But when deciding whether saving should be required of them or not, they should consider the consequences of full compliance of all generations, past and future, to the chosen principle—saving by all generations or dis-saving by all generations. When this is the choice, maximizing rationality will guide them to choose saving, and at a rate of saving that would be the most advantageous to the current generation on the assumption of full compliance.

---

[19] Rawls (1971: 145, italics added).

No doubt full compliance is an unrealistic assumption in the intergenerational context and, therefore, might be considered implausible. But no more implausible than in the intragenerational context. Moreover, its unrealistic quality is consistent with Rawls's insistence on working out the principles of ideal theory prior to addressing problems of application in more realistic circumstances that include non-compliance.

In light of this, describing the choice situation for a principle of saving on the assumption of full compliance seems a promising method for incorporating a universalizing trait into a Rawlsian theory of justice between generations and introducing mutuality into the original position. Hubin, though he does not develop this thought, suggests that strict compliance as a constraint on the knowledge available to the participants in the original position will result in the acceptance of a principle of saving.[20] English too believes that full or strict compliance will generate a just savings principle without the need to modify the motivation assumption. But she rejects this way of proceeding on the grounds that intergenerational justice ought to be based on non-ideal theory where the assumption of full compliance does not apply.[21] Rawls himself appears to have accepted this solution in his later works. Yet relying upon full compliance becomes hardly passable once the justification of the constraint and the persons to whom it applies are examined. Rawls's purpose of introducing the condition of full compliance is not to assure mutuality or any kind of symmetry in the original position, but to guarantee the utility of participating in the original position.[22] The participants in the original position know that their counterparts are fair, that they are endowed with a sense of justice, and that they will comply with the principles that will be chosen and agreed to, whatever they may be. The constraint of full compliance directs the participants to choose a principle that everyone could comply with, that would not be self-defeating in practice. But it primarily relieves them from the worry about circumstances in which collective compliance with a principle might be best for everyone, but individual non-compliance might be better for the defiant individual. The same reasoning made by each and every individual would lead to general non-compliance and would turn futile the whole project. Guaranteeing full compliance of *all those who are parties to the original position* solves this free-rider problem and makes participation worthwhile. But the problem in the intergenerational context is that under the present time of entry interpretation this includes *the current generation alone*.[23] That is to say,

---

[20] Hubin (1976/7: 74–5).   [21] English (1977: 98).   [22] Rawls (1971: 145) quoted above.
[23] By this I mean the generation to which the parties to the original position belong, not necessarily our generation.

only the cooperation and compliance of the present participating generation is assured. Thus, even with the condition of full compliance (by the present generation) the rational choice in the original position—a choice that will neither bind previous generations nor affect their choices—remains not to save. The condition of full compliance as a means to introduce mutuality into the original position fails the efficacy criterion—it is not effective in generating a plausible principle of saving.

E. *Narrowing choice*

A second option for incorporating universalization in the original position is the formal constraint of universality. Together with the other formal constraints of generality and publicity, it limits the range of principles from which the parties to the original position must choose the principles of justice.

> Principles are to be universal in application. They must hold for everyone in virtue of their being moral persons. A principle is to be ruled out if it would be self-contradictory, or self-defeating, for everyone to act upon it. Similarly, should a principle be reasonable to follow only when others conform to a different one, it is also inadmissible. Principles are to be chosen in view of the consequences of everyone's complying with them.[24]

The list of principles of justice available to the parties in the original position, the list from which they must choose, is narrowed down by the constraint of universality. To qualify for the list the principle must apply universally to every moral person as such, and it must be thought worthwhile to follow only on the condition that everyone follows the same principle. The application of this constraint to the intergenerational sphere is clear: a policy of dis-saving will be self-beneficial only on the condition that previous generations have followed a policy of saving. If we are to assume that all generations follow the same principle, the choice of saving is the most expedient.[25]

Subjecting the list of principles to the constraint of universality is designed to attain mutuality in the original position. The principles of justice ought to be chosen and agreed upon under circumstances of mutuality, constructed in conformity with the criterion of fairness. Equality and freedom are provided by the veil of ignorance. In the intergenerational context, under the present time of entry interpretation, this includes not knowing to which generation one belongs. Only with the introduction of universality as a formal constraint on principles does this become sufficient to guarantee mutuality.[26] The principles

---

[24] Rawls (1971: 132).
[25] Rawls points out that the formal constraints rule out all forms of egoism (1971: 136). In the intergenerational context we can say that it rules out 'generational egoism'.
[26] Rawls (2001: 86).

chosen in circumstances modelling fairness such as these would hold just as well in the real world, where mutuality might not exist. This is precisely the constructivist idea of the mechanism of the original position. This way more is drawn out of the hat than was put into it beforehand: the person motivated by self-interest alone, under conditions modelling mutuality, will rationally choose just principles of distribution and saving.

Let me summarize the main differences between the condition of universality and the condition of full compliance. First, full compliance is a constraint on the *knowledge* available in the original position; universality is a constraint on the available principles on the *menu* from which the participants are to choose. Second, full compliance is aimed at relieving the participants to the original position of the worry that a *free-rider problem* would make their participation futile; the point of universality and other formal constraints (like that of the veil of ignorance) is to achieve the required *symmetry*, of free and equal status, among participants to the original position. Third, to achieve its stated purpose, full compliance need only apply to those who are *bound* by the agreement (under present time of entry this includes the present generation alone); to realize its goal universality must apply to those whose interests ought to be *represented* (this includes all generations).

In *Theory* Rawls does not proceed along the lines of justifying a saving principle on the basis of either one of the universalizing constraints. He introduces instead a modification in the motivation of the parties to the original position. Only in later works does Rawls take on board this idea, which he attributes to Nagel and Parfit.[27] It remains quite baffling how such a simple idea could have been missed by Rawls in the first place. It doesn't become more comprehensible when we come across the following allusion in *Theory* to this universalizing constraint:

Thus the persons in the original position are to ask themselves how much they would be willing to save at each stage of advance *on the assumption that all other generations are to save at the same rates.*[28]

It might be objected that I have ignored in the discussion so far the crucial problem of the first generation. Going back to the prisoner's dilemma modelling of the intergenerational situation, the matrix presented at the beginning of this paper does not represent the preferences of the first generation. Since there is no generation preceding it that could save, improve its position, and make saving worthwhile, the first generation has no incentive to choose saving. Since participants in the original position do not know to which

---

[27] Rawls (1996: 274n; 2001: 160n).   [28] Rawls (1971: 287, italics added).

generation they belong—specifically they can't be sure that they are not the first generation—assuming the worst, as maximin guides them to do, they would choose not to save, universality notwithstanding.

Now, on a practical level this problem seems to me very much contrived. The concept of a first generation, involving as it must a theological idea of creation, appears more suited to mythology than to philosophy. Yet even if we accept the idea that there must have been a first generation, whose interests and preferences are not captured by the prisoner's dilemma matrix, it is far from clear what relevance this has for 'you and me, here and now'. We know with certainty that we are not the first generation, that there is not a single living person among us who has known a member of the first generation, or has a second-order acquaintance with members of the first generation. The same holds for the first generation to have saved, or the first generation to have saved some of what they had discovered or produced. It needs a fair amount of mendaciousness to pretend that we cannot reach an agreement in the original position since, for all we know, we might be the first generation or the first to have saved.

But beyond these pragmatic concerns there is a further theoretical reason to disregard the problem of the first generation. Assume that we are the first generation to have saved or to have considered saving, that all previous generations have not saved. The problem we are facing is the losses that we will endure in moving from a no-saving unjust situation to a presumably just situation that involves some saving. This is a typical question of transitional justice of which Rawls says 'are covered by non-ideal theory and not by the principles of justice for a well-ordered society'.[29] In other words, the hypothetical possibility that we are the first to abide by the principles of justice has no bearing on the question of what these principles might be. Where we happen to be situated in the long succession of generations is a morally irrelevant fact about the world. The original position generates a duty to save on the assumption that all generations save following the same principle whether or not previous generations have in fact done so.

3. Generating a Just Saving Principle

A. *Rawls's principle of just saving*

Participants in the original position situated behind a veil of ignorance lack knowledge as to what social position and what generation they belong, though

---

[29] Rawls (1996: 18).

they know they all belong to the same generation (present time of entry). They also know that they are choosing principles to be followed by all generations and not merely their own (universality constraint). Motivated by their own interest alone (mutual disinterest), what kind of principle of justice between generations would they choose? Aiming (among other things) to receive as much income and wealth as possible, the particular circumstances of the original position make maximin the most reasonable principle of choice.[30] The participants choose a principle that would set the degree of inequality and the rate of saving such as to maximize the expectations of the least advantaged within a generation.

Inequality affects consumption of the least advantaged (C) in two opposing ways. On the one hand, a greater degree of inequality can raise the *productivity* of society due to, among other factors, the incentive structure, thus increasing the total wealth available for distribution. Hence, the degree of inequality can *positively* affect C. On the other hand, a greater degree of inequality will increase the funds forgone for the sake of compensating the talented, thus reducing the share of the total product accruing to the least advantaged. Hence the degree of inequality can *negatively* affect consumption. In other words consumption increases as a function of inequality until a maximum is reached where it begins to decrease.

Saving affects consumption of the least advantaged (C) in two opposing ways. On the one hand, a higher rate of saving undertaken, particularly by previous generations, will increase both the *initial capital*, the total wealth in terms of machines, material, buildings, and so on, that G_n inherits, and the *growth factor*, a function of the level of technology, scientific knowledge, methods of production and division of labour that were developed or preserved and passed on to G_n from preceding generations. Assuming the distributive pattern within the generation remains unchanged, the rate of saving can thus *positively* affect C. On the other hand, a higher rate of saving undertaken, particularly by the current generation, will increase the total wealth that G_n bequeaths to the next generation, thus reducing the amount remaining for their own consumption, and that of the least advantaged in particular. Thus the rate of saving can *negatively* affect C. In other words C increases as a function of saving until a maximum is reached, beyond which it decreases.

The parties to the original position aim to maximize C within the constraints of the veil of ignorance and universality. The *just degree of inequality* is that which maximizes consumption for the worst off. That is the degree of inequality

---

[30] This is of course a contentious issue famously criticized by Harsanyi (1975) and more recently by Roemer (2002). For a defence see Rawls (1974; 2001: 97–100).

that would be set by the principle chosen in the original position. The *optimal rate of saving* is that which (undertaken by both by G_n and G_{n-1})[31] maximizes consumption for the worst off of G_n.

The choice in the original position is a maximin optimizing choice—intragenerationally, not knowing to which social position one belongs, maximizing the expectations of the least advantaged whoever they may turn out to be; inter-generationally, knowing that one belongs to the current generation, a rate of saving that when applied to all generations optimizes income for the *current* least advantaged is chosen. This is not prioritarianism of generations, but prioritarianism *over* generations. The focus of our concern remains the least advantaged of the current generation. But we take the synchronic (distributive) dimension as well as the diachronic (saving) dimension as means to the improvement of their position. Rather than two separate principles, in effect just one principle with two dimensions: it is in this sense a *trans*-generational difference principle.

I have so far entirely ignored what is perhaps the central aspect of Rawls's conception of justice between generations. It is the idea that saving is only required up to a certain level and for a certain purpose. The purpose is to provide the material base necessary to establish and to maintain institutions of justice over generations. Moreover, saving from one generation to the next beyond that point, indefinitely raising the material standard of living of all, including that of the least advantaged, is not only unnecessary but might well be damaging.

Justice does not require that early generations save so that later ones are simply more wealthy. Saving is demanded as a condition of bringing about the full realization of just institutions and the fair value of liberty. If additional accumulation is to be undertaken, it is for other reasons. It is a mistake to believe that a just and good society must wait upon a high material standard of life ... In fact beyond some point it is more likely to be a positive hindrance, a meaningless distraction at best if not a temptation to indulgence and emptiness.[32]

Rawls endorses in effect a two-stage conception of justice between generations.[33] A first stage of accumulation where the burden of setting up the material base required for the establishment and maintenance of just institutions is fairly shared among the various generations; and a steady-state stage where no more saving is required.

---

[31] 'In attempting to estimate the fair rate of saving the persons in the original position ask what is reasonable for members of *adjacent* generations to expect of one another at each level of advance'. Rawls (1971: 289, italics added).

[32] Rawls (1971: 290).   [33] Gosseries (2001: 311–7).

Rawls's two-stage principle of saving raises at least two difficult problems: (1) *the derivation problem*—how can the construction of the original position as set out above, based on mutual disinterest and universality (or full compliance) generate the two-stage principle Rawls ends up endorsing? (2) *the inconsistency problem*—the requirement of saving at the accumulation stage seems to conflict with the difference principle. How can this be justified or how can this apparent conflict be resolved? I shall first introduce the problems and how they were addressed by commentators, and then present my own proposal for a resolution.

B. *The derivation problem*

Rawls's argument for saving at the accumulation stage, the argument from full compliance (or universality), is based on the self-interested motivation of the participants in the original position. It is thus informed by a notion of saving for the material benefit of future generations. But as we have seen, Rawls denies that the saving principle requires this. Its only goal is the establishment and maintenance of just institutions, which is why once a sufficient level is reached no more saving is required, even though it would still be conceivable that more saving will continue to benefit future generations. Thus, as Roger Paden points out, the self-interested reasoning for the first accumulation stage is at odds with the justice-motivated reasoning for the second steady-state stage and with the entire rationale for saving. Paden urges us to abandon the just saving principle that would be adopted by the participants in the original position aiming to maximize the long run expectations over generations. Instead, both stages of the saving principle should be based on a sense of justice rather than on a self-interested motivation.[34]

One problem with Paden's interpretation is that Rawls does not introduce a sense of justice as a motivation *in the original position*. The parties are not expected to choose the principles of justice that would most fit their sense of justice. It is introduced as an assumption about *the real world*, as a piece of knowledge available to original position participants so that they can be assured that their project is not in vain. Real people outside the original position will act according to duty even if it might not be in their self-interest. As Rawls puts it: 'In reaching an agreement, then, they know that their undertaking is not in vain: their capacity for a sense of justice insures that the principles chosen will be respected'.[35] Secondly, it is difficult to see what kind of saving principle substantively could follow from a sense of justice; if,

---

[34] Paden (1997: 39, 41 ff.).   [35] Rawls (1971: 145); See also (1993: 315–6).

that is to say, the introduction of a sense of justice is supposed to convey anything more than the idea that, whatever principle would be accepted, a sense of justice will guarantee that it is complied with. Moreover, to introduce non-self-interested motivations such as this in the original position weakens the general argument. This is why Rawls was criticized for adjusting his motivational assumption and why he ultimately rejected it in favour of the full compliance assumption. Finally, the saving principle based on full compliance (or universality) seems to be Rawls's considered opinion. He adopts it in *Political Liberalism* and then reaffirms it in *Justice as Fairness*. It is an embarrassing consequence of Paden's interpretation that such a central position for Rawls, a position he pronounces repeatedly, has to be discarded for the sake of consistency.

Steven Wall argues for the opposite conclusion. Rawls affirms a weighted-prioritarian saving principle, that is to say, a principle that gives a certain rather than an absolute priority to the worse off so that sufficient gains for those who are better off might justify the worst off ending up in a position slightly below the maximum they could possibly hope for. Thus future generations will be made much better if only the members of the present generation, the least favoured included, will undertake a slight sacrifice. This according to Wall must be the rationale for saving at the accumulation stage.

On this supposition, Rawls's claim that justice never requires saving beyond the basic level is almost certainly false. A savings schedule that complies with the [weighted] prioritarian savings principle will sometimes require earlier generations to make sacrifices beyond that specified by the basic level. This will be true in cases … where a small sacrifice could lead to substantial benefit for later generations.[36]

If this is the kind of thinking that leads to the adoption of a savings principle then a steady-state, no saving, stage is incompatible with the reasoning of the original position. Since future generations could often be made better with a slight sacrifice to the present generation, why would saving ever stop? Participants in the original position will choose to continue saving indefinitely under such circumstances. It is indeed difficult to see why, behind the veil of ignorance, motivated by a desire to maximize their material benefits, participants would choose a saving principle that comes to a halt. But again this plainly contradicts Rawls's insistence that the only purpose of saving is enabling the establishment and maintenance of just institutions.

Paden and Wall agree on the following: self-interested motivation (together with full compliance) cannot generate the two-stage principle of saving. They

---

[36] Wall (2003: 88).

diverge in their proposed solutions: either reject the self-interested construction of the original position in favour of a justice-oriented motivation; or reject the two-stage principle in favour of indefinite accumulation. Both solutions are at odds with what seems to be Rawls's established view.

C. The inconsistency problem

According to Paden, saving, as required by the just saving principle, must be borne by the earlier less well-off generation. This appears contrary to the requirements of the difference principle to maximally improve the position of the least advantaged.

> ... the just savings principle requires that money be diverted from immediate consumption (specifically from the funds that a just society would otherwise reserve to raise the income level of the least well-off) to support the creation and long-term stability of a just social structure.[37]

Paden proposes to view the relation between the two principles such that the just savings principle has priority over the difference principle (though not over the principles of equal liberty and fair equality of opportunity). Saving is required during the accumulation stage, contrary to the dictates of the difference principle, but only until the point that justice can be instituted and maintained. Beyond that, saving for reasons other than justice is permitted but no longer required.

Axel Gosseries agrees that the concern for achieving justice that informs the just savings principle at the accumulation stage overrides the concern for the position of the worst off of the present generation that is at the basis of the difference principle. However, he convincingly argues, once we enter the steady-state stage, institutions of justice are well established and maintained, further improvements in the position of future generations can no longer be permitted since they conflict with priority for the intergenerational worst off—that is to say, the worst off of the earlier generation. So contrary to Rawls's explicit view, further savings at the steady state stage are not only not required, they are not even permitted.[38]

Steven Wall too identifies a conflict between the absolute-prioritarian difference principle (interpreted as giving absolute priority to the least advantaged), and the weighted-prioritarian savings principle (understood as giving weighted priority to the least advantaged, so that a small sacrifice might be outweighed by a greater gain to some who are better off).[39] A savings principle under

---

[37] Paden (1997: 35).   [38] Gosseries (2001: 325–7).
[39] Somewhat confusingly Wall terms these 'egalitarian' and 'prioritarian' respectively.

Table 7.2

	Plan I	Plan II
G_n	(10, 15, 20)	(9, 14, 18)
G_{n+1}	(10, 15, 20)	(13, 18, 22)

typical assumptions of growth will be inconsistent with an absolute concern for the intergenerational least advantaged.

Wall conveniently provides a numerical example. Say we have a choice between two plans. Under Plan I no saving is undertaken. The benefits of the various social positions remain the same over generations. Under Plan II, saving undertaken by the earlier generation (G_n) slightly reduces the benefits to all social positions, the least advantaged in particular, of a greater benefit to all social positions of the later generation (G_{n+1}), the least advantaged in particular. This is shown in Table 7.2.

Plan II should be preferred according to Wall because of a principle of weighted-prioritarianism that must lie at the basis a just savings principle. But this contradicts absolute-prioritarianism that could not permit the sacrifice made by the least advantaged of G_n.[40] Wall proposes to unify Rawls's theory by reinterpreting the difference principle as a weighted priority rule. He maintains that in practice, weighted priority and absolute priority coincide within a generation. But if we take the intergenerational view, absolute priority will not permit any saving at all, and so Rawls's endorsement of a savings principle must reveal his true commitment to weighted prioritarianism.

Paden, Gosseries, and Wall are in agreement on at least one point: there is some tension within Rawls's theory between the intragenerational and the intergenerational aspects, i.e. between the difference principle and the savings principle. The numerical example provided by Wall exemplifies the kind of inconsistency they envisage: any saving undertaken for the sake of the least advantaged of later generations would be at the expense of the less well off least advantaged of earlier generations. Paden and Gosseries propose to explain this conflict by reference to a priority of justice over the difference principle; Wall proposes to reinterpret the difference principle and Rawls's general prioritarian conception. Paden and Gosseries are led to deny the permissibility of saving at the steady state stage; Wall's proposal constitutes a radical revision of the difference principle. Both seem at odds with Rawls's stated views.

---

[40] Wall (2003: 84).

D. *Resolving the problems*

I shall address the inconsistency problem first. Plan II, possibly sanctioned by the savings principle, is thought by Rawls's critics to violate the difference principle because it fails to maximize the position of the least advantaged group within the current generation. Without savings the situation of the least advantaged would be better, thus saving appears to contradict the maximin rationale at the basis of the difference principle. There are two points one could make in response.

First, at least under an interpretation I want to offer here, Plan II does not violate the difference principle. The focus of the difference principle, its subject, so to speak, is the inequalities it sanctions, permits, or forbids. It is not the expectations of the least advantaged. These are merely a test for the justifiability of the inequality. In elaborating the meaning and significance of the difference principle Rawls writes: 'the *inequality* in expectations is permissible only if lowering it would make the working class even more worse off'.[41] Thus it requires limiting inequalities to a degree that benefits the worst off. A greater inequality that would fail to improve or at least if it worsens the position of the least advantaged would be unacceptable.

The difference principle does not require, however, maximally benefiting the worst off by means other than distribution. It is not a principle of efficiency. The length of a normal working day, for example, is not set by the difference principle. Using natural resources and labour productively is not a concern of justice. Nor are the better off obliged to work even harder than they do merely because this might further improve the position of the worst off,[42] and an inefficient economy is not as such unjust. All the principle says is that to the extent that productivity and raising material well being are desired by a society, they may harness incentive-generating inequalities up to the point where those who are expected to gain least are maximally benefited.

To be sure, the effect of saving is to shift down the expectations curve as a function of inequality. Thus everyone, the least advantaged included, will get less than they could if they were not to save. But this says nothing about how unequal the distribution is. So the fact the intra-generational least advantaged get less under Plan II than they get under Plan I is not, by itself, sufficient to show that the difference principle is violated. If saving does not upset the inequality, making the distribution within the generation more unequal, then saving does not violate the difference principle. The distribution of benefits under Plan II appears in fact more equal, on most measures, than Plan I.

---

[41] Rawls (1971: 78).
[42] For an opposing view see Cohen (1992; 1995; 1997). Cf. Williams (1998).

Of course, this might be an accidental property of an arbitrary numerical example. Yet we can generalize that so long as the burden of saving falls proportionately across all social positions, or if the more advantaged bear a greater burden, saving-tax is progressively instituted, so that the better off forgo a larger proportion of their income than the worse off, the result of saving will be a more equal intra-generational distribution *ipso facto* consistent with the requirements of the difference principle.

The second point in response to the claim that saving conflicts with the difference principle draws attention to the fact that the income of the least advantaged of the current generation is the result of saving undertaken by previous generations. So their '9' under Plan II is more than it would have been had no saving taken place at all. In other words, taking a continuous diachronic point of view rather than a snapshot synchronic perspective, saving in fact *improves* the position of the worst off further to the benefits they derive from the intra-generational inequality. Thus, even on the maximinimizing understanding of the difference principle (implicitly assumed by Paden, Gosseries, and Wall) it need not be violated by the application of a just savings principle.

I turn now to address the derivation problem. Should we reject the self-interested construction of the original position in favour of a justice-oriented motivation, or should we rather reject the two-stage principle in favour of a principle of indefinite accumulation? I shall argue that neither is necessary. A two-stage principle of justice can be derived from the original position under the present time of entry interpretation with the constraint of universality and on the basis of the participants' self-interested motivation. To see how this may be done I shall draw attention to some further aspects of Rawls's theory, specifically to the primary good of self-respect, and to the possibility of a moderate non-materialistic conception of the good. Moreover, I shall argue that the two-stage configuration of the trans-generational difference principle applies not only to the diachronic saving aspect of the principle but also to its synchronic inequality aspect.

If their own income and wealth are not what motivates participants in the original position, then not only would saving be required merely to the point necessary for the establishment of justice, but it would also be unclear how *inequality* within a generation beyond that point may be required by justice even though it might raise the material well-being of the least advantaged. That is to say, the same rationale that justifies saving for establishing justice and not simply to raise the standard of living indefinitely should also apply to the intra-generational principle so that inequalities too would not be justified by a maximinimizing fervour but only by the need to establish and maintain just institutions. If participants to the original position *are* motivated by income and wealth then not only would they permit any inequality that optimizes their (the least advantaged) income, but also they would permit an ever increasing rate of saving perpetually so long as this optimizes their trans-generational income. That is to say, participants in the original position do not have split personalities. Their motivation must be identical whether applied to the issue of intra-generational distribution, or to the issue of savings.

To see how reference to self-respect might be helpful in generating a two-stage principle we should look at Rawls's argument for the priority of liberty. Rawls says that 'the most important primary good is that of self respect'.[43] Though nowhere does he make explicit how self-respect or its social bases ought to be distributed, it seems that he is committed to an equal distribution of self-respect.[44] Now, for self-respect to be distributed equally, its bases must be distributed equally. Either self-respect will be based on the distribution of liberties or it will be based on the distribution of income and wealth. Beyond some point, after the urgent and basic wants of all persons have been satisfied, 'the marginal significance for our good of further economic and social advantages diminishes relative to the interests of liberty'.[45] At this point of guaranteed economic adequacy for all, the least advantaged included, maximal and equal liberty is to be preferred to further raising the economic standard of living. This grounds the priority of liberty to wealth and income. Why can't these material goods function as the bases of self respect so that they, rather than liberty, be distributed equally? Rawls provides three, not very convincing, arguments. First, according to Rawls, if self-respect is going to be based on relative income shares, it will be impossible to improve one person's position without lowering that of someone else.[46] Rawls views income as the basis of self-respect to be a positional good. However, it could be a semi-positional good—in the sense that having less than others can negatively affect one's self-respect, whereas having more than others will have no positive effect on one's self-respect. Thus an equal distribution might plausibly increase overall self-respect. Rawls's second argument is that since an unequal distribution of income and wealth can work to everyone's benefit, it would be irrational to insist on an equal division of these primary goods.[47] But this begs the question, since to the extent that an equal distribution of income is necessary to secure everyone's sense of self-respect (the most important primary good), then an unequal distribution would not necessarily make everyone's circumstances

---

[43] Rawls (1971: 440).
[44] This implicit idea is apparent for example at (1971: 546). See Shue (1975: 198) and Eyal (2005: 197). This short exposition of Rawls's argument for the priority of liberty relies heavily on Shue.
[45] Rawls (1971: 542).   [46] Ibid., 545.   [47] Ibid., 546.

better, all things considered. The third argument proposed by Rawls is that social envy and jealousy that could trigger a loss of self-respect due to income disparities 'should not be excessive, at least not when the priority of liberty is effectively upheld'.[48] Perhaps Rawls is right that they ought not be erosive of self-respect, but still they might, and he concedes that this may be so:

> To some extent men's sense of their own worth may hinge upon their institutional position and their income share. [...] theoretically we can if necessary include self-respect in the primary goods, the index of which defines expectations. Then in applications of the difference principle, this index can allow for the effects of excusable envy; the expectations of the least advantaged are lower the more severe these effects. *Whether some adjustment for self-respect has to be made is best decided from the standpoint of the legislative stage* where the parties have more information about social circumstances...[49]

So here we have it. At least with respect to the intra-generational aspect of the difference principle, maximizing the position of the least advantaged is obligatory until a threshold of adequacy is reached. At this point everyone's basic and urgent needs are met, and the institutions of justice are established. Once that level is reached it is possible that inequalities in income will harm individuals' self-respect. To take account of this participants to the original position will allow inequalities to fall short of the maximinimizing point, so long as they do not go beyond it. To what extent individuals' self-respect is harmed and the degree of equality that would rectify it is a matter they would leave to political deliberation. Thus a two-stage principle emerges. The first stage *requires* maximizing the position of the (trans-generational) least advantaged. Its aim is to reach an adequacy threshold as soon as possible. Inequalities and savings are a means to this end, but they must work to the maximal benefit of the least advantaged. The point at which they do, Rawls refers to as 'perfectly just'. The second stage *permits* continued saving and inequalities beyond the threshold level. Its aim is to further improve the material condition of everyone, subject to securing the self-respect of individuals and within the range limited by the point of maximum benefit to the least advantaged. A range Rawls refers to as 'just throughout'.[50]

Additional support for a two-stage principle can be found in Rawls's incidental remark about Mill's stationary state. According to Rawls the difference principle...

> does not require continual economic growth over generations to maximize upward indefinitely the expectations of the least advantaged (assessed in terms of income and wealth). That would not be a reasonable conception of justice. We should not rule out

---

[48] Rawls (1971: 546).   [49] Ibid., 546 (italics added).   [50] Rawls (1971: 78f).

Mill's idea of a society in a just stationary state where (real) capital accumulation may cease.[51]

In his *Principles of Political Economy* J. S. Mill laments political economists' excessive focus on growth as a means to well being. Rather than fear the necessary stationary state at which all economic growth must eventually converge, Mill asks us to embrace it. He draws an ideal of a society more concerned with cultural, moral and social improvement, the preservation of nature, the reduction of labour, and *an equal distribution of wealth*.[52] In the above Rawls accepts the possibility of a moderately non-materialist conception of the good. Beyond an adequacy threshold society may prefer, in line with Mill's vision, to improve its moral well being rather than continuously raising its material standard of living. Participants to the original position would not want to bind the persons they represent to a materialistic conception of the good that values economic growth above other non-materialistic aspects of well-being. To allow for this possibility, once basic needs are met and institutions of justice maintained, the trans-generational difference principle permits, but no longer requires, saving and inequality to the maximum benefit of the least advantaged. Thus the possibility of a non-materialistic conception of the good provides supplementary grounds, with the concern for self respect, for a two-stage trans-generational principle of justice.

4. Conclusion

I have urged an understanding of the just saving principle, not as an external constraint limiting the application of the difference principle, but as a clause in its full articulation. Saving takes the diachronic intergenerational dimension as a means to improve the position of the least well off, in much the same way that inequality treats the synchronic intra-generational dimension. As such it shifts the viewpoint from that of the least advantaged within a generation to that of the trans-generational least advantaged. As Rawls puts it: 'the appropriate expectation in applying the difference principle is that of the long-term prospects of the least favoured extending over future generations'.[53] Rawls's initial response to the issue of justice between generations was intuitively correct. Viewing the participants in the original position as representing family lines with bonds of affection and natural concern is substantively similar to the thought of shifting the focus of concern to the least advantaged extended over generations.

---

[51] Rawls (2001: 63f).   [52] Mill (1994: 124–30).   [53] Rawls (1971: 285).

The problem was to coherently introduce this idea into the original position. Rather than amending motivations in the original position, a modification that significantly weakens the argument for the principles of justice, Rawls was led in the development of his thought to rely on the notion of full compliance. I suggested that, given Rawls's understanding of the idea of full compliance, it is wrong to do so. Instead the desired result can be achieved on the basis of the formal constraint of universality. Nevertheless, not a lot hinges on this. The present time of entry interpretation highlighting the formal constraint of universality, or assuming full compliance of all generations, can generate a principle of saving. But then, a further problem ensues: the specification of the original position so far fails to generate the kind of two-stage principle of saving Rawls endorses. This has led commentators either to reject the idea of principles chosen on the basis of self-interested motivation, or to reject the idea of a two-stage principle.

Highlighting two further aspects of Rawls's theory—namely, the centrality of self-respect and the allowance for a non-materialistic conception the good—I suggested that a two-stage principle such as that endorsed by Rawls may be generated from the original position under the present time of entry interpretation and without amending the parties' self-interested motivation. However, the two-stage configuration would apply to both saving and inequality. Hence, a full articulation of the trans-generational difference principle would be as follows:

(1) inequality and saving are *obligatory* to reach a threshold material level; (2) inequality and saving are *permitted* to further improve the material well being of society beyond the basic level; (3) inequality and saving at both stages are *prohibited* beyond the rates that would maximize the position of the trans-generational least advantaged.

References

BARRY, B. (1977), 'Justice Between Generations', in P. M. S. Hacker and J. Raz (eds.), *Law, Morality and Society* (Oxford: Oxford University Press), 268–84.

——(1978), 'Circumstances of Justice and Future Generations', in I. Sikora and B. Barry (eds.) *Obligations to Future Generations* (Philadelphia: Temple University Press), 204–48.

——(1989), *A Treatise on Social Justice, i: Theories of Justice* (Hemel Hempstead: Harvester Wheatsheaf).

BRINK, D. O. (1989), *Moral Realism and the Foundations of Ethics* (Cambridge: Cambridge University Press).

COHEN, G. A. (1992), 'Incentives, inequality and community', *The Tanner Lectures on Human Values Volume XIII* (Salt Lake City: University of Utah Press).

—— (1995), 'The Pareto argument for inequality', *Social Philosophy and Policy*, 12: 160–85.

—— (1997), 'Where the action is: On the site of distributive justice' *Philosophy and Public Affairs*, 26: 3–30.

ENGLISH, J. (1977), 'Justice between Generations' *Philosophical Studies*, 31: 91–104.

EYAL, N. (2005), ' "Perhaps the most important primary good": Self-respect and Rawls's principles of justice', *Politics, Philosophy and Economics*, 4: 195–219.

GOSSERIES, A. P. (2001), 'What Do We Owe the Next Generation(s)?', *Loyola of Los Angeles Law Review*, 35: 293–355.

HARE, R. M. (1973), 'Critical Study—Rawls' Theory of Justice—II', *Philosophical Quarterly*, 23: 241–52.

HARSANYI, J. (1975), 'Can the Maximin Principle Serve as a Basis for Morality? A Critique of John Rawls's Theory', *American Political Science Review*, 69: 594–606.

HILL, T. E. (1992), 'Kantian Constructivism in Ethics', in *Dignity and Practical Reason in Kant's Moral Philosophy* (Ithaca: Cornell University Press).

HUBIN, D. C. (1976/7), 'Justice and Future Generations', *Philosophy and Public Affairs*, 6: 70–83.

MILL, J. S. (1994), *Principles of Political Economy: and Chapters on Socialism* (Oxford: Oxford University Press), 450 p.

O'NEILL, O. (1989), *Constructions of Reason: Explorations of Kant's Practical Philosophy* (Cambridge: Cambridge University Press), 249 p.

PADEN, R. (1997), 'Rawls's Just Savings Principle and the Sense of Justice', *Social Theory and Practice*, 23(1): 27–51.

PARFIT, D. (1984), *Reasons and Persons* (Oxford: Oxford University Press), 543 p.

RAWLS, J. (1971), *A Theory of Justice* (Oxford: Oxford University Press), 607 p.

—— (1974), 'Some Reasons for the Maximin Criterion', *American Economic Review*, 64: 141–6.

—— (1996), *Political Liberalism* (New York: Columbia University Press), 464 p.

—— (2001), *Justice as Fairness: a Restatement* (Cambridge: Harvard University Press), 214 p.

ROEMER, J. (2002), 'Egalitarianism Against the Veil of Ignorance' *Journal of Philosophy*, 46: 167–184.

SHUE, H. (1975), 'Liberty and Self-Respect', *Ethics*, 85: 195–203.

WALL, S. (2003), 'Just Saving and the Difference Principle', *Philosophical Studies*, 116: 79–102.

WILLIAMS, A. (1998), 'Incentives, Inequality and Publicity', *Philosophy and Public Affairs*, 27: 225–47.

8

Enough for the Future

LUKAS H. MEYER AND DOMINIC ROSER

1. Introduction

What do we owe to future people as a matter of social justice? We follow a broad understanding of intergenerational justice: justice considerations are relevant to decisions that are likely to affect the existence, number and identity of future people if—with respect to these decisions—future generations can be viewed as holding legitimate claims or rights against present generations, who in turn stand under correlative duties to future generations. This chapter proposes a framework for the normative interpretation and assessment of intergenerational relations: we will delineate how to understand the welfare rights and distributive justice claims of future people vis-à-vis currently living people. We argue that we have strong and particular reasons for interpreting intergenerational justice in terms of a sufficientarian conception of justice. The sufficientarian interpretation of currently living people's duties of intergenerational justice (and future people's correlative rights) can guide our decision-making with respect to decisions that will have an impact on both the well-being of future people as well as the composition of future people, that is, on the number, existence, and identity of future people.

We will begin our discussion of intergenerational justice by distinguishing between sufficientarian and egalitarian conceptions of justice. We will then (in sections 3 and 4) argue in favour of a sufficientarian understanding of intergenerational justice in response to the so-called non-identity problem. Our argument here has two stages. First, we argue that by relying on a threshold conception of harm we can respond to the non-identity problem. Second, we argue that we have reasons to specify the threshold in terms of a sufficientarian understanding of justice. Finally, in section 5, we submit further reasons for intergenerational sufficientarianism.

2. Egalitarian and Sufficientarian Conceptions of Justice

According to Thomas W. Scanlon, egalitarian (or 'strictly egalitarian'—as we will call them) reasons are 'unspecific in not being concerned with the absolute level of benefits that individuals enjoy'. Rather, on the basis of these reasons inequalities are to be objected because relative differences between the states of persons are seen as something 'which is itself to be eliminated or reduced.'[1] Proponents of sufficientarianism, in contrast, hold the view that what primarily matters is that everybody is well off, i.e. has well-being above a certain given threshold which is considered 'sufficient' (this may or may not be a 'minimal' threshold). They also hold that one person being worse off than another is irrelevant if those persons are both well off. They reject the egalitarian understanding, at least for those people who are well off. Of course, equality and sufficiency are not the only promising distributive principles but, together with priority, they are deemed the most worthy of discussion in the contemporary debate. And so we will focus on these principles.

A strictly egalitarian position by which we understand a position that holds equality to be of intrinsic value is open to the so-called levelling-down-objection.[2] This objection is based on the fact that such an egalitarian understanding can recommend that the state of the better-off persons be worsened for the sake of equality even if this is not good for anyone. Indeed, most such strict egalitarians believe that a state of affairs in which nobody is well off but they are equally so, is better, in one respect, than a state in which some people are not well off and others are well off. For this such egalitarians assume that equality has intrinsic value. They will quickly want to add that, of course, equality at a low level of well-being is only better than inequality at a high level of well-being *in one respect*. In an all-things-considered view the other respects—such as the total sum of well-being—might easily outweigh the importance of equality. Thus also such a value-pluralist egalitarian might, when considering all things, prefer not to level down. But adding such value-pluralism to egalitarianism does not pull the sting out of the levelling-down-objection. For the objection already concerns the judgement that a state with equal but low well-being is better than a state with high but unequal well-being *in one respect*: the value-pluralist egalitarian, too, is committed

---

[1] Scanlon (2005: 6).

[2] If we follow Parfit (1997, 2000) deontological egalitarianism is not open to this objection. For a critical discussion of this claim, see Lippert-Rasmussen (2007).

to the view that in at least one respect the former state of affairs is better even though it is better for no one and worse for some. By claiming that a state of affairs can be better in some respect, even though it is better for no one, such a strictly egalitarian position must give up a person-affecting view, i.e. the view that the moral quality of a state of affairs must crucially depend on how the interests of (particular and actual) persons are being affected.[3]

The levelling-down-objection may seem to speak generally against egalitarian intuitions or, put more carefully, one may attempt to suggest a reformulation of these intuitions and without relying on the notion that what matters is equality as such. Derek Parfit's priority view is such a reformulation.[4] One plausible version of his priority view is:

Priority View: To benefit persons matters more the worse off the person is to whom the benefits accrue, the more people are being benefited and the greater the benefits in question.

According to the priority view equality, as such, does not matter. The view is thus not open to the levelling-down-objection. At the same time the priority

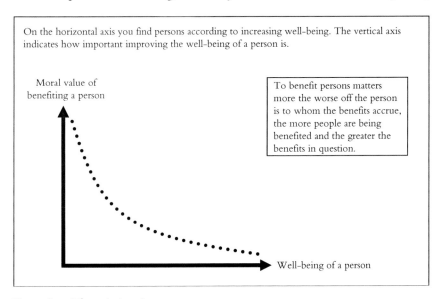

Figure 8.1. The priority view

---

[3] See also n. 14 below. The term 'crucially' is of course less than precise and the reader is referred to Holtug (2007: 139–46) who carefully spells out how egalitarianism (and possibly prioritarianism) conflict with different versions of person-affecting views.

[4] See Parfit (1997: 213).

view clearly has a built-in tendency towards equality. To this extent it is correctly described as non-relational egalitarianism. The reason for this built-in tendency towards equality is found in the fact that the priority view accepts the following egalitarian condition: if X is worse off than Y, we have at least a *prima facie* reason for promoting the well-being of X rather than of Y. Even if priorit-arians do not see anything intrinsically bad in social, economic, and other differ-ences, their priority view is a derivatively egalitarian view. In the following, we will understand egalitarian conceptions of justice to include those that are based on strictly egalitarian reasons (reflecting the notion of the intrinsic value of equality) as well as those that give greater weight to benefiting less well-off per-sons, where these reasons apply quite apart from how well off these persons are.

The position of weak sufficientarianism qualifies the priority view. We can distinguish between weak and strong interpretations of sufficientarianism.[5] While, as we will explain below, the position of strong sufficientarianism qualifies the maximin view (i.e. lexical priority ought to be given to the worst off), the position of weak sufficientarianism can be understood as a qualified priority view: the latter claims that the priority to be given to the position of the not well off decreases to zero at a certain threshold of well-being, at which people are sufficiently well off, whereas the priority view claims that this is only the case if people's well-being is perfect, that is, when it simply cannot be improved further. Accordingly we can summarize the position of weak sufficientarianism as follows:

Weak Sufficientarianism: To benefit persons below the threshold matters more the worse off they are. Above the threshold there are no priorities. The priority to be given to the position of the not well off decreases to zero at the threshold and above the threshold there are no priorities. To benefit persons matters more the more people are being benefited and the greater the benefits in question.

As with the priority view, the position of sufficientarianism also holds that equality as such does not matter. And, likewise, sufficientarianism has a built-in tendency towards equality. However, this tendency is restricted in the following way: To benefit person X is more important than to benefit person Y, if X is below the threshold and if Y is better off than X. On a low level of well-being, equality is of derivative value. So, concerning the improvement of the position of those who are less well off than others, sufficientarianism holds both a positive and a negative thesis: it is more important to benefit people below the threshold than above the threshold (this being the positive thesis;

---

[5] So far the discussion has not led to a consensus on the concept of sufficientarianism. See, generally, Frankfurt (1987); Crisp (2003); Casal (2007).

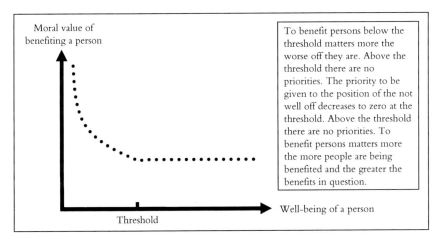

Moral value of benefiting a person

To benefit persons below the threshold matters more the worse off they are. Above the threshold there are no priorities. The priority to be given to the position of the not well off decreases to zero at the threshold. Above the threshold there are no priorities. To benefit persons matters more the more people are being benefited and the greater the benefits in question.

Well-being of a person

Threshold

Figure 8.2. Weak sufficientarianism

in our versions of sufficientarianism people below the threshold get treated according to the priority view), and above the threshold the improvement of the position of the less well off is of no particular concern (this being the negative thesis).[6]

As explained, the position of weak sufficientarianism can be understood as a qualified priority view. The position of strong sufficientarianism, however, can be understood as a qualified maximin view. Strong sufficientarianism differs from weak sufficientarianism in how it interprets the priority of persons below the threshold. Strong sufficientarianism attributes much stronger priority, namely lexical priority, to those whose well-being is below the threshold (while according to weak sufficientarianism the priority decreases to zero at the threshold). This amounts to giving a person just below the threshold absolute priority over a person just above the threshold. Versions of sufficientarianism are stronger the greater the priority they attribute to those below the threshold. With a lexically prioritarian threshold strong sufficientarianism also rejects the view that it always matters more to benefit persons the more people are being benefited and the greater the benefits in question.

According to both weak sufficientarianism and the priority view, we ought to benefit those who are already well off if it is the case that, given the number of those benefited by our action and the extent of benefits accruing to them, we will do more good even if we take into account that benefiting

---

[6] For a general distinction between a positive and negative thesis for characterising sufficientarianism see Casal (2007: 297f.): 'The positive thesis stresses the importance of people living above a certain threshold, free from deprivation. The negative thesis denies the relevance of certain additional distributive requirements.'

people below the threshold has particular weight. This is what proponents of strong sufficientarianism reject and also those who defend the maximin principle.[7] In contrast to maximin strong sufficientarianism does not propose that the smallest improvement of the smallest number of the worst off ought to be given absolute priority over any improvement of people in the next worst off group. Strong sufficientarianism qualifies this view by making two assumptions:

Strong Sufficientarianism: First, the improvement in well-being of those whose level of well-being is below the threshold has absolute or lexical priority; and to benefit persons below the threshold matters more the worse off they are. Second, both below and above the threshold it matters more to benefit persons the more persons are being benefited and the greater the benefits in question. But: Trade-offs between persons above and below the threshold are precluded.

The position of strong sufficientarianism is absolutist in the sense that it attributes absolute or lexical priority to the improvement of the not well off. The position is single-level in so far as it attributes special moral significance to only one level of well-being.[8] As the position is single-level, it can be

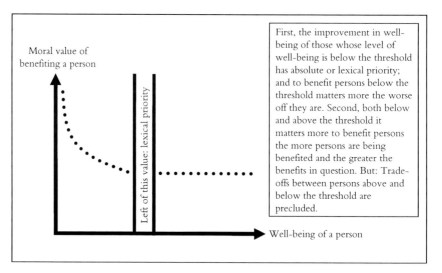

Figure 8.3. Strong sufficientarianism

---

[7] However, the maximin principle does not specify an absolute level of well-being for determining who ought to be given priority but rather demands that whoever is the worst-off be given lexical priority. Thus, maximin can demand the prioritarian treatment of people who are well off or very well off.

[8] Sufficientarian conceptions can be distinguished according to whether they specify one or more threshold values. For this and further differentiations see Meyer and Roser (2006: 235f.).

heterogeneous by specifying different principles of distribution below and above the threshold.[9]

To thresholds and especially such ones that designate an absolute priority—as is characteristic of the position of strong sufficientarianism—Richard Arneson[10] and others have objected that we cannot avoid an arbitrary specification of such priority thresholds. It can further be criticized, that such thresholds are incompatible with our distributive convictions' being non-heterogeneous—that is, that they all can be accounted for by means of one principle of distribution. The existence of thresholds where a tiny change (such as enhancing the well-being of an individual just below the threshold so as to place her just above the threshold) dramatically changes our evaluation of the total outcome, can be claimed to be alien to our moral intuitions.

So, if we cannot specify such a privileged level of well-being, as Arneson and others contend, the priority view seems to provide the best account of our basic intuition that we ought to give some priority to benefiting people who are not well off. According to the priority view a bad life in terms of well-being is rightly considered a morally bad state of affairs. At the same time we do not draw a categorical (qualitative) difference between a good and a bad life. Rather, formulations such as 'he fares badly' or 'she is doing well' are imprecise formulations that each refer (usually in a context-dependent manner) to a whole range of differing levels of well-being and where the border between the different levels does not have any special moral significance.

We therefore assume that the priority view is a plausible candidate for an adequate principle of distribution among contemporaries. However, in the following subsections 3 to 5 we show that we have special and strong reasons for a sufficientarian conception of intergenerational justice. We assume that one can justify a threshold, namely as specified by strong sufficientarianism, for intergenerational relations.[11]

---

[9] And any multi-level sufficientarianism can, of course, be even more heterogeneous by specifying a different distributional principle above every relevant threshold.

[10] See esp. Arneson (1999), (2000).

[11] The most promising approach for justifying a priority threshold relies upon the distinction between needs and (mere) wishes. Here, a short sketch of the argument may suffice: If person X has a need for something (needs something) that person Y wishes to have but does not need, then, *prima facie*, we ought to fulfil the needs of person X. But how do we distinguish between needs and mere wishes? Whether a need deserves the moral priority as indicated entirely depends upon whether the needy person would be badly off if the need in question is not fulfilled. Thus, an interpretation of the moral significance of needs suggests the commitment to a morally privileged priority line of well-being. If person X has the need for something that person Y wishes to have but does not need—in the sense that person X would not be well off if his need is not fulfilled, but person Y would still be well off if his wish is not fulfilled—then fulfilling the need of person X is *prima facie* more important than fulfilling the wish of Y. Of course, we would have to defend the argument as sketched against a good number of

Our discussion so far in section 2 enables us to specify what we will understand by egalitarian and sufficientarian conceptions of justice: Egalitarian conceptions comprise first those that include strictly egalitarian reasons for action as Scanlon understands them—reflecting the notion of equality as having intrinsic value—and, secondly, those conceptions that have a continuous tendency to lead to equality, and in particular the priority view. Conceptions of weak and strong sufficientarianism differ from both egalitarian understandings. Sufficientarian conceptions have a tendency to lead to equality only below the threshold. Above the threshold neither improving the position of the worse off nor even promoting equality as such are of concern. To simplify matters, we will identify sufficientarian justice with strong sufficientarianism. The conception of strong sufficientarianism differs most clearly from both egalitarian understandings. Furthermore, strong sufficientarianism differs from both weak sufficientarianism and the priority view in precluding trade offs between persons above and below the threshold.

We start our discussion by inquiring into particular reasons for holding that a sufficientarian understanding of justice is appropriate for the relations between currently living people and future non-contemporaries. We will then take up the question of the relevance of certain reasons often cited in favour of international sufficientarianism. These reasons, we hope to show, speak more strongly in favour of intergenerational than international sufficientarianism. We shall invite attention, too, to the fact that some of the more common instrumental reasons in favour of an egalitarian conception of justice are irrelevant in the intergenerational realm.

3. A Specific Case for Sufficientarianism (1): Responding to the Non-Identity Problem

A particular reason for holding a sufficientarian understanding of intergenerational justice relies upon a certain response to the so-called non-identity problem.[12] The non-identity problem rests upon the contingency of future people upon currently living people's decisions and actions. We know, of course, that when we harm future people's interests and violate their rights, specific persons are harmed. But the decision we make often counts as a

---

objections. Additionally, we would have to show that the argument will justify a substantial threshold that has absolute priority. For that we would also have to specify what activities or capabilities (or secure access to what goods) are necessary for a sufficiently good life.

[12] See Schwartz (1978); Kavka (1982); and esp. Parfit (1984), part IV.

necessary condition of the very existence of this genetically and numerically specific set of people at some future point in time. Consider a policy of making intensive and extensive use of exhaustible resources for the aim of increasing the welfare of currently living people. If the policy is criticized for harming future people on the ground that this policy will predictably worsen their conditions of life and, thus, is likely to violate their welfare rights, a defender of the policy could reply by saying: many, if not all of our actions have (indirect) effects not only on the conditions of life, but also on the composition of future persons, that is, on the number, existence, and identity of future persons. This is also true for actions that allegedly harm future persons. If the omission of the allegedly harmed action meant that the allegedly harmed person did not come into existence, then that person cannot be said to have been harmed by this action—or, at any rate, not according to the normal understanding of harm.[13] With respect to persons whose existence is dependent upon the allegedly harming action, they cannot be worse off owing to this action than they would have been had this action not been carried out, for in that case they would not have existed.

In responding to the non-identity problem and the skepticism linked to it with respect to the very possibility of future people having welfare rights vis-à-vis those currently living, we develop a two-stage argument. First, we introduce and defend a threshold notion of harm. Second, we argue that a (strongly) sufficientarian interpretation of the threshold is to be preferred.

A threshold understanding of harm (as an element of what we call the combined view of harm) allows us to justify the following propositions: The dependency (or contingency) of the number and specific identity of future people upon our decisions does not matter where the question is our potentially harming future people's interests and violating their rights. Considerations of justice, namely the welfare rights claims of future people vis-à-vis currently living people can guide us in choosing among long-term policies. Finally, such considerations can also guide prospective parents in deciding whether they ought to revise their decision to conceive out of regard for the children they would thereby beget.

These widely held convictions can be supported by an interpretation of harm that requires a subjunctive comparison with a threshold as its baseline (hereinafter: subjunctive-threshold interpretation). We presuppose a person-affecting view of ethics, which holds that the moral quality of an action has

---

[13] The common understanding is the subjunctive-historical interpretation of harm: An action (or inaction) at time t_1 harms someone only if the agent causes (allows) this person to be worse off at some later time t_2 than the person would have been at t_2 had the agent not interacted with (or acted with respect to) this person at all. For a detailed discussion see Meyer (2003: 147–49 and 155–58).

to be assessed on the basis of how it affects the interests of particular and actual persons. In the context of intergenerational justice, the person-affecting view has the implication that only the rights and interests of those persons whose identity is beyond manipulation by the acts (or social policies) under evaluation are to be regarded as morally relevant.[14] The person-affecting view stands in contrast to an impersonal view according to which the value of states of affairs is not reducible to their effects on the interests of actual people.

Some philosophers hold the view that future people whose existence depends upon currently living people's actions cannot have rights vis-à-vis the latter people's actions. Others argue that currently living people can violate the rights of future people even if the former cannot harm the latter.[15] If currently living people cannot affect the welfare of future people, future people cannot have welfare rights vis-à-vis currently living people. Or we can attempt to limit the practical significance of the non-identity problem. Some have suggested limiting the relevant actions to those that are not only likely but indeed necessary conditions of the existence of the concerned person.[16] Or, and this is the response we argue for, we may delineate an alternative understanding of harm, the so-called threshold conception of harm,[17] according to which future people can be said to be harmed by currently living people's actions even if these actions are among the necessary conditions of the existence, identity or number of future people. According to a threshold understanding of harm an action harms a person if as a consequence of that action the person falls under a normatively defined threshold—this is to be understood as a sufficient condition of harming a person.[18] The threshold understanding is unaffected by the non-identity problem, for here the finding of harm does not require a hypothetical comparison with the situation that would have occurred in the absence of the harming action. Such a notion of harm limits the practical significance of the non-identity problem to different degrees depending upon how the threshold is substantially defined.[19]

---

[14] For the person-affecting view see esp. Heyd (1992: 80–90 and passim). As Heyd we do not believe in a knock-down argument for the person-affecting and against the impersonal. Rather, by relying upon the method of wide reflective equilibrium the person-affecting view is to be assessed in comparison to an impersonal view, namely as an element of a philosophical account of, *inter alia*, intergenerational justice—taking into account their respective implications in dependence upon other assumptions (see Daniels (1979)).

[15] Kumar (2003).   [16] Roberts (1998).

[17] This understanding can be expressed in the formula: an action (or inaction) at time t_1 harms someone only if the agent thereby causes (allows) this person's life to fall below some specified threshold. See also Shiffrin (1999).

[18] Meyer (2003: 152–8).   [19] Meyer (2008: section 4).

The threshold interpretation of harm relies on the idea that we have a general duty to people not to cause them to be worse off than they ought to be. By our actions and omissions we can cause a person to be worse off than *that* person is entitled to be. The threshold interpretation of harm relies, *inter alia*, on our being able to specify a standard of well-being that enables us to assess the likely consequences of a long-term policy as harming future people. The threshold conception presupposes our being able to describe positively a level of well-being in such a way that a person's right is violated if we do not fulfill our negative duty to refrain from carrying out actions that would cause this person to fall below the specified standard. In addition, and in accordance with this understanding of harm, we can stand under the positive duty of seeing to it that persons reach a level of well-being at or above the threshold level of well-being. In so far as our specifying the relevant level of well-being reflects the idea of people *qua* people having rights vis-à-vis currently living people, our correlative duties set a normative framework that describes the level of protection owed to future people as bearers of general (human) rights.

In the following we will argue that a (strongly) sufficientarian interpretation of the threshold is to be preferred. While the threshold standard can substantively be defined in numerous ways we will argue that neither of the egalitarian conceptions of justice, by itself, can plausibly define the standard. But before we turn to this second stage of our argument for intergenerational sufficientarianism we would like to point out that the proposed solution to the non-identity problem also provides plausible guidance in the contexts of both procreational decision-making and population policies and with respect to the question whether we ought to bring into existence those people who are best off. Joined with the person-affecting view the threshold conception does not support the claim that if a possible person were to have a good enough life, but a different person could instead be brought into existence who would have an even better life, there is then an obligation to bring into existence the second child, rather than the first.[20] This is true for individual decisions about procreation as well as for collective policy decisions. Under the named conditions present generations have no obligation to bring into

---

[20] The priority view does not specify a threshold. Joined with the person-affecting approach the priority view will require that actual persons are to be taken into account according to how well off or less than well off they are—and likewise for future people from the time of their conception. This is also how we can interpret a strictly egalitarian understanding that takes equality to be intrinsically valuable: in conjunction with a person-affecting approach such an understanding will require that we diminish the relative differences among actual (future) people. However, such an egalitarian understanding that takes relative differences seriously can also be understood to specify a threshold such that future people have a claim to be not much worse off than either their contemporaries or the currently living people. For a discussion see below, section 4.

existence only those whose lives, among possible future persons, would be optimal, or even the obligation to bring into existence those whose lives would be comparatively better.

The following example illustrates this:[21] A woman knows that she is suffering from a particular disease which means that if she conceives a child now, that child will have a certain slight handicap, but will enjoy a life above the threshold, however specified. Fortunately, there is a treatment for this disease assuring that afterwards the woman will be able to conceive a perfectly healthy child. The treatment lasts three months. There is, thus, no way that this *particular* child can be born without the handicap. Can the woman be said to owe it to her child to postpone conception until after she has been treated for the disease? According to the threshold conception of harm, she cannot be said to owe this to her child.[22] She might, however, have good reasons to decide to receive the medical treatment and conceive later. These reasons will reflect her interests and those of her partner as well as the interests of other present and future people.[23] Such interests may well be important enough to give rise to an obligation on the part of the parents, namely, to postpone conception until after the treatment. We can then have obligations not to bring into existence persons whose lives, though still (far) above the threshold, are less worth living than the lives of others whom we might bring into existence in different circumstances, but these obligations are not grounded on considerations of harm to the future children in question.

To support the claim that parents *do* owe it to their prospective child to bring into existence the possible child who, among the options available to them, enjoys the highest level of well-being, we will have to rely on a different notion of harm—namely a notion of harm based upon the comparison of the state of a person to the counterfactual state of another person who could have been brought into existence instead.[24] Analogously, decisions concerning long-term policies are likely to have an impact on the size of the future population. Thus, if we wish to support a claim analogous to that just made with respect to the parents at the collective level, namely, that we owe it to

---

[21] This is a variation of Parfit's example of 'The 14-Year-Old Girl'. See Parfit (1984: 358, 364).

[22] See Meyer (1997a: 203–7); Woodward (1986: 815, n. 12); Woodward (1987: 808f.).

[23] According to the priority view people's claims to improvements in their well-being are the stronger, the worse off they are. If a person comes to existence and that person is not well off, others will stand under the corresponding duties. Conceiving a person who is likely not to be well off (due to genetic or other medical causes) will give rise to especially high demands on that person's future contemporaries. Analogously, a strictly egalitarian understanding requiring that relative differences be diminished will justify strong claims when a person comes into existence who is much worse off than most of his contemporaries.

[24] See Parfit's 'same number quality claim' (principle Q) in Parfit (1984: 360); Kavka (1982: 98f.).

possible future people to bring into existence those who will enjoy the highest level of well-being, we will also have to allow for different numbers.[25] The relevant understanding of harm can be expressed in the following formula: Having brought about a person's existence at time t_1, the agent thereby harms someone only if the agent causes this person to be worse off at some later time t_2 than other persons—whose existence the agent could have brought about instead—would have been at t_2 had the agent acted differently.[26]

If we follow this understanding of harm, a person whose quality of life is above the threshold will be considered harmed if there is a possible state of affairs in which, although this person would not have existed, another person or other persons would have existed and would have realized an even higher quality of life. According to the person-affecting approach and from the perspective of the allegedly harmed person, however, such a comparison makes no sense. We cannot simply proceed by drawing plausible intrapersonal comparisons of the life of this person and the counterfactual state of affairs in which, although this person would never have existed, another person or other persons would have existed.

The value of non-existence in the sense of never existing at all[27] cannot be compared with the value of the life of an actually existing person. As David Heyd argues: 'the comparison between life and nonexistence is blocked by two considerations: the valuelessness of nonexistence as such and the unattributability of its alleged value to individual subjects. The two considerations are intimately connected: one of the reasons for denying value to nonexistence *of* people is the very fact that it cannot be attached *to* people.'[28] A person can retrospectively prefer not to have been brought into existence, but it does not follow that this person would have been better off had he never been brought into existence.[29] To be sure, we can attribute to an existing person the state of 'nonexistence before conception' just as we can attribute to this person the state of 'having ceased to exist'.[30] This does not mean, however, that never existing at all can be understood as a (dis-)value vis-à-vis that person.

Those who claim, contrariwise, that we can meaningfully compare future states of affairs with different people (and different numbers of people)

---

[25] This can be true for procreative decisions also: Prospective parents might bring about more or less people (one child, twins, triplets etc.) depending upon their decisions.

[26] Compare the formulae in nn 13 and 17 above.

[27] Here we assume that comparing the state of an existing person with the state of the person had the person not been conceived amounts to comparing the state of an existing person with the state of the person had the person never existed at all.

[28] Heyd (1992: 37 and see 113).

[29] But see Roberts (1998: 151) (assigning zero-value to never having existed).

[30] See Meyer (1997a: 205); Meyer (2005: 95–99).

presuppose an impersonal approach: the value of states of affairs is not reducible to their effects on the interests of actual people; instead we can and have to compare possible future states of affairs with different people. Joined with an impersonal approach, the priority view (just like classical utilitarianism) leads to a repugnant conclusion, namely:[31] According to the priority view we aggregate the value realized for each possible world whereby the sum depends *inter alia* upon the number of persons who contribute to the realization of the value; thus, a possible world populated by persons all of whose lives are sufficiently good (according to a plausible threshold) or even better and very good, is to be judged worse than an alternative possible world populated by a large enough number of people whose lives are not sufficiently good but better than not-worth-living, even if only barely so. Principles with such features as these will recommend the creation of a large population whose people have lives worth living—and most theorists agree, this implication is repugnant and ought to be avoided.[32] A sufficiency principle specifying a minimal threshold for all people clearly does not imply the repugnant conclusion adumbrated here.[33]

We should also note that our argument for a threshold notion of harm is not meant to replace the more common notion of harm that requires a subjunctive comparison with a historical baseline.[34] Rather, we hold the view that the threshold notion of harm and the subjunctive-historical notion of harm can and are to be combined. According to the combined view the necessary condition for harming is the disjunction of the conditions of harming as set out by the threshold and the subjunctive-historical notion of harm.[35] The combined view is compatible with the response to the non-identity problem we argue for in this chapter: in assessing what we owe to future people we can employ the threshold interpretation of harm where the common understanding of harm does not apply. At the same time, the combined view allows us to rely on the common subjunctive-historical interpretation of harm whenever it is applicable, that is, when we will harm an actual person. In these cases the common notion provides us with a straightforward interpretation of the harm caused.[36]

---

[31] Parfit (1976); (1982); (1984), ch. 17.

[32] See Parfit (as in n. 31); Heyd (1992), ch. 2; and see the contributions in Ryberg und Tännsjö (2004).

[33] See also Blackorby et al. (2003: 354–60).

[34] See nn. 13 and 17, above, for the formulae of these notions of harm.

[35] The combined view can be expressed in the following formula: An action (or inaction) at time t_1 harms someone only if either the agent thereby causes (allows) this person's life to fall below some specified threshold; or the agent causes (allows) this person to be worse off at some later time t_2 than the person would have been at t_2 had the agent not interacted with (or acted with respect to) this person at all.

[36] For a detailed interpretation and defence of the combined view, see Meyer (2003: 152–8).

4. A Specific Case for Sufficientarianism (2): Specifying the Threshold of Harm

Responding to the non-identity problem as outlined in section 3—namely, by relying on a threshold notion of harm—does not by itself support a conception of intergenerational sufficientarianism. To be sure, the above-mentioned considerations as well as the interpretations of examples we submitted do suggest a specification of the relevant threshold as a *sufficientarian* standard. But for this substantive claim we need to provide further arguments.

Some have suggested defining the relevant sufficientarian standard in terms of absolute, noncomparative conditions.[37] One could hold a unitary view of the threshold according to which one and the same threshold would be applicable to all decisions. Even if we held that the same list of rights were attributable to all people (wherever and whenever they live), for example, those which are meant to protect basic capabilities of human beings, what these rights amount to will reflect contemporary social, economic, and cultural conditions.[38]

Specifying the standard by attributing equal minimal rights to people is only one possible interpretation of the threshold. We might, instead, want to define the threshold in accordance with either of the egalitarian conceptions introduced in section 2. First, strictly egalitarian considerations that address relative differences between people can help to specify the standard—and in at least two ways. We might hold that the standing of people relative to their contemporaries is important[39] and that the threshold notion of harm ought to reflect, say, the average level of well-being that people realize, or that future people will realize: the higher the average level of well-being the higher the threshold level of harm should be set. According to one interpretation of such an egalitarian reading, presently existing people harm future people by causing them to realize a (much) lower level of well-being than their own contemporaries.[40] In addition or alternatively, we might hold that the threshold level ought to reflect, say, the average level of well-being of the present generations upon whose decisions the existence, identity, and well-being of future people depend. According to such an interpretation,

---

[37] See Shiffrin (1999: 123f.); McMahan (1998: 223f.); and Meyer (1997a).

[38] See, e.g., Sen (1984); Nussbaum (2000b: 132f.).

[39] This would be the case since equality is of intrinsic value. See section 2 above, and see Marmor (2003); Steiner (2003). Responding to Marmor and Steiner, Raz (2003, 264f.) points out that what counts as sufficient might depend on how many people reach what levels of well-being and that this can be the case without our presupposing that equality is of intrinsic value. See also Gosepath (2004: 454–63); Brighouse and Swift (2006); Holtug and Lippert-Rasmussen (2007).

[40] Sher (1979: 389).

presently existing people harm future people by causing them to realize a (much) lower level of well-being than they enjoy themselves.[41] Still, even if egalitarian considerations that reflect a concern with the relative differences between people can contribute to the specification of the threshold, a plausible threshold is not going to be based on that concern, but will reflect primarily a concern with the absolute level of well-being of persons. Otherwise—this is an implication of the first interpretation—any level of well-being would be considered justified as long as all future people fare equally badly. This presupposes attributing intrinsic value exclusively to equality—an implausible view.[42] Moreover, to define the threshold standard of well-being of future people as the level of well-being achieved by currently living people (whatever it may be) is less than plausible, unless we were to attribute intrinsic value exclusively to intergenerational equality, so understood.[43] This view would deny that currently living people may stand under a duty of justice positively to save for future people so that they will achieve a sufficientarian level of well-being.[44]

The second way in which egalitarian considerations can help to identify the standard is to rely on the priority view for specifying the threshold. On this interpretation, future people fall under the threshold unless they are as well off as the priority view requires. However, this understanding is likely to be unreasonably demanding on the currently living. In the intergenerational context the priority view has most misleading implications even if it is coupled with the person-affecting approach. For, given the large number of future people whose level of well-being can be affected by the decisions and actions of currently living people, the priority view will make unreasonable demands on the currently living. In assessing alternative options we would have to weigh the claims to improvements as well as to take into account both the size of the benefit and the number of beneficiaries; if the number of future people is sufficiently large, we would then have to choose the option that improves their well-being even if both their claims to improvements in well-being are weak and the benefits they receive are small. If the number of future people

---

[41] See Barry (1999: 109). See also our remarks on the irrelevance of common instrumental justifications for more equality in section 5 below.

[42] See the above discussion regarding the levelling-down-objection. A monistic value egalitarianism will also have unacceptable implications when applied to contemporaries: the state of affairs in which all have lives barely worth living is to be preferred to a state in which all have good or very good lives but some are better off than others.

[43] See literature referred to in n. 39 above.

[44] Rawls (2001: 159) proposes a duty to save positively 'to make possible the conditions needed to establish and to preserve a just basic structure over time.' For discussion of the role of a principle of sufficiency in justifying this duty see Gaspart and Gosseries (2007: 200).

is sufficiently large, currently living people will stand under an obligation to improve the well-being of those future people even if in fulfilling that obligation the currently living people will lose (very) much in well-being and the improvements in well-being of future people will be small or even trivial.[45]

The objections to specifying the threshold in terms of the egalitarian conceptions as distinguished here present a particular reason for holding that the specification of the threshold ought to be informed by a sufficientarian understanding of justice, at least for intergenerational relations. In defining the relevant threshold we may also rely on considerations that reflect the significance of relative differences among future people or people who belong to different generations including the currently living. Considerations characteristic of the priority view may, also, be considered relevant for the specification of the threshold. It is implausible, however, to hold the view that we might define the relevant standard as reflecting solely egalitarian reasons of the two types distinguished: reasons for diminishing relative differences among people and those for the prioritarian weighting of claims to improvements in well-being. By defining a threshold of well-being according to which both currently and future living people are able to reach a sufficientarian conception allows us to avoid the misleading implications of both egalitarian conceptions. First, avoiding or reducing differences must not lead to a state of affairs in which people are worse off than they ought to be. Secondly, claims against currently living people are unreasonable if in fulfilling them the currently living people will bring about minimal or even trivial improvements of the well-being of future people but suffer losses themselves, causing them to fall under a plausible threshold level of well-being.

If these objections are valid, we have strong particular reasons for interpreting intergenerational justice in terms of a conception for which a sufficientarian threshold is of central significance. At the same time, the reasons for a sufficientarian understanding of intergenerational justice are not equally relevant for the relations among existing contemporaries—never mind whether we think of these contemporaries simply as people wherever they may live, or as members of a well-ordered liberal society, or as found in different basic political units. For the reasons reflect particular features of intergenerational

---

[45] The position of weak sufficientarianism can have this implication, too. For, even if we attribute particular weight to improving the well-being of people below the threshold, we might be able to do more good (in total) by benefiting many more people who are well-off already (compare, above, p. 224, last paragraph). This is an implication of both the priority view and the position of weak sufficientarianism even if the number of people to be considered is fixed; thus, it can arise in situations involving contemporaries only, as noted by Casal for the priority view (2007: 319f.).

relations: the non-identity problem simply does not arise in relations among existing contemporaries. The problem does not arise among institutionalised transgenerational legal entities such as Rawls's peoples or states understood as subjects of public international law, either. Also, as shown in sections 3 and 4 the (strength of) objections to egalitarian conceptions of intergenerational justice—to both the prioritarian conception and the conception relying on the notion that equality is of intrinsic value—reflect, in part, particular features of intergenerational relations. Thus, the reasons for a sufficientarian understanding of intergenerational justice are at least in part specific reasons and are not relevant for understanding either global justice or the notion of justice that holds among contemporary members of well-ordered societies.[46]

5. Further Reasons for Intergenerational Sufficientarianism

Next, we should like to turn to some of the often-cited reasons for a sufficientarian understanding of global justice. They concern, first, the prerequisites of implementing welfare rights, second, the possibility of measuring (relative) differences, and third, the significance of co-citizenship as well as instrumental justifications for an egalitarian distribution. We will ask whether these reasons are relevant to an understanding of intergenerational relations and whether they, in fact, speak more strongly on behalf of a sufficientarian conception of intergenerational relations than on behalf of such a conception of international relations. We hope to show that this is, indeed, the case. The reasons that are said to speak on behalf of a sufficientarian understanding of global justice turn out to be relevant to our understanding of intergenerational justice, and this owing to other special non-contingent features of intergenerational relations: the unchangeable power asymmetry as well as the impossibility of interaction between non-contemporaries, and not least of all our uncertainty as to how in particular our actions will affect future people. If so, there are weighty and specific reasons that speak on behalf of a sufficientarian conception of intergenerational justice and that are independent of the reasons we delineated in sections 3 and 4.

First, some authors[47] raise the criticism that the egalitarian understandings of global justice is negatively utopian: regulating world politics in accordance

---

[46] On the notion of well-ordered societies see Rawls (2001: 8f.); Rawls (1999).
[47] See Kersting (2001: 282–91); Miller (2005: 72f.).

with such demanding conceptions of justice—aiming either at globally establishing an equal distribution of well-being (and at a high level) or at giving weighted significance to globally improving the well-being of the not-well-off people—would require a world welfare state with far-reaching powers and authoritative means of implementation. For reasons familiar since Kant,[48] we cannot wish to live in a world state and in particular not in a world welfare state with regulatory powers. A world welfare state is likely to threaten seriously the liberty rights of all. We cannot hope to establish a sustainable well-ordered global state or its functional equivalent, or so the critics argue. On the other hand, a sufficientarian understanding is thought to specify a standard of distributive justice for international relations that could be implemented by means of co-ordinated efforts within a decentralized system (of a plurality) of basic political units. Of course, showing that a sufficientarian understanding of global justice is positively utopian would require further discussion. Here we just note that it is likely to be a less demanding goal of global justice.

We will not go into assessing the validity of the quasi-empirical claim that an egalitarian understanding of global justice is utopian in a negative sense, as its implementation will require a world state with far-reaching competencies and powers. Our point is simply the comparative one that we have additional and weighty reasons for believing that a world welfare state is a prerequisite for carrying out principles of intergenerational justice that require—in either of the ways specified—an egalitarian consideration of people whenever they live: solving so-called world problems[49] requires the global implementation of adequate measures. It is one thing, however, to aim at solving such problems without violating sufficiency standards; to aim at solving such problems and at the same time to pursue the goal of implementing an egalitarian conception of justice is quite another. The latter will demand a great deal both of currently living people (and as argued with respect to the priority view in section 4 possibly unreasonably much) and of international and intergenerational cooperation. Egalitarian solutions in particular will depend upon the reliable and stable

---

[48] See Kant (1795), (1784), (1793), and (1798), all in Kant (1968); but see Horn (1996); Höffe (1999); the so-called Clark-Sohn plan is the best-known post-World-War II proposal for the establishment of a world government. See Clark and Sohn (1960); see further, Suganami (1989) (who systematically compares and discusses alternative proposals for restructuring international society in accordance with its domestic counterparts).

[49] On 'world problems' see Opitz (2001). If we could realize intergenerational justice within well-ordered single states, we would not have to rely on a world state for its implementation. Here we do not discuss the problems of justice between age groups with respect to single-state cooperative schemes, e.g. social security systems. Rather, we take up problems of intergenerational justice among non-contemporaries. One such problem turns on the consequences of climate change and its normative implications.

cooperation of many influential actors in international politics; thus egalitarian solutions would require a world state or its functional equivalent:[50] If the solutions are meant to be just in accordance with an egalitarian conception and with respect to the claims of future people, a world welfare state is very likely presupposed. The implementation of measures aimed at securing the welfare rights of future people is particularly difficult. Non-contemporaries cannot give expression to and stand for their interests and they cannot impose sanctions on currently living people who do not carry out their obligations vis-à-vis them. Furthermore, the implementation of such measures is often dependent upon transgenerational cooperation. Both the fair representation of the interests of non-contemporaries and the securing of conditions of trans-generational cooperation require strong and stable institutions. Thus, if we hold that the implementation of an egalitarian understanding of global justice among contemporaries requires the institutions of a world welfare state, this will be true *a fortiori* for the implementation of an egalitarian understanding of global *and* intergenerational justice.[51] To the extent that we do not wish to live in a world state, the objection is valid for egalitarian conceptions of intergenerational relations; this is especially so for the reason that such a state would have to be enormously powerful in order to be able to implement egalitarian intergenerational obligations. At the same time, the particular reasons for the prerequisite of a world state, where intergenerational justice is concerned, reflect non-contingent features of intergenerational relations, namely, the unchangeable power asymmetry that holds between present and (remote) future generations and the impossibility of interaction between them.[52]

The second justificatory argument is connected with an argument on the level of practical validity. Some authors[53] claim that we cannot measure

---

[50] See Gardiner (2002: 406–416).

[51] Other factors may support the implementation of an egalitarian ideal in the intergenerational context, or, at the very least, there are amoral factors that contribute to the improvement of the well-being of future people. For example, many parents hope that their children will be better off than they themselves; this may contribute to the well-being of future people generally. Saving for future people comes with an interest yield, and this may induce an additional motivation for such savings. Also, if people are motivated to act in such ways that enhance their prospects of being better off in, say, 30 years, this may have the (unintended) side-effect of improving the well-being of future people in, say, 80 years.

[52] These features, one might well want to argue, require transgenerationally stable world state structures even for implementing the far less demanding conception of an intergenerational (minimal) sufficientarianism. However, our claim in this section is a comparative one: The world state or its functional equivalent is in all likelihood an institutional prerequisite if we are to fulfil intergenerational duties vis-à-vis (remote) future people and if (these) duties are interpreted in accordance with an egalitarian conception of justice, and less likely if we are to fulfil duties vis-à-vis (geographically distant) contemporaries and if (these) duties are interpreted in a non-egalitarian way.

[53] Miller (2005: 4–10); Brock (2005: 348–350).

globally what we would need to measure in order to be able to determine what in accordance with egalitarian conceptions of justice is owed to people who belong to different societies. We cannot say what an egalitarian justice, to quote David Miller, 'means in a culturally plural world'[54], for we can neither assess the relative differences among people who live in very different, historically formed cultural and social contexts, nor can we determine how well off they are in a way that bears on the prioritarian attribution of weighted claims to improvements in well-being. In response, we ought to consider whether the alleged difficulties of measurement are simply greater than the difficulties of measurement in single societies[55] or whether the difficulties of measurement are principally different and of a kind that they should be regarded as insuperable given the global pluralism of conceptions of the good and socially shared forms of life. Proponents of both egalitarian and non-egalitarian conceptions of justice agree that no problems principally different arise with respect to the measurement of some goods and especially the basic goods of survival when compared with the well-being of people wherever they might live. This is not to deny, of course, that the means necessary for supplying these goods vary and thus also the costs involved in providing and securing them; reaching, for example, the tolerable minimum of well-being in an OECD country requires secure access to a different set of goods than in a country of the so-called Third World. Applying a minimal sufficientarian threshold globally rather than within a single society does not, however, seem to entail principally different problems of measurement.

Problems principally different might arise, however, where we compare goods that are relevant for people's well-being above such a minimal threshold. People's well-being depends upon access to valuable options whose existence depends in turn upon collective and, often, also participatory goods whose supply is secured within bounded societies whose members share a particular historically and culturally formed understanding as to why these options are valuable to them.[56] Access to such options—professions, social roles, being a mother or a father, and societal activities in sports and culture—is of vital importance to the well-being and social status of members of a society. For realising the value of self-respect, backed by social recognition, depends upon having access to such options and having success in pursuing them.

It is, however, not obvious why we should face principally different problems when we compare access to such goods globally. Instead one might want to

[54] Miller (2005: 9).
[55] For an example of an author who focuses on the problems which already arise within a single society, see Rosenberg (1995).
[56] For an account see Meyer (2000).

argue that access to such options and success in pursuing them are goods whose comparative assessment in accordance with a conception of justice will rely upon a value that people can be said to hold in common transculturally, say, the value of self-respect. The sources of and the prerequisites for self-respect may well differ from society to society (this is true, for example, for the significance of belonging to certain professions) or culturally (this is true, for example, for such life options as having your own family), but not the significance of the value of self-respect. If the impact of life options on the value of self-respect counts from the perspective of justice[57] and if we are in a position to compare the impact of very different life options on the value of self-respect globally, then the great plurality of ways of life globally will not carry with it principled problems in measuring the relative well-being of people or the level of well-being they realize.

Further, Joseph Raz in particular holds that the value of such options even within a single (well-ordered liberal) society can be incommensurable in the strong sense of being incomparable: 'Two valuable options are incommensurable if (1) neither is better than the other, and (2) there is (or could be) another option which is better than one but is not better than the other.'[58] If so, the shared cultural-historical and social context within which these options exist does not guarantee their comparability for those who have access to these options. This might well not be decisive, however, if looked at from the perspective of an egalitarian understanding of justice. What counts is that people do have access to (morally acceptable) sources of self-respect quite apart from the options, whatever they may be, open to them in their particular cultural and social contexts. We may well be in a position to assess the impact of such options on the self-respect of people, even though, in other respects, these options are incommensurable.

It seems plausible both that problems of comparatively measuring the well-being of individuals both within single societies and globally will vary depending upon which goods we compare and that we will face problems of measurements more often in international relations given the far more far-reaching global pluralism of both conceptions of the good and available life options when compared with a reasonable pluralism within a single (Rawlsian well-ordered liberal) society. Thus, a conception of global egalitarian justice will be able to take into account only a selection of goods—which raises

---

[57] Of course we would have to show that the value of self-respect (or some other value) could play this central role for transculturally comparative judgements of justice. For self-respect as a central aspect of well-being or primary good, see Raz (1994: 24–26) and Rawls (2001: 58–61).

[58] Raz (1986: 325). Raz identifies incommensurability with the failure of transitivity. See also Raz (1991) und (1997), and Griffin's response (1991) to Raz.

questions about the meaningful applicability of the conception—or will have to make generalized assumptions about the significance of various goods for the realization, say, of the value of self-respect. The assumption, given that the value of self-respect is equally transculturally significant, is that we can rely upon the value of self-respect for comparative measurements of the well-being of people (or for the prioritarian assessment of weighted claims to improvements in well-being).

Comparatively to measure the well-being of people is even more difficult in intergenerational relations, however. For our knowledge of the relevant conditions of life of future people is limited and this epistemic situation of ours seems insuperable. At least two considerations support the view that in our efforts to carry out such measurements with respect to future people we face principally different problems:

- The particular way of life of future people is likely to depend in part upon those new and today unknown technologies to which they will have access. However, we cannot or can only with great difficulty predict technological developments.[59]
- The collective way of life of future people will depend, in part, upon their own individual and collective decisions. We are not in a position to predict how they will decide to organize their lives socially or how they will want to live individually and we cannot hope to determine these decisions either, that is, where we believe that the individual and collective autonomy of future people ought to be secured.[60] We also know that the decisions of their predecessors will have an impact on what options more remote future people will have as individuals and collectively; we cannot hope to determine the decisions of intervening generations either and for the same reason.

Thus, it might well be true that we are in no position to know what we owe to more remote future non-contemporaries in accordance with egalitarian conceptions of justice.[61] We are in no position to determine their pertinent relative differences, for the particular historically formed cultural and social contexts that the lives of remote future people will have are uncertain to us. We do know, however, that these particular contexts will be of decisive importance for the particular level of well-being that future people will enjoy.

---

[59] See Birnbacher (1988: 168f.).   [60] See Meyer (1997b: 145−50).

[61] It might be well to stress, at this point, that the argument in favour of sufficientarianism in response to the non-identity problem and as the more plausible specification of the intergenerational threshold conception (sections 3 and 4) is independent of the epistemic considerations we have discussed in this section.

Accordingly, over and above the satisfaction of certain general or basic needs or preferences[62] which can be estimated with a certain level of reliability we cannot hope to determine today how well off future[63] people will be. We are in no position to know what impact our actions will have on the relative well-being of future people or their particular level of well-being, for their individual well-being will depend to a large part on socially shared understandings of what options are valuable as well as on who has access to them and how successful they are in pursuing them.[64]

Third, some of the reasons that have been advanced against an egalitarian conception of global justice and in favour of global sufficientarianism do speak in favour of intergenerational sufficientarianism. This is owing to further particular features of intergenerational relations. Some have argued that institutional relationships among citizens ought to be regulated by an egalitarian understanding of justice if and to the extent that such a conception legitimately regulates citizens' claims to benefits in a scheme of cooperation that is made possible by authoritative rules that the state will enforce, where necessary, by means of coercion.[65] Non-contemporaries cannot be regarded as co-citizens in the relevant sense, however; there is no interaction possible among non-contemporaries, and future people cannot take part in today's political decision-making. The legitimacy of principles of intergenerational justice

---

[62] See Barry (1977: 261f.) and (1989: 347).

[63] It can also be difficult to have a positive impact on the well-being of geographically distant people. However, in this instance we can learn from experience; the predictability of the consequences of our actions is not restricted due to the two reasons that characterise our epistemic situation with respect to more remote future people as mentioned in the text above (see nn. 56–7 and text).

[64] We would need to analyse more precisely what the problems of comparative measurement are, namely with respect to the subject-matter that we assess (in the sense of the so-called *Equality of What?*-debate). In the contemporary debate on justice the more common alternatives are to focus on resources or basic goods (see, e.g., Rawls (1971: 92–4); Dworkin (2000: 65–119)) or capabilities (see, e.g., Nussbaum (2000a: 78–80); Sen (1999)). As Pogge (2002) has convincingly shown, a highly advanced primary goods approach not only allows but requires us to take into account many of the factors Sen has identified as decisive for the quality of life people enjoy. Among these factors are: the significance of relative differences in access to goods for, e.g., self-respect; the significance of the particular social conditions (e.g., the availability of public goods—such as a tertiary educational system or advanced health care—or the crime rate within a society) for the value of claims and rights to, e.g., physical and psychic integrity of people and that they may move and reside freely within the territory of their societies; the significance of the quality of the natural environment and of its change; the value of having a job at a particular place and in a particular society. If, in our attempts comparatively to measure quality of life, we are to take into account these and similar factors and considerations, we will find that we cannot know for certain (or by relying on generalised hypotheses with little accuracy) how well off (more remote) future people will be (relative to their contemporaries). And this, in particular, for the reason that we would have to take into account that their conditions of life will depend, in part, upon their predecessors' decisions and actions.

[65] See for alternative interpretations of this view Dworkin (2000: 6); Blake (2002); Nagel (2005); Scanlon (2005: 10f.).

cannot depend upon future people's approval of these principles in any real sense. Further, there is no correlation between economic and political equality among non-contemporaries. This is one of the more common justifications for greater equality among citizens of one society: Large differences in wealth or income will make it possible for the rich to exercise impermissible power over the poor, which might, is indeed likely to, lead to unacceptable inequalities in people's liberty rights. There is, however, an unchangeable power asymmetry between non-contemporaries.[66] Furthermore, other instrumental advantages of equality among contemporaries are of very little, if any, relevance where relations among non-contemporaries are concerned. It makes no sense to claim that greater income equality among non-contemporaries will further intergenerational harmony, reduce intergenerational envy, or strengthen a sense of intergenerational solidarity or communal belonging.[67] And, finally, one further consideration might be noted: if we hold the view that the validity of calling for obligations of justice depends, in part, upon whether we can effectively fulfil them,[68] then, again, we have reasons for doubting that this is the case in calling for obligations of egalitarian justice vis-à-vis future people and, in particular, more remote future people. This is due, in part, to our dependency on transgenerational cooperation in fulfilling duties vis-à-vis more remote future people.[69]

6. Concluding Remarks

We have particular and strong reasons for understanding the justice claims of future people vis-à-vis currently living people in terms of intergenerational sufficientarianism. This view is developed in response to the non-identity problem and other considerations that reflect the normative significance of non-contingent features of intergenerational relations, which include the dependency of the number and identity of future people on currently living people's decisions, the uncertainty as to how current people's actions will affect the relative well-being of future people, the problems of measuring relative differences of well-being of people whose particular conditions of life differ to a large degree, and the impossibility of interaction between non-contemporaries and their not sharing membership in a common polity.

Of course, many of us have concerns for future people that cannot be accounted for by considerations of justice: Duties of intergenerational justice

---

[66] See Barry (1989: 189, 246).   [67] See Beckerman and Pasek (2001: 49f.).
[68] See Scanlon (1998: 224f.); for discussion see Wenar (2001: 8of.).
[69] See Gardiner (2002: 402–6); Birnbacher (1988: 157–64).

(and the correlative rights of future people) can account neither for the concern that there be future people at all nor that they share a particular way of life nor that future people should have a life well above the level of a sufficientarian level of well-being. We might want to argue that over and above what currently living people owe future people as a matter of justice, they can stand under additional duties to benefit future people so that they will be able to continue their way of life and enjoy a level of well-being that is above any plausible understanding of a sufficientarian threshold. But going into these issues is a matter for another occasion.[70]

Bibliography

ARNESON, R. J. (1999), 'Egalitarianism and Responsibility', *Journal of Ethics* 3: 225–47.

—— (2000), 'Luck Egalitarianism and Prioritarianism', *Ethics* 110: 339–49.

BARRY, B. (1977), 'Justice between Generations', in P. M. S. Hacker and Joseph Raz (eds.), *Law, Morality and Society. Essays in Honour of H. L. A. Hart* (Oxford: Clarendon Press), 268–84; reprinted in Barry, B. (1991), *Liberty and Justice. Essays in Political Theory 2* (Oxford: Clarendon Press), 211–41.

—— (1989), *Theories of Justice. A Treatise on Social Justice*, Band Vol. 1 (Berkeley: University of California Press).

—— (1999), 'Sustainability and Intergenerational Justice', in Andrew Dobson (ed.), *Fairness and Futurity. Essays on Environmental Sustainability* (Oxford: Oxford University Press), 93–117.

BECKERMAN, W., and PASEK, J. (2001), *Justice, Posterity, and the Environment* (Oxford: Oxford University Press).

BIRNBACHER, D. (1988), *Verantwortung für zukünftige Generationen* (Stuttgart: Reclam).

BLACKORBY, C., BOSSERT, W., and DONALDSON, D. (2003), 'The Axiomatic Approach to Population Ethics', *Politics, Philosophy and Economics*, 2: 342–81.

BLAKE, M. (2002), 'Distributive Justice, State Coercion, and Autonomy', *Philosophy & Public Affairs*, 30: 257–96.

BRIGHOUSE, H., and SWIFT, A. (2006), 'Equality, Priority, and Positional Goods', *Ethics*, 116: 471–97.

BROCK, G. (2005), 'The Difference Principle, Equality of Opportunity, and Cosmopolitan Justice', *Journal of Moral Philosophy*, 2: 333–51.

BUCHANAN, A. (2004), *Justice, Legitimacy, and Self-Determination. Moral Foundations for International Law* (Oxford: Oxford University Press).

CASAL, P. (2007), 'Why Sufficiency Is Not Enough', *Ethics*, 117: 296–326.

CLARK, G., and SOHN, L. B. (1960), *World Peace Through World Law*, 2nd edn (Cambridge: Harvard University Press).

---

[70] See Meyer (1997b) and (2005: chs. 4 and 5).

COHEN, J., and SABEL, C. (2006), 'Extra Rempublicam Nulla Justitia?', *Philosophy & Public Affairs*, 34: 147–75.

CRISP, R. (2003), 'Equality, Priority, and Compassion', *Ethics*, 113: 745–63.

DANIELS, N. (1979), 'Wide Reflective Equilibrium and Theory Acceptance in Ethics', *Journal of Philosophy*, 76: 256–82.

DWORKIN, R. (2000), *Sovereign Virtue. The Theory and Practice of Equality* (Cambridge: Harvard University Press).

FRANKFURT, H. G. (1987), 'Equality as a Moral Ideal', *Ethics*, 98: 21–43.

GARDINER, S. (2002), 'The Real Tragedy of Commons', *Philosophy & Public Affairs*, 30: 387–416.

GASPART, F. and GOSSERIES, A. (2007), 'Are Generational Savings Unjust?', *Politics, Philosophy & Economics*, 6: 193–217.

GOSEPATH, S. (2004), *Gleiche Gerechtigkeit. Grundlagen eines liberalen Egalitarismus* (Frankfurt: Suhrkamp).

GRIFFIN, J. (1991), 'Mixing Values', *Aristotelian Society*, Supplementary Vol. LXV: 101–18.

HEYD, D. (1992), *Genethics. Moral Issues in the Creation of People* (Berkeley: University of California Press).

HÖFFE, O. (1999), *Demokratie im Zeitalter der Globalisierung* (Munich: C.H. Beck).

HOLTUG, N. (2007), 'Prioritarianism', in N. Holtug and K. Lippert-Rasmussen (eds.), *Egalitarianism. New Essays on the Nature and Value of Equality* (Oxford: Oxford University Press), 125–56.

——and LIPPERT-RASMUSSEN, K. (2007), 'An Introduction to Contemporary Egalitarianism', in N. Holtug and K. Lippert-Rasmussen (eds.). *Egalitarianism. New Essays on the Nature and Value of Equality* (Oxford: Oxford University Press), 1–38.

HORN, C. (1996), 'Philosophische Argumente für einen Weltstaat', *Allgemeine Zeitschrift für Philosophie*, 21: 229–51.

JULIUS, A. J. (2006), 'Nagel's Atlas', *Philosophy & Public Affairs*, 34: 176–92.

KANT, I. (1968), *Kants Werke*, vol. VIII (Akademie Werkausgabe, Wilhelm Weischedel (ed.), Berlin: Walter de Gruyter); the vol. contains: 'Zum Ewigen Frieden. Ein philosophischer Entwurf' (1795); 'Idee zu einer allgemeinen Geschichte in weltbürgerlicher Absicht' (1784); 'Über den Gemeinspruch: Das mag in der Theorie richtig sein, taugt aber nicht für die Praxis' (1793); 'Der Streit der Fakultäten' (1798). All essays in English translations in Kant (1970), *Kant's Political Writings*, Hans Reiss (ed.) (Cambridge: Cambridge University Press).

KAVKA, G. (1982), 'The Paradox of Future Individuals', *Philosophy & Public Affairs*, 11: 93–112.

KERSTING, W. (2001), 'Suffizienzorientierung versus Gleichheitsorientierung. Bemerkungen zur Konzeption einer internationalen Verteilungsgerechtigkeit', in K. G. Ballestrem (ed.), *Internationale Gerechtigkeit* (Opladen: Leske and Budrich), 278–315.

KUMAR, R. (2003), 'Who Can Be Wronged?', *Philosophy and Public Affairs*, 31: 99–118.

LIPPERT-RASMUSSEN, K. (2007), 'The Insignificance of the Distinction Between Telic and Deontic Egalitarianism', in N. Holtug and K. Lippert-Rasmussen (eds.), *Egalitarianism. New Essays on the Nature and Value of Equality* (Oxford: Clarendon Press), 101–24.

MARMOR, A. (2003), 'The Intrinsic Value of Economic Equality', in L. H. Meyer, S. L. Paulson, and T. W. Pogge (eds.), *Rights, Culture, and the Law. Themes from the Legal and Political Philosophy of Joseph Raz* (Oxford: Oxford University Press), 127–41.

McMAHAN, J. (1998), 'Wrongful Life: Paradoxes in the Morality of Causing People to Exist', in J. Coleman and C. Morris (eds.), *Rational Commitment and Social Justice. Essays for Gregory Kavka* (Cambridge: Cambridge University Press), 208–47.

MEYER, L. H. (1997a), 'Can Actual Future People Have a Right to Non-Existence?', *Archives for Philosophy of Law and Social Philosophy, Beiheft 67: Rights*, 200–9.

——(1997b), 'More Than They Have a Right to. Future People and Our Future Oriented Projects', in N. Fotion and J. C. Heller (eds.), *Contingent Future Persons. On the Ethics of Deciding Who Will Live, or Not, in the Future* (Dordrecht, Boston and London: Kluwer Academic Publishers), 137–56.

——(2000), 'Cosmopolitan Communities', in A. Coates (ed.). *International Justice* (Aldershot and Brookfield: Ashgate), 89–110.

——(2003), 'Past and Future. The Case for a Threshold Notion of Harm', in L. H. Meyer, S. L. Paulson, and T. W. Pogge (eds.), *Rights, Culture, and the Law. Themes from the Legal and Political Philosophy of Joseph Raz* (Oxford: Oxford University Press), 143–59.

——(2005), *Historische Gerechtigkeit* (Berlin and New York: Walter de Gruyter).

——(2008), 'Intergenerational Justice', in E. N. Zalta (ed.). *The Stanford Encyclopedia of Philosophy (Spring 2008 Edition)*. Available at <http://plato.stanford.edu/archives/spr2008/entries/justice-intergenerational/>.

——and ROSER, D. (2006), 'Distributive Justice and Climate Change', *Analyse & Kritik*, 28: 223–49.

MILLER, D. (2005), 'Against Global Egalitarianism', *The Journal of Ethics*, 9: 55–79.

NAGEL, T. (2005), 'The Problem of Global Justice', *Philosophy & Public Affairs*, 33, 113–47.

NUSSBAUM, M. C. (2000a), *Women and Human Development. The Capabilities Approach* (Cambridge: Cambridge University Press).

——(2000b), 'Aristotle, Politics, and Human Capabilities. A Response to Antony, Arneson, Charlesworthy, and Mulgan', *Ethics*, 111: 102–40.

OPITZ, P. J. (ed.) (2001), *Weltprobleme im 21. Jahrhundert* (Munich: Fink).

PARFIT, D. (1976), 'On Doing the Best for Our Children', in M. D. Bayles (ed.), *Ethics and Population* (Cambridge, Mass.: Schenkman), 100–15.

——(1982), 'Future Generations. Further Problems', *Philosophy & Public Affairs*, 11: 113–72.

——(1984), *Reasons and Persons* (Oxford: Clarendon Press).

PARFIT, D. (1997), 'Equality and Priority', *Ratio*, 10: 202–21.

—— (2000), 'Equality or Priority?', in M. Clayton and A. Williams (eds.), *The Ideal of Equality* (New York: St. Martin's Press), 81–125.

POGGE, T. W. (1989), *Realizing Rawls* (Ithaca: Cornell University Press).

—— (2002), 'Can the Capability Approach be Justified?', in M. Nussbaum and C. Flanders (eds.), *Global Inequalities*, Special issue of *Philosophical Topics* 30: 167–228.

RAWLS, J. (1971), *A Theory of Justice* (Oxford: Oxford University Press).

—— (1999), *The Law of Peoples* (Cambridge: Harvard University Press).

—— (2001), *Justice as Fairness. A Restatement* (Cambridge: Harvard University Press).

RAZ, J. (1986), *The Morality of Freedom* (Oxford: Clarendon Press).

—— (1991), 'Mixing Values', *Aristotelian Society*, Supplementary Vol. LXV: 83–100.

—— (1994), 'Duties of Well-Being', in J. Raz, *Ethics in the Public Domain. Essays in the Morality of Law and Politics* (Oxford: Clarendon Press), 3–28.

—— (1997), 'Incommensurability and Agency', in Ruth Chang (ed.). *Incommensurability, Incomparability, and Practical Reason* (Cambridge: Harvard University Press), 110–28.

—— (2003), 'Responses', in L. H. Meyer, S. L. Paulson and T. W. Pogge (eds.), *Rights, Culture, and the Law. Themes from the Legal and Political Philosophy of Joseph Raz* (Oxford: Oxford University Press), 253–73.

ROBERTS, M. A. (1998), *Child versus Childmaker. Future Persons and Present Duties in Ethics and the Law* (Lanham: Rowman & Littlefield).

ROSENBERG, A. (1995), 'Equality, Sufficiency, and Opportunity in the Just Society', *Social Philosophy and Policy*, 12: 54–71.

RYBERG, J., and TÄNNSJÖ, T. (eds.) (2004), *The Repugnant Conclusion. Essays on Population Ethics* (Dordrecht et al.: Kluwer).

SCANLON, T. M. (1998), *What We Owe To Each Other* (Cambridge: Harvard University Press).

—— (2005), *When Does Equality Matter?*, Ms. (presentation, British Academy, December 2005), 31pp.

SCHWARTZ, T. (1978), 'Obligations to Posterity', in R. I. Sikora and B. Barry (eds.), *Obligations to Future Generations* (Philadelphia: Temple University Press), 3–13.

SEN, A. K. (1984), *Resources, Values and Development* (Cambridge: Harvard University Press).

—— (1999), *Choice, Welfare and Measurement* (Cambridge: Harvard University Press).

SHER, G. (1979), 'Compensation and Transworld Personal Identity', *Monist*, 62: 378–91.

SHIFFRIN, S. (1999), 'Wrongful Life, Procreative Responsibility, and the Significance of Harm', *Legal Theory*, 5: 117–48.

STEINER, H. (2003), 'Equality, Incommensurability, and Rights', in L. H. Meyer, S. L. Paulson, and T. W. Pogge (eds.), *Rights, Culture, and the Law. Themes from the Legal and Political Philosophy of Joseph Raz* (Oxford: Oxford University Press), 119–26.

SUGANAMI, H. (1989), *The Domestic Analogy and World Order Proposals* (Cambridge: Cambridge University Press).

WENAR, L. (2001), 'Contractualism and Global Economic Justice', *Metaphilosophy*, 32: 79–94.

WOODWARD, J. (1986), 'The Non-Identity Problem', *Ethics*, 96: 804–31.

—— (1987), 'Reply to Parfit', *Ethics*, 96: 800–17.

PART II
Specific Issues

9

Wronging Future People: A Contractualist Proposal

RAHUL KUMAR

1. Can Future People Resent Us?

Some moral wrongs—call them *interpersonal wrongs*—involve one person wronging another. If you tell me a secret and I swear, at your request, not to tell anyone, but then I tell it to several others, you have a legitimate claim to have been wronged by me, insofar as my promise obligated me *to you* not to disclose your secret. But not all moral wrongs are appropriately characterized as interpersonal; some are better thought of as *impersonal moral wrongs*. Many, for instance, find intuitive the idea that it would be morally wrong to cover the ceiling of the Sistine Chapel with graffiti, quite apart from the implications of its desecration for the interests of those deprived of the experience of it, or those who have some particular personal interest in it. And according to a familiar and, to many, attractive philosophical characterization of moral wrongness, choosing a course of conduct that results in a state of affairs obtaining that is worse than would have obtained had another available course of action been chosen is morally wrong, even if it is the case that there is no one for whom that state of affairs can be said to be worse than that which would likely have obtained had the alternative course been chosen. That is, it can be morally wrong to do something even if no one stands to be wronged if it is done.[1]

Work on this paper was generously supported by a Laurence S. Rockefeller Visiting Fellowship at Princeton's University Center for Human Values.

[1] The distinction between impersonal and interpersonal characterizations of moral wrongness is meant to capture the same point as Derek Parfit's distinction between person-affecting and non-person affecting principles. The important difference is that Parfit treats person affecting views as appealing exclusively to considerations having to do with how a person is worse off than she otherwise would have been had some other choice been made. An interpersonal characterization of wrongness, as I

The dominant position in the philosophical literature on obligations to future generations holds that they are best characterized in impersonal terms. We ought not, the thought goes, to collectively pursue certain policies because they are likely to result in there coming into existence in the further future individuals with lives that are not as good as those who are likely to exist if some other policy is chosen. It isn't the case, though, that we *owe it to* anyone who will live in the further future not to make the morally wrong choice. But that doesn't mean that choosing such policies is not morally wrong.

There are several reasons for the appeal of this approach to understanding obligations to future generations, the most important of which is what Derek Parfit calls the *non-identity* problem. At the heart of the problem is the thought that in order to have a legitimate claim to have been wronged by what another does, it must be the case that one has been left worse off than one would have been had it not been for what was done.[2] This condition, though, is one that is not satisfied in cases in which the act in question is an *identity-fixing* fact. In such cases, if it weren't for the conduct or choice in question, the individual who is supposed to have been wronged would not have been conceived at even roughly the time she was conceived. So if it weren't for the wrongdoing, she in particular would not now exist; someone else would. But if a person would not now exist were it not for a particular choice or act, and she has a life worth living, that choice or act cannot be said to have made her worse off than she otherwise would have been. *A fortiori*, she has not been wronged.

If we make the reasonable assumption that many of the policy choices facing us have implications not just for the quality of life likely to be available to those who will live in the further future, but for who in particular will exist in the further future, what the non-identity problem brings into focus is that our thinking about what policy choice is morally defensible cannot be framed in terms of whether or not those who will live in the further future stand to be wronged if we adopt a particular policy. As it is intuitively plausible to think that there are moral constraints on the choice between policies that have implications for the quality of life that will be available to those who will live in the further future, this suggests that reasoning about the moral defensibility of choosing a particular policy is best characterized in impersonal terms. That

---

am using the term, is more capacious. It only requires that the justification for thinking that a person has been wronged by a particular choice appeal to considerations having to do with an individual's interests, but not that she has been made worse off than she otherwise would have been.

[2] This thought is often expressed as: you can only be wronged if you've been harmed, and harming requires that you have been made worse off than you otherwise would have been. Here I prefer the more general form of the point, which says that you can only have been wronged if you have been made worse off than you otherwise would have been.

is, we have a duty to ensure those who live in the further future have a certain quality of life available to them, but it is misleading to think of this duty as an obligation *owed to* those who will live in the further future.

It seems to me that an interpersonal characterization of the basis of our obligations to future generations is more intuitively plausible than an impersonal one, as the former does justice to the idea that the object of our concern when we worry about the implications of a policy choice for future generations is what our choices will mean for *them* rather than the value of the state of affairs likely to obtain as a consequence of our choice. But perhaps that is neither here nor there. The non-identity problem, after all, is a clear and compelling reason to reject the intuition that what we do now may be wronging future generations. And it isn't as if an impersonal characterization of such obligations is so radically at odds with what I'm taking to be the more intuitive view—it doesn't amount to a denial, after all, of our having particular duties with respect to future generations; it only denies that they are obligations owed to future generations.[3]

The suggestion, then, that not a lot hangs on the choice between an impersonal and an interpersonal characterization of the basis of obligations to future generations has, at least initially, considerable plausibility, particularly if we think about such obligations solely from the point of living individuals deliberating about a policy that has implications for the lives of those who will live in the further future.[4] But if we shift our attention to the point of view of those who end up living in the further future and are faced with the prospect of at best a poor quality of life as a consequence of a past moral wrongdoing, the idea that little hangs on whether the basis of obligations to future generations are characterized impersonally or interpersonally starts to sound suspect. Should we really accept, after all, that individuals faced with only poor life prospects, who know that their situation is a foreseen consequence of choices made in the past that could have been avoided with only a little additional sacrifice, are not justified in, for instance, resenting us for how we have wronged them by our choices, just because they in particular would not now exist had better choices been made? Further, the idea that those who will live in the further future cannot be wronged by what we do now is at odds with an intuitively familiar

---

[3] Any justification of duties to future generations that not only impersonal but consequentialist has to deal with well-known problems concerning how the demands of such duties are to be plausibly limited. For present purposes, I will assume that an impersonal justification need not be consequentialist.

[4] This seems to me to be true with respect to deliberations concerning the implications of our choices for future generations, but not true in the context of pre-conception reproductive decisions, where it is harder to deny that characterizing the basis of the relevant obligations in impersonal terms is revisionist.

understanding of certain kinds of demands for reparations for past injustice as owed to living individuals wronged by what was done several generations ago. We have, then, reasons to doubt the truth of the assertion that little hangs on whether obligations to future generations are characterized interpersonally or impersonally.

In this paper, I want to set aside questions about the prospects for plausibly characterizing obligations to future generations in impersonal terms, in favour of offering a positive case for an interpersonal characterization of the basis of such obligations. In particular, I believe a plausible characterization of this kind is readily available if we understand their basis in Scanlonian contractualist terms.[5]

Scanlonian contractualism, as I will understand it here, offers an explication of an interpersonal sense of 'morally wrong' central to commonsense morality. On this account, A wrongs B by failing to give B the kind of deliberative consideration of her relevant interests to which she is entitled, where what she is entitled to expect by way of consideration is fixed by a relevant principle for the general regulation of that type of situation that no one can reasonably reject.

The prospects for employing Scanlonian contractualism to illumine the basis of our obligations to future generations have to date received little attention. This has much to do with the common tendency to associate Scanlon's contractualism with Rawls's contractualist account of justice, one that is widely thought to be of little value as a framework for developing a better understanding of the basis and content of our obligations to future generations.[6] But while some of the objections to using the Rawlsian apparatus to make progress on these questions also have force against Scanlon's contractualism, and thus need to be addressed as part of a defense of the contractualist approach in this context, many do not. In particular, Rawls takes the problem to which the principles of justice answer as that of fixing fair terms of social co-operation for an on-going society amongst individuals who belong to a single society and single generation. Using Rawls's apparatus to justify the claim that we have certain obligations to future generations that we owe to them as a matter of fairness therefore appears then to require that, at the very least, generations be treated as engaged in co-operative activities with one

---

[5] The most complete statement of Scanlon's contractualist theory is that offered in T. M. Scanlon (1998), *What We Owe to Each Other* (Harvard University Press).

[6] See B. Barry (1977), 'Justice Between Generations', in P. M. S. Hacker and J. Raz (eds.), *Law, Morality and Society: Essays in Honour of H.L.A. Hart* (Oxford: Clarendon Press), 268–84 and B. Barry (1978), 'Circumstances of Justice and Future Generations', in R. Sikora and B. Barry (eds.), *Obligations to Future Generations* (Philadelphia: Temple University Press), 268–84.

another, which strikes many as, if not wholly implausible, at least very difficult to defend.[7] This kind of objection has no purchase against a characterization of our obligations to future generations in Scanlonian contractualist terms, as no notion of either social co-operation or reciprocity plays a role in that account.

Properly understood, Scanlon's contractualism offers a way of thinking about the basis and content of obligations to future generations that has, I believe, considerable intuitive appeal.[8] This is especially so for two reasons. First, the non-identity problem cannot get started within the terms of the contractualist account of wronging. So the fact that who *in particular* will live in the further future is not independent of whether or not a particular policy is adopted has, on this view, no bearing on whether or not those who will live in the further future are wronged by our adopting that policy. Second, contractualism treats the reason we have to be concerned about avoiding wronging those who will live in the further future as no different than the reason we each have to be concerned with not wronging those now living. On this account, then, there are no distinctive philosophical issues regarding the normative basis of such obligations that need to be addressed. The difficult questions are all substantive, concerning how exactly we are required to constrain our present choices in order to avoid undermining the interests of those who will live in the further future.

The case for understanding obligations to future generations in contractualist terms is presented in the next five sections. Sections 2 and 3 sketch the general contractualist approach to what it is for one person to have wronged another, with particular attention to aspects of it that are of particular relevance to the issue at hand. Section 4 argues that these aspects of the account, properly understood, show contractualism to be immune to the non-identity problem. Section 5 argues for the claim that on the contractualist account, the reason a person has to care about the justifiability of her conduct to those who now exist is also the reason she has to care about the justifiability of her conduct to those who will live in the further future, even if who in particular exists in

---

[7] J. Reiman (2007), in 'Being Fair to Future People: The Non-Identity Problem in the Original Position', *Philosophy and Public Affairs*, 35/1: 69–92 argues, on Rawlsian grounds, that we have obligations to future generations as a matter of fairness. But he does not appear to offer an argument as to why we owe anything to those who will live in the further future as a matter of fairness, in the sense of fairness that Rawls identifies as central to the justification of domestic obligations of justice that contemporaries in a society owe to one another.

[8] Scanlon does not discuss the issue in any detail in *What We Owe to Each Other*, noting only that the question of whether or not we have wronged someone by making a particular choice if it is the case that the wronged would not now exist were it not for that choice is a substantive question about when we have wronged someone, not a question concerning who can be wronged (Scanlon 1998: 186–87).

the further future is not independent of her present choices. Section 6 briefly considers the relevance of the line of argument developed in the previous sections for thinking about the claims of living individuals to reparations for past wrongdoing or injustice.

2. Non-Consequentialist Wronging and the Non-identity Problem

Central to the contractualist account of what it is for one person to have wronged another is a general thought that it shares with certain other non-consequentialist accounts of wronging: that how one person relates to another has a moral significance that is wholly independent of what happens to the other as a consequence of having been related to in that way. The intuitive force of this idea can be illustrated with a simple example. Say I am injured in a skiing accident because I didn't know that the slope conditions were hazardous. It then comes to light that a disgruntled former student, seeing where I was heading, removed the 'Warning: conditions on this run are hazardous' sign that would have stopped me from making the run (I'm not a risk taker). The emergence of this fact doesn't change the extent of my injury, but it does bring to light that I am not just harmed, but have been *wronged*, for my predicament is not the result of mere bad luck, but of another having *put me* in harm's way.[9]

Is having been harmed even a necessary condition of having been wronged? Let's say I'm lucky—I come through the run unscathed, so I'm in no respect worse off as a result of the student's malicious conduct. That doesn't change the fact that I've been wronged. After all, though not harmed, I was still *put* in harm's way (the sign did not, after all, just get blown off the signpost by a strong wind). It is enough for me to have a claim to have been wronged that

---

[9] In (2004) 'Harms and Wrongs', *Buffalo Criminal Law Review*, 4: 101–33, Anthony Duff suggests that what cases like this show is that there is a special class of harms that cannot be brought about by just any causal chain, but can only be brought about through human agency. The harm of vandalism, for instance, is distinct from the harm of having one's property destroyed or damaged, as the harm can only be understood through an intentional description that includes the fact that the damage or destruction was intentionally brought about through the agency of another. Duff is certainly right to think that certain kinds of harms are best described using thick ethical concepts whose description is internally related to having been wronged, but this doesn't show that the harm of, say, vandalism is a kind of harm that can only be brought about through human agency. It only shows that what happened as a result of the vandalism, which could have come about some other way, has a special significance for the wronged that can only be made sense of by attention to how it came about.

he deliberately did what was necessary to interfere with my life, even if my good luck prevented his plan from succeeding.[10] [11]

What non-consequentialist accounts like contractualism take this show is not just that a person can be wronged without being harmed—a perfectly familiar point (think of harmless trespass)—but that what it is for one person to have wronged another ought always to be explicated without appeal to how the victim has been harmed, or generally, what has happened to her. This move has clear implications for assessing the challenge of the non-identity problem, as standard formulations of it assume an understanding of what it is for a person to have been wronged as that person having been made worse off than she otherwise would have been were it not for the wrongdoing. The non-consequentialist's proposed approach to the explication of wronging promises, therefore, a way of understanding wronging in which the non-identity problem can't get started.

Realizing this promise is not, however, a straightforward matter. Standard formulations of the non-identity problem do assume an understanding of having been wronged as 'having been made worse off than one would otherwise have been'. But that is just a convenient way of articulating its central insight: that for a *particular* person to have been wronged by another, it must be the case that she does not owe the fact of her existence to the wrongdoing. If there is such a dependence, the question can then be pressed against the non-consequentialist: you claim, roughly, that if a particular person has been wronged, the wrongdoer has related to her in a way that does not appropriately respect her standing as a person. But if the existence of the wronged is not independent of the wrongdoing, whose standing as a person was it exactly that the wrongdoer failed to appropriately take account of in her deliberations? The challenge of the non-identity problem, that of explaining how it is that a particular person could be wronged by another's failure to take the requirements of respect for her status as a person seriously when she

---

[10] A suggestion made by Axel Gosseries is that perhaps the harm in this kind of case is just the harm of another acting disrespectfully with regards to your interests. That is, disrespect is intrinsically harmful (which is compatible one having benefited overall as a result of the harmful action). Part of the difficulty with this proposal is understanding how to characterize the state that the disrespectful action has caused one to be in. On the standard understanding of harm suggests that an individual could be caused to be in a harmed state in a number of different ways, which makes the harmed state (what happens) independent of how it was brought about. To make sense of the idea that someone relating to you disrespectfully is necessarily harmful, some characterization of the state that a person is caused to be by the disrespectful treatment is called for other than saying that one is in a state of having been disrespected which makes it clear how being treated with disrespect is intrinsically damaging, as opposed to, say, offensive.

[11] See Arthur Ripstein's important discussion of the harmless trespass case, in Arthur Ripstein (2006), 'Beyond the harm principle', *Philosophy and Public Affairs*, 34/3: 215–45.

in particular would not now exist were it not for that very failure, remains standing.

3. Contractualism: Basic Framework

It seems to me that the general non-consequentialist approach to what it is for one person to have wronged another briefly sketched in the previous section does contain the seeds of a promising approach to thinking about wronging that is not derailed, in the relevant range of cases, by the non-identity problem. But to realize this promise, we have to move from certain general non-consequentialist ideas concerning wronging to a particular non-consequentialist account in which these general ideas are better fleshed out, namely Scanlonian contractualism.

Contractualism aims characterize the basis of one set of moral norms, those concerning the obligations we owe to one another as a matter of respect for the value of one another as persons. In particular, contractualism holds that one person wrongs another by relating to her in a way disallowed by any system of principles for the general regulation of behaviour that no one could reasonably reject as a basis of unforced, informed, general agreement. Anyone, that is, who values how she relates to others being justifiable to any other by appeal to principles no one could reasonably reject.

Though there is a great deal to be said about this characterization of what it is for one person to wrong another, what is of particular relevance for present purposes is the role of principles as fixing the terms of how individuals ought to relate to one another if they are to do so on a basis of mutual respect for one another's value as persons. In particular, principles fix the kind of deliberative consideration of her relevant interests that a person is entitled to legitimately expect and demand, in a particular type of situation, of another (and that it is legitimate for another to expect and demand of her) as a matter of respect for her value, or the value of another, as a person.

The understanding of 'value of a person' here is best characterized in terms of two general ideas concerning what appropriate deliberative recognition of a person's value requires. First, a person must be recognized as a creature capable of recognizing, and acting upon, reasons. Second, a person must be recognized as having 'the capacity to select among the various ways there is reason to want a life to go, and therefore to govern and live that life in an active sense' (Scanlon 1998: 105). That is, a person must be recognized as one who has the capacity not only to be guided by her beliefs about reasons, but also to reflect upon whether her beliefs are correct, select among her beliefs in ways that allow her to shape her life in distinctive ways, and reflect upon the quality of her selections. It is this general capacity, without which self-knowledge would not be possible, which distinguishes persons from other animals capable of intentional behaviour. More importantly, it is in virtue of this capacity that there is the possibility of what Philippa Foot refers to as 'second-order evil' in human life, which has to do with 'the consciousness of being disregarded, lonely or oppressed'.[12] The capacity to be conscious of reasons results, then, in a distinct kind of vulnerability, a vulnerability to what another's reasons, or reasoning, concerning how it is appropriate to relate to oneself says about oneself.[13]

This account holds that what it is for one person to have *wronged* another is for the wrongdoer to have culpably failed to regulate her practical deliberations in the way that the wronged was legitimately entitled to expect and demand of her.[14] But why think that the failure to give another the kind of consideration in a particular type of situation to which she is entitled amounts to *wronging* her, rather than just having done something morally wrong? Reflection on the kinds of considerations relevant in contractualist moral argument for justifying a principle that fixes it that persons, in situations of a certain type, are entitled to a certain degree of deliberative consideration by others, suggests a possible answer. In the contractualist account, the relevant range of considerations is marked out by what has come to be known as the *individual reasons restriction*, which delimits the kinds of considerations relevant for the assessment of a principle's validity to those implications (broadly construed) to which an individual could appeal to as having a bearing on *her* being able to live a rationally self-governed, meaningful life.[15] Amongst the kinds of considerations excluded by this restriction are impersonal considerations, such as the implications of a particular principle for the impersonal value of the outcome likely to obtain as a consequence of the principle's adoption (like the diversity of plant life in a certain area of the Antarctic) and less personal considerations, such as a principle's implications for a group of people (in cases

---

[12] Philippa Foot (1994), 'Rationality and Virtue', in H. Pauer-Studer (ed.), *Norms, Values, and Society*, (Netherlands: Kluwer), 210.

[13] The last part of this paragraph is taken from R. Kumar (2003), 'Who Can Be Wronged?', *Philosophy and Public Affairs*, 31/2: 99–118.

[14] 'Practical deliberations' should be understood broadly, having to do with what a person takes there to be reason to do, think, or feel. Such assessments do not require that there be anything like conscious deliberative assessment of reasons.

[15] See Scanlon 1998: 204–6, and R. Kumar (2004), 'Reasonable Reasons in Contractualist Moral Argument', *Ethics*, 114: 6–37.

where there is no story to be told about the distinctive interest of individuals served by group membership).

The intuitive appeal of understanding what it is to have been wronged as having to do with having been made worse off as a result of another's conduct than one otherwise would have been lies in the thought that what justifies the wronged's entitlement—not shared by others—to press a specific complaint about the wrongdoer's conduct is that something has *happened to her* that justifies her claim to stand in a relation to the wrongdoer as victim. The demarcation of relevant considerations by the individual reasons restriction aims to capture this same idea. It does so because it connects the idea of having failed to give another the kind of consideration of her interests to which she is entitled to a failure of the wrongdoer to appropriately recognize the value of *her life*. This is not quite the same as the idea of one person's life having been damaged as a result of another's conduct (the worse off view), but it occupies the same conceptual space, without requiring that anything have happened to a person in order for her to stand in a particular relation to the wrongdoer as the one who has been (metaphorically) attacked by wrongdoer's conduct.

4. Immunity to the Non-identity Problem?

The discussion so far has focused on contractualism's claim to offer an interpersonal characterization of what it is for one person to have wronged another that does not require that anything have happened to a person in order for her to have been wronged. The challenge at the end of section 2, however, has yet to be directly addressed: how it is that a failure to give another the kind of consideration she is owed can be said to have wronged her if there was no particular other who, at the time of acting, could be picked out as the one *to whom* a certain degree of consideration is *owed*?

The best contractualist response to this challenge, I believe, is one that takes to be significant the way in which the system of principles in contractualism is relevantly analogous to a legal system, in that the principles set out the kind of deliberative consideration that persons are entitled to expect of one another in different *types* of situation.[16] A 'type' of situation is not, of course, an actual situation, but a way of referring to a cluster of normatively relevant

---

[16] The system of principles is analogous to a legal system in two respects. First, it allows individuals to know in advance roughly what can be demanded of them by others, and what they are entitled to expect of others. Second, it provides a shared basis among persons for the assessment and criticism of conduct.

characteristics that can be found together in various actual situations. To say that a principle is for the regulation of a type of situation is just to say that the principle's role is to guide individuals in situations of that type as to the kinds of interests of others that they must, must not, and may take into account in assessing what is morally permissible in a situation of that type.[17]

Persons, like situations, figure in the specification of principles as type characterizations. And just as a type of situation is not an actual, fully determinate situation, a *type* of person is not a particular, fully determinate person. Rather, a type of person is just a way of referring to a cluster of normatively significant characteristics (and related interests) that may aptly characterize certain actual particular individuals in actual situations in which they find themselves. One can, for example, meaningfully discuss and argue about what principles regulating how employers are to relate to their employees specify by way of consideration of an employee's interests in different types of situation, such as what kind of warning and assistance is due to an employee whose performance is coming close to warranting dismissal.[18] What the principle specifies is not what is owed by way of consideration to a particular employee (who has a particular token identity), but what is owed to an individual in virtue of satisfying a certain *type* description, namely being an employee at risk of dismissal. Any particular individual will exemplify many different type descriptions in virtue of her various characteristics. What a particular individual is owed by way of consideration in a particular situation will depend on (a) the type of situation, (b) the kind of consideration that can be defended as owed by individuals to one another by appeal to the relevant principle for the regulation of that type of situation, and (c) the relevant type descriptions that are applicable to the particular relevant individuals in that situation.

The general point here, which is key to understanding contractualism's claim to immunity to the non-identity problem, is that for there to be a fact of the matter concerning what it is one owes another to whom stands in a particular type of relationship, it is enough that the other to whom consideration is owed be characterizable in normative terms, by a relevant type description. There need be no fact of the matter concerning the particular token identity of that individual, as her token identity is irrelevant for fixing what it is she is owed as

---

[17] The application of principles to situations does, of course, require judgment, as a principle is not a statable rule. Rather, someone whose judgment about what it is permissible to do is guided by and expresses an understanding of a particular principle is one who grasps (though need not be able to articulate) a complex rationale for requiring that individuals take certain considerations into account as reasons, and set aside other considerations as reason giving, in deliberating about what there is, all things considered, reason to do in the type of situation she finds herself in. See Scanlon 1998: 197–202.

[18] Here I have in mind what employees are morally entitled to as a matter of fairness, not what they are legally entitled to.

a matter of respect for her value as a person. As I've previously argued in the context of thinking about preconception obligations, if a woman intends to have a child, there is a fact of the matter about what she owes her child by way of due care to ensure the child is born healthy. If she culpably fails to comply with those requirements, her child, irrespective of the child's token identity, will have a legitimate claim to have been wronged, as the requirements that were not complied with are requirements demanded by the proper recognition of the value of *the child's* life.[19]

Note, however, that in this sort of case, the intention to have a child places the mother in a normatively significant relation to another, her child, a relationship regulated by certain moral principles that fix the kind of consideration she owes her child (even before there is a particular existing individual who is, or will become, her child). The choice between policies that have implications for both who will live in the further future and what kind of life will be available to them is relevantly disanalogous, insofar as it is hard to see what familiar type of relationship we stand in to those who will live in the further future that is relevantly analogous to other types of relationship—like that of parent and child—such that it makes sense to speak of what it is we owe *them* in virtue of the particular type of relationship we stand in to *them*. In the absence of any such concretely characterizable relationship that living individuals stand in with respect to those who will live in the further future, one might well wonder whether a contractualist defense of what we owe to those who will live in the further future is really available after all.

5. In What Relation Do We Stand to Those Who Will Live in the Further Future?

Let's grant that we don't stand in any concretely characterizable relationship to those who will live in the further future. Does that undermine the case for thinking that if we now make choices without appropriate regard for the implications of such choices for their interests, we will have wronged them—such that any one of the wronged will be justified, for instance, in taking herself to have privileged standing to complain, resent the attitude towards her embodied by our choices, hold us accountable for our failure, etc.?[20]

---

[19] See Kumar, 2003.
[20] Here I have in mind what P. F. Strawson (1982) calls 'reactive attitudes'. See his 'Freedom and Resentment', in Gary Watson (ed.), *Free Will* (Oxford: Oxford University Press), 59–80.

Grounds for thinking that it does not are suggested by reflection on the understanding of moral motivation that lies at the heart of the contractualist account. Contractualism, recall, holds that a person is wronged if another relates to her in a particular way that, under the circumstances, is disallowed by principles for the general regulation of behaviour that no one could reasonably reject as a basis for informed, unforced, general agreement. A valid principle, fixing the deliberative consideration in a particular type of situation that persons are entitled to expect and demand of another in virtue of their status as persons, must, on this view, be *justifiable to anyone* on grounds she could not reasonably reject. Anyone, that is, who values living her life on terms justifiable to others on grounds no one can reasonably reject.

The requirement that a valid principle must be justifiable to any *one* on grounds she could not reasonably reject in order to count as impartially justifiable rests on two ideas. First, that impartial moral justification requires that the life of each person be taken into account as intrinsically no more important than any other. Second, that the appropriate way to take a person into account is as one capable of assessing reasons and justifications, and living her life guided by her assessments and choices amongst competing reasons.

What it is to take a person into account as one capable of assessing reasons and justifications is to consider whether or not a proposed principle for the general regulation of how individuals relate to one another in a certain type of situation is one that, as assessed from her own standpoint, she has reason to accept (or not reasonably reject)—assuming that she values her conduct being justifiable to others on grounds no one can reasonably reject.[21] [22] A principle that can be so justified is one that she can be understood to have *licensed* you (and others) to be guided by in how you relate to her in situations of the relevant type. Having another be guided in how she relates to you by a principle that you (for good reason) authorized her to be guided by in how she relates to you, on this account, is constitutive of what it is to have one's value as a creature capable of assessing reasons, evaluating justifications, and making reason guided decisions concerning how to live, respected.

An impartially justified principle—one that takes into account the value of each person's life in the same way—is one, then, that is justifiable *to any individual* as one that she has reason, as assessed from her standpoint (assuming she values being guided in how she relates to others by principles no one can reasonably reject), to license others to be guided by in how they relate to her

---

[21] See Scanlon's discussion of 'standpoints' at Scanlon 1998: 202–6.

[22] Assessment of the reasonable rejectability of a principle from a particular standpoint or point of view, recall, is limited to taking into account those considerations that the individual reasons restriction allows as relevant.

in that type of situation. Even if we do not, therefore, stand in any particular concrete type of relationship to those who will live in the further future, this understanding of impartial justification suggests that we do stand in a morally relevant relation to them, as choices we make now that have implications for the quality of life likely to be available to them must be justifiable to any one of them by appeal a principle that no one can reasonably reject. They are owed this kind of consideration simply in virtue being persons; that there is no fact about the matter concerning their particular identities (because they do not now exist) is irrelevant to their claim on us that our choices be constrained by considerations having to do with what it justifiable to each of them.

This last point is unquestionably contentious, as no reason has yet been given for thinking that the scope of the 'no one' in 'no one can reasonably reject' includes those who do not now exist, and may never exist depending on the choices we make now. Isn't it more plausible to restrict the scope of those to whom principles must be justifiable to those who are currently living?

An objection of this kind, it seems, to me is naturally suggested by the invocation of the notion of 'agreement' in the contractualist characterization of what it is for one person to have wronged another. But it is nevertheless misplaced. For on this account, what one to whom living her life in conformity with the requirements of principles no one can reasonably reject is important cares about is not whether or not others recognize that she lives her life on terms respectful of the value of others as persons; nor is the motivation rooted in the prospect of so living making it more likely that others will relate to her on terms respectful of her value as a person. What matters is that the principle guiding her choices and actions in a particular type of situation be *in fact* justifiable to any other on grounds no one can reasonably reject, whether or not any other either knows or cares that her conduct is so justifiable.

Living in conformity with the requirements of principles no one can reasonably reject puts one in a relation of 'mutual recognition' with others, a kind of relationship that is worthwhile for its own sake as a way of living with others (Scanlon 1998: 162). The appeal of the ideal of standing in a relationship of mutual recognition with others partially accounts, contractualism holds, for the distinctive reason giving force of the judgement that e.g. acting in a certain way would wrong another. Unlike familiar kinds of relationships valued for their own sake, though, in which interaction, shared history, and some knowledge of mutual regard for one another is necessary, what matters to one who values standing in a relationship of mutual of recognition to others is that anyone, *at any time or place*, when assessing e.g. her choice made in a particular situation, have reason to assess that choice as permitted by a principle which that person cannot reasonably reject.[23]

One might still be inclined to think that the central puzzle has yet to be addressed: what sense does it make to speak of justifiability to those who do not presently exist, and who may not exist depending on what choices are now made?[24] The argument so far, that a valid principle must be justifiable to anyone on grounds no individual could reasonably reject, whether or not that individual presently exists, does not, it could be argued, settle the matter. For it does not take seriously the distinction between justifiability to those whom we know will live in the further future whose particular identities are independent of the choices we make now, and those whose identities are dependent on the kind of choice whose moral permissibility is in question. In the later case, there is still a serious question as to whether it makes sense to ask whether a principle that permits the kind of choice in question is one that is justifiable *to* them.

What this worry reveals is the deceptive allure of understanding the question of whether a particular principle is, or is not, one that no one could reasonably reject as a matter of assessing the objections to a particular principle pressed by actual persons. But the contractualist position, recall, is that assessment of a principle requires consideration of its implications, both positive and negative, from the points of view, or standpoints, of a plurality of individuals characterized as types, where a 'type' of individual is just a way of referring to a normatively significant cluster of relevant interests that a person might well have in virtue of certain general features of that person and the circumstances in which she finds herself.[25]

There may, then, be no existing individuals whose point of view, in the relevant respects, is aptly characterized by the cluster of interests constitutive of a certain standpoint, and it may be unlikely (though not impossible) that there ever will be any such particular individuals. But that has no bearing on the relevance of that standpoint to the assessment of the particular principle.

---

[23] That the time or place on the globe in which a person lives is in principle irrelevant follows once the crucial move that distinguishes Hobbesian contractarian approaches to moral reasoning from contractualism is made, namely what matters is *that* one's choice or action is justifiable to any other as respectful of the value of her life. There is no further goal, such as co-operation for the sake of mutual advantage, sought that would justify limiting the scope of those to whom justification is owed.

[24] As Barry dryly observes, making an analogous point, 'we are bound to worry about the good sense of choosing principles to advance the interests of potential people most of whom will never exist'; B. Barry (1989), *Theories of Justice* (Berkeley: University of California Press), 195.

[25] Scanlon calls these *generic reasons*, where a generic reason is 'one that we can see people have in virtue of certain general characteristics; it is not attributed to specific individuals' (Scanlon 1998: 204–5).

For what matters to one who values standing in a relation to others of mutual recognition is that if a particular individual were to come into existence whose particular point of view is aptly characterized by the cluster of interests constitutive of a certain standpoint, it will be true that that, in living in conformity with principles no one could reasonably reject, one will have given appropriate consideration to the relevant interests of *that* individual.

On this picture, then, the consideration that who in particular will exist in the future is not independent of the choices we make now is one that has *no relevance* for the question of what principles ought to regulate choices that have implications for those who will live in the further future. Those who will live in the further future figure in moral thought as a standpoint of relevant interests. In asking whether or not those who will live in the further future have grounds for reasonably rejecting a particular principle, what is of concern is the objections to the principle in light of its implications that could be pressed from that standpoint; who (if anyone) in particular exists in the further future, whose relevant interests are captured by that standpoint, is neither here nor there.

It could be objected that this line of argument simply relocates the difficulty of thinking about obligations to future generations in contractualist terms. For even if it is agreed that the non-identity problem can't get started on contractualist terms, the view still requires us to be able to make sense of what the interests are of those who will live in the further future. Is that remotely reasonable? How do we know what will reasonably matter to those who will live in the further future?[26]

Assessing this concern requires a more extensive discussion than I can give it here, but a few points are worth making. As stated, the objection is vague; in order to assess it, it is worth distinguishing three questions: first, what if human beings who live in the further future have adapted such that certain things that reasonably matter to us no longer reasonably matter to them? Second, what if human beings in the future having enhanced capacities that make their interests very different from the interests of human beings as we now know them? And three, what if human beings in the further future have interests like ours, but have adapted in various ways that make those interests much easier to satisfy than they are for us?[27]

With respect to the first question, it may be that those who live in the further future have adapted in certain ways such that they no longer seek to secure

---

[26] I am grateful to an audience at the Arizona State University Law School for pressing me on this issue.

[27] It is, for instance, sometimes suggested that we need not worry unduly about the implications of global warming.

or pursue a certain interest. But the relevant question, on the contractualist account, is whether if someone did seek to pursue to secure that interest, would they have reason to do so? If they would have reason to do so, the permissibility of doing now what will undermine that possibility in the further future needs to be assessed. The second question, which appeals to the spectre of what is sometimes spoken of as 'post-humans', raises a general issue of how, on the contractualist account, we are to think about our duties to non-human animals. That is an important issue, but not one specific to thinking about obligations to future generations. The third question, it seems to me, is not a foundational question but a substantive issue: in assessing the extent to which pursuit of a particular policy risks the interests of future generations, how much technological and social advancement over time are we entitled to assume in assessing the seriousness of the risk? This kind of question, however, can only be helpfully vetted in light of details concerning the type of policy in question and the specific kinds of foreseeable implications for those who will live in the further future.

6. The Relevance of Reparations

Earlier, I suggested that what is intuitively resonant about the idea of a person being wronged by what was done several generations ago, even in cases in which it is arguably true that she would not now exist were it not for that wrongdoing, is that claims to be wronged of this type are often implicit in certain ways of framing certain claims to reparations for historical injustice, such as those pressed by African Americans for the injustice of chattel slavery. The discussion so far, however, has focused exclusively on the case of doing now what has implications for those who will live in the further future, such as rapidly depleting resources in such a way that the deleterious consequences create a serious risk of harm for those who will live many generations from now. In this section, I want to briefly consider what bearing the approach to thinking about intergenerational obligations on offer will have on how the basis of claims to reparations are best understood.

Some approaches to thinking about the reparations claims of the living treat the relevant issues as distinct from those concerning our obligations to future generations. One reason for thinking that this is the methodologically correct view is that, for example, the claims of living African-Americans to reparations for chattel slavery concern a wrong that has arguably wronged several generations of African-Americans since the time of chattel slavery. Questions concerning obligations to future generations need not be intergenerational in this way, as often the risk of harm created by certain policy choices now will not threaten the interests of anyone for several hundred years.

If we characterize obligations to future generations in contractualist terms, this difference proves to be greatly exaggerated. Roughly put, in both the chattel slavery case and the resource depletion case, the wrongdoing has to do with certain choices or decisions being made that are not consistent with what respect for the value of a certain type of individual requires. As a result, all tokens of the type have a claim to be wronged. The difference is that in the chattel slavery case, there have been several generations of living tokens of the type, but in many resource depletion cases, tokens of the type whose interests are jeopardized by certain policy choices will not exist for another few hundred years.

But can the contractualist framework really be deployed to illumine the basis of the claims of the living to reparations for a wrongdoing that took place, in some cases, several hundred years ago? Here is why one might well think its value in this context is very limited: say we accept that those who will live in the further future can be wronged by what is done today. Won't it be true of them (provided they have lives worth living) that though they have a claim to be wronged by past choices, this at most shows that a certain degree of anger, or resentment, directed towards those who made those choices in the past is justifiable? But since (let us assume) they wouldn't now exist had those choices not been made, they are not entitled to anything like compensation for the wrongdoing. After all, it isn't the case that *they in particular* would be now better off were it not for the past wrongdoing. This conclusion is, note, compatible with there still being good reason to acknowledge the past wrongdoing and publicly discuss the history and its consequences in order to learn from it, in the spirit of 'never again!'.[28]

There are two distinct intuitions at work in this challenge that are worth pulling apart. The first is that those who would not now exist were it not for past wrongdoing ought, in some sense, to be glad that the wrong was done. After all, they now have lives worth living, and that is an unqualifiedly good thing. That they are wronged by what was done in the past is neither here nor there, as it is just an unfortunate fact about them they in particular could not exist other than as wronged.[29] One can accept, then, that they are wronged by

---

[28] For pressing this objection, and for helpful discussion of how to respond to it, I am grateful to Lukas Meyer.

[29] Melinda Roberts proposes an approach to non-identity issues that denies that this is so, but for present purposes I will set aside the complications that consideration of her view would introduce. See M. Roberts (1998), *Child versus Childmaker* (Boston: Rowman Littlefield).

what was done in the past, but deny that they are entitled to anything in virtue of the wrongdoing, as they have benefited as a result of it. The second is the corollary of this thought, that one may have a claim to have been wronged by past wrongdoing, but because one has not been harmed, nothing is owed.

Does having benefited from a past wrongdoing undermine a claim to redress in virtue of having been wronged? Consideration of a simple example suggests the idea is dubious: say my lover betrays me, and I am destitute because of what she has done. To help with my depression, I join a therapy group, and there I meet someone wonderful, and we have a very happy life together, much happier than the one I could have had with my ex-lover. But does it then follow that when we happen to run into one another years later, she has no reason to apologize for what she did, and I am wrong to think that I am entitled to an apology? My own intuition here is that I am so entitled, and that her apologizing is completely appropriate.

What this example draws our attention to is a general point: the thought that one is not entitled to demand redress or reparation for past wrongdoing if one would not now exist were it not for that wrongdoing implicitly assumes that if one is entitled to redress for past wrongdoing, one is committed to the claim that *it would have been better* had the wrongdoing not been done. But that assumption needs to be argued for. In particular, some argument is needed to explain why it is that one who takes herself to be entitled to redress in virtue of how she has been wronged must be committed to anything more than what was morally wrong, taking no stand on the question of whether it would have been better had it not been done.[30]

Arguably, even if this argument is sound, all it shows is that those who could not now exist other than as wronged are owed some kind of symbolic acknowledgment, or apology, by the wrongdoer. Reparations claims, though, are often characterized as demands for both symbolic and material redress. What the second intuition suggests is that one is only owed material compensation if one has been harmed, not just wronged, by past wrongdoing. So, for instance, with respect to African-Americans, the suggestion is that living African-Americans may have a claim to be insulted by chattel slavery, but they have no claim to have been injured by it. They have, therefore, no claim to material compensation for chattel slavery and its consequences.

There are at least two ways of resisting this conclusion. The first is to reject an understanding of harm presupposed by this argument, one that requires

---

[30] In some cases there will be no existing wrongdoer(s), or any person or institution who stands in the right relation to the wrongdoer(s) to hold accountable. But that doesn't undermine the entitlement of those who have been wronged by what was done in the past to hold those who wronged them accountable.

the truth of a counterfactual claim, and turn instead to a non-comparative understanding of harm.[31] The other is to call into question the idea that what is relevant for the assessment of what the wronged is owed is best understood as the eradication of harm done in any sense. This idea of appropriate redress as eradication of harm has a natural home in tort law, where damages are awarded to the wronged as a remedy in order to make it as if the person had never been wronged. But it is a mistake to therefore assume that it has ready application in thinking about what the wronged is morally entitled to demand of the wrongdoer by way of holding her accountable for what she has done. It may be enough for purposes of a moral claim to material redress that the wronged faces certain serious disadvantages or is badly off in ways systematically related to what the wrongdoer has done.

I won't here attempt to elaborate this later strategy. For present purposes, the salient point is that there is no reason to think that a justification on contractualist terms is not available for why those wronged by what was done many generations ago may be entitled to some form of material redress, not just symbolic acknowledgment of past wrongdoing (even if they would not now be better off were it not for the past wrongdoing).

7. Conclusion

My aim in this discussion has been to sketch a case for framing substantive questions concerning intergenerational obligations, such as those owed to future generations and those owed to those wronged by historical injustice, in contractualist terms. Doing so allows us to circumvent many of the conceptual difficulties that are often thought to block characterizing such obligations as *owed to* those who will live in further future. Those who end up living in the further future can be wronged by what we do now, even in cases in which who in particular lives in the further future is not independent of whether or not a choice is made now that wrongs them. Temporal distance, like spatial distance, has no bearing on the question of whether a person can in principle be wronged. That doesn't show, of course, that such considerations are necessarily irrelevant. What does follow is that the relevance of temporal distance as a consideration to be taken into account in working out what the substance is of our obligations to those who will live in the further future needs to be justified, just as the relevance of spatial distance needs to be justified in

---

[31] A suggestion developed by Lukas Meyer in, most recently, (2006), 'Reparations and Symbolic Restitution', *Journal of Social Philosophy*, 37/3, 406–22.

working out the substantive content of what it is that the affluent owe to the distance needy.

In fact, it is an implication of this discussion that most of the interesting questions concerning obligations to future generations are not foundational, but substantive. For what has been argued for here is not just that the contractualist account does a good job of making sense of reasoning about what it is we owe to those who will live in the further future, but it does so without introducing any innovations to the contractualist account in order to allow it to better account for obligations to future generations. That is, on this account, thinking about what we owe to future generations raises no foundational questions that are different from those involved in understanding interpersonal obligations that those now living owe one another. The difficult issues have to do with, for instance, how much can be demanded of us now in the name of not imposing a serious risk of harm on those who will live in the further future, a question that raises issues analogous to those that arise in thinking about the demandingness of obligations to help alleviate the plight of the distant needy.

I say 'most of the interesting questions' because there is one important question regarding future generations that might be thought to appeal to moral norms that fall outside that aspect of morality which contractualism aims to illumine. What has been offered here is a way of thinking about what is owed by way of consideration to those who will live in the further future, assuming there will be people living in the further future. But it appears to say nothing about the idea that there is something morally objectionable about doing what will ensure that *no one* is living in the further future. It is an open question as to whether anything at all can be said to better illumine this idea, to the extent it is defensible, by appeal to ideas implicit in the contractualist framework.[32]

References

BARRY, B. (1977), 'Justice Between Generations', in P. M. S. Hacker and J. Raz (eds.), *Law, Morality and Society: Essays in Honour of H. L. A. Hart* (Oxford: Clarendon Press), 268–84.

—— (1978), 'Circumstances of Justice and Future Generations', in R. Sikora and B. Barry (eds.), *Obligations to Future Generations* (Philadelphia: Temple University Press), 268–84.

—— (1989), *Theories of Justice* (Berkeley: University of California Press).

---

[32] A good discussion of the issue is J. Lenman (2002), 'On Becoming Extinct', *Pacific Philosophical Quarterly*, 83: 253–69.

DUFF, A. (2004), 'Harms and Wrongs', *Buffalo Criminal Law Review*, 4: 101–33.

FOOT, P. (1994), 'Rationality and Virtue', in *Norms, Values, and Society*, ed. Herlinde Pauer-Studer (Netherlands: Kluwer), 210.

KUMAR, R. (2003), 'Who Can Be Wronged?', *Philosophy and Public Affairs* 31/2: 99–118.

——(2004), 'Reasonable Reasons in Contractualist Moral Argument', *Ethics*, 114: 6–37.

LENMAN, J. (2002), 'On Becoming Extinct', *Pacific Philosophical Quarterly*, 83: 253–69.

MEYER, L. (2006), 'Reparations and Symbolic Restitution', *Journal of Social Philosophy*, 37/3: 406–22.

REIMAN, J. (2007), in 'Being Fair to Future People: The Non-Identity Problem in the Original Position', *Philosophy and Public Affairs*, 35/1: 69–92.

RIPSTEIN, A. (2006), 'Beyond the harm principle', *Philosophy and Public Affairs*, 34/3: 215–45.

ROBERTS, M. (1998), *Child versus Childmaker* (Boston: Rowman Littlefield).

SCANLON, T. M. (1998), *What We Owe to Each Other* (Cambridge, Mass.: Harvard University Press).

STRAWSON, P. F. (1982), 'Freedom and Resentment', in G. Watson (ed.), *Free Will* (Oxford: Oxford University Press), 59–80.

10

What Motivates Us to Care for the (Distant) Future?

DIETER BIRNBACHER

1. The 'Motivation Problem'

'Motivation problem' is not a well-established term in future ethics or, for that matter, in any other branch of ethics. It is taken here as a convenient label for an inquiry into the conditions that have to be fulfilled in order to make a recommendation, norm, prescription or any other action-guiding statement effective in the sense of making the addressee of such a statement behave in conformity with it. Normative statements, whether in ethics, aesthetics, or technology cannot, by themselves, compel conformity. All they do is to prescribe, or recommend, a certain course of action. In order to make someone act accordingly they have to rely on further factors. In each case the rules formulated by the system appeal to certain dispositions of the addressee of these rules: self-interest, rationality, sensibility, and moral attitudes. Even if the prescription, or recommendation, is categorical, their addressee is in principle free to follow it or not.

Attempts to deal with the 'motivation problem' in ethics—sometimes called 'motivation *aporia*'[1]—date back to the beginnings of moral philosophy. The question of what factors are necessary and sufficient to act in conformity with a given rule has been extensively discussed in the ethical systems of Plato, Spinoza, Hume, and Kant, and these discussions keep reverberating through the recent debate between internalists and externalists about moral reasons. Internalists like Bernard Williams[2] thought that having moral reasons for an action is inseparable from being motivated to act in accordance with it, even though not necessarily to the extent that the action is actually carried out. Externalists like H. A. Prichard[3] claimed that having moral reasons for an action

---

[1] cf. Wieland 1989: 25 ff.   [2] cf., e.g., Williams 1981, ch. 8.
[3] cf. Korsgaard 1986, section II.

and being motivated to carry it out are distinct items, so that a psychological mechanism independent of the acceptance of the moral rule is needed to explain action in conformity with it.

Though the problem of moral motivation is mostly formulated in terms of bridging the psychological gap between the *acceptance* of a rule, on the one hand, and of *acting* in accordance with it, on the other, a finer-grained analysis might distinguish two further steps in the transition from acceptance to action so that we get four items: *acceptance, adoption, application,* and *action.* In morality, a necessary condition of acting in accordance with a rule is that the addressee *accepts* the rule, in the sense of judging it to be right and justified. Second he must *adopt* the rule as a principle by which to guide his behaviour, to incorporate it, as it were, into his own identity. Third, he must *apply* it to situations of the appropriate kind, i.e. identify situations to which the rule is relevant, which, in the case of consequentialist rules, can require considerable effort. Fourth and finally, he must *act* as the respective rule says he should act in the given situation or, in cases where the rule commands a series of actions, to decide on a strategy reaching from the present into the future.

It is a moot question whether all four of these motivational steps are logically distinct. It is unclear, for example, whether the distinction between *acceptance* in the sense of judging a rule to be justified and *adoption* of a rule can coherently be upheld. Moral psychologists tend to insist on this distinction because empirical evidence strongly suggests that the capacity to make, for example, moral judgements is largely independent of the readiness to act in accordance with them.[4] In philosophy, internalists about moral motivation will dispute the distinction between accepting and adopting a moral rule and maintain the impossibility of purely intellectually accepting a moral rule without integrating it into one's moral outlook, at least to a certain extent. From this point of view, even accepting a rule cannot be conceived as a purely cognitive act but involves at least a modicum of affective identification. This, again, is taken to imply a motivation to act in accordance with the rule, if only to an extent that leaves it open whether the rule is actually followed. Some meta-ethical prescriptivists like Hare have even gone so far as to maintain that only action in conformity with a rule is sufficient proof that is has been accepted. Though they do not want to deny the reality of weakness of will, they insist that at least continued non-conformity is incompatible with saying that a rule has been accepted.[5] On this view, the motivation problem is not the problem of closing the gap between accepting a rule and following it, but rather it is the problem

---

[4] cf., e.g., Montada 1993: 268 and Baumgartner 2005: 114.   [5] cf. Hare 1963: 82 ff.

of the difference between merely asserting that one accepts a rule and really accepting it.

It is less controversial that these four motivational conditions are empirically interdependent and that, partly in consequence of this, there can be considerable problems in attributing a failure to act in accordance with a rule to any one of these in particular. A strongly internalized moral or prudential conviction will, as a rule, be accompanied by a more reliable conformity in action than a weaker moral or prudential belief. On the other hand, a moral or prudential principle will be more easily accepted if it corresponds to an already established way of acting. This interdependence is, however, far from perfect. Rule competence in the sense of being able to make valid normative judgements need not go together with rule competence in the sense of being able to rightly identify the situations in which these have to be applied. Even less does it imply moral performance in the sense of acting in conformity with these judgements. In cases where there are strong motives to deviate from an accepted rule, the empirically well-established theory of cognitive dissonance[6] predicts that even the capacity to identify the situations in which it should be applied will be considerably weakened. We not only fail to observe the principles we have adopted but even fail to see that we do so by unconsciously, or half-consciously, misrepresenting the situation to ourselves. The same motives that make us act in ways incompatible with our principles blind us about the nature, and, given the case, the consequences of our actions.

All this contributes to the complexities of attributing a failure to act in conformity with a professed rule retrospectively. In principle, a failure to follow one's practical beliefs can be attributed to weakness of will, to an insufficiently developed capacity to identify situations for which these beliefs are relevant, or to the fact that these beliefs are only asserted and not fully internalised. The fact that these factors are interdependent does not make it easier to pinpoint the exact source of defection.

2. Why Motivation to Care for the Future is a Special Case

Future ethics poses more stringent problems of motivation than other branches of practical philosophy because there is a more striking discrepancy between the motivation to accept principles of future ethics and the motivation to act in

---

[6] Festinger 1957.

accordance with them than in other areas of ethics. Furthermore, future ethics poses special difficulties in rightly identifying situations to which its principles are relevant. I will comment on these points in turn.

The motivation to *accept* future ethical principles is much less problematic than the motivation to *adopt* such principles because it is more or less natural to extend the principles relating to our dealings with present people to our dealings with future people. We live in a moral culture deeply impregnated with the universalistic moral tradition of the Enlightenment. Most people who accept a fundamental moral maxim like *neminem laede* as a rule of behaviour (Schopenhauer's 'principle of justice') will hardly object to generalizing this maxim in such a way that not only present but also future beings susceptible of being harmed are included in its domain. There does not seem to be a big difference between what motivates the unextended and what motivates the extended maxim. Once a maxim of non-harming is accepted it seems plausible to include potential future 'moral patients' in addition to potential present 'moral patients'. The point made by Henry Sidgwick at the end of the 19th century, that the temporal position of who is harmed by a present action cannot be relevant to its moral evaluation,[7] can be expected to seem compelling to most moralists.

Within the universalistic paradigm of morality, the irrelevance of the temporal position of a moral patient is indeed obvious. Though moral principles containing temporal relations (such as the principle to treat one's children better than one's grandchildren) are not—*pace* Hare[8]—incompatible with the meta-ethical principle of universalization, discrimination against future persons by excluding them from the range of moral principles seems incompatible with the ideal of impartiality characteristic of the universalistic paradigm. It is part and parcel of this paradigm that actions and their consequences are judged from a standpoint of maximal impartiality, a standpoint beyond personal preferences and the limited horizon of personal sympathies. One of the reasons for this is that only evaluations of a sufficiently impartial kind have a chance of making true the claim to universal assent, which is a condition equally characteristic of the universalistic paradigm. Given that the *moral* point of view is a point of view beyond all particular perspectives—the 'view from nowhere'—any attempt to defend a privileged treatment of present people (and, perhaps, people of the near future) over people in the more distant future, seems systematically misguided. It is no accident that for Kant, who endowed the universalistic paradigm of morality with his own metaphysical emphasis, it was more or less a matter of course that whoever is motivated to accept moral principles

---

[7] Sidgwick 1907: 381.   [8] Hare 1981: 100 ff.

in his dealings with present people is thereby also motivated to accept these principles in his dealings with future people, and to judge the good and bad of people in the future as no more and no less morally considerable than the good and bad of people in the present. In one of his late essays on the philosophy of history, he boldly asserted that 'human nature is so constituted that it cannot be indifferent to goods and bads that happen at the most distant epoch, if only they happen to our species and can be expected with certainty'.[9]

Roughly the same, however, holds at least for some variants of the particularistic, or communitarian, paradigm of morality for which the range of moral norms is restricted to the members of a certain group or community.[10] Though the moral norms recognized in such communities have only a limited range and do not extend to members of different communities, they generally include the future members of the community along with its present members.[11] Since the motivation to accept the norms of the community is, in this paradigm, not their plausibility judged from an impartial and rational perspective but group loyalty and adherence to the group's customs and traditions, these motivations extend as naturally to the future members of the community in question as the universalistic motivations to future mankind. Temporal universalization is, therefore, no exclusive feature of universalistic morality, despite the fact that intergenerational moral responsibility has always been a theme more prominent in universalistic systems of ethics such as Kantianism and Utilitarianism. The crucial difference between the universalistic and the particularistic paradigm, it seems, is not its tendency to go beyond temporal but to go beyond ethnic, social, and cultural limits.[12]

Universalists and particularists in ethics, then, go together in including future generations into the scope of their principles. Nevertheless, the 'motivation problem' tends to be more acute for universalists because of their indifference to psychological distance based on ethnic, social, or cultural differences. In successively extending the range of 'moral patients' that have to be taken into consideration in judging the morality of action, the Enlightenment has deeply challenged the anthropological drive towards keeping morality within

---

[9] Kant 1912: 27.

[10] For an early elaboration of this contrast combined with a speculation as to their psychological origins see Bergson 1932: 27 ff.

[11] An early example of such a theory is Golding 1981 who writes: 'Future generations are members of our moral community because, and insofar as, our social ideal is relevant to them, given what they are and their conditions of life.' (68). A more explicit conception of 'transgenerational communities' on the basis of what he calls 'moral similarity' is developed by De-Shalit in De-Shalit 1995, ch. 1.

[12] It may be, of course, that it is not really possible to go beyond temporal limits without at the same time going beyond these other limits, so that the long-term ethnic, social and cultural identity presupposed in such a view is an illusion.

the limits of emotional bonds. There can be no more conspicuous contrast than that between what universalistic ethical systems such as Kantianism and Utilitarianism expect of moral motivation and the evolutionary origins of morality in the low-distance-morality of the family, the clan and the tribe. While this origin is deliberately disavowed in the *principles* of these moralities, it stubbornly reappears in the limits of *motivation* documented by moral psychology. Moral emotions such as love of humanity, a sense of justice and international solidarity are readily affirmed in the abstract but rarely lived in the concrete.[13] Their motivational force is throughout inferior to competing low-distance emotions such as egoism, family bonds, group solidarity and patriotism. It has even to be doubted whether the whole of humanity, spread out in past, present and future, can at all be a proper object of love. Taken all in all, experience confirms Hume's sceptical view that

in general, it may be affirm'd, that there is no such passion in human minds, as love of mankind, merely as such, independent of personal qualities, of services, or of relation to ourself. 'Tis true, there is no human, and indeed no sensible, creature, whose happiness or misery does not, in some measure, affect us, when brought near to us, and represented in lively colours: But this proceeds merely from sympathy, and is no proof of such an universal affection to mankind, since this concern extends itself beyond our own species.[14]

Though the high-minded principles of a universalistic morality include the totality of peoples, cultures and generations, the limited possibilities of practised solidarity make our practical morality focus on small islands within an ocean of moral indifference. Even if, in theory, we recognize the rights of those most distant to us along with those nearer to us, this is rarely sufficient to make them effective. Even those who heroically postulated the universal brotherhood of men usually restricted the solidarity they demanded to an in-group of the righteous and excluded the unbrotherly, the tyrants, the heathens, or the capitalists. In the same Sermon of the Mount in which Jesus preaches the love of our enemies (Mt. 5, 44), he invokes the fire of hell on those who offend their brother by calling him a fool (Mt. 5, 22).[15]

Despite these differences in the problems of motivation facing universalistic and particularistic moralities, the motivational problems posed by obligations

---

[13] cf. Baumgartner 2005: 26 with relation to environmental values. See also Bierhoff 1990: 63 ff. and Bierhoff 2002:160 on the importance of sympathy for altruistic behaviour.

[14] Hume 1888: 481 ff.

[15] There may be other kinds of gap between the motivation to accept moral principles and the motivation to act accordingly which do not result from the fact that our principles are *stricter* than human nature allows but from the fact that they are *less strict* than human nature dictates. A pertinent case is the incest taboo.

towards the future, and especially towards the distant future (i.e. those generations that we have no chance to get into direct contact with during our lifetimes) are more or less alike, at least to the extent that particularistic moralities include distant future people as persons to whom the present generation owes moral concern. In our days, the moral imperative of taking the interests of future generations into account is firmly established in most parts of the industrialized world. Only few people in the more well-to-do countries of the world would deny that the present generation has responsibilities towards future generations. The diagnosis given by Tocqueville in the 19th century about North America that 'people want to think only about the following day'[16] is no longer true, neither of North America nor of Europe. On the contrary, the long-term preservation of the natural conditions on which human life depends and the preservation of a satisfactory quality of life seem to be widely recognized values, and the same seems to hold for what Hans Jonas has called the 'first commandment' of future ethics,[17] the imperative not to endanger the future existence of mankind.

Evidence for that comes from the international treaties on environmental protection and nature conservation that have been concluded in the last decades such as the CITES convention of 1973, the Montreal Protocol on the protection of the ozone layer of 1987, and the Kyoto protocol of 1997. It is further evidenced by empirical data. In a recent empirical study of attitudes to anthropogenic climate change, Russell et al. found that imposing climate changes on future generations by present energy use is predominantly judged to be morally unjust to these generations. They also found a clear correlation between the feeling of injustice and the expressed readiness to act in ways appropriate to reduce the risk of long-term climate change.[18] Similar results were found in a study of attitudes to the environment conducted by the American ecologists Minteer and Manning. The primary aim of this study, which was based on a representative sample of the population of Vermont, USA, was to find out what matters to people in policies of environmental protection.[19] One of the results was that there is a considerable pluralism of environmental values even within the relatively closed New England population. Not surprisingly, values with a religious background are more important to some than to others. The most interesting result was, however, that the three values which were the most often nominated and on which there is the highest degree of agreement were also the three values with the highest values in relative importance, namely 'future generations' (with the representative

---

[16] Tocqueville 1961: 156.   [17] Jonas 1979: 186.   [18] Russell et al. 2003: 167.
[19] Minteer and Manning 1999.

statement 'Nature will be important to future generations'), 'quality of life' (with the representative statement 'Nature adds to the quality of our lives (for example, outdoor recreation, natural beauty)'), and 'ecological surviv- al' (with the representative statement 'Human survival depends on nature and natural processes'). This points to the conclusion that a justification of environmental protection can be expected to be the more successful the more it invokes anthropocentric but unselfish values of a roughly 'pruden- tial' sort: the values of stewardship and of keeping nature intact for future generations.

However well-established such future ethical principles are, they compete with other, more present-oriented motivations, and it is far from guaranteed that the high-minded future ethical principles expressed by respondents are given priority in concrete practice. Empirical data strongly support the 'low cost hypothesis'[20] according to which moral principles concerning nature conservation will be the more easily observed the less this creates costs or opportunity costs for the individual. The difficulty is illustrated by the problems of keeping greenhouse emissions within the narrow limits of the Kyoto protocol. It must be doubted whether a tax on fossil fuels high enough to curb the further expansion of motorized traffic would be politically feasible except under conditions of acute crisis such as the oil crisis of the 1980s. An empirical study of a representative sample of the population of Baden-Württemberg in 2001 showed that though 50 per cent of the people interviewed associated the climate problem with a 'high' or even 'very high' catastrophe potential and 54 per cent saw great or very great societal dangers in it, this did not correlate with a willingness to find the causes for this problem in their own behaviour. Only 11 per cent associated the responsibility for climate change with their own ways of acting.[21] Similar data were reported from the US[22] exhibiting the same psychological pattern of denial.[23] If long- term objectives require changes in the habitual behaviours and consumption patterns of a society, we should be pessimistic about their prospects of being translated into action under non-critical conditions. Any attempt to change the fundamental behaviour patterns in a society by political initiatives seems doomed to failure if the necessity of these changes is only motivated by possible or future rather than by present dangers.[24]

---

[20] Baumgartner 2005: 87.   [21] Zwick 2001: 302.   [22] Leiserowitz 2006: 56.
[23] Stoll-Kleemann, O'Riordan, and Jaeger 2001: 111.

[24] These data suggest that the 'discounting' of future utility accepted in most economic models should be understood to refer to a motivational problem rather than to a valuational one. A person who discounts the gains or losses he expects for the future does not *underrate* the true size of these gains and losses, in the way a mountaineer underrates the height he has to climb in order to reach a shelter, but is

In the following, I will focus on temporally distant generations of humans and leave aside the question of temporally distant animals and other non-human beings. I will also leave aside overlapping generations for which the 'motivation problem' is less acute. There seem to be two principal factors to explain this relative weakness of motivation to act on one's own principles in the context of future ethics as far as temporally distant generations are concerned. The one is that actively taking responsibility for the distant future is more exclusively dependent on genuinely *moral* motives than other kinds of responsibility. The other is that the effectiveness of present action in altering the future course of events to the better is, in general, less *certain* than in other kinds of responsible behaviour.

3. Moral and Quasi-moral Motives to Care for the (Distant) Future

In principle, there are three kinds of motives from which a morally required act can be done: from moral motives, from quasi-moral motives, and from non-moral motives (or any combination of these). A morally required act is done from *moral* motives if it is done precisely because it is morally required, i.e. from conscientiousness or a feeling of duty. It is done from *quasi-moral* motives if it is done from altruistic motives such as love, compassion, solidarity, generosity or spontaneous impulses to care for others, i.e. from motives that often lead to the same courses of action as genuinely moral motives, without being dependent on the adoption of a particular system of morality. (Indeed, some systems of moral philosophy, like those of Hume and Schopenhauer, rely heavily, or even exclusively, on quasi-moral motivations in this sense.) Non-moral motivations comprise both self-centred and non-self-centred motivations that result in morally required action accidentally, such as the desire for self-respect, social integration and recognition, and the pursuit of personal ideals from which others happen to profit. (These are only the ideal types. In reality, there may be all kinds of combinations of these kinds of motive.)

According to psychological internalism, not only the adoption of a moral principle as a personal maxim, but even the judgement that a certain principle is right and proper implies a certain motivation to act in accordance with it. This is a rather strong position. Nevertheless, it seems more plausible than the externalist one that construes acceptance of a moral principle as a

less *motivated* to act in accordance with his expectations (cf. Birnbacher 2003: 45). This is obscured both by the expression 'myopia' and by Pigou's (1932: 25) metaphor of the defective 'telescopic faculty'.

purely cognitive act. To accept a moral principle means more than to accept a descriptive statement of fact. It implies that the principle in question is introduced, to a certain extent, not only into one's system of beliefs but also into one's system of motivation. Whoever accepts a moral principle has a reason to act in certain ways rather than in others. However, the internalist position is perfectly compatible with maintaining that the acceptance of moral principles is insufficient to motivate action in conformity with these principles in cases where competing motivations can be assumed to be present. Since this latter condition is fulfilled more often than not, pure acceptance of a moral principle is rarely sufficient for its practical observance. Even on internalist premises there are reasons to think that there have to be additional motivations, of another kind, to make moral principles effective.

This gives us at least part of an explanation for why there is a *special* 'motivation problem' in future ethics. Moral motives are usually too weak to effect appropriate action unless supported by quasi-moral and non-moral motives pointing in the same direction. Moreover, the quasi-moral motives potentially supporting moral motivation such as love and sympathy are significantly absent in this field because they essentially depend on face-to-face relations with their objects. Apart from some of the members of the generations of our children and grandchildren, future generations are faceless and invisible. Future people are objects of thought and calculation. They come into view only as abstract recipients of goods and potential victims of harms, as anonymous items, and do not offer themselves as concrete and experientially accessible objects of attitudes such as love, friendship, reverence, or solidarity. But it seems that our moral sensibilities are primarily attuned to 'identified' and not to 'statistical' beneficiaries and victims. As Calabresi and Bobbitt have shown, emotions are aroused primarily by people who are threatened by death or other harm under our eyes (the victims of mining accidents, the victims of earthquakes, the patient needing immediate help), and these emotions make us act for their survival and good health even in cases in which cold calculation would tell us that it would be more rational to use the resources for preventive measures.[25]

Our spontaneous quasi-moral motives are primarily directed to what lies next to our own person in terms of temporal, spatial and social distance. A bad conscience is much more likely with someone who behaves in a way harmful to people in his or her vicinity than to someone who behaves in a way harmful to people in the distant future. In this respect, Nietzsche's polemical concept

---

[25] Calabresi and Bobbitt 1978. Cf. also the list of conditions influencing the extent to which people are prepared to give money to alleviate distant needs in Unger 1996: 73. The most important of these conditions are also satisfied by situations in the distant future.

of *Fernstenliebe* (love of the most distant), the verbal opposite of *Nächstenliebe*, the love of one's neighbour, points to a real paradox.[26]

One important aspect of the necessary abstractness of future generations is that it is more difficult to present a vivid and realistic picture of future situations than of present situations in the media.[27] TV reports about disasters can be expected to stimulate a quite remarkable willingness to give money for their alleviation, provided these disasters are perceived as caused by external factors such as uncontrollable natural forces or military attacks from foreign states. It is much more difficult to present potential future disasters such as a rapid progress of desertification by changes in the global climate with a vividness and credibility that stimulates preventive action with comparable effectiveness.

4. Non-moral Motives to Care for the Future

Roughly the same holds for non-moral motivations potentially supportive of moral responsibilities to the distant future. There is not very much the future can do for a present moral agent, and those few things it can do lack motivation potential. Later generations can erect monuments for 'great men of the past', they can cultivate their memory by commemoration services, by re-editions of their works, or by naming streets, buildings or scientific discoveries after them. These manifestations of retrospective recognition and gratitude, however, are necessarily symbolical and do not actually effect the agent during his lifetime. Though there may be some motivating potential in the hope for posthumous fame (as in the notable case of Horace who prided himself of having created a work *aere perennius*), this is relevant only for a small elite, mainly for those occupying important positions in society, politics, religion or culture already during their lives. I personally doubt whether a less exclusive future-directed motivation such as the thought of being remembered by one's descendants is a particularly strong motivation to act for their benefit.

An even more important factor in weakening the motivation to act for the distant future is the impossibility of direct and indirect negative sanctions. While children and grandchildren are in a position to claim their legitimate share and to protest against future burdens (such as the burden of paying

---

[26] Nietzsche 1980: 77. A similar paradox is involved in Schopenhauer's attempt to extend the concept of *compassion* to cover an indefinite multitude of potential moral patients in the context of the *Mitleidsethik* (cf. Birnbacher 1990: 30 ff.). The more abstract the objects of compassion or pity become, the more the specific meaning of these concepts is lost.

[27] The importance of vivid representation as a precondition of sympathy with remote victims was already clearly stated by Hume, see the quotation above, p.280.

back international debts over a long period of time in the future), our grand-grandchildren necessarily remain silent. If they have a voice, it is only vicariously, through the advocacy of people who protect their interests and rights against the short-sighted loyalties of the present.

This, however, is only one of the obstacles lying in the way of future ethical motivation. The other is the *uncertainty* about which actions will have morally significant effects in the future. Though the general direction of future-oriented action may be clear (as, for example, reducing emissions of greenhouse gases in the case of the problem of global warming), there is more than one dimension of uncertainty to create doubts about whether future-oriented behaviour will really make a difference to future people. First, there is the uncertainty about the validity of the theories and scenarios on which the prognosis of future risks is based. Second, there is the uncertainty about whether and, if so, at what point of time alternative ways will be found to neutralize or to reduce future hazards. A third factor of uncertainty is the synergistic and cumulative nature of most long-term conservation strategies, both synchronically and diachronically. Potential impacts of present action are threatened by the potential lack of co-operation of present agents as well as by the potential lack of co-operation of future agents. The impact of present energy saving by one agent on future resources may be seen as negligible without the certainty that others join in. In order to attain their goal long-term strategies have to be undertaken by a series of successively co-operating generations. No single individual and no single collective can be sure, however, that its descendants will honour their efforts by carrying on the process into the distant future. There can be, in the nature of the case, no certainty that countervailing interests of later generations will not annul the beneficial effects of the efforts of the first generation.

Given these uncertainties (which apply especially to the distant future), the causal relevance of present action on future conditions is much less open to empirical control than the causal relevance of present action on spatially distant regions of the world. Acting for the future is inherently more risky than acting for the present or for the immediate future. It essentially involves the risk of squandering moral resources on projects that fail to achieve their intended aims by factors beyond the agent's control. That these risks have a considerable psychological impact on behaviour has been shown in several relevant areas. One of the preconditions for action motivation seems to be a relevant 'control belief', i.e. the belief that appropriate action will be effective in attaining the desired goal. Without relevant 'control beliefs', the motivation to enter upon a course of action can be expected to be unstable.[28]

---

[28] cf. for the case of air pollution Evans and Jacobs 1981: 116 ff.

Each of the factors listed above contributes to weaken the practical effect-iveness of moral beliefs about obligations to the future. Some of these factors are specific to future ethics: future ethics has to do without the help of most of the quasi-moral and non-moral motivations that support the effectiveness of moral beliefs about obligations to present people. It further faces the problem that identifying actions by which the benefit of future generations can be secured is much more riddled with uncertainties than identifying actions by which the benefit of present people (or people in the near future) can be secured.

5. Indirect Motivations

This pessimistic picture is, however, too pessimistic to be realistic. It leaves out what, in future ethics, may be a far more potent motivational resource than the motivations discussed so far, *indirect* motivations. The distinction between direct and indirect motivations cuts across the distinction between moral, quasi-moral, or non-moral motivations introduced above. Indirect motivations can be moral, quasi-moral, or non-moral. Their distinctive mark is that they produce a certain value or good as a side-effect. In an intergenerational context, indirect motivations do not aim at the production of goods or the prevention of evils befalling future people, but aim at objectives in the present or in the near future. They are nevertheless indirect motivations to act for the distant future in so far as they can be assumed to work for the good of people in the long term and to contribute to the realization of the same ends as those underlying the principles of future ethics.

The advantage of indirect motivations from a practical point of view is their more reliable emotional basis and their potentially greater effectiveness in guiding behaviour. Differently from direct motivations, indirect motivations are supported by a broader range of emotional factors. This is not to say that a purely moral motivation to act responsibly towards the future is without emotions. These emotions, however, are necessarily abstract and impersonal. The future individuals (at least those in the far future) figure in them only as blanks. Indirect motivations, on the contrary, are able to make use of the full scope of quasi-moral motives, such as love, compassion, care, and solidarity, directed to objects accessible to experience.

The most well-known construction of an indirect motivation in future ethics is Passmore's idea of a 'chain of love'. 'Chain of love' means the intergenerational concatenation of each generation's love for its children and grandchildren. According to this model, each generation cares exclusively for the generation of its children and grandchildren, with the result that the sequence of limited responsibilities has the same or even better effects on the whole series of generations than postulates of a more future-oriented responsibility.[29] These advantages are both cognitive and motivational. Each generation is in a better position to judge what serves the well-being of the next generation than of what serves the well-being of the second or third generation coming after it. And each generation pursues the well-being of the next generation with higher intensity than that of the second or third generation coming after it because of the presence of stronger quasi-moral and non-moral motives.

The model can be interpreted and filled out in various ways, differing in the explanation given for why each generation cares for the generation of their children. One is to assume a natural and inborn propensity on the part of parents to make provisions for their children's future and to make sacrifices for their good. In this case, each generation is assumed to be motivated to care for its children independently of whether the generation of its own parents has similarly cared for itself. In a second variant the motivation is made to depend on a process of social learning. The motivation of the children's generation to care for their children is acquired by a process of model learning: each generation takes over the future-directed behaviour of their parents (and possibly grandparents) in their relations to their children (and grandchildren). The only external motivation necessary for triggering the concatenation of sympathies is the initial motivation of the first generation. Everything else follows, as it were, by chain reaction.

The chain of love-model is a quite powerful one. This is evident from the fact that even future disasters like a potential running out of a fundamental (non-substitutable) exhaustible resource such as energy can be modelled in such a way that even generations with a limited 'sympathy horizon' extending over no more than the two following generations have a reason to act so as to prevent or at least mitigate the future calamity. Even a generation not covered by the altruism of the first generation, such as the third generation coming after it, can be better off, in this model, than under the assumption that it is covered by the altruism of the first generation. This result essentially depends on the condition that though the aim of each generation's intergenerational sympathy is only the welfare of the directly following generations, this welfare is a compound of its own egoistic welfare and the altruistic welfare resulting from the anticipation of the welfare of subsequent generations. By aiming

---

[29] Passmore 1980: 88 ff.

at the welfare of the directly following generations, each generation thereby unintentionally sympathises with the welfare of the generations with which its directly following generations sympathise and therefore, by concatenation, with all future generations. Each generation aims at the welfare of no more than the two following generations. But in fact, as an unintended result, it promotes the welfare of the whole chain.

Assume, for example, that the compound welfare $U_{tot}s_n$ of each generation s_n is the sum of three utilities, its egoistic welfare $U_{ego}s_n$, a part of the compound welfare of the generation of its children, $U_{tot}s_{n+1}$, and a part of the compound welfare of the generation of its grandchildren, $U_{tot}s_{n+2}$.[30] Let the compound welfare of generation s_n, $U_{tot}s_n$ be defined as $U_{tot}s_n = U_{ego}s_n + 0.5\ U_{tot}s_{n+1} + 0.25\ U_{tot}s_{n+2}$, with 0.5 and 0.25 as 'sympathy factors' representing the degree to which the welfare of each generation depends on the welfare it perceives or anticipates subsequent generations to enjoy. It is easily shown that under these assumptions foreseen negative developments starting only during the lifetime of generation 4, which lies beyond the 'sympathy horizon' of generation 1, nevertheless have an impact on the welfare of generation 1.

Let us assume that after an initial period of growth, a foreseeable shortage occurs during the adult years of generation 4 leading to a decline in welfare of all subsequent generations (with generation 6 as the last generation):

generation	1	2	3	4	5	6
net welfare	2	3	3	1	1	1

As a consequence, the welfare of all earlier generations is affected:

generation	1	2	3	4	5	6
compound welfare	5.938	5.688	4.375	2	1.5	1

This distribution compares unfavourably with an alternative scenario in which generation 1 sacrifices part of its net welfare to invest in the prevention of the foreseeable shortage so that the level of net welfare rises instead of falling during the lifetime of generation 4. Think, for example, of heavy investments in the development of energy production from nuclear fusion in generation 1, resulting in a substitution of fossil fuels from generation 4 on.

---

[30] For a generalized model of iterated sympathy relations between subsequent generations see Dasgupta 1974: 413 ff.

generation	1	2	3	4	5	6
net welfare	1	3	3	4	4	4

In this case, the corresponding values for the compound welfare are:

generation	1	2	3	4	5	6
compound welfare	7.75	9.25	8.5	8	6	4

What makes the 'chain-of-love' model attractive is the weakness of the conditions on which it is based. It demands neither moral heroism nor dramatic sacrifices but only foresight and the effort to make each generation's sympathies for subsequent generations effective in future-oriented strategies. The motive of parents to see to the future of their children is a reliable motive mainly for two reasons: first, because it in fact seems 'natural' that parents have an interest in the future well-being of their children; and second, because many parents can be assumed to have an interest in securing assistance from their children in case they have to depend on them in old age.[31]

Furthermore, the model incorporates the empirical findings on the importance of model learning for intergenerational behaviour. How a generation behaves toward its immediate descendants seems to a large extent determined by the behaviour of the previous generation towards this generation. In a series of experiments on the distribution of a given quantity of resources between oneself and subsequent subjects (representing subsequent generations), Wade-Benzoni impressively showed that the preparedness to generosity toward future subjects heavily depends on the generosity experienced or attributed to the previous owner of the resource.[32] In conformity with Bandura's theory of social learning in moral contexts[33] the generosity or non-generosity of the previous owner from whom the initial stock of the resource has been inherited is interpreted as a social norm and mimicked by one's own preparedness to make sacrifices for the future. There is empirical evidence that even the form in which parents provide for the future of their children (i.e. by bequest, financial assistance, investment in their education etc.) is closely correlated with the kind of provisions their own parents made for them.[34]

At the same time, the chain-of-love model is hopelessly unrealistic as far as it construes whole generations as homogeneous, whereas, in reality, agency lies with politicians, economic planners, and the heads of families and dynasties

---

[31] See Becker and Murphy 1988: 5 ff.   [32] Wade-Benzoni 2002.   [33] Bandura 1969.
[34] Arrondel and Masson 2001: 417 ff.

with highly diverse possibilities of determining the welfare of subsequent generations. Well-to-do family heads usually bequeath their wealth to children who would be well-to-do even without the bequest, whereas older people with modest means usually have little to spare. The parts of the world in which future shortages are most likely to have an impact on the overall welfare of subsequent generations (and in which they do so already now) are also the least likely to have the means to make the investments necessary to prevent shortages in the future.

A second model of indirect motivations to care for the distant future was adumbrated by Passmore and then elaborated by Visser't Hooft.[35] In this model, indirect motivation is not aimed at *persons*, but at *goods* valued for their own sake, either natural or cultural. The idea of the model is that the long-term conservation of a certain good is best assured by establishing a tradition of valuing this good. This is plausible, first of all, for environmental goods such as beautiful landscapes and wilderness areas. It does not come as a surprise that, in an empirical study, Kals et al. found that emotional affinity towards nature proved to be an important predictor of the willingness to protect nature.[36] This is plausible, however, also for cultural goods such as forms of art, music, literature, philosophy, science, social virtues, and political institutions. Valuing these goods is closely linked, psychologically, to motivations to contribute to the conservation of these values and their manifestations. Whoever loves, for example, the music of Bach can be expected to have an interest in preserving this music from being lost or forgotten. That implies that he must be interested in conserving or even strengthening attitudes likely to respect the integrity of these values. He must be a conservative in respect to a certain form of life. It is hardly imaginable to subscribe to a cultural value like classical music, scientific truth or the democratic state without the hope that they will 'never die'. Indeed, Nietzsche's line according to which 'alle Lust will Ewigkeit' (all pleasure wants eternity)[37] seems to apply more to the objects of pleasure, satisfaction and valuation than to pleasure itself. It is not pleasure that we want to exist forever, but the objects of pleasure.

An anticipation of this model with respect to natural values is one of the pioneering conceptions of ecological ethics, Aldo Leopold's 'land ethic'. Leopold proposed the 'land ethic' because he was convinced that direct motives of nature conservation based on future ethical considerations are insufficiently effective in motivating ecologically correct action. Therefore, he thought, a functional substitute was needed; in his own words, 'a mode of guidance for meeting ecological situations so new or intricate, or involving

---

[35] Visser't Hooft 1999: 122.   [36] Kals et al. 1999.   [37] Nietzsche 1980: 404.

such deferred reactions, that the path of social expediency is not discernible to the average individual.'[38] Leopold's 'land ethic', though designed for ultimately anthropocentric purposes, has an ecocentric orientation. It expects the agent to see himself not as a conqueror but as part of nature and to define his role as serving nature instead of dominating it. It furthermore includes the cultivation of emotions such as love, respect and admiration of nature for its own sake.[39]

This characteristic indirectness of motivation is also present in some attempts within the communitarian school of social thought to incorporate future ethics into the communitarian framework. Philosophers in the communitarian tradition like De-Shalit have drawn attention to the close relations between the fact of being firmly embedded in a social group and the motivation to care for its future.[40] Concern about the future well-being of a group to which one has a close emotional relationship can be expected to be more reliable than the interest in the well-being of abstractions like humanity or future generations. Caring for the future of one's reference group can even be part of one's own moral identity. Whoever defines himself as German, Christian, or as a scientist, can hardly be indifferent to the future of the group to which his identity refers, though, with a plurality of identities and loyalties, their may be conflicts between the future-directed motivations associated with each. In a pioneering paper on the 'motivation problem' in future ethics, this source of motivation was called 'community bonding'.[41] The essential motivational factor in community bonding is the 'sense of belonging to some joint enterprise with others'. One's own contribution to the future is seen as a contribution to a common cause which one expects to be carried further by an indefinite number of subsequent generations of members of the same community.

Future-oriented motivations by specific loyalties are further supported by the fact that quite a number of collectives are either defined by a certain long-term project, as, e.g. 'movements' for x where x is a value or good of an intergenerational kind, or are so efficient in inculcating long-term objectives in their adherents that these have no room for long-term projects and ideals of their own. From the perspective of future ethics, such collective objectives are, however, a mixed blessing. They are too often directly averse to the well-being of future mankind, rationally conceived, as has been shown by the projects of imperialism, colonialism, and the world revolution.

This does not close the list of indirect motivations relevant to actively pursuing the good of future generations. There is one further indirect motivation to act for the future that can be expected to become even more important in the

---

[38] Leopold 1949: 203.   [39] Leopold 1949: 204, 209, 223.   [40] De-Shalit 1995.
[41] Care 1982: 207.

future, which is the motivation to give meaning to one's life by embedding it in a transgenerational context of solidarity. In the developed world, a spiritual vacuum has made itself felt that can be traced back both to the continuing historical process of secularization and to saturation with purely economic private and collective objectives. There is a high degree of preparedness to contribute to causes or projects that reach further than one's own person, one's own personal context, and one's own lifetime. Ernest Partridge has called such motives motives of 'self-transcendence'.[42] Future orientation and responsibility to the future offer themselves as the natural candidates for the longing for existential meaning in a secularized world. Acting for the future fits such motives most neatly because a commitment to the future makes the individual feel his own value and makes him feel embedded in a wider context of meaning which reaches from the past into the far future. By acting for the future, the individual is given the chance to see himself as an element in a chain of generations held together by an intergenerational feeling of community, which combines obligations in the direction of the future with feelings of gratitude in the direction of the past. However modest his contribution, he thereby situates himself in a context transcending the individual both in personal and temporal respects.

This motive will gain particular momentum when it is combined with the communitarian motive and supported by the feeling that one's own contribution is part of the objectives of a larger community. The best term to characterize such a feeling of transcending the bounds of one's existence seems to be *elevation*, a word characteristically used by Stendhal when he wrote, in an age more given to enthusiasm than ours: '... sacrifice du présent à l'avenir; rien *n'élève* l'âme comme le pouvoir et l'habitude de faire de tels sacrifices' (... sacrificing the present to the future; nothing elevates the soul like the power and the habit of such sacrifices).[43] Of course, at least part of the robustness of this motivation depends on the fact that it cannot be disappointed by experience. In this respect, motivations to act for the future resemble religious commitments of a more literally transcendent kind. Both are, for the present agent, unfalsifiable. Partly in consequence thereof, they are liable to be abused. Whether there will in fact be the temporally overarching community with shared objectives and values and shared feelings of solidarity implicitly assumed to exist in this motivation is highly uncertain. It is an open question whether our descendants will recognize, or honour by acting in accordance with them, the present generation's principles of intergenerational responsibility and visions of intergenerational justice. The more remote in time

---

[42] Partridge 1980: 204.   [43] Stendhal 1959: 246 ff. (my italics).

a later generation is situated and the more its principles are shaped by a long series of intermediary generations coming between ours and theirs, the less certain we can be that they will in fact be, as this motivation presupposes, part of the same moral community.[44] As historical examples of powerful ideologies like Marxism have shown, however, the risk of illusion does not necessarily detract from the strength of this motivation.

It should be mentioned that all four models discussed, though potentially quite effective in stimulating actions and omissions with long-term impact, have serious limits. The most important limit is the risk of wasting moral energies on the world's future that might more profitably be invested in solving the world's present problems. Each of these models might mislead the present generation in making provisions for the future that the future will not in fact need. It may, e.g., be doubted whether future generations would actually suffer from not having the chance to see live members of those biological species that will by that time have become extinct unless kept alive by the present generation's efforts. It is an open question whether the libraries of classical literature we try to preserve now will be of much use for the people of a distant future in which people's interests might have radically changed. On the other hand, there is a substantial risk that we are currently wasting resources that will prove to be much more vital for the basic needs of future people than we can possibly expect.

6. Self-binding as a Supportive Device

Hope for long-term policies does not come only from indirect motivations but also from *self-binding*. Self-binding functions either by raising the threshold to deviate from the road of virtue defined by one's own principles, or by limiting one's freedom to deviate from these principles. In either case, an attempt is made to control in advance the extent to which future motivations deviating from one's principles result in undesired behaviour, either by deliberately making deviations more difficult or less attractive, or by deliberately restricting future options. In the first case, the motivational mechanism is similar to the replacement of direct motives by indirect motives: whoever binds himself by a long-term contract and pre-commits himself to a certain course of action complements the direct motivation for long-term provisions or long-term beneficence by the indirect motivation to escape the short-term consequences of breaking or changing the contract.

---

[44] cf. Auerbach 1995: 79 ff.

The paradigmatic field of operation of self-binding mechanisms is the field of prudential maxims like paying one's debts, saving a portion of one's income, or not resuming smoking after having given it up. The agent pre-commits himself to live up to his maxims by delegating control to an external personal or institutional agency, thus protecting himself from his own opportunism. Self-binding must be attractive to anyone who thinks that he is inclined to impulses by which he risks jeopardizing his long-term objectives.

Self-binding can take various forms. *Internal* self-binding consists in self-binding relying on mechanisms internal to the agent. In the case of the individual, internal self-binding can assume the form of adopting maxims by which internal sanctions are activated to avoid opportunistic deviations from one's principles, so that deviations are 'punished' e.g. by feelings of guilt or shame. Feelings of guilt or shame are mobilized whenever the person does not live up to the obligations of his moral identity. Once these internal sanctions have been established, even the most extreme egoist has a reason to take these sanctions into account. In the case of collectives, internal self-binding can consist in establishing institutions within a society by which collective decisions are controlled and potentially revised. *External* self-binding consists in delegating these sanctions to an external agency, either by making it raise the threshold for deviations or by restricting the options open to oneself. Delegating the power to make one follow a rule according to the Ulysses-and-the-Sirens pattern can be thought of as a kind of self-paternalism, which, however, is without the moral problems characteristic of other forms of paternalism since the subject and object of paternalistic intervention are one and the same.

Self-binding is clearly relevant to future-oriented action. Given the psychological facts about time preference and the limited intergenerational sympathy horizon (which rarely exceeds the generations of children and grandchildren), self-binding is, in principle, a potent device in effectively caring for the future. A case for introducing such self-binding mechanisms in the context of future ethics was recently made by Baumgartner.[45] According to this author, future-oriented moral values can play the role of internal self-binding mechanisms if they are sufficiently firmly embedded in an individual's moral identity. The individual's moral identity is not a given. It can be modelled by morally significant experience and by a process of reflective working through of this experience. Self-binding is effected by moral experiences that are intense enough to have an impact on a person's moral identity.

The problem with individual self-binding, however, is that it is difficult to manipulate one's moral experience at will. Changes in fundamental value

---

[45] Baumgartner 2005: 283 ff.

orientation do not usually occur deliberately. It must be doubted, therefore, whether internal self-binding on the level of the *individual* is a good candidate for compensating for other kinds of future ethical motivation wherever these are lacking. A further problem is that even a conscience reliable enough to constitute a moral identity is not immune to corruption. Internal moral sanctions are often too weak to overcome temptation. On the whole, delegation of control to an external agency seems more effective.

This is true, however, only on the level of the individual. On the social level, internal self-binding might serve as a potent instrument of protecting collective long-term concerns from being weakened by myopic temptations, both by formal and informal means. The most important formal means are legal and constitutional safeguards; the most important informal means are educational policies. By educating the young generation in the spirit of sustainability and by creating an atmosphere in which foresight, cautious use of resources, nature conservation, and the long-term stability of social security are strengthened against countervailing short-term interests, society deliberately builds up pressure from below to keep its own opportunistic tendencies under control. This pressure then might act as a kind of 'social conscience' against the temptations of politicians to serve themselves or their constituencies at the cost of the future. This is not say that social self-binding mechanisms are by themselves supportive of sustainability and long-term objectives. On the contrary, in many welfare states the legal realities are such that long-term political objectives (such as lowering the national debt) are made more difficult by legally established social rights.

Compared to legal safeguards against social myopia, constitutional safeguards are clearly more reliable. They are not only less easy to change than simple laws, they can also be expected to pre-commit future generations of politicians and other decision-makers, thus contributing to continuity in the pursuit of transgenerational objectives.[46] Though there can be, in the nature of the case, no guarantee that they will remain in force during future generations, they provide as much certainty that the projects of today are carried on in the future as one can possibly hope for. Besides that, constitutions usually provide a certain degree of protection against politics being excessively dominated by short-term objectives, through both procedural and material safeguards. One of the procedural safeguards designed to control short-term orientation in political decision-making is the institution of indirect democracy, which requires that the members of the legislative organs are bound exclusively by their own conscience and/or party discipline and not by an imperative

---

[46] cf. Elster 1979: 95.

mandate. By assigning the control of the executive not to the constituencies themselves but to their elected representatives, potential pressure from the basis to prioritize short-term objectives over long-term objectives of preservation and development is effectively reduced. Again, this assignment of control will work in favour of long-term orientations only to the extent that the decisions taken by political representatives are in fact less myopic than those hypothetically taken by their constituencies. Whether this is so, is open to doubt.

Another procedural safeguard is the institution of an independent constitutional court with the power to control government policies by constitutional principles. Most constitutions contain material principles limiting the extent to which governments may indulge in 'obliviousness of the future'. In the German *Grundgesetz,* there are two articles to that effect: article 115 which limits the national debt to the sum total of national investments, and the recently introduced article 20a, which contains an explicit commitment to care adequately for the needs of future generations, especially by preserving resources and by protecting the natural environment.

There are other hopeful developments in establishing self-binding mechanisms by which collective agents keep their own myopia under control. In a number of political areas, such as economics, science, technology, environment, medicine and social security, there is a growing number of independent bodies whose counsel is heard, and often respected, in practical politics. Examples of such independent bodies are, on the one hand, research institutions, think tanks, and foundations designed to exist over longer periods of time and wholly or partly financed by the state, and, on the other hand, committees and commissions expected to work on more limited tasks. The intention in setting up these bodies is, partly, to make them act as a kind of collective 'future ethical conscience', a role which politics is often unable to play because of pressures of lobbying, party politics and election campaigns. Of course, there is no guarantee that the advice of these committees and commissions (even where it is unanimous) is respected. The advice coming from these bodies binds those to whom it is addressed as little as advice from a friend binds an individual. The alternative of endowing these bodies with executive or legislative powers, however, would not be compatible with basic democratic principles. The sovereignty of the people, or of its representatives, must not be usurped by experts.

Experience shows that it may take quite a long time until the warnings of experts from these bodies about future dangers have an impact on politics. In some cases, it takes twenty or thirty years until the warnings about long-term hazards are taken seriously by politicians, as, for example, in the case of climate changes caused by the emission of greenhouse gases. (One may well wonder how long it will take for the dangers inherent in the dramatic changes in the distribution of age groups to be fully recognized by political planners.) In part, these delays are not unreasonable given the fact that neither every warning is well-founded nor every catastrophe scenario realistic (think of such insufficiently founded warnings as the *Waldsterben* or the potentially fatal erosion of the oxygen content of the atmosphere). In part they are due, however, to the reluctance of politicians to meet new challenges and to confront their constituencies with truths they do not like.

7. External Self-binding Mechanisms

On the level of the individual, self-binding by an external agency is the more attractive the more firmly an individual wants to act on its long-term principles and the higher its risk of impulsiveness. An extreme case is the situation of gambling addicts, some of whom have gone so far as to demand legal possibilities to make gambling casinos restrict access to them on an international scale. A milder form of self-restraint by external self-binding would be to make one's decision to quit smoking public and to expose oneself to the mockery of friends in case of defection (cf. Bayertz 2004, 172).

Since time preference is a universal phenomenon, delegating responsibility for long-term provisions to an external agency like the state is often rational even for those who are less prone to succumb to their impulses. For one, control costs are shifted to an external institution. Self-restraint is wholly or partly replaced by restrictions coming from outside. Second, the individual can be more certain that his individual investment has an effect on the future in all cases where a cumulative effort is needed to make a difference. Third, it is more probable that the burdens of realizing long-term objectives are fairly distributed and that free riding on the idealism of others is ruled out. Fourth, there are advantages of a moral division of labour made possible by institutional solutions. Instead of each individual making its own provisions for the future, those with an intrinsic interest in the class of objects to be protected can be assigned the task of keeping them in good order, with environmentalists caring for the conservation of nature, and economists caring for the conservation of capital. Empirical surveys repeatedly show that a large proportion of citizens is interested in the conservation of nature but that very few are willing to actively contribute to it by voluntary work. In all such cases it is rational to lay these widely shared aims into the hands of those who are intrinsically motivated.

On the level of the collective, several external self-binding mechanisms with a clear relevance to future ethics are already in operation, some of them taking the form of international law and international contracts, others taking the form of transnational organizations and authorities. A model of an internationally effective agency able not only to give advice to national governments but also to implement their future directed policies independently of national politics is the European Central Bank. It functions independently of national governments and is bound exclusively by the criteria of the European Union Treaty. Important functions of an external control of government policies in the sphere of future objectives are international contracts like the Maastricht Treaty (concerning the limits set to the national debt) and the Kyoto Protocol (concerning the emission of greenhouse gases into the atmosphere). However, given the fact that governments are the key agents of most future hazards such as the destruction of large parts of tropical rain forest, the reduction of biodiversity, and the degradation of soils by intensive agriculture, there is still much to be done. There are quite a number of proposals about how this may be effected. One option that should be taken into consideration is the global court for future issues proposed, together with other options, by Weiss.[47] Such a court, even if it lacks the authority to check the 'obliviousness of the future' of national governments by issuing sanctions, would at least be able to protest against policies that endanger the interests of future people and to encourage the search for sustainable alternatives.

8. Conclusion

The 'motivation problem', the problem of bridging the psychological gap between the acceptance of a rule and acting in accordance with it, is not only a practical challenge to politicians and educators, but also a theoretical challenge to moral psychology and moral philosophy. The challenge is to identify factors that might help to motivate an agent not only to accept responsibility in the abstract but also to adopt it as a part of his moral identity and to take appropriate action. Though internalists about moral motivation are probably right in thinking that accepting a moral rule is more than a purely intellectual act of assent and involves some motivation to act in accordance with it, this motivation by itself is, in general, too weak to resist the temptations of more immediate and more controllable objectives.

---

[47] Weiss 1989: 121.

Motivation to make provisions for the more distant future is a particular challenge for any theory of moral motivation. Moral norms to care for the distant future do not only share the problems of motivation common to all moral norms but face particular difficulties resulting from the facelessness of future people and the inevitable abstractness of obligations to act for the future. Moreover, the motivation to act responsibly towards the future tends to be weakened by a number of uncertainties, among them the uncertainty about what our descendants will value, the uncertainty about whether present sacrifices will have an effect on future well-being, and the uncertainty about whether subsequent generations will co-operate in the long-term effort to preserve essential natural resources (such as energy resources) and important cultural resources (such as the democratic state).

The picture resulting from an exclusive consideration of direct motivations to act for the future is unduly pessimistic, however. It leaves out the important role of indirect motivations. In the context of future ethics, indirect motivations, whether moral, quasi-moral or non-moral, can be expected to have a more reliable emotional basis than direct motivations and to be more effective in guiding behaviour. Taking indirect motivations into account makes the prospects of future-oriented action appear much less gloomy. Among these are the love of one's children and grandchildren (and the expectation to receive something from them in exchange in a later period of life), group loyalties, the high valuation of transgenerational projects and ideals for their own sakes, and the satisfaction gained by embedding one's own limited existence into a 'self-transcending' chain of contributions to a transgenerational cause. These motivations hold at least a limited promise of effectively shaping the decisions of the present generation in a way compatible with widely shared principles of future ethics, especially if these motivations are supported by mechanisms of external self-binding on the level of the individual and by mechanisms of internal and external self-binding on the level of collectives like states and companies.

References

ARRONDEL, L., and MASSON, A. (2001), 'Family transfers involving three generations', *Scandinavian Journal of Economics*, 103: 415–44.

AUERBACH, B. E. (1995), *Unto the Thousandth Generation. Conceptualizing Intergenerational Justice* (New York: Peter Lang).

BANDURA, A. (1969), 'Social learning of moral judgements', *Journal of Personality and Social Psychology*, 11: 275–9.

BAUMGARTNER, C. (2005), *Umweltethik—Umwelthandeln. Ein Beitrag zur Lösung des Motivationsproblems* (Paderborn: Mentis).

BAYERTZ, K. (2004), *Warum überhaupt moralisch sein?* (Munich: Beck).

BECKER, G. S., and MURPHY, K. M. (1988), 'The family and the state', *Journal of Law and Economics*, 31: 1−18.

BERGSON, H. (1932), *Les deux sources de la moralité et de la religion* (Paris: Alcan).

BIERHOFF, H.-W. (1990), *Psychologie hilfreichen Verhaltens* (Stuttgart: Kohlhammer).

—— (2002), *Prosocial Behaviour* (Hove: Psychology Press).

BIRNBACHER, D. (1990), 'Schopenhauers Idee einer rekonstruktiven Ethik (mit Anwendungen auf die moderne Medizinethik)', *Schopenhauer-Jahrbuch,* 71: 26−44.

—— (2003), 'Can discounting be justified?', *International Journal of Sustainable Development*, 6: 42−51.

CALABRESI, G., and BOBBITT, P. (1978), *Tragic Choices* (New York: Norton).

CARE, N. S. (1982), 'Future generations, public policy, and the motivation problem', *Environmental Ethics*, 4: 195−213.

DASGUPTA, P. (1974), 'On some alternative criteria for justice between generations', *Journal of Public Economics*, 3: 405−23.

DE-SHALIT, A. (1995), *Why Posterity Matters. Environmental Policies and Future Generations* (London/New York: Routledge).

ELSTER, J. (1979), *Ulysses and the Sirens. Studies in Rationality and Irrationality* (Cambridge/Paris: Cambridge University Press).

EVANS, G. W., and JACOBS, S. (1981), 'Air pollution and human behavior', *Journal of Social Issues*, 37: 95−125.

FESTINGER, L. (1957), *A Theory of Cognitive Dissonance* (Stanford: Stanford University Press).

GOLDING, M. (1981), 'Obligations to future generations', in E. Partridge (ed.), *Responsibilities to Future Generations* (Buffalo (N. Y.): Prometheus Books), 61−72.

HARE, R. M. (1963), *Freedom and Reason* (Oxford: Clarendon Press).

—— (1981), *Moral Thinking: Its Levels, Method and Point* (Oxford: Clarendon Press).

HUME, D. (1888), *Treatise on Human Nature* (Oxford: Oxford University Press).

JONAS, H. (1979), *Das Prinzip Verantwortung. Versuch einer Ethik für die technologische Zivilisation* (Frankfurt/M.: Insel).

KALS, E., SCHUMACHER, D., and MONTADA, L. (1999), 'Emotional affinity toward nature as a motivational basis to protect nature', *Environment & Behaviour*, 31: 178−202.

KANT, I. (1912), 'Idee zu einer allgemeinen Geschichte in weltbürgerlicher Absicht', in *Werke* (Akademie-Ausgabe) (Berlin: Reimer), 8.

KORSGAARD, C. M. (1986), 'Skepticism about practical reason', *Journal of Philosophy*, 83: 5−25.

LEISEROWITZ, A. (2006), 'Climate change risk perception and policy preferences: The role of affect, imagery, and values', *Climatic Change*, 77: 45−72.

LEOPOLD, A. (1949), 'The land ethic', in *A Sand County Almanac and Sketches Here and There* (New York: Oxford University Press), 201–26.

MINTEER, B. A., and MANNING, R. E. (1999), 'Pragmatism in environmental ethics: Democracy, pluralism, and the management of nature', *Environmental Ethics*, 21: 191–207.

MONTADA, L. (1993), 'Moralische Gefühle', in Edelstein,W., Nunner-Winkler, G., and Noam, G. (eds.), *Moral und Person* (Frankfurt/M.: Suhrkamp), 259–77.

NIETZSCHE, F. (1980), *Also sprach Zarathustra* (F. Nietzsche: *Sämtliche Werke. Kritische Studienausgabe.* Ed. Colli/Montinari, vol. 4, Munich/Berlin: dtv/de Gruyter).

PARTRIDGE, E. (1980), 'Why care about the future?', in E. Partridge (ed.), *Responsibilities to Future Generations* (Buffalo (N. Y.): Prometheus Books), 203–20.

PASSMORE, J. (1980), *Man's Responsibility for Nature. Ecological Problems and Western Traditions* (2nd edn., London: Duckworth).

PIGOU, A. C. (1932), *The Economics of Welfare* (4th edn., London: Macmillan).

RUSSELL, Y., KALS, E., and MONTADA, L. (2003), 'Generationengerechtigkeit im allgemeinen Bewußtsein?—Eine umweltpsychologische Untersuchung', in Stiftung für die Rechte zukünftiger Generationen (ed.), *Handbuch Generationengerechtigkeit* (Munich: ökom), 153–71.

SIDGWICK, H. (1907), *The Methods of Ethics* (7th edn., London: Macmillan).

STENDHAL (1959), *De l'Amour* (Paris: Garnier Frères).

STOLL-KLEEMANN, S., O'RIORDAN, T., and JAEGER, C. C. (2001), 'The pychology of denial concerning climate mitigation measures: Evidence from Swiss focus groups', *Global Envrionmental Change* 11: 107–17.

TOCQUEVILLE, A. de (1961), *De la Démocratie en Amérique* (Œuvres complètes, tome 1) (Paris: Gallimard).

UNGER, P. (1996), *Living High and Letting Die. Our Illusion of Innocence* (New York: Oxford University Press).

VISSER'T HOOFT, H. P. (1999), *Justice to Future Generations and the Environment* (Dordrecht: Kluwer).

WADE-BENZONI, K. A. (2002). 'A Golden Rule over time: Reciprocity in intergenerational allocation decisions', *Academy of Management Journal*, 45: 1011–28.

WEISS, E. B. (1989), *In Fairness to Future Generations: International Law, Common Patrimony, and Intergenerational Equity* (Tokyo/Dobbsferry (N. Y.): United Nations University/Transnational Publishers).

WIELAND, W. (1989), *Aporien der praktischen Vernunft* (Frankfurt am Main: Klostermann).

WILLIAMS, B. (1981), *Moral Luck. Philosophical Papers 1973–1980* (Cambridge: Cambridge University Press).

ZWICK, M. M. (2001), 'Der globale Klimawandel in der Wahrnehmung der Öffentlichkeit', *Gaia*, 10, 299–303.

11

Preference-formation and Intergenerational Justice

KRISTER BYKVIST

1. Introduction

We all agree that we should be concerned with the well-being of future generations. But it is notoriously difficult to spell out this concern in more detail without generating contradictions. In particular, it has been proved to be extremely difficult to find a theory of beneficence that would provide both a coherent and plausible account of our responsibilities to future generations.[1] What makes this so difficult is that in many cases—the so-called *different people cases*—we can affect the identities of future people.[2] Our standard principles of beneficence were formulated to take care of *same people cases* where the identities of people are fixed, but when they are generalized to different people cases they often have unpalatable consequences.

One unpalatable consequence is the non-identity problem. If we are choosing between creating a child who we know would have a handicap that would make her life barely worth living and creating another child later who would not have this handicap, it seems difficult to say that it is better to wait and create the healthy child. How can this be better if it would not be better for anyone? The healthy child would not be better off living than not having a life at all. Similarly, how can it be worse to create the handicapped child if she would not have been better off if we had not created her?

Another unpalatable consequence is the Repugnant Conclusion. If we want to promote total well-being, we can do this by either making existing people happier or making new happy people. But this seems to licence a policy that encourage people to create as many children as possible even if their and their

---

[1] For some excellent discussions about these difficulties, see, for instance, Arrhenius (2000), Broome (2004), and Parfit (1992).

[2] The labels 'different people cases' and 'same people cases' are taken from Parfit (1992), pp. 355–6.

parents' lives will be only barely worth living. Furthermore, if the number of new children is sufficiently large, then this policy must be deemed better than a policy that would encourage people to have fewer but extremely happy children.

Matters seem to be even worse if we adopt a desire-based theory of well-being. If we assume that the well-being of a person crucially depends on how well her preferences are satisfied, then we get a new form of non-identity problem, one that involves not just the non-identity of persons but also the non-identity of desires. Not only do we have to worry about which persons to create, we also have to worry about which desires to create.

One challenge for the desire-based theory here is to specify which option is better when the desires and preferences that define what is good and better for people will themselves be shaped by our choices. More generally, it seems difficult to talk meaningfully about maximizing the satisfaction of desires and preferences when there is no fixed set of desires and preferences to satisfy.

Another challenge is that if desire-satisfaction is all that counts, it does not seem to matter how the fit between desires and the world is achieved. Other things being equal, it seems better to bring up our children to become adults with easily satisfied desires, rather than adults with normal and more demanding aspirations. But this seems to favour an education system that would aim at making people able to adjust their desires to whatever circumstances their lives will offer, no matter how worthless these circumstances might be.

I shall argue that these challenges can be met if proper attention is paid to two important but often neglected distinctions: the distinction between comparative desires (preferences) and absolute desires (pro- and con-attitudes), and the distinction between desires for worthless things and desires for worthwhile things. A satisfactory desire-theory, I shall argue, must define what is better for a person in terms of his absolute desires, not his comparative ones, and discriminate between desires on the basis of the values of their objects.

The outline of the paper is the following. In the next section, I start by stating some important presuppositions. In section 3, I show that desire-based theories that define the standard of betterness in terms of preferences is threatened by indeterminacy in the sense that in some cases there is no determinate answer to the question of which preferences it is best to inculcate in a person. In section 4, I show that even in cases where no indeterminacy of this kind is at stake, the theory will lead to inconsistencies if certain plausible assumptions about good-for and bad-for are accepted. In sections 5 and 6, I argue that the problems of indeterminacy and inconsistency are best solved by adopting a polarity-based desire-theory that defines betterness in terms of absolute desires, i.e., favouring, disfavouring and indifference. In section 7, I turn to the problem of desire-adjustment and show that what is at issue is not whether our desires are easily satisfied but whether they concern worthwhile things. I argue that the right response to this problem is to adopt a discriminating desire-theory that defines well-being in terms of desires that match up with objective values.

2. Presuppositions

Before I get down to business I need to state some presuppositions. It should be stressed that my aim in this essay is not to defend a complete theory of intergenerational justice. A complete theory would have something to say about desire fairness, and equality. This paper deals only with those aspects of intergenerational justice that concern the promotion of well-being. Nor is my aim to provide a full defence of a desire-based theory of well-being. My main aim is rather to show that there is a version of the desire-based theory that can tackle some of the most difficult theoretical obstacles and provide a coherent and plausible view on preference-formation in cases in which the identity of people is fixed but the identity of their desires is not.

My discussion will be conducted at the axiological level, in terms of what is better or worse from the perspective of beneficence and in terms of what is better or worse, good or bad, for individual persons. I assume that facts about what is better or worse from the perspective of beneficence are normatively relevant, but not that they fully determine what we ought to do. Perhaps there are other considerations, deontological side constraints, for instance, that also have a bearing on what we ought to do. Nor do I assume that what is better or worse from the perspective of beneficence is also better or worse *all things considered*. In particular, considerations about equality and desert will be put aside in this essay, since they might plausibly be seen as falling outside the scope of the morality of beneficence, narrowly conceived.[3]

I am mainly interested in *outcome*-evaluations, but for ease of exposition I will sometimes talk loosely about the values of actions. So, whenever I say that it is better (or better for a person) that one action is done rather than another,

---

[3] Drawing the boundaries of the morality of beneficence in this way will exclude the possibility that inequality is *intrinsically bad for people*, a possibility that is embraced by some people. See, for instance, Broome (1991), pp. 181–2. I think this is an implausible position, but I do not have the space to argue this. In any case, my decision to rule out this possibility will not affect the main points of my arguments.

this should be seen as a loose way of saying that the outcome of the first action is better (or better for the person) than that of the second.

Desire-theories of well-being usually assume that what is good or better for a person is determined by the person's *intrinsic* desires, the desires he has for things, in and for themselves, and not because they are means for the fulfilment of some of his other desires. I will follow the common lead here, but to avoid cluttering the exposition, I will suppress the qualifier 'intrinsic'.

To simplify the discussion, I will for the most part only consider people's *global* desires, the desires they have for their lives taken as a whole. Though this restriction is somewhat controversial, it enables us to illuminate the desire-theories under discussion in a clear and simple way. It should be noted that this restriction is not wholly implausible. It seems reasonable to give priority to global desires since they are more comprehensive than local desires about particular states of affairs. Global desires concern the way these states of affairs make up bigger wholes, for instance, the way they unfold in time and make up temporal wholes. And our attitudes towards these holistic features of our lives seem crucial to the overall value of our lives.

It is commonplace that a person's desires can differ radically across time. I will sidestep the temporal problem here and assume that the desire theory has a plausible solution to offer.[4] So, when I say that a person desires a certain life (or part of a life) in a certain world this is to be understood as the person *timelessly* desires it, where his timeless desire is some kind of amalgamation of his past, present, and future desires in this world. Alternatively, we could assume, unrealistically, that there is simply no conflict in desires across time.

3. Indeterminacy

On most theories, same people choices pose no special problems. A desire-based theory, however, will have problems even in these cases, since the future desires of people might be contingent on our present decisions. Even if the present decision does not determine who is going to be around in the future, the choice might determine which future desires these people will have. Same people choices are not always same desires choices.

It is well-known that desire-based theories have a hard time deciding which outcome is better for a person when his preferences over the available outcomes

---

[4] I have addressed this problem elsewhere. See Bykvist (2003).

depend on which outcome is realized.[5] To take a familiar example, suppose that you are considering getting married. The problem is that you know that if you get married, you will prefer being unmarried to being married, and if you stay unmarried, you will prefer being married to being unmarried. The reason is that if you get married you will adopt certain perfectionist marital ideals about marriage and think that your marriage is less than perfect. On the other hand, if you stay unmarried, you will be an unhappy single. Which outcome is better for you? From the perspective of the outcome in which you are married, being married seems to be worse for you since here you prefer to be unmarried. But from the perspective of the outcome in which you are unmarried, being married seems to be better for you, since here you prefer to be married. Note that you may be undecided at the time of choice, so you can't rely on your present preferences in order to decide what to do.

Similar problems might occur when we consider choices that affect other generations, for which ideals and values our children will adopt depend crucially on which schools they attend, which people they marry, which people they befriend, which careers they choose, and which roles the play in society. But these are all factors that to a large extent are contingent on our present choices. Consider the following cases:

(i) You have to choose a school for your child, and the choice is between a religious school and a secular one. If you send your child to a religious school, she will become deeply religious and prefer being in a religious school to being in a secular school. If you send your child to the secular school, she will adopt a secular lifestyle and prefer being in a secular school to being in religious one.[6] Which option is better for you child? Note that your child might be undecided at the time of choice, so you may not be able to rely on your child's present preferences.

(ii) The government is considering whether to encourage young people to live in the countryside, and they want to know if that would be better for them. They know that if people were to move to the countryside, they would come to appreciate the values of living close to nature and prefer this life to a life in the city. However, they also know that if people were to stay in the city, they would appreciate the values of city life, and prefer city life to country life. How can the government decide

---

[5] For other illustrations of this problem, see, for instance, Bricker (1980) and Gibbard (1992).

[6] For a similar case, see Gibbard (1992), pp. 176–7.

which option is better for the people? Note that the young people might at the time of decision be undecided between these options, so the government cannot rely on their current preferences.

In the above cases, since it is indeterminate which outcome people will prefer, the desire-based theory seems forced to say that it is indeterminate which outcome is better for them. One way to avoid this indeterminacy would be to take into account the preferences in each outcome and satisfy the strongest preferences. So, for instance, if my child's preference for being in a secular school would be stronger than her preference for being in a religious school, it is better for her to go to the secular school. However, I will show in the next section that this move is not enough to save the theory from inconsistency.[7]

4. Inconsistency

It might seem that the desire-based theory will be safe in cases where it is determinate which outcome people will prefer. As I will argue, however, this is not so. To see this, consider the following variation of the school example above. Suppose, again, that if you send your child to the secular school, she will adopt a secular lifestyle, and prefer being in this school to being in a religious school. However, suppose that if you send your child to the religious school, she will become religious but prefer being in a secular school to being in a religious school. Perhaps she would be taught the virtues of tolerance and multi-faith dialogue and would prefer to be in a secular school where she would be able interact with non-believers. In this case, if preferences provide the standard of betterness, it might seem straightforward that sending your child to the secular school would be better for your child, for no matter which option is chosen your child will prefer being in the secular school. If we assume that no other preference would be affected, then sending your child to this school seems also to be the better option all things considered.

This conclusion is problematic, however, because we have not yet said anything about whether your child would *like* or *dislike* her being in these

<hr />

[7] Another move would be to let the uniquely actual preferences decide the matter. Here 'actual' is supposed to refer rigidly to the preferences we have here in our world. What is actual in this sense will then not change from one world to another, so indeterminacy will be avoided. But this comes at a very high price. There does not seem to be any special reason to give exclusive weight to the preferences we happen to have here in our world. Surely, we want to give weight to counterfactual preferences as well.

schools, respectively. Suppose, for instance, that if your child went to the religious school, she would *love* her life in this school but she would love it even more to be in a secular school where she would be able interact with non-believers. If she went to a secular school, she would *hate* it, since it would offer poor education in overcrowded classrooms. Since she would adopt a secular lifestyle, she would not be able to see the virtues of a religious education and therefore hate that option even more. But, surely, whether an outcome would be favoured, disfavoured, or seen as neutral, and whether it would be strongly or weakly favoured or disfavoured, is something that is crucial for deciding the value of the outcome for people. More specifically, these attitudes seem crucial when we determine what is good or bad for a person. It seems clear that a life (or a part of a life) is good for a person just in case he would favour it, i.e., have a positive attitude towards it, if he were to lead it, and bad for him just in case he would disfavour it, i.e., have a negative attitude towards it, if he were to lead it. According to these principles, what matters for the goodness or badness of a certain possible life of a person is how he would feel about his life were he to lead it. This seems right. How he would feel about this life, had he lead a different life, is irrelevant, at least if his desires in these lives are equally autonomous, rational, and well-informed.

But if we add these principles to the desire-based theory, we will get an inconsistency. The desire-based theory under consideration claims that since your child would prefer being in a secular school no matter which school she was sent to, she would be better off in the secular school than in a religious school. But if we accept the above definitions of good-for and bad-for, we also get the conclusion that your child's life in the secular school is bad for her, since she would disfavour her life in this school, whereas being in a religious school is good for her, since she would favour her life in this school. These two conclusions cannot both be true, for the simple reason a bad thing cannot be better than a good thing.

What creates this problem is that preferring one life (or part of a life) to another is compatible with taking very different absolute attitudes towards the compared lives (parts of lives). More generally, preferring A to B is compatible with either of the following possibilities:

(a) A is favoured, B is favoured less.
(b) A is favoured, B is seen as neutral.
(c) A is favoured, B is disfavoured.
(d) A is seen as neutral, B is disfavoured.
(e) A is disfavoured, B is disfavoured more.

One might try to evade these difficulties by saying that if we only consider fully rational or ideal desires, the desires we would have in an epistemically ideal situation, these cases will never occur. The reason why the comparative or absolute desires are contingent in the examples above is that at least one of the person's contingent selves lacks some crucial information about the alternatives.

This response assumes not only that the desire-based theory should favour ideal desires, which is in itself a controversial assumption, but also that these ideal desires will be insensitive to a person's character traits and personality. In order to defend this, it would have to be shown that the specification of the ideal epistemic situation will somehow guarantee that the resulting ideal desires do not vary with even the most drastic changes in the character and personality of the person. However, this is a tall order, and there are plenty of reasons to be sceptical about this. The personalities, character traits and belief systems of persons may differ radically from one outcome to another. It will not do to say that an ideal epistemic situation is one in which the person has all the relevant factual information and makes no mistakes in reasoning.[8] Obviously, what a person would desire in a situation like this depends crucially on his actual psychological make-up.

But couldn't the friend of ideal desires respond that if each contingent self of a person was fully informed not just about the objects of his attitudes but also about what would happen to his attitudes if these objects were realized, they would no longer disagree in their ideal desires? For instance, if a bachelor knew that he would not favour being married if he were married, then he would no longer favour being married. He might think: 'What is the point in being married if I won't favour it?' Similarly, if your child knew that she would hate being in a secular school if she went there, she would no longer favour it.

I think this response will work for some of the cases. It will work for those cases in which a person's attitude is *conditional on its own persistence*: she favours X only on the condition that were X realized, she would still favour it.[9] But one's attitudes might be based on *personal ideals*, and it is a characteristic (if not defining) feature of ideals that they are not conditional on their own persistence. I might favour being married because my religious or perfectionist ideals tell me that matrimony is sacred, and therefore has a value that does not depend on whether I would still favour being married if I got married. To take

---

[8] This characterisation of the ideal situation is can be found in Harsanyi (1990), p. 55. Similar views can be found in Brandt (1979), chs. 6–7, and Rawls (1971), p. 417 ff.

[9] This kind of conditionality is discussed in Parfit (1992), p. 151.

another example, my desire now to be an honest and healthy person in the future is not conditional on my desiring it then. I want now that I am honest and healthy even in the future scenario in which I do not care about being honest and healthy.

This response has therefore only limited success: it will only take care of cases in which the attitudes are conditional on their own persistence. But we still have cases in which the attitudes are expressive of personal ideals, and there is no guarantee that these attitudes must converge, even if they were properly idealized. So something has to give. Either we have to go for a strict preference-based approach that claims that the whole story about whether an outcome is better than another for a person is captured by her preferences concerning these outcomes; or we have to define better-for in terms of positive and negative attitudes. I shall argue that the right option is to abandon the preference-based approach. This will give us a theory that can deal more successfully with the cases we have discussed so far. But to show this I will need to spell out my theory a bit more.

5. The Polarity-based Desire Theory

A polarity-based desire theory is one that takes the *polarity* or *valence* of attitudes into account.[10] Very roughly put, to have a positive attitude (a pro-attitude) towards x is to be positively oriented towards x in your actions, emotions, feelings or evaluative responses. So, if you have a positive attitude towards x, you tend to be motivated to bring it about, to be glad and happy when you think it obtains, to have pleasant thoughts about it, or to see it in a good light. To have a negative attitude (a con-attitude) towards x is then to be negatively oriented towards x in your actions, emotions, feelings or evaluative responses. You tend to be motivated to avoid it, to be sad and unhappy when you think it obtains, to have unpleasant thoughts about it, or to see it in a bad light. I also assume that an attitude can have zero valence and thus be an attitude of indifference, accompanied by indifference in actions, emotions, feelings, or evaluative responses.

It is important to distinguish favouring in this sense from wanting, if wanting x is simply defined as preferring x to its negation. Suppose you want not to have a headache, understood as your preferring not having a headache to having a headache. Then this implies that when this want is satisfied something positively

---

[10] For a similar account of the polarity of attitudes, see Hurka (2001), pp. 13–14.

good occurs in your life. It also implies that if you create anti-headache wants in order to satisfy them you make your life better, other things being equal. But if you are like me you take a *neutral* attitude towards not having a headache, and a negative attitude towards having a headache. Therefore, it seems more sensible to say that it is good for you to get what you *favour*, i.e., what you have a positive attitude towards.

Similar points apply to want-frustration. It is not true that frustrating a person's want is always bad for him. Whether it is bad for him depends on what attitude he takes towards not getting what he wants. Suppose I want to get an unexpected gift and I do not get it. This need not be bad for me, since I may take a neutral attitude towards not getting an unexpected gift. It is therefore seriously misleading to say that desire-theories assign positive value to want-satisfactions and negative to want-frustrations.[11]

Having spelled out the conditions for good-for and bad-for, it is time to say something about better-for. To decide whether an outcome x is better for a person than another outcome y we should see what absolute attitude he *would* have towards x, if x obtained, and compare that attitude with the absolute attitude he *would* have towards y, if y obtained.[12] More exactly:

x is better for S than y iff:

> (i) S would *favour* his life in x *more*, if x obtained, than he would *favour* his life in y, if y obtained, or
> (ii) S would *disfavour* his life in x *less*, if x obtained, than he would *disfavour* his life in y, if y obtained, or
> (iii) S would *favour* his life in x, if x obtained, and he would *disfavour* his life in y, if y obtained, or
> (iv) S would *favour* his life in x, if x obtained, and he would be *indifferent* towards his life in y, if y obtained, or
> (v) S would be *indifferent* towards his life in x, if x obtained, and he would *disfavour* his life in y, if y obtained.

---

[11]   This is also pointed out by Brülde (1998), pp. 35–7.

[12]   There is an alternative way of understanding this suggestion. I have assumed so far that what is good for a person is the *object* of her favouring. But the polarity-based theory could instead assign value, not to the object of her favouring, but to *the fact that her favouring is satisfied*. To see the difference between these approaches, suppose that Eric favours to drink pink champagne. The object-oriented approach would say that it is the drinking of pink champagne that is good for Eric, whereas the satisfaction-oriented approach would say that what is good for Eric is the whole state of affairs consisting of Eric's favouring of drinking pink champagne and his drinking this champagne. The satisfaction-oriented approach will also be immune to the problems that afflict the preference-based theory. I will not argue for this here, but instead stick to the object-oriented approach. For more on the distinction between these two approaches, see Bykvist (1998), Rabinowicz and Österberg (1996), and Persson (1995).

A shorter but slightly misleading formulation of this principle would be: x is better for S than y iff S's x-self wants x more than his y-self wants y.[13]

Equality in value can now be defined in a similar way:

x is equally as good for S as y iff:

  (i) S would favour his life in x, if x obtained, as much as he would favour his life in y, if y obtained, or,
  (ii) S would disfavour his life in x, if x obtained, as much as he would favour his life in y, if y obtained, or,
  (iii) S would be indifferent towards his life in x, if x obtained, and he would be indifferent towards his life in y, if y obtained.

In short: x is equally as good for S as y iff S's x-self want x as much as his y-self wants y.[14]

One might object to these principles on the grounds that they seem to presuppose that absolute attitudes are primitive and can't be reduced to comparative ones. But this is not so. These principles could be defended even if we defined favouring, disfavouring, and indifference in terms of preference in the following way:

S favours x iff S prefers x to something he is indifferent towards.

S disfavours x iff S prefers y to x and y is something S is indifferent towards.

S is indifferent towards x iff S is indifferent between x and the negation of x.[15]

Of course, I do have to assume that it makes sense to compare attitudes of different contingent selves of the same person. I see no problem in comparing absolute attitudes with different polarity: favourings with disfavourings, favourings with indifferent attitudes, and disfavourings with indifferent attitudes. What could create a problem are comparisons of absolute attitudes that have the same positive or negative polarity. What does it mean to say that one contingent self favours x more than another contingent self favours y? In

---

[13] Bricker (1980) seems to suggest a similar principle, but he does not make use of the attitudes of favouring, disfavouring and indifference. Instead he defines his theory in terms of utility functions representing preferences on a ratio scale without arguing for the meaningfulness of this numerical representation.

[14] Note that analogous principles can be formulated for *interpersonal* comparisons of well-being: x is better for S than y is for T (S is better off in x than T is in y) iff S's x-self wants x more than T's y-self wants y. x is equally as good for S as y is for T iff S's x-self wants x as much as T's y-self wants y.

[15] Note that the same manoeuvre can be applied to goodness. What is good is what is better than something indifferent, and something is indifferent if its presence is as good as its absence. See Chisholm (1966).

reply, I would say that if favourings can be defined in terms of preferences along the lines presented above, then a comparison of favourings boils down to a comparison of preferences. To decide whether my x-self favours x more than my y-self favours y, we should compare my x-self's preference for x over something he is indifferent towards with my y-self's preference for y over something he is indifferent towards. Comparisons of favourings will then be comparisons of preference *differences*. The same reasoning can of course be applied to comparisons of disfavourings. Note that this shows that the proponent of the preference-based approach has no advantage, if he assumes that we can compare preference differences across people. We are in the same boat. We both need to make sense of comparisons of preference differences.

It is important to note that, even if favourings and disfavourings can be reduced to preferences, to say that my x-self would favour x more than my y-self would favour y is *not* to say that my x-self's preference for x over y is stronger than my y-self's preference for y over x. My x-self might favour x even though she does not have a preference for x over y. My x-self might be indifferent between x and y but favour both. Or she might prefer y to x and favour x less than she favour y.

6. Why the Polarity-based Theory Works Better

It is now time to see how the polarity-based theory will cope with the problems we have discussed so far. First, indeterminacy is no longer a problem. To decide what is better for the person, we should look into each outcome and see what he would feel about his life in that outcome. An outcome x is better for a person than another outcome y just in case her x-self would want x more than her y-self would want y. So, for instance, if I would *hate* being married but hate being unmarried more, whereas, as a bachelor, I would *love* being unmarried but love being married more, it is better for me to be unmarried. It is better for me to lead a life he would love than to lead a life he would hate. And this evaluation does not depend on which outcome is realized. Similarly, to decide what is better for your child, you should look into each school scenario and see what your child would feel about her life in that scenario. It is, for instance, better for your child to be in a school that she would love than be in a school that she would hate. Again, this evaluation does not depend on which outcome is realized. Finally, the same considerations apply to the government's choice problem. They should look into each outcome and find out what the people would feel about their lives if they were to lead them. So, for instance, if the country-bumpkins would favour their lives more than the city-slickers would favour theirs, it is better for the people to move to the countryside.

Second, the polarity-based theory will not lead to any inconsistencies in the school case where your child would prefer going to the secular school no matter which school she went to. It is better for your child to go to the religious school than to go to the secular school, since she would favour her life in the religious school, and would disfavour her life in the secular school. There is no contradiction involved here, since, according to the polarity-based approach, the fact your child would prefer being in the secular school no matter which school she went to does not show that being in the secular school is better for her.

There is one remaining worry, however, and that is that the polarity-based theory does not seem to fare better than its preference-based sibling when it comes to the problem of desire-adjustment: if we can't change the world to fit our desires, we should make our desires fit the world. Here the distinction between comparative and absolute desires is of no avail. It does not help to say that what matters is the fit between absolute desires and the world rather than the fit between preferences and the world. The polarity-based theory still seems to favour people with easily satisfied *positive attitudes*, people whose *favourings* would adjust to whatever conditions their lives would offer. As we will see in the next section, this is a problem that calls for a more radical refinement of the desire-based theory.

7. The Problem of Easily Satisfied Desires

Desire-based theories seem to be committed to creating easily satisfied desires. It is important to note, however, that since my theory is polarity-based, it avoids some of the most counterintuitive cases. Suppose that we can affect the attitudes of our children so that they will grow up to become adults who do not care about anything else than living a pain-free life. Now, if we can make sure that most of their desires for not being in pain are satisfied, we seem to have strong reason to create these pain-free but dull lives. However, a desire for not being in pain is usually based on a *neutral* attitude towards not being in pain and a *negative* attitude towards being in pain. A polarity-based account would therefore claim that by creating and satisfying anti-pain desires we are not creating good lives; we are only creating neutral lives. In order for a life to be good it is not enough that it is full of things you want in the sense that you prefer their presence to their absence; it must be full of things you *favour*, i.e., have a positive attitude towards.

This reply will not take care of all cases, however. My theory seems still committed to what has been dubbed the Stoic Slogan: if you cannot make the world conform to people's desires, you should make their desires conform to the world. Rawls complains that following the Stoic Slogan reduces us to bare persons who 'are ready to consider any new convictions and aims, and even abandon attachments and loyalties, when doing this promises a life with greater overall satisfaction'.[16] This means, he continues, that as a bare person you cannot lead a life 'expressive of character and of devotion to specific ends'.[17] This argument can of course be applied to cases where we are considering the well-being of other people. If I can turn someone else into a bare person, the Slogan seems to tell me that it is better to do so.

Four common responses

A common response from desire-theorists is to say that it is not clear that bare persons would be better off in terms of overall desire-satisfaction.[18] Since a bare person cannot have deep commitments and projects, he cannot have any deeply held desires. But since deep-seated desires last longer and are usually stronger and than desires that change from one moment to another, satisfying deep-seated desires may therefore count more towards overall desire-satisfaction than satisfying more transient ones. Furthermore, since not all of us have easy access to indirect means such as brain-washing and hypnosis, it will not, in general, be easy to change our most deeply held desires and we have to expect significant psychological costs in terms of frustrated desires.

This response does not get to the heart of the matter, because is easy to think of cases where the new desires will be as deep-seated as the old ones and where no serious costs would be involved. Suppose that your child suffers from an illness that will develop into autism with the consequence that your child's dominant desire will be to count the blades of grass on public lawns.[19] A cure is offered that would prevent autism and allow your child to form normal aspirations. Now, since it will be easier to satisfy the desire for grass-counting (supposing there is an abundance of public lawns), then it must be better to refuse this cure. To take an even more extreme case, suppose that there is a complacency pill available that would transform anyone who took it to a person whose desires would be completely satisfied with all circumstances

---

[16] Rawls (1990), p. 181.   [17] Rawls (1990), p. 181.
[18] See, for instance, Goodin (1991), pp. 114–15.   [19] This example is from Rawls (1971), p. 432.

of his life, come what may.[20] Then, again, if desire-satisfaction is all that counts, we seem to be forced to say that the best thing to do is to distribute this pill.

Now, there are many different replies the defenders of the desire-based account could offer. The first reply is to invoke what we may call *presentism*, the principle that we should give extra, or perhaps all weight, to people's present desires in deciding what is better for these people. (This account is most plausible if we assume that only ideal desires count, the desires we would have in some ideal epistemic situation.) One could then argue that allowing people to turn into grass-counters or making them complacent does not make them better off, since, normally, at the time of decision, people do not want to change their characters in such a radical way. On this view, people would not be better off after the grass-counting therapy or taking the complacency pill, for whether a person is better off depends wholly on their present (ideal) desires.

This is not an especially attractive option, however. To begin with, it saddles us with a form of relativism about well-being. Since our desires, including our ideal desires, may change across time, we cannot say that a person is better off in one outcome A than in another B; we have to say that he is better off in A than in B *relative to a time*.

Another problem with presentism is that it does not give enough weight to future well-being. It is true that a person's future well-being will be given indirect weight when his present self happens to care about his future selves, or would care if properly idealized. But if he values spontaneity and thinks that the moment itself is all that counts, then what happens to his future self may not matter at all, since there seems to be no guarantee that his obsession with the present moment would disappear even if he were fully informed and reasoned carefully. It would not help to define 'careful reasoning' in terms of a proper concern for one's future well-being, since this would give us a circular account of well-being: well-being is defined by present ideal desires, which in turn are defined by a proper concern for well-being.

Presentism might look attractive if we fail to distinguish between *what it is rational for an agent* and what is good for him.[21] It might be argued that what is rational for a person to do depends crucially on his present attitudes. For instance, whether it is rational for me *now* to prepare to go to a concert a year from now may depend decisively on my present attitudes towards this future event. This dependency is uncontroversial if we talk about what rational to do *given our present beliefs and desires*. But whether it will benefit me to go

---

[20] This example is from Bricker (1980), p. 384.   [21] Here I follow Darwall (2002), pp. 34–5.

to the concert does not seem to depend on my present attitudes. So, if the prudentially right thing to do is determined by all prudential values, including the future ones, it is quite possible that prudence and practical rationality will give us conflicting prescriptions in many cases.

No matter whether presentism is seen as a theory about prudence or a theory about practical rationality, accepting presentism makes it difficult to plan your life according to what is prudentially or rationally best for you, since what is best for you will vary with time. You may end up implementing a plan that you will have no reason to complete at a later time. Assume that you have a desire to write a Ph.D. thesis in philosophy and that you therefore start preparing for this. You may then find yourself with no reason to complete your thesis once you have started working on it, for by that time you might have changed your mind about philosophy. This change need not be irrational, e.g. based on a mistaken belief about what it means to study philosophy. It might just be that you acquired a new and stronger interest in something else, investment banking, for instance. Now, assume that you know that you will change your mind about your philosophy career. On presentist assumptions, how should you then plan your life?

Another reply to the problem with following the Stoic Slogan would be to say that we should become *necessitarians* and take into account only our necessary desires, the desires that would exist independently of the choice to be made.[22] This will then include past and present desires, and those future desires that are fixed, i.e., will exist no matter how we choose. One could then argue that we should discount the desires we would have if our personalities were transformed since these desires are contingent on our choice and not fixed.

Necessitarianism and presentism will have the same implications in practice since in most cases we have the opportunity to kill ourselves. In these cases, all future desires will be contingent; they will exist only if we do not kill ourselves. And necessitarianism would imply that they should not be taken into account. But the mere fact that a person can kill himself should not let him off the hook. He has still prudential reasons to take care of his future self.

The final reply to the Stoic Slogan is to claim that what makes the desires of the grass-counters and complacent people problematic is their *genesis*.[23] Their desires seem to be induced in a manipulative way, 'behind the back'.

---

[22] This position is defended in Arneson (1990), pp. 172–4.
[23] The autonomy restriction on preferences is defended in Elster (1990). See also Sumner (1996), pp. 166–71, who defends similar restrictions on a pro-attitude he calls 'life satisfaction'.

Therefore, they are not autonomous and should be disregarded. Only people's autonomous desires can determine their well-being. I have nothing against adopting a constraint like this, provided that we can make sense of autonomous desires in a way that would not exclude the vast range of normal desires that are to some extent the result of social pressures and biological factors. But adopting this constraint will not get to the heart of the matter.

Desire for the good

To find an acceptable solution, we need to do is to get a bit clearer about what exactly makes the problematic desires so problematic. It can't be the mere fact that the desires are easily satisfied. Much more important, I think, is the fact that the desires do not seem to be about things that are *worthy of concern*. For instance, a person whose main aim is to count the blades of grass on public lawns seems to have desires that are seriously misplaced. The strength of this desire does not seem to match the value of the activity. I am not saying that there is no value in counting the blades of grass—perhaps there is some excellence involved, endurance, for instance, so that the achievement merits an entry in the Guinness Book of World Records. But to make grass-counting your main aim is care too much about something that has only minor value. Similarly, a person who would be completely satisfied with the circumstances of his life, no matter what they turned out to be, shows no sensitivity at all to the value of what he desires. Finally, what makes a bare person such an odd figure is not that he is willing to change his desires, but that he is willing to change his desires no matter whether the new desires will be for something more valuable. Replacing one's old aims and convictions with new ones is appropriate when the old aims and convictions were concerned with things of little or no value. Similarly, abandoning loyalties and attachments is perfectly acceptable when they concern people who are not worthy of our concern.

If this diagnosis is right, is not enough to adopt an autonomy constraint. Since this constraint rules out desires only on the basis of their genesis and not on the basis of their content, there is no guarantee that autonomous desires will match up with worthwhile activities. An autonomous grass-counter or a bare person is not a logical impossibility. For instance, a bare person is surely autonomous if she freely adopts the Stoic Slogan and decides to live by it despite the objections raised by her family and friends.

What we need to do is to adopt a more discriminating desire theory. What makes a person better off is not just simply that he gets what he would favour more. It is also important that his favourings are about things that are worthy of concern.[24] This is of course to reject desire theory in its purest form. But note that on this view, nothing can be good for a person if it is not favoured by that person. So, this theory is radically different from a pluralist theory that would accord value to worthwhile activities even if they were not endorsed.

At this point, some might object that my well-being theory is unstable.[25] Once it is recognized that the objective value of achievements matter to well-being, why not give some independent weight to excellent achievements? In reply, I would say that we have to distinguish between the different kinds of value a life can possess. A life full of artistic or scientific achievements will have instrumental value for the society as a whole, even if the person herself does not see the point of what she is doing and thus fails to endorse her life. This life can also have perfectionist value and be a good instance of its kind, a good artistic or scientific life, for instance. But I maintain that if she is cold and indifferent towards her life, it is not *good for her* even though it may be good for others, and a good artistic or scientific life. The discrepancy between what is worthwhile in her life and her attitudes explains what is so tragic about a depressed but successful achiever. She had it all in terms of objective value but was unable to endorse it.

Of course, much more need to be said before we have a complete theory of well-being. One major task is to give an account of the values that merit a positive response. It is of course important to exclude prudential values. We would get a circular account if we said that something is good for a person because he favours it and it is good for him.[26] What we are looking for are non-prudential values and excellences. There is no need to restrict the values to only one kind of excellence, such as moral virtue. That would give us an all too moralized conception of well-being. It is more promising to embrace the whole range of excellences and values, including moral, social, intellectual, aesthetic, and athletic ones.

What is important for my purposes here is that this revised polarity-based theory is able to discriminate between favourings on the basis of their content and not just their strength. This means that transforming a person into a bare person, a grass-counter, or a completely complacent person is not always the best option even if the person displaying either of these odd character traits would favour his life strongly. Allowing or making sure that a person develops into a normal person with normal aspirations is usually the better option

---

[24] This mixed desire theory, or endorsement theory as it is often called, has gained a lot of popularity in recent years. See, for instance, Dworkin (2002), ch. 6, Darwall (1999), Kraut (1994), and Parfit (1992), p. 502.

[25] An anonymous referee pressed me on this point.

[26] This circularity problem is stated in Sumner (1996), pp. 164–5.

since this person's favourings will be more in line with what is objectively valuable.[27] More generally, the revised account takes the edge off the Stoic Slogan. Whereas the pure polarity-based theory tells us that it is better to make our favourings conform to the world, the revised theory tells us, much more plausibly, that it better to make our favourings conform to what is *worthwhile* or *valuable* in the world.

A final worry is that this stress on what is objectively worthwhile and valuable might seem to licence a paternalistic approach to child-rearing and education. One could imagine a nightmare scenario in which pushy parents spend all their time and energy to make sure that their children are exposed to 'high culture' from a very young age. Instead of relaxing and engaging in pleasant idle play with their children, the parents will be hot-housing their young ones by, if necessary, coercing them to read classic literature, go to museums, learn to play a musical instrument, and take ballet lessons.

This objection assumes that the objective values at stake only involve intellectually, aesthetically, or physically demanding activities. But nothing in the revised desire-theory requires us to take such a narrow view on objective values. Some important values will be found in close intimate relationships that can only develop if enough time is set apart for spontaneous interaction.

Even if greater objective value is attached to the more demanding excellences, we need to remember that these objective values do not provide intrinsic benefits if they are not properly endorsed. If these values are pursued by our children only because they want to please us or avoid negative sanctions, they are not properly endorsed. To endorse these values, they need to appreciate them for their own sakes. By hot-housing our children we might succeed in getting them to pursue valuable activities, but if they can't see the point of these activities, they will not reap any intrinsic benefits from them.[28]

8. Conclusions

I have argued that a desire-based theory will encounter insurmountable problems if it insists that what determines whether one outcome is better for a person than another is that he would prefer the former outcome to the latter.

---

[27] I am not assuming that the lives of these odd characters must be bad for them and not worth living. I am just saying that they will normally have lives that are less good than the lives of normal people.

[28] Similar anti-paternalistic implications of the revised desire-theory are discussed by Dworkin (2002), ch. 6.

It will generate indeterminacies in same number cases where the identities of people are fixed, but the preferences are not. What is better for a person will then depend on which outcome is realized. In cases where both the identities of people and their preferences are fixed, it will often give the wrong results, for even if the preferences are fixed, the polarity of the underlying attitudes might change. In particular, a preference-based theory implies that it is sometimes better to bring about an outcome in which all people would hate their lives than to bring about an outcome in which all people would love their lives. What is worse, a preference-based theory will in this case generate the contradiction that a bad life can be better than a good life, since a plausible desire theory must say that what is bad for a person is what he would disfavour and what is good for a person is what he would favour.

The proper response to these problems is not to ditch the desire-based theory; it is instead to abandon the assumption that what is better for a person is what he would prefer. What is better for a person should be defined in terms of the polarities of the absolute attitudes he would form in the respective outcomes. Roughly put, an outcome A is better for a person than an outcome B just in case his A-self wants his life in A more than his B-self wants his life in B. But this means that we will avoid the contradiction that the preference-based theory was saddled with. If a person's A-self *favours* his life in A and his B-self *disfavours* his life in B, then A is better for him than B, and this holds even if both his A-self and his B-self prefer B to A. More generally, this polarity-based theory will be able to meet all the challenges that faced the preference-based theory.

The problem of desire-adjustment calls for a more radical revision of the desire theory. In order to avoid the conclusion that we should sometimes favour people who are able to adjust their desires to worthless things, we have to impose content-restrictions on desires. What makes a person better off is not just simply that he gets what he would favour more. It is also important that his favourings are about things that are worthy of concern.

I am of course aware that much more needs to be said about the exact contours of a content-restricted polarity-based theory. But I hope that I have at least shown that it is a theory of well-being worth taking seriously when we consider our moral responsibilities to other generations.

References

ARRHENIUS, G. (2003), 'The Person Affecting Restriction, Comparativism, and the Moral Status of Potential People', *Ethical Perspectives*, 10: 3–4.

—— (2000), *Future Generations: A Challenge for Moral Theory* (Uppsala: University Printers).

ARNESON, R. (1990), 'Liberalism, Distributive Subjectivism, and Equal Opportunity for Welfare', *Philosophy and Public Affairs*, 19/2: 158–94.

BRANDT, R. (1979), *A Theory of the Good and the Right* (Oxford: Clarendon Press).

BRICKER, P. (1980), 'Prudence', *Journal of Philosophy*, 77/7: 381–401.

BROOME, J. (1991), *Weighing Goods: Equality, Uncertainty and Time* (Oxford: Blackwell).

—— (2004), *Weighing Lives* (Oxford: Oxford University Press).

BRÜLDE, B. (1998), *The Human Good* (Ph.D thesis, University of Gothenburg, Acta Universitatis Gothoburgensis).

BYKVIST, K. (1998), *Changing Preferences: A Study in Preferentialism* (Ph.D. Dissertation, Uppsala University).

—— (2003), 'The Moral Relevance of Past Preferences', in H. Dyke (ed.), *Time and Ethics: Essays at the Intersection* (Dordrecht: Kluwer Academic), 115–36.

CARLSON, E., and OLSSON, E. (2001), 'Existence, Beneficence, and Design', in E. Carlson and R. Sliwinski (eds.), *Omnium-gatherum, Uppsala Philosophical Studies 50* (Department of Philosophy, Uppsala University, Uppsala), 79–92.

CHISHOLM, R., and SOSA, E. (1966), 'On the Logic of Intrinsically Better', *American Philosophical Quarterly*, 3: 244–9.

DARWALL, S. (1999), 'Valuing Activity', in E. Paul, F. Miller, and J. Paul (eds.), *Human Flourishing* (Cambridge: Cambridge University Press), 176–196.

—— (2002), *Welfare and Rational Care* (Princeton: Princeton University Press).

DWORKIN, R. (2002), *Sovereign Virtue* (Harvard: Harvard University Press).

ELSTER, J. (1990), 'Sour grapes: Utilitarianism and the Genesis of Wants', in A. Sen and B. Williams (eds.), 219–38.

GIBBARD, A. (1992), 'Interpersonal comparisons: preference, good, and the intrinsic reward of a life', in J. Elster and A. Hylland (eds.), *Foundations of Social Choice Theory* (Cambridge: Cambridge University Press), 165–93.

GOODIN, R. E. (1991), 'Actual Preferences, Actual People', *Utilitas*, 3: 113–19.

HARSANYI, J. (1990), 'Morality and the Theory of Rational Behaviour', in A. Sen and B. Williams, *Utilitarianism and Beyond* (Cambridge: Cambridge University Press), 36–62.

HOLTUG, N. (1996), 'In Defence of the Slogan', in Rabinowicz (ed.), *Preference and Value. Preferentialism in Ethics* (Studies in Philosophy, Department of Philosophy, Lund), 64–89.

—— (2001), 'On the value of coming into existence', *The Journal of Ethics*, 5: 361–84.

HURKA, T. (2001), *Virtue, Vice, and Value* (Oxford: Oxford University Press).

KRAUT, R. (1994), 'Desire and the Human Good', *Proceedings and Addresses of the American Philosophical Association*, 68/2: 39–54.

MCMAHAN, J. (ed.) (1998), *Rational Commitments and Social Justice* (Oxford: Oxford University Press).

MEYER, L. (2003), 'Past and Future', in L. Meyer, S. Paulson, and T. Pogge (eds.), *Rights, Culture, and the Law* (Oxford: Oxford University Press).

PARFIT, D. (1992), *Reasons and Persons* (Oxford: Clarendon Press).

PERSSON, I. (1995), 'Peter Singer on why persons are irreplaceable', *Utilitas*, 7: 55–66.

RABINOWICZ, W., and ÖSTERBERG, J. (1996), 'Value based on preferences. On two interpretations of Preference Utilitarianism', *Economics and Philosophy*, 12: 1–27.

RAWLS, J. (1971), *A Theory of Justice* (Cambridge: Harvard University Press).

—— (1990), 'Social Unity and primary goods', in A. Sen and B. Williams *Utilitarianism and Beyond* (Cambridge: Cambridge University Press) 159–185.

RYBERG, J., (1995), 'Do possible people have moral standing?', *Danish Yearbook of Philosophy* 30: 96–118.

SEN, A., and WILLIAMS, B. (eds.) (1990), *Utilitarianism and Beyond* (Cambridge: Cambridge University Press).

SUMNER, W. (1996), *Welfare, Happiness, and Ethics* (Oxford: Oxford University Press).

12

Egalitarianism and Population Change

GUSTAF ARRHENIUS

1. Introduction

Consider the following populations:

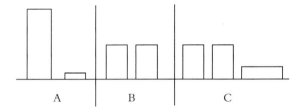

Diagram 1

Diagram 1 shows three populations: A, B, and C. The width of each block represents the number of people, and the height represents their lifetime welfare. These populations could consist of all the past, present and future lives, or all the present and future lives, or all the lives during some shorter time span in the future such as the next generation, or all the lives that are causally affected by, or consequences of a certain action or series of actions, and so forth. All the lives in diagram 1 have positive welfare, or, as we also

I would like to thank Krister Bykvist, Lars Bergström, John Broome, Erik Carlson, Sven Danielsson, Marc Fleurbaey, Axel Gosseries, Tom Hurka, Lukas Meyer, Wlodek Rabinowicz, Howard Sobel, Wayne Sumner, Folke Tersman, Olle Torpman, Torbjörn Tännsjö, and two anonymous referees for their very helpful and detailed comments. Thanks also to the Oxford Uehiro Centre for Practical Ethics and Jesus College, Oxford, for being such generous hosts during some of the time when this paper were written. Financial support from the Bank of Sweden Tercentenary Foundation and the Swedish Collegium for Advanced Study is gratefully acknowledged.

could put it, have lives worth living.[1] Population A consists of one group of people with very high welfare and a same sized group with very low positive welfare. B is a perfectly equal population of the same size as A and with the same total and average welfare as A. C consists of the B-people and an extra group of people with lower positive welfare than the B-people.

How should we rank these populations? I take it that most of us would agree that B is better than A. The two populations are equally large and have the same total and average welfare. The only difference is that there is inequality in A whereas B is perfectly equal. Hence, A is worse than B since it is worse in regards to equality.[2]

Consider now population B and C. The number of best-off people is the same in these two populations. The only difference between these two populations is that in the C, there is a number of 'extra' people whose lives are of poor quality but worth living. Could the existence of these extra lives which are worth living make C worse than B? Some would say yes since the C-population is worse in regards to equality: There is perfect equality in B but inequality in C, and this inequality counts against C.[3] Moreover, we have already granted that inequality can play a role in the ranking of populations since we appealed to it when we compared population A and B.

Some theorists deny, however, that egalitarian concerns are applicable in different number cases, that is, when the number of people differs in the

---

[1] We shall say that a life has neutral welfare if and only if it has the same welfare as a life without any good or bad welfare components, and that a life has positive (negative) welfare if and only if it has higher (lower) welfare than a life with neutral welfare. A hedonist, for example, would typically say that pain is bad and pleasure is good for a person, and that a life without any pain and pleasure has neutral welfare. This definition can be combined with other welfarist axiologies, such as desire and objective list theories (see below for a discussion of the 'currency' of egalitarian justice). There is a number of alternative definitions of a life with positive (negative, neutral) welfare in the literature. For a discussion of these, see Arrhenius (2000) and Broome (1999). For a discussion of this issue in connection to the Repugnant Conclusion, see Fehige (1998), Tännsjö (1998; 2005), Arrhenius (2000), and Broome (2004). Also cf. Parfit (1984), p. 358.

[2] Of course, I am assuming here that we can compare populations such as A and B without any further information. Some theorists would deny this since they think an outcome can only be better or worse if it is better or worse for somebody, which might not be the case if A and B consist of different people. To apply these so-called 'person affecting views', we also need to know the identities of the individuals in the compared populations. I have discussed this approach at length elsewhere (Arrhenius 2000, 2003c, 2006) and showed that it entails very counterintuitive results, so I shall not dwell on it further here. For the purpose of the present paper, I shall assume that we can compare the value of populations without knowledge of the specific identities of the individuals in the compared populations (this approach is sometimes, misleadingly in my view, called the 'impersonal view').

[3] C is also worse than B in respect to average well-being. However, Average Utilitarianism has a number of very counterintuitive implications in different number cases so we can safely put it to the side. See Arrhenius (2000), section 3.3, and Parfit (1984), section 143.

compared populations. As Derek Parfit puts it, '[s]ince the inequality in [C] is produced by Mere Addition [as is the case in diagram 1], this inequality does not make [C] worse than B'.[4] Moreover, there is a higher total of welfare in C, so even if we grant that C is worse in regards to equality, could this really outweigh the goodness of the extra welfare in C? Would it have been better if the 'extra' people in C with lives worth living had never existed? It might strike one as implausible to claim that C is worse than B, merely because there are additional people with lives worth living. Hence, egalitarian considerations are not relevant in different number cases, or so it seems.

As this example and the title of this paper indicate, I'm going to discuss the role of equality in the evaluation of populations of different sizes in respect to their goodness. One approach is to investigate rankings of populations in respect to equality alone, that is, how they can be ordered by the relation 'is at least as equal as'. It would then be a further question how such a ranking would play in to the all things considered rankings of populations where we also have to consider other aspects such as the total wellbeing in a population.[5]

I shall take a more direct approach and discuss the relevance of egalitarian considerations for all things considered evaluations in some key cases. The field of population ethics has been riddled with paradoxes which purport to show that our considered beliefs are inconsistent in cases where the number of people and their welfare varies. Parfit's well-known Mere Addition Paradox is a case in point. These paradoxes challenge at a fundamental level the existence of a satisfactory theory of our duties to future generations and intergenerational justice. Since consistency in our considered moral beliefs is, arguably, a necessary condition for moral justification, these paradoxes seem to force us to conclude that there is no theory regarding our moral duties to future generations and intergenerational justice which can be justified.[6] The main question of my paper is whether egalitarian concerns can help us solve these paradoxes.

My result is going to be mainly negative. Although I think there is a *prima facie* plausibility to the claim that egalitarian considerations are applicable in different number cases and can solve the Mere Addition paradox, I shall contend that such considerations are not of much help in another paradox that

---

[4] Parfit (1984), p. 425.

[5] This is the approach in Temkin's (1993) influential work on inequality.

[6] For more on the connection between population ethics and intergenerational justice, see Meyer (2003) and Gosseries (2001, 2003). For a discussion of the possible meta-ethical implications of these paradoxes, see Arrhenius (2000), ch. 12.

involves logically weaker and intuitively more compelling conditions than the ones used in the former paradox. En route, we shall also discuss whether the so-called Priority View might be able to explain all of our purportedly egalitarian intuitions. I shall suggest that although there is a good case for this being true in same number cases, it isn't true in different number cases. We shall also take a look at some different ways of conceptualizing and measuring equality of welfare.

Before turning to the main questions of this paper, let me say a bit more about what kind of equality we shall discuss in this paper. Equality clearly plays a fundamental role in moral and political reasoning. Views about equality can differ immensely, however, depending on a number of factors: what kind of equality one is seeking (political, legal, moral, and so forth); the 'currency' of equality (welfare, opportunity, rights, and so forth); among what kind of objects equality is supposed to hold (citizens, human beings, sentient beings, possible beings, groups, and so forth). It goes without saying that a full treatment of this subject is far beyond the reach of the present essay. We shall only consider one kind of equality: equality of welfare among people. The fundamental question in population ethics turns around how to rank populations where the number of people and their welfare varies.

This does not mean that we are committed to welfarism—the view that welfare is the only value that matters from the moral point of view. On the contrary, other considerations such as fairness, liberty, fulfilment of rights, autonomy, knowledge, cultural diversity, and the like may figure in the ranking of populations. We shall only assume that welfare at least matters when all other things are equal, that is, when the compared populations are roughly equally good in regard to other axiologically relevant aspects. Although we shall not defend this claim, this assumption is arguably a minimal adequacy condition for any moral theory.

Lastly, the concept of welfare used here is a broad one. For the present discussion, it doesn't matter whether welfare is understood along the lines of experientialist, desire or objective list theories.[7] Hence, many of the views presented in the debate on the currency of egalitarian justice as alternatives to welfare, for example Rawls' influential list of primary goods, will fall under the heading of welfare as the term is used in this paper.[8]

---

[7] For experientialist theories, see e.g., Sumner (1996), Feldman (1997, 2004), and Tännsjö (1998). For desire theories, see e.g Barry (1989), Bykvist (1998), Griffin (1986), Hare (1981), Harsanyi (1992), Singer (1993), Raz (1986), and Goodin (1991). For objective list theories, see e.g. Braybrooke (1987), Finnis (1980), Hurka (1993), Rawls (1971), and Sen (1980, 1992, 1993).

[8] For this debate, see Rawls (1971), Sen (1980, 1992, 1993), Dworkin (1981a, 1981b, 2000), Cohen (1989, 1993), Arneson (1989), and Nielsen (1996).

2. The Mere Addition Paradox

Here is a version of Parfit's well-known axiological population paradox, the Mere Addition Paradox:[9]

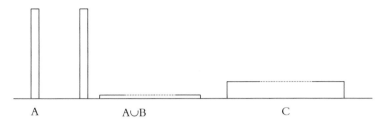

Diagram 2

In diagram 2, A is a population of people with very high welfare, B is a much larger population than A but consisting of people with very low positive welfare, and C is a population of the same size as A ∪ B (that is, the population consisting of all the lives in both A and B). Everybody in C has very low positive welfare but they are all better off than the people in B. Moreover, there is perfect equality in C and the total and average welfare in C is higher than in A ∪ B.

How should we rank these populations? Consider first population A and A ∪ B. Since the B-people have lives worth living, many would agree that A ∪ B is at least not worse than A (see also the discussion above of population B and C in diagram 1). Here's a principle that expresses this view:

The Mere Addition Condition: An addition of people with positive welfare does not make a population worse, other things being equal.[10]

What about A ∪ B and C? Since there is perfect equality in C and higher total and average utility in C as compared to A ∪ B, it seems reasonable to

[9] For a formal proof with slightly weaker conditions, see Arrhenius (2000), section 10.6. It should be stressed that the above paradox is not identical to Parfit's (1984), pp. 419 ff, Mere Addition Paradox since it involves stronger assumptions. This version is similar to the one presented in Ng (1989), p. 240. A formal proof with slightly stronger assumptions than Ng's can be found in Blackorby and Donaldson (1991).

[10] Cf. Parfit (1984), p. 420, Hudson (1987), Ng (1989), and Sider (1991). We have included a *ceteris paribus* clause in the formulation of the Mere Addition Condition and the conditions below. As I indicated above, the idea is that people's welfare is the only axiologically relevant aspect which may be different in the compared populations, and that the compared populations are roughly equally good in regard to other axiologically relevant aspects. That welfare can vary implies that the number of people and the distribution of welfare can vary in the compared populations. See Arrhenius (2000, 2005).

claim that C is better than A ∪ B. Perhaps the following principle captures our intuition:

The Non-Anti Egalitarianism Condition: A population with perfect equality is better than a population with the same number of people, inequality, and lower average (and thus total) welfare, other things being equal.[11]

Lastly, how should we rank A and C? Parfit's famous Repugnant Conclusion seems to express most people's intuition about the relative value of A and C:

The Repugnant Conclusion: For any perfectly equal population with very high positive welfare, there is a population with very low positive welfare which is better, other things being equal.[12]

As the name indicates, Parfit finds this conclusion unacceptable. To avoid the Repugnant Conclusion, we could claim that A is better than C, a belief expressed by the following principle:

The Quality Condition: There is at least one perfectly equal population with very high positive welfare which is better than any population with very low positive welfare, other things being equal.

By now, we have contradicted ourselves. If C is better than A ∪ B, and A is better than C, then by transitivity of 'better than', it follows that A is better than A ∪ B. But we said that A ∪ B is not worse than A, that is, A is not better than A ∪ B. Hence, these valuations imply a contradiction: A is better than A ∪ B and A is not better than A ∪ B.

When faced with an impossibility result like the one just described, that is, a situation in which our beliefs entail a contradiction, a sensible response is to question the principles involved and try to find reasons to reject one of them. One could for example reject the Mere Addition Condition by claiming that A ∪ B is worse than A since there is inequality in the former population but not in the latter. So here is a case where welfarist egalitarian considerations

---

[11] See Ng (1989), p. 238 for a similar principle. It seems to be unanimously agreed in the literature that inequality aversion of some kind is a prerequisite for an acceptable population axiology. Ng (p. 239, n. 4), states that 'Non-Antiegalitarianism is extremely compelling' and Carlson (1998), p. 288; claims that '[r]ejecting NAE [the Non-Anti Egalitarianism Principle] is … a very unattractive option'. Blackorby et al. (1997), p. 13, hold that 'weak inequality aversion is satisfied by all ethically attractive … principles'. Fehige (1998), p. 12, rhetorically asks '… if one world has more utility than the other and distributes it equally, whereas the other doesn't, then how can it fail to be better?' See also Sider (1991), p. 270, n. 10. There are, however, reasons for rejecting the Non-Anti Egalitarianism principle. See Arrhenius (2000), section 6.2.

[12] See Parfit (1984), p. 388. My formulation is more general than Parfit's, except that he does not demand that the people with very high welfare are equally well off.

might help us solve a population paradox. Let us consider this idea in more detail.[13]

3. Welfarist Egalitarianism and the Priority View

One can distinguish two kinds of Welfarist Egalitarians: monists and pluralists. The former think that equality of welfare is the sole consideration when ranking populations, whereas the latter think that equality of welfare is one among other relevant factors in ranking populations. Probably, no one has ever held the position of the Monist Welfarist Egalitarian since it implies clearly unacceptable conclusions. For example, it implies that a population with very high welfare and some inequality is worse than a population of equally tormented people. Monist Welfarist Egalitarianism violates the following very plausible condition:

The Weak Dominance Condition: If population A contains the same number of people as population B, and every person in A has positive welfare and every person in B has negative welfare, then A is better than B, other things being equal.

Monist Welfarist Egalitarianism has a number of other counter-intuitive implications in same-number cases, but let us leave those aside for now and turn to Pluralist Welfarist Egalitarianism. A reasonable pluralist limits the importance of equality of welfare so that her theory satisfies the Weak Dominance Condition. Thus, it is fair to ask: in which cases can equality of welfare make a difference in the ranking of populations? This is a tricky question that the Pluralist Welfarist Egalitarian has to answer.

As a matter of fact, I doubt that many people, on reflection, really believe that equality of welfare has a value in itself. This might seem surprising since equality is such an entrenched value in moral and political reasoning. Most of us believe in some kind of equality (I certainly do), such as equality before the law, equal rights, political equality, 'similar cases should be treated equally', 'everyone's interests matter and matter equally', and so forth.[14] These ideas of equality are very important but different from the idea of equality of welfare. One reason why appeals to equality of welfare look attractive at first sight

---

[13] For a survey of proposed solutions to the Mere Addition Paradox, see Arrhenius (2000) and Arrhenius et al(2006).

[14] Kymlicka (1990), p. 4, suggests that all modern moral and political theories are based on some conception of equality.

is, I think, that these other kinds of equality are important and reasonable considerations. There is nothing inconsistent, however, in endorsing those kinds of equality and rejecting appeals to equality of welfare.

It is also important to remember that to reject the idea that equality of welfare has value in itself is not to deny that equality of welfare may have good effects and that inequality may have bad effects. Inequality of welfare can undermine people's self-respect, cause envy and thus undermine the cohesion of society, be bad for the economy, and so forth. Consequently, inequality of welfare can diminish the general welfare in a population. As true as this might be, this is beside the point of the matter since if any such factors are at play, then the effects are already included in the specification of people's welfare. What we are considering is whether equality of welfare has a value in itself, apart from any instrumental value it might have in bringing about other good effects.

Many might still find my claim about the role of equality of welfare in our moral reasoning perplexing since there are so many cases where we clearly appeal to exactly such considerations. Typically, they would point to cases like the following:

A   B

Diagram 3

The two populations A and B in diagram 3 are equally large and have the same total welfare. The only difference is that there is inequality in A whereas B is perfectly equal. Is it not obvious that B is better than A and does that not show that equality of welfare is a value in itself? Why would we otherwise rank B as better than A?

I certainly agree that B is better than A but this is not because I value equality of welfare as such, but because the worst off are better off in B than in A, and because I think that the loss sustained by the best off is more than compensated for by the gain enjoyed by the worst off. In other words, I think that we mistake intuitions about the value of equality of welfare with intuitions about priority of the welfare of the worst off. Roughly, the idea is that we should maximize welfare, but increases in welfare matter more, the worse off people are, and decreases in welfare matter less, the better off people are. Let us call this idea, following Parfit, the Priority View.[15]

Another way to express this intuition is to say that the contributive value of welfare is diminishing: if John has higher welfare than Wlodek, then an extra unit of welfare in Wlodek's life increases the value of a population more than an extra unit of welfare in John's life. One can achieve this result by applying a strictly increasing concave transformation to the numerical representation of people's welfare before summing them up.[16] This description of the Priority View is not very exact but precise enough to explain cases, such as the one depicted in diagram 3, where the gain enjoyed by the worst off equals the loss endured by the best off. Since, according to the Priority View, the marginal value of the gain enjoyed by the worst off is higher than the marginal value of the loss incurred by the best off, the value of population B is higher than population A.

In general, if we are to distribute a fixed amount of welfare among a fixed number of people, the Priority View opts for a completely equal distribution. Consequently, in such cases our beliefs are equally well explained by the Priority View as by appeals to equality of welfare.[17] Moreover, the Priority View implies the Weak Dominance Condition.

One of the adequacy conditions used in the Mere Addition Paradox above, the Non-Anti Egalitarianism Condition, seems to involve an appeal to equality. Certainly, people who believe in equality of welfare would endorse this condition. But so too would those who believe in the Priority View. We could have called it the 'Non-Anti Priority Condition' or 'Non-Priority to the Best off Condition'. It is, however, a weaker condition than the Priority View since it is compatible with principles that give no extra weight to the welfare of the worst off, such as Total Utilitarianism.

Although it is reasonable to give extra weight to the welfare of the worst off, it is unreasonable to prioritise a small increase in the welfare of one slightly

---

[15] Parfit's formulation of the Priority view is, however, different from mine: 'Benefiting people matters more the worse off people are.' See Parfit (1993), p. 57. For simplicity, I have added a maximizing component to the statement of the Priority View above. As I shall discuss below, I don't think maximization is a proper part of the Priority View.

[16] See Broome (1991), ch. 9. This way of expressing the Priority View is analogous to the idea of diminishing marginal value used in economics: The more money a person already has, the less good an extra pound will do her.

[17] Another explanation, suggested to me by Axel Gosseries, as to why people believe they are egalitarians even if they actually are prioritarians is that in the majority of practical cases, policies advocated by one or the other coincides, since the reduction of inequalities generally benefit the worst off.

bad off person at any cost to the general welfare. An acceptable version of the Priority View should satisfy the following condition:

The Non-Extreme Priority Condition: There is a number n of lives such that a population consisting of n lives with very high welfare and a single life with slightly negative welfare, is at least as good as a population consisting of $n + 1$ lives with very low positive welfare, other things being equal.[18]

Roughly, principles that violate the Non-Extreme Priority Condition imply that the slightest gain in welfare for one person with negative welfare outweighs a very large loss in welfare, from very high welfare to very low positive welfare, for *any* number of people. Unsurprisingly, Monist Welfarist Egalitarianism violates this condition but since it is a good illustration of the condition, let's take a closer look. Assume that A consists of a very large number of people with very high welfare and one person with slightly negative welfare. In B, we have a small increase in the welfare of the worst off in A but a large decrease in welfare of all the best off in A: everybody has the same very low positive welfare in B. According to Monist Welfarist Egalitarianism, B is better than A. Of course, this would hold even if there was no increase in the welfare of the worst off and everybody else's welfare was decreased to slightly negative welfare. Again, a reasonable Pluralist Welfarist Egalitarian reduces the importance of equality to avoid these kind of conclusions.

A well-known egalitarian principle that violates the Non-Extreme Priority Condition is the Maximin Principle. Maximin ranks populations according to the welfare of the worst off: the lower the welfare of the worst off, the worse the population, and if the worst off enjoy the same welfare in two populations, then these populations are equally good. In other words, Maximin gives maximal priority to the welfare of the worst off. The same holds true for Maximin's cousin, Leximin. According to Leximin, if the worst off in A are better off than the worst off in B, then A is better than B. If the worst off in A and B have the same welfare, then A is better than B if the second worst off in A are better off than the second worst off in B, and so forth.[19] In cases where

---

[18] This is a slightly simplified version of the condition with the same name presented in Arrhenius (2000) where a formalized statement of this condition also can be found.

[19] How does Leximin compare populations of different size? As I take Leximin, one compares the worst off in both populations, then the second worst off, and so forth, until one has compared all the lives in the smaller population with some life in the larger population. For example, let's say that A consists of two lives with one unit of welfare and B consists of one life with one unit of welfare. On my interpretation of Leximin, A and B are equally good. On another interpretation, suggested by an anonymous referee, one adds neutral life to the smaller population to get a population of the same size as the larger population, and then the comparison between the two same sized populations determines the ranking of the original populations. In my example, we should compare A and B*, where B* consists of one life with one unit of welfare and one life with neutral welfare. This version of Leximin

the worst off in the compared populations is a person with slightly negative welfare, both of these principles violate the Non-Extreme Priority Condition. Maximin and Leximin do not only rule out trade-offs in such cases, but in all cases where a gain for the worst off is at stake.

I think that the Priority View can explain our beliefs about distribution of welfare in same-number cases at least as well as an appeal to equality. We have not properly shown this, however, since we have only looked at cases which involve comparisons of perfectly equal populations with unequal populations. One also has to consider cases where both of the compared populations involve inequality of welfare. To be applicable to such case, the prioritarian has to specify the degree of priority given to the worse off, whereas the Welfarist Egalitarian has to devise some method of measuring degrees of inequality.[20] There are a number of different suggestions, more or less convincing, but it would take us too far away from the main topic to consider them all.[21] Let us instead turn to egalitarian and prioritarian considerations in different number cases.

4. Egalitarianism and Different Number Cases

Is there a reasonable egalitarian objection to the Mere Addition Condition? Consider population A and A ∪ B again. According to Maximin and Leximin, A ∪ B is worse than A.[22] However, as we saw above, we have to reject these principles since they violate the Non-Extreme Priority Condition. Still, it is not unreasonable to claim that A ∪ B is more unequal than A, and that A ∪ B is in that respect worse than A. For example, according to Temkin, 'the ultimate intuition underlying egalitarianism is that it is bad ... for some to be worse off than others through no fault of their own'.[23] Clearly, this is the case in A ∪ B since the B people have not done anything to deserve to be worse off than the

---

thus ranks A as better than B. I find this interpretation of Leximin somewhat more unattractive than the one that I propose above since it implies, for instance, that a population of one billion lives with very high welfare is *worse* than a population of one billion and one lives with very low positive welfare. I am indebted to an anonymous referee for reminding me about this ambiguity in the formulation of Leximin.

[20] This might come to the same thing since, as argued by Fleurbaey (forthcoming), for any version of the Priority View, there is an extensionally equivalent version of Welfarist Egalitarianism.

[21] For arguments to the effect that the Priority View *cannot* explain our beliefs about distribution of welfare in same-number cases better than egalitarianism, see Temkin (1993, 2003a). There has been a quite intensive discussion during the last few years of the pro and cons of egalitarianism and the priority view in same number cases, and whether they really are distinct views. See, among others, Broome (forthcoming), Crisp (2003a, b), Fleurbaey (forthcoming), Persson (2001), Rabinowicz (2002), Temkin (2003b), Tungodden (2003), and Vallentyne (2000).

[22] Cf. n. 19.   [23] Temkin (1993), p. 200 and elsewhere.

A-people. Moreover, as suggested by Temkin, one might hold the view that the greater the number of worst off, the worse the inequality.[24] Consequently, since the B-population in the Mere Addition Paradox has to be enormous to reach the C population by redistribution of welfare in the A ∪ B-population, the inequality in A ∪ B would thus be considerable.

The crucial question, however, is whether this inequality makes A ∪ B worse than A all things considered. Since A ∪ B is clearly better than A in respect to total welfare, the pluralist egalitarian has to limit the importance of total welfare relative to the importance of inequality to reach this judgment. There are, I surmise, three plausible ways the pluralist egalitarian could do this. Firstly, she could put such a negative value on inequality that the negative value of the resulting inequality from the addition of one life with very low positive welfare to a high welfare population outweighs the resulting extra total welfare. This view in combination with the idea that the negative value of inequality increases linearly with the number of worse off lives yields the sought after judgment (view 1 in diagram 4).

A more moderate egalitarian could claim that the contributive value of extra total welfare in lives at a low level of well-being diminishes so that

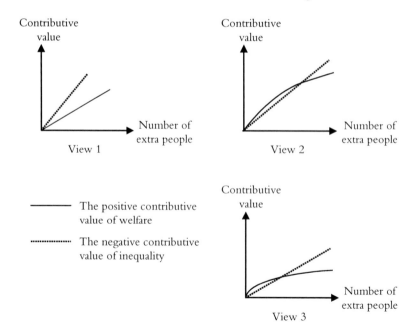

Diagram 4

[24] See Temkin (1993), p. 200–2. Cf. Persson (2003) for a similar view.

even if there is no upper boundary to this value, it will at some point be overtaken by the negative value of the increased inequality (view 2 in diagram 4). Lastly, the pluralist egalitarian could put an upper limit to the value of total welfare that comes in lives with very low welfare which is approached asymptotically (the value of extra welfare is always increasing but it cannot go beyond a certain limit). If the negative value of inequality has no upper boundary, or an upper boundary that is higher than the upper boundary of the value of total welfare, it will at some point overtake the bounded value of total welfare that comes in lives with very low positive welfare (view 3 in diagram 4).

What all of these views have in common is that the addition of a certain number of lives or more with very low positive welfare to a population with very high welfare will have negative contributive value, and more negative the greater the number of added lives, because of the negative value of the resulting inequality. Consequently, such additions make the ensuing population worse than the original because of the inequality introduced.

Clearly, these proposals have to be tested against other cases for us to be able to judge their general appeal and my hunch is that they will run into trouble (I shall point out one problem for these views in the last section). For the purpose here, however, it is sufficient to note that these views have an intuitive appeal from an egalitarian perspective and that there is a *prima facie* case that egalitarian concerns can solve the Mere Addition Paradox.

5. The Priority View and Different Number Cases

What implications would the Priority View have in regard to the Mere Addition Condition? As a matter of fact, as we have stated the Priority View, it implies the Mere Addition Condition. Moreover, in diagram 2 it ranks A ∪ B as better than A, and C as better than A, since it ranks populations according to the total sum of people's transformed welfare. Not only that, it will also imply the Repugnant Conclusion with a vengeance since it will rank C as better than A even in cases where the total welfare in C is less than in A.[25]

Here is a simple illustration. Assume that the welfare per person is a hundred units in A and one unit in C and that the population size of A and C are n respectively $20n$. Then the total welfare in A is $100n$ whereas the total welfare in C is $20n$. Hence, A is better than C both in respect to total and

---

[25] Holtug (1999) makes the same point.

average welfare. Assume now that we use the square root function as the prioritarian transformation function. According to this version of the Priority View, the value of A is $n\sqrt{100} = 10n$ and the value of B is $20n\sqrt{1} = 20n$. Analogous results can be shown for any choice of the strictly increasing concave transformation function. Hence, it seems that the Priority View implies that an outcome with lower total and average positive welfare can be better, which is quite bizarre.

But of course, using summing as an aggregation method is as contentious with transformation of individual welfare as without it. We assumed it above just for reasons of simplicity. The core idea of the Priority View—that gains in welfare matter more, the worse off people are, and losses in welfare matter less, the better off people are—can be combined with other aggregation methods, such as, for example, the one used in Average Utilitarianism. Combined with this aggregation method, the Priority View would yield the same results in same-number cases as the ones described above, whereas its results in different-number cases would be pretty much the same as those of Average Utilitarianism, e.g. it would rank A as better than A ∪ B. The same holds for a combination of the Priority View with other aggregation methods.[26]

No specific method for aggregating the (transformed) welfare of different lives seems to follow from the Priority View, so it is hard to see how this idea could explain our evaluation of different-number cases such as the one discussed here. Whatever aggregation method one combines with the Priority View, the main work in different-number comparisons will be done by the aggregation method, not by the Priority View.[27] Hence, there is little hope of finding the key to the solution of the problems of population ethics in the prioritarian idea.

It seems that the Priority View is an idea mainly about how to distribute welfare among a fixed number of people. Since welfarist egalitarians do have something to say about the Mere Addition Condition, it follows that there seems to be some intuitions about equality of welfare that the Priority View cannot explain away: In different number cases, Welfarist Egalitarianism and the Priority View come apart.

---

[26] For a survey of these alternative aggregation methods, see Arrhenius (2000), ch. 4–6, 8, and Arrhenius et al. (2006).

[27] Hence, I find Holtug's (1999) argument to the effect that the Priority View leads to worse Repugnant Conclusions as compared to Total Utilitarianism question-begging. All we can say is that a summing version of the Priority View leads to worse Repugnant Conclusions than Total Utilitarianism. Holtug has recently abandoned his (1999) argument against the Priority View and moved to a position similar to mine, see Holtug (2007).

6. A Harder Paradox

So far, so good, for the pluralist egalitarian. However, there are problems ahead. As I've showed elsewhere, one can construct impossibility results with logically weaker and intuitively more compelling conditions than the one used in the Mere Addition Paradox.[28] Those results don't make use of the controversial Mere Addition Principle. Roughly speaking, the Mere Addition conditions are replaced by two other conditions.[29] Let's look at the first one of these conditions:

The Weak Quality Addition Condition: For any population X, there is at least one perfectly equal population with very high positive welfare such that its addition to X is at least as good as an addition of any population with very low positive welfare to X, other things being equal.[30]

Here is a case where an egalitarian might object to the Weak Quality Addition Condition:

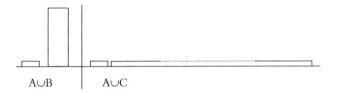

Diagram 5

According to the Weak Quality Addition Condition, for any population X, there is at least one perfectly equal population with very high positive welfare such that its addition to X is at least as good as an addition of any population with very low positive welfare to X. Assume that population B in diagram 5 is such a high welfare population in relation to population A. In population A ∪ B, B has been added to population A with very low positive welfare. In A ∪ C, instead of population B, the very large population C with the same very low positive welfare as A has been added. According to the Weak Quality Addition Condition, A ∪ B is at least as good as A ∪ C. One might object to this valuation and hold that A ∪ C is better than A ∪ B, since there

---

[28] See Arrhenius (2000, 2001). Cf. Arrhenius (2003a).

[29] Apart from the two conditions discussed below, the impossibility theorem involves a weak non-priority to the best off condition, a weak egalitarian dominance condition, and a weaker version of the Non-Extreme Priority Condition discussed above.

[30] For a formalized statement of this condition and the one discussed below, see Arrhenius (2000, 2001).

is inequality in the latter population whereas there is perfect equality in the former population.

A Monist Welfarist Egalitarian would rank A ∪ C as better than A ∪ B. As we have seen, this view has highly counter-intuitive implications in same-number cases. Its implications in different number choices are no different. Assume that the A-people and the C-people in diagram 5 do not enjoy positive welfare but, rather, they experience very negative welfare—they all have terrible lives. According to the Monist Welfarist Egalitarian, it would be better to add the terrible C-lives rather than the excellent B-lives since the resulting population of the former addition would be perfectly equal.

A Pluralist Welfarist Egalitarian could avoid this conclusion by also assigning importance to the total welfare. Can the pluralist give us a good reason to discard the Weak Quality Addition Condition? I do not think so. Indeed, one can hold that A ∪ C is in one respect better than A ∪ B since there is perfect equality in the former population but not in the latter one, but it seems clear that this aspect is outweighed by the greater quality of life in the B-population as compared to the C-population. If a Pluralist Welfarist Egalitarian theory put such a value on equality of welfare that it implied that A ∪ C is better than A ∪ B, then that would constitute a good argument against that version of Welfarist Egalitarianism, I surmise. An example of the case described in diagram 5 could be that the A-people either have children who enjoy very high welfare or that they have more children with the same poor welfare (perhaps because of lack of resources) as themselves. It seems indeed odd that the prospective parents should opt for the latter alternative for reasons of equality.

More importantly, there is further problem for the Pluralist Welfarist Egalitarian that rejects Weak Quality Addition Condition. Consider the following population:

B∪D

Diagram 6

In diagram 6, D is a population with the same very low positive welfare as populations A and C in diagram 5. The size of B ∪ D equals A ∪ C. Relative B ∪ D, A ∪ C is an extreme case of levelling down. Recall that population B can be as big and enjoy as high positive welfare as we suppose. Thus, to avoid implying extreme versions of levelling down, a reasonable Pluralist Welfarist

Egalitarian has to rank B ∪ D as better than A ∪ C. Assume now that we reject the Weak Quality Addition Condition and rank A ∪ C as better than A ∪ B.[31] By transitivity, it follows that B ∪ D is better than A ∪ B.

Now, recall that to reject the Mere Addition Principle in order to avoid the Mere Addition Paradox, the Pluralist Welfarist Egalitarian had to hold the view that the greater the number of worst off, the worse the inequality, and that the negative value of inequality at some point overcomes the positive value of extra positive welfare that comes in lives with very low positive welfare. Since C can be of any finite size, D can also be of any finite size. Thus, we can assume that the point where the negative value of inequality overcomes the positive value of extra positive welfare has already been reached with population D relative to population B. Moreover, since D can be of any finite size, we can assume that D is bigger than A.

The difference between B ∪ D and A ∪ B is thus that there are many more lives with very low positive welfare in B ∪ D as compared to A ∪ B. Hence, according to the version of Pluralist Welfarist Egalitarianism that avoids the Mere Addition Paradox, the addition of D to B has negative contributive value and a greater negative contributive value than the addition of A to B (which might not be negative at all). It follows that B ∪ D is worse than A ∪ B, which contradicts the result we reached above by rejecting the Weak Quality Addition Condition. Consequently, a Pluralist Welfarist Egalitarian that wants to avoid extreme levelling down and solve the Mere Addition Paradox cannot reject the Weak Quality Addition Condition.

Here is the second condition:

The Weak Non-Sadism Condition: There is a negative welfare level and a number of lives at this level such that an addition of any number of people with positive welfare is at least as good as an addition of the lives with negative welfare, other things being equal.

Might a Welfarist Egalitarian object to the Weak Non-Sadism Condition? Let's say that A consists of one life with very high welfare, B consists of great number n of lives with very negative welfare such that the antecedent of the Weak Non-Sadism Conditions is satisfied, and C consists of an even larger number m of lives but with very low positive welfare, as shown in diagram 7.

The difference between population A ∪ B and A ∪ C is thus that in the former population, n lives with very negative welfare has been added to

---

[31] I am disregarding the possibility of incommensurability here. For a discussion of incommensurability in population ethics, see Arrhenius (2000), section 5.1.1, Broome (2004), ch. 12., and Blackorby et al. (2005), ch. 7.

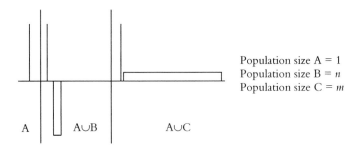

Diagram 7

A, whereas in the latter population, a larger number of lives *m* with very low positive welfare have been added to A. Consequently, according to the Weak Non-Sadism Condition, A ∪ C is at least as good as A ∪ B.

Now, someone might claim that A ∪ B is better than A ∪ C, since it is better in regard to equality of welfare. It is, of course, by no means apparent how this could be the case. Here we have to compare two populations that both involve inequality. Hence, how to evaluate these populations from a Welfarist Egalitarian perspective all depends on how to measure degrees of inequality. On one measure—the difference in welfare between the best off and worst off—A ∪ B is worse than A ∪ C in regard to inequality. Moreover, the worst off are worse off in A ∪ B as compared to A ∪ C. But, as we saw above, according to another view entertained by Larry Temkin, what matters, among other things, is the number of the worst off: the greater the number of worst off, the worse the inequality.[32] According to this view, if C is sufficiently larger than B, then A ∪ B is better than A ∪ C in regard to inequality. On still another view, proposed by Parfit, the reverse holds true: if the proportion of worst off increases, then the inequality decreases.[33]

Since it is Temkin's suggestion that might challenge the Weak Non-Sadism Condition, let us take a closer look at it. Unfortunately, Temkin never states

---

[32] See Temkin (1993), p. 200–2. Cf. Persson (2003) for a similar view.

[33] Parfit compares two populations, A+ and Alpha. A+ consists of two groups of people of the same size, one with 100 units of welfare per person, and one with 50 units of welfare per person. Alpha consists of one group of the same size as A+ but with 105 units of welfare per person and a very large group of people with 45 units of welfare per person. He writes: 'The inequality in Alpha is in one way worse than the inequality in A+, since the gap between the better-off and the worse-off people is slightly greater. But in another way the inequality is less bad. This is a matter of the relative numbers of, or the *ratio* between, those who are better-off and those who are worse-off. Half of the people in A+ are better off than the other half. This is a worse inequality than a situation in which almost everyone is equally well off, and those who are better off are only a fraction of one per cent. ... All things considered, the natural inequality in Alpha is not worse than the natural inequality in A+.' Parfit (1986), p. 156.

his theory in a precise manner. Instead, he presents his view in a series of arguments against what he calls the Standard View:

The Standard View: Proportional variations in the number of better- and worse-off do not affect inequality.

According to the Standard View, a population D with one person with very high positive welfare and ten with very low positive welfare is as unequal as a population E with ten persons with very high positive welfare and a hundred persons with very low positive welfare. As Temkin points out, this position can be challenged: '…if it is bad for one person to be worse off through no fault of his own, it should be even worse for two people to be in such a position. … After all, to paraphrase the basic insight of the utilitarians, more of the bad is worse than less of the bad, and in many respects there is, in the end, more of what the egalitarian regards as bad in [E] than in [D]'.[34] Temkin concludes from this and other arguments that we have to reject the Standard View.

No clear implications follows from this, however, regarding the comparison of the inequality in A ∪ B and A ∪ C since these populations do not only differ in regard to proportional variations of the number of best and worst off, they also differ in respect to other egalitarian considerations. As pointed out above, A ∪ B is worse than A ∪ C in regard to the difference in welfare between the best and worst off. Moreover, the worst off are worse off in A ∪ B than in A ∪ C, and they have very bad lives. Actually, it is not clear that Temkin would consider A ∪ B worse than A ∪ C in regard to inequality since this conclusion is analogous to a devastating objection that Temkin directs against his own proposal:

The Repellant Conclusion: For any world F, let F's population be as large (though finite) as one likes, and let the gaps between F's better- and worse-off be as extreme as one likes, there will be some unequal world, G, whose population is 'sufficiently' large such that no matter how small G's gaps between the better- and worse-off might be G's inequality will be worse than F's (even if everyone in G is better off than everyone in F).[35]

In other words, if a theory implies that A ∪ B is worse than A ∪ C in regard to equality, then that might even be considered as an argument against that particular theory of equality.

Secondly, even if Temkin's theory in the end would imply that A ∪ C is less unequal than A ∪ B, he would probably not consider A ∪ C better than

[34] Temkin (1993), pp. 200, 201.   [35] Temkin (1993), p. 218.

A ∪ B *all things considered*, since he is not a Monist Welfarist Egalitarian. For example, he considers and rejects the following argument directed against his view of equality:

> ... [One] may object that if proportional increases worsen inequality, then proportional decreases should improve it. Thus the egalitarian should favor a *Shrinking World*. More particularly, for any pattern of inequality, the *best* world will be the one with the *smallest* number of people in the better- and worse-off groups consistent with that pattern. This, it may be contended, is absurd.—Surely, it *would* be absurd to claim that a two-person world with the same pattern of equality as A and B [two worlds with much more people] ... would be better than A and B *all things considered*.—Put simply, I am unpersuaded that this objection seriously challenges [my arguments] ...—Why shouldn't the egalitarian insist that the former worlds are better than the latter one[s] regarding inequality, but admit that they are worse *all things considered*?'[36]

To sum up: It is not clear which one of populations A ∪ B and A ∪ C is better in regard to equality since different reasonable egalitarian considerations pull in different directions. There is a bigger gap between the best off and the worst off, and the worst off are worse off in A ∪ B as compared to A ∪ C; on the other hand, there is a greater number of worst off in A ∪ C. Our intuitive *all things considered* ranking of these two populations is, however, pretty robust—intuitively, it seems clear that an addition of a huge number of lives with very negative welfare cannot be better than an addition of people with positive welfare. An argument to the effect that we should give up this intuitive judgement must be very convincing. As we have seen, egalitarian concerns are pulling in different directions and are thus indecisive in cases such as these. Consequently, egalitarian concerns can hardly give us any reason to change our all things considered ranking of A ∪ B and A ∪ C.

One might object to the argument above by imagining an analogous argument against utilitarianism. Consider a population A that contains more pleasure (which is some utilitarians' idea of welfare) and population B that contains more desire fulfilment (which is some other utilitarians' idea of welfare). A utilitarian that conceives of welfare as pleasure would thus rank A as better than B, whereas a utilitarian that conceives of welfare as desire fulfilment would rank B as better than A. We could then conclude, following the style of the argument above, that appeals to maximizing utility are indecisive in such cases, which clearly is not a good argument.[37]

---

[36] Temkin (1993), pp. 216–7.   [37] This argument was suggested by an anonymous referee.

The above argument is not, however, analogous to the argument I made above. I made an epistemic point about what is a reasonable stance when one and the same person's considered intuitions are pulling in different directions. I suggest that this actually is the case for most of us in regards to the welfarist egalitarian intuitions considered above. These intuitions points in different directions and none strongly outweigh the others. In other words, they do not together give any strong support for ranking the considered populations one way or the other. Another intuition (the all things considered intuition) strongly points in one direction. Hence, it is reasonable to rank the populations according to the latter intuition, and the former intuitions are in that sense indecisive in such cases. The former intuitions are, so to speak, dwarfed by the strength of the latter intuition. The analogous case would be someone who considered *both* maximization of desire fulfilment and pleasure as relevant when ranking populations A and B but who also, taking other aspects into account, has a strong all things considered intuition that, say, A is better than B. If the reasons steaming from considerations of maximization of desire fulfilment and pleasure are roughly equally strong, one pointing in favour of A and the other pointing in favour of B, then these considerations do not give her a strong reason to prefer anyone of the populations, and thus to change her all things considered judgement.

7. Conclusions

Population ethics, with cases involving population change, is one of the hardest, if not the hardest, challenge for moral theory. The Priority View might be able to explain all the distributive intuitions that we have in same number cases but seems to have little to add to the discussion of different number cases. Welfarist Egalitarians, on the other hand, do have something to say about different number cases and can help us solve the Mere Addition Paradox. Hence, there seems to be some intuitions about equality of welfare that the Priority View cannot explain away. However, egalitarian considerations cannot yield convincing arguments against the adequacy conditions involved in the impossibility result discussed above. Thus, the paradoxes of population ethics cannot be solved by an appeal to welfarist egalitarianism, and our theories regarding moral duties to future generations and intergenerational justice are still on shaky ground.

References

ANDERSON, E. (1999), 'What is the point of equality?', *Ethics*, 109: 287–337.

ARNESON, R. (1989), 'Equality of Opportunity for Welfare', *Philosophical Studies*, 56: 77–93.

ARRHENIUS, G. (2000), *Future Generations: A Challenge for Moral Theory* (Uppsala: University Printers). Also available at <http://people.su.se/~guarr/>.

——(2001), 'What Österberg's Population Theory has in Common with Plato's', in E. Carlson and R. Sliwinski (eds.), *Omnium-gatherum, Uppsala Philosophical Studies 50* (Uppsala: Department of Philosophy, Uppsala University). Also available at <http://people.su.se/~guarr/>.

——(2003a), 'The Very Repugnant Conclusion', in Krister Segerberg and Rysiek Sliwinski (eds.) *Logic, Law, Morality: Thirteen Essays in Practical Philosophy, Uppsala Philosophical Studies, vol. 51* (Uppsala: Department of Philosophy, Uppsala University). Also available at <http://people.su.se/~guarr/>.

——(2003b), 'Feldman's Desert-Adjusted Utilitarianism and Population Ethics', *Utilitas*, 15/2: 225–36.

——(2003c), 'The Person Affecting Restriction, Comparativism, and the Moral Status of Potential People', *Ethical Perspectives*, 10/3–4: 185–95.

——(2005) 'The Paradoxes of Future Generations and Normative Theory', in J. Ryberg and T. Tännsjö (eds.), *The Repugnant Conclusion: Essays on Population Ethics* (Dordrecht: Kluwer Academic Publisher).

——(2006), 'The Moral Status of Potential People' (mimeo, Dept. of Philosophy, Stockholm University). Available at <http://people.su.se/~guarr/>.

——(2006), RYBERG, J., and TÄNNSJÖ, T., 'The Repugnant Conclusion', *Stanford Encyclopaedia of Philosophy*, <http://plato.stanford.edu/>.

BARRY, B. (1989), 'Utilitarianism and Preference Change', *Utilitas*, 1: 278–82.

BLACKORBY, C., and DONALDSON, D., (1991) 'Normative Population Theory: A Comment', *Social Choice and Welfare*, 8: 261–7.

——Bossert, W., and Donaldson, D. (1997), 'Critical-Level Utilitarianism and the Population-Ethics Dilemma', *Economics and Philosophy*, 13: 197–230.

——(2005) *Population Issues in Social Choice Theory, Welfare Economics, and Ethics* (Cambridge: CUP).

BRAYBROOKE, D. (1987), *Meeting Needs* (Princeton: Princeton University Press).

BROOME, J. (1991), *Weighing Goods* (Oxford: Basil Blackwell).

——(1999), *Ethics out of Economics* (Cambridge: Cambridge University Press).

——(2004), *Weighing Lives* (Oxford: Oxford University Press).

——(forthcoming), 'Equality versus Priority: a Useful Distinction', in D. Wikler et al. (eds.), *Fairness and Goodness in Health* (World Health Organization).

BYKVIST, K. (1998), *Changing Preferences: A Study in Preferentialism* (Uppsala: University Printers).

CARLSON, E. (1998), 'Mere Addition and Two Trilemmas of Population Ethics', *Economics and Philosophy*, 14: 283–306.

COHEN, G. A. (1989), 'On the Currency of Egalitarian Justice', *Ethics* 99: 906–44.

—— (1993) 'Equality of What? On Welfare, Goods and Capabilities', in M. Nussbaum and A. Sen (eds.), *The Quality of Life* (Oxford: Clarendon Press).

CRISP, R. (2003a), 'Equality, Priority, and Compassion', *Ethics*, 113: 745–63.

—— (2003b) 'Egalitarianism and Compassion', *Ethics*, 114: 119–26.

DWORKIN, R. (1981a), 'What is Equality? Part 1: Equality of Welfare', *Philosophy and Public Affairs*, 10/3: 185–246.

—— (1981b), 'What is Equality? Part 2: Equality of Resources', *Philosophy and Public Affairs* 10/4: 283–345.

—— (2000), *Sovereign Virtue: The Theory and Practice of Equality* (Cambridge, Mass.: Harvard University Press).

FEHIGE, C. (1998), 'A Pareto Principle for Possible People', in C. Fehige and U. Wessels (eds.), *Preferences* (Berlin: de Gruyter), 509–43.

FELDMAN, F. (1997), *Utilitarianism, Hedonism, and Desert: Essays in Moral Philosophy* (Cambridge: Cambridge University Press).

—— (2004), *Pleasure and the Good Life: On the Nature, Varieties, and Plausibility of Hedonism* (Oxford: Oxford University Press).

FINNIS, J. (1980), *Natural Law and Natural Rights* (Clarendon Law Series, Oxford: Oxford University Press).

FLEURBAEY, M. (forthcoming), 'Equality versus Priority: How Relevant is the Distinction?' in D. Wikler et al. (eds.) *Fairness and Goodness in Health* (World Health Organization).

GOODIN, R. E. (1991), 'Actual Preferences, Actual People', *Utilitas*, 3/1: 113–9.

GOSSERIES, A. P. (2001), 'What Do We Owe the Next Generation(s)?', *The Loyola of Los Angeles Law Review*, 35/1: 293–354.

—— (2003), 'Intergenerational justice' in H. LaFollette (ed.) *Oxford Handbook of Practical Ethics* (Oxford: Oxford University Press).

GRIFFIN, J. (1986) [1990], *Well-Being: Its Meaning, Measurement, and Moral Importance* (Oxford: Clarendon Press).

HARE, R. M. (1981), *Moral Thinking: Its Levels, Method, and Point* (Oxford: Clarendon Press).

HARSANYI, J. C. (1992), 'Utilities, Preferences and Substantive Goods', Research Paper 101 (WIDER, The United Nations University).

HOLTUG, N. (1999), 'Utility, Priority and Possible People', *Utilitas*, 11/1: 16–36.

—— (2007), 'On Giving Priority to Possible Future People', in T. Rønnow-Rasmussen, B. Petersson, J. Josefsson, and D. Egonsson (eds.) *Hommage à Wlodek: Philosophical Papers Dedicated to Wlodek Rabinowicz*. Available at <www.fil.lu.se/hommageawlodek/index.htm>.

HUDSON, J. L. (1987), 'The Diminishing Marginal Value of Happy People', *Philosophical Studies*, 51: 123–37.

HURKA, T. (1993), *Perfectionism* (New York: Oxford University Press).

KYMLICKA, W. (1990), *Contemporary Political Philosophy* (Oxford: Clarendon Press).

MEYER, L. (2003), 'Intergenerational Justice', *The Stanford Encyclopedia of Philosophy* (Summer 2003 Edition), Edward N. Zalta (ed.). Available at <http://plato.stanford. edu/archives/sum2003/entries/justice-intergenerational/>.

NG, Y-K. (1989), 'What Should We Do About Future Generations? Impossibility of Parfit's Theory X', *Economics and Philosophy* 5/2: 235−53.

NIELSEN, K. (1996), 'Radical Egalitarianism Revisited: On Going Beyond the Difference Principle', *Windsor Yearbook of Access to Justice*, 15: 121−48.

PARFIT, D. (1984), [1991] *Reasons and Persons* (Oxford: Clarendon Press).

——(1986), 'Overpopulation and the Quality of Life', in P. Singer (ed.), *Applied Ethics* (Oxford University Press), 145−64.

——(1993), 'Does Equality Matter?,' in J. R. Richards (ed.), *Philosophical Problems of Equality* (Milton Keynes: Open University).

PERSSON, I. (2001), 'Equality, Priority and Person-Affecting Value', *Ethical Theory and Moral Practice* 4/1: 23−39.

——(2003), 'The Badness of Unjust Inequality', *Theoria*, 69/1−2, 108−23.

RABINOWICZ, W. (2002), 'Prioritarianism for Prospects', *Utilitas* 14: 2−21.

——(2003), 'The Size of Inequality and Its Badness—Some Reflections around Temkin's Inequality', *Theoria* 69: 60−84.

RAWLS, J. (1971), *A Theory of Justice* (Cambridge, Mass.: Harvard University Press).

RAZ, J. (1986), *The Morality of Freedom* (Oxford: Clarendon Press).

SEN, A. (1980), 'Equality of What?', in S. McMurrin (ed.), *The Tanner Lecture on Human Values* (Cambridge: Cambridge University Press).

——(1992), *Inequality Reexamined* (Cambridge, Mass.: Cambridge University Press).

——(1993), 'Capability and Well-Being', in M. Nussbaum & A. Sen (eds.), *The Quality of Life* (Oxford: Clarendon Press).

SIDER, T. R. (1991), 'Might Theory X Be a Theory of Diminishing Marginal Value?', *Analysis*, 51/4: 265−71.

SINGER, P. (1993), *Practical Ethics*, 2nd edn. (Cambridge: Cambridge University Press).

SUMNER, L. W. (1996), *Welfare, Happiness, and Ethics* (Oxford: Clarendon Press).

TÄNNSJÖ, T. 1998, *Hedonistic Utilitarianism* (Edinburgh: Edinburgh University Press).

——(2005), 'Why We Ought to Accept the Repugnant Conclusion', in J. Ryberg and T. Tännsjö (eds.), *The Repugnant Conclusion: Essays on Population Ethics* (Dordrecht: Kluwer Academic Publisher).

TEMKIN, L. S. (1993), *Inequality* (Oxford: Oxford University Press).

——(2003a), 'Equality, Priority Or What?', *Economics and Philosophy*, 19: 61−88.

——(2003b) 'Egalitarianism Defended', *Ethics*, 113: 764−82.

TUNGODDEN, B. (2003), 'The Value of Equality', *Economics and Philosophy*, 19: 1−44.

VALLENTYNE, P. (2000), 'Equality, Efficiency, and the Priority of the Worse-off', *Economics and Philosophy*, 16: 1−19.

13

Intergenerational Justice, Human Needs, and Climate Policy

CLARK WOLF

1. Environmental Change and Intergenerational Justice

Because present actions will shape the world inherited by our children and by later generations, we can influence their lives for good or for ill. Anthropogenic climate change and the resultant environmental damage presents an especially pressing instance of this influence. There is now no room for serious doubt that human activities, especially those that have occurred over the past fifty years, have warmed the earth and influenced the global climate. Evidence of this influence is not difficult to find: data indicate that the surface temperature of the earth is rising, as are sea levels. Recent decades have seen dramatic increases in the rate of retreat of glaciers and polar ice and permafrost. Biologists record the migration of species up the slopes of mountains and farther from equatorial latitudes as their environment has changed as a result of global warming. In addition to these indicators of change, we have substantial data documenting increased levels of CO_2 and other greenhouse gases in the earth's atmosphere, and good evidence that these increases are the result of human activities. Finally we have a plausible hypothesis linking warming trends to the presence of these gasses in our atmosphere. Under the circumstances, it would be surprising if we found that anthropogenic emissions were *not* influencing global climate.[1]

I would like to thank an anonymous reviewer who provided generous comments on an earlier draft of this paper. I would like to extend special thanks to Axel Gosseries, who read successive drafts of this paper and whose penetrating comments prevented many errors. I alone am responsible for those that remain.

[1] See for example the reports from the Intergovernmental Panel on Climate Change (2001) and (2007), as well as the Millenium Ecosystem Assessment (2005a, 2005b). Flannery (2005) and Maslin (2004) both discuss the mechanisms involved in climate change and some of the likely effects.

It is difficult to predict the effects of climate change, but there is reason for serious concern that global warming may be disastrous for the environmental systems of the earth, with consequent disastrous effects on human welfare. When climate patterns shift, this destabilizes environmental systems on which people depend, putting human lives and human welfare at risk. Global warming increases the risk that people in equatorial regions will suffer from drought, and that higher temperatures will further compromise agricultural self-sufficiency in less developed countries of the global south. Global warming may also result in an increase in the rate of extreme weather events, including hurricanes, tornados, floods, and droughts. While it is sometimes urged that those most urgently at risk are the poor inhabitants of less developed countries in the global South, hurricane Katrina clearly demonstrated in 2005 that the risks associated with extreme weather events threaten those in developed nations as well.[2] In sum, global warming increases the risk of famine and misery for those who will live in the warmer world we cede to later generations. This paper will take these empirical facts as *given* since they are well confirmed, and since, in any case, they could not be settled by *a priori* philosophical inquiry. I will assume that anthropogenic climate change significantly increases the risk that many future people will be unable to meet their most basic needs. As I will urge, this makes the problem of global climate change, and environmental change in general, a central problem for a theory of intergenerational justice.

The intergenerational effects of present policies often raise important questions of fairness and justice. When present choices influence the distribution of burdens and benefits born and enjoyed by people who will exist at different times, we may reasonably ask whether the resultant distribution is equitable, fair, or just. Questions of fairness may arise if present activities impose unfair costs on the future, but they may also arise if our choices place unfair burdens on present generations. For example, policies and treaties designed to mitigate the effects of climate change, like the Kyoto agreement, have sometimes been rejected on the ground that they cost too much, and that those who pay for them will not reap any of the benefits. There is a generational lag between the present cost of implementing mitigation policy, and the much later benefits that such a policy would generate: those who pay are not likely to live long enough to see the benefits of their investment. Can we justify imposing these costs on present people for the benefit of future people? In most contexts, it is reasonable to ask why some people should pay for others' benefits. On the

---

[2] While weather events like hurricane Katrina can be somewhat indiscriminate in their ability to distribute misery, it is noteworthy that those who were unable to escape were mostly the poor, powerless, and the disabled. Wealthy New Orleaneans were mostly able to leave the city before the storm arrived.

other hand, we might reasonably ask whether an appropriate climate policy imposes *costs* on present people. We might instead understand such policies as a way to prevent present generations from unfairly taking advantages for ourselves by imposing the costs of our own behavior on to future people who are not yet here to defend themselves. If we frame the choice in the first way ('Must we accept the cost of climate policy?'), then it appears that we must overcome a presumption against shifting burdens to the present from the future. But if we frame it in the second way ('May we shift costs to future generations by failing to adopt a climate policy?'), then we are forced to ask whether we are justified in imposing these costs on the future.

To find the appropriate way to frame the decisions we face, we need to situate these choices within broader considerations of justice. This paper offers an account of intergenerational justice that provides guidance in circumstances where present choices will influence the intertemporal distribution of burdens and benefits as they do in the case of climate policy. Sections 2 through 5 develop an account of justice, including intergenerational justice, built from elements of the theory articulated by John Rawls. Rawls's work has become a touchstone for discussions of distributive justice in general and intergenerational justice in particular. But while I begin with Rawls, the account I develop here is Rawlsian only by extension, and is very much at odds with the usual understanding of his view. I do not assume that Rawls would agree. The evaluation of the view as a theory of justice must depend on its philosophical merits, and not on what some might regard as a tenuous connection to Rawls's work. Sections 6 and 7 take some steps to apply this theory to the special problems presented by global environmental change, and climate policy in particular.

2. Liberalism and Intergenerational Justice

Rawls on intergenerational justice

John Rawls's account of justice among contemporaries is familiar, but his account of intergenerational justice has received considerably less attention. This is surprising, since Rawls incorporates the intergenerational aspect of justice into the foundational description of his project: principles of justice, he writes, are those that will support a 'fair system of cooperation over time, from one generation to the next.'[3] In his well-known account, Rawls argues that a theory of justice is constituted by the principles we would choose

---

[3] Rawls (1993) p. 14.

from an original position behind a veil of ignorance that blinds each person to any facts about him or herself that might introduce bias. The purpose of the veil is to prevent bias, prejudice, or unequal bargaining power from distorting the choice of principles. According to Rawls, parties to the original position will select what he calls the 'conception of justice as fairness' as the theory best suited to protect their rights and interests. This conception of justice includes two principles. The first principle, the 'equal liberty principle', specifies that each person is to have an equal right to the most extensive total system of equal basic liberties compatible with a similar system for all. It is lexically prior to the second principle, which governs social and economic inequalities. This second principle is itself composed of two sub-principles: the 'open offices' principle, which stipulates that social and economic inequalities must be attached to offices and positions open to all under conditions of fair equality of opportunity, and the 'difference principle' which specifies that social and economic inequalities must be organized so that they are maximally advantageous to the worst off members of society. Rawls argues that the equal liberty principle must be lexically prior to equal opportunity (the open offices principle) which is itself prior to the difference principle.[4]

In his discussion of justice between generations, Rawls restricts his attention to the problem of just *saving*. He asks, 'When is it <permissible or required or impermissible> for a generation to save for the benefit of later generations?' In his answer to this question, Rawls adopts a two-stage view. If people live in circumstances in which there are inadequate resources to implement just institutions, they have an obligation to save so that later generations will not be in the same predicament. In this first 'accumulation stage', saving is required since it is necessary to secure justice for later generations. Just institutions protect basic rights and liberties as required by the equal liberty principle, and to secure fair equality of opportunity and distributive justice as required by the second principle of justice.[5] Once just institutions have been established, Rawls argues, there is no need for further accumulation of wealth just to make later generations richer. It is simply necessary to preserve the existing stock so that subsequent generations will also be able to live under institutions that are stable and just. This second stage in Rawls's account of intergenerational justice is sometimes called the 'steady state' stage.[6] As Rawls writes:

The purpose of a just (real) savings principle is to establish (reasonably) just institutions for a free constitutional democratic society (or any well-ordered society) and to secure a

---

[4] Rawls (1971) Ch. II.
[5] Gosseries (2001) offers the clearest account of Rawls's two-stage view.
[6] For instance, by Gosseries (2005a, 2005b), Rawls (1999b) p. 107.

social world that makes possible a worthwhile life for all its citizens. Accordingly, savings may stop once just (or decent) basic institutions have been established. At this point, real saving may fall to zero; and existing stock only needs to be maintained or replaced, and nonrenewable resources carefully husbanded for future use as appropriate.[7]

While he does not expressly state the assumption, it would seem that Rawls's model assumes zero population growth at the steady-state stage. He assumes that maintaining a stable stock of capital will ultimately be sufficient to secure justice over time and effectively to protect liberties. But it is easy to think of circumstances under which this assumption would be unjustified. For example, if later generations are simply more numerous, then increasing capital reserves might be necessary to guarantee appropriate institutions for them all.[8] In addition, even after the necessary steady state capital stock was achieved, it might be possible to predict that later generations will face serious challenges that will put the institutions of justice at risk. In such a case additional protective saving might be necessary for the maintenance of just institutions over time.

Rawls and the priority of basic needs

In his later works, Rawls considered and briefly proposed incorporating an additional principle in the theory of justice, requiring that basic needs must be met. Surprisingly, he claims that such a principle should have lexical priority over the other two principles of justice. He writes:

... the first principle covering the equal basic rights and liberties may easily be preceded by a lexically prior principle requiring that citizens' basic needs be met, at least insofar as their being met is necessary for citizens to understand and to be able fruitfully to exercise [their] rights and liberties. Certainly any such principle must be assumed in applying the first principle.[9]

This remarkable passage proposes a *needs principle,* and assigns it lexical priority over the other principles of justice. If this proposal were taken seriously, it would constitute a major change in Rawls's theory. While Rawls never developed this suggestion, I propose to take it very seriously in my discussion here.

The view Rawls indicates in this last quotation might be described as a form of *moderate sufficientarianism.* Rawls justifies it, in part, by its association with the liberties and rights discussed in the other two principles of justice. *Extreme*

---

[7] Rawls (1999b) p. 107.

[8] It is worthwhile to note that it may not be possible to restrict population growth in a way consistent with justice. Sen (1994) urges that population control policies are likely to violate basic rights and liberties.

[9] Rawls (1993) p. 7. For further discussion of this needs principle, see pp. 166 and 228–9.

sufficientarian theories hold that justice requires that peoples basic needs be met so that they are provided with a sufficient minimum, but do not incorporate additional requirements of justice. *Moderate sufficientarian* views similarly hold that justice requires that people be provided with a sufficient minimum. Where resources are too scarce to meet needs, it might require that we minimize unmet needs. But *moderate sufficientarians* would regard this as only one principle within a broader account of justice.

If justice includes other requirements in addition to a sufficiency principle, then priority rules are needed to provide direction when different requirements conflict. Rawls indicates a reason why a needs principle should have priority over the principle protecting equal liberties: only if people have sufficient means to satisfy basic needs will other rights and liberties have any significance for them. Where needs come into conflict with the other principles of justice, the obligation to meet needs will take priority.

Since it has priority over the equal liberty principle, the needs principle will *a fortiori* take priority over the principles governing tolerable inequalities. Still, one might wonder whether a needs principle could ever come in conflict with the difference principle. While both principles oblige concern with those who are very badly off, it turns out that there are circumstances in which they systematically diverge. A needs principle may be fully satisfied even where vast inequalities persist, but the difference principle will continue to generate requirements even where all needs are met. If a needs principle is formulated to require minimization of unmet need, then there are even circumstances where a needs principle will generate requirements that are inconsistent with the difference principle. Sometimes we will most effectively minimize unmet need by focusing our efforts on those needy people who will benefit most, instead of focusing on those who are worst off. While the difference principle would direct us to give priority to those who are worst off, the requirement to minimize unmet need, in such circumstances, would require us to engage in triage. Since the needs principle and the difference principle can conflict, we need higher-level rules to arbitrate conflicts between them. Priority rules settle such disputes by giving the egalitarian focus of the difference principle second place to the requirement to meet people's basic needs.

Four arguments for a needs principle

What reasons might be given for the claim that parties to the original position would choose a needs principle and give it lexical priority over other principles of justice? And more broadly, what additional justification (if any) can be given for including such a principle within Rawls's theory or any other liberal conception of justice? There are several arguments that might be given on the principle's behalf: First, the suggestion that basic needs should be a high priority of justice is broadly consistent with the underlying concern that social institutions must be defensible to every member of society. Those who are worst off and those whose basic needs are unmet are the most likely to have a legitimate complaint against the institutions of society, and are the least likely to have sufficient reason to accept the principles that animate those institutions. If satisfaction of basic needs is the first priority of justice, then institutions that conform to the requirements of justice can be defended to the needy on the ground that their needs are not merely a high public priority but the first public priority. If scarcity dictates that some people's needs cannot be met, just institutions will still be defensible to those who suffer deprivation: no alternative institutions would serve the fundamental needs of the worst off any better than the existing institutions. This argument may be stated in brief: Liberal theories of justice are distinguished, in part, by the view that public institutions and the conception of justice animating these institutions must be justifiable to every person who is subject to them. Institutions that avoidably leave some peoples most basic needs unmet cannot be justified to those whose needs are avoidably unmet. Thus only institutions that satisfy a needs principle will be publicly justifiable to all. So liberal conceptions of justice must satisfy the needs principle.[10]

Second, a needs principle gains support from many other considerations that can be used to motivate and justify the difference principle. The needs principle may be understood to reinforce the difference principle, especially its highest priority requirements.[11] For example, Rawls describes parties to the original position as making their choices under circumstances that satisfy the conditions for the rationality of maximin reasoning. These conditions are three: (1) the downside risk is great if the outcome is bad; (2) the upside benefit is relatively small if the outcome is optimal; and (3) the parties have no basis to assign probability values to alternative outcomes.[12] One can easily imagine parties in such a situation acting to choose a principle that would put a 'floor' on the

---

[10] A version of this needs principle might be made consistent with 'luck egalitarianism' (see Gosseries 2005b). For example, one might regard those whose present needs are unmet because they have squandered their opportunities to have relinquished their claims on basic institutions. Their deprivation is not the result of simple bad luck, since their own choices are involved. On the other hand, one might plausibly urge that people's most fundamental needs should be met, when possible, even if their present deprivation *is* the result of bad choices and not bad luck. I will not investigate here the details of these alternative interpretations of the needs principle, but either of them should be consistent with the discussion that follows.

[11] Note that this argument, if successful, might give a needs principle priority over the difference principle, but not over other prior principles.

[12] Rawls (1971) pp. 154–5.

downside risks, especially the very serious risk that one's basic needs might not be met. The prior choice of a needs principle would neatly accomplish this. Once a needs principle has been selected, however, one might argue that the parties are *no longer* in circumstances that satisfy the conditions for maximin reasoning. It will be important to consider how this might change other aspects of Rawls's view, including especially the argument for the difference principle itself.

A third justification for a needs principle (and its priority) is implicit in the insight that having ones needs met is 'necessary for citizens to understand and to be able fruitfully to exercise [their] rights and liberties.'[13] Satisfaction of basic needs is a precondition for the significance of the equal liberty principle and the value of the rights and liberties it guarantees. Without prior satisfaction of basic needs, rights and liberties would be valueless to those who possess them, but who would lack any ability to exercise or understand them. Within Rawls's framework, this consideration gives parties to the original position a strong reason to choose a needs principle first. It should also be a compelling argument for those who may be skeptical of Rawls's project. We have good reason to accept that the objective to meet basic needs must be a fundamental priority for any plausible theory of liberal justice.

But this argument may raise a special kind of concern: since the argument makes the justification of the need principle depend, at least in part, on the values protected by the equal liberty principle, it might be thought to support the notion that the needs principle should be subsequent, not prior, to the equal liberty principle.[14] But there is an important distinction to be made between practical priority and justificatory priority. The reasoning behind this argument would not make the needs principle subsequent to the equal liberty principle in any practical sense: where the two conflict, the needs principle would be prior. In fact, in practice the needs principle would be *lexically* prior, since needs must be met first, before equal liberties can be secured. This practical lexical priority of needs is fully consistent with Rawls's suggestion that the justification of the needs principle may depend, in part, on the relationship between needs, liberties, and rights.

Fourth and finally, it is plausible to think that a liberal theory of justice should place high priority on meeting basic needs simply because having basic needs met is a very important objective from the moral point of view. Meeting basic needs has a higher moral significance than most other values that can be secured and protected by public institutions. It is easy to see why Rawlsian contractors, interested to protect their most fundamental and most general

---

[13] Rawls (1993) p. 7.   [14] I thank Axel Gosseries for calling this concern to my attention.

interests, might agree to such a principle from behind Rawls's veil of ignorance as a first principle of justice, and why such a principle should have a high priority within any liberal conception of justice. In what follows I will consider some of the implications of a lexically prior needs principle for a theory of intergenerational justice.

Theoretical costs

However plausible it may be in the abstract, it is not at all clear that the addition of this principle can come without cost for Rawls's theory, and Rawls himself may not have considered all of the implications of this change. In particular, an important argument for the difference principle may be substantially altered by the inclusion of a needs principle among the basic principles of justice. As Rawls describes the choice behind the veil of ignorance, the choice of lexically prior principles takes place first, and the implications of prior principles change the context in which later choices are made. If the choice of a distribution principle is made after the choice of a lexically prior needs principle, as well as the equal liberties principle, this eliminates a significant portion of the 'downside risk' associated with the choice of alternatives to the difference principle. This in turn undermines the claim that the original position choice meets the conditions for maximin reasoning. This is especially important since the argument from maximin is often regarded as a central justificatory foundation of the difference principle.

Perhaps Rawls recognized this. It may partly explain why his later discussions (for example, in Rawls (2001)) place much less emphasis on the argument from maximin reasoning, and offer alternative grounds for the difference principle. As I will interpret Rawls's proposal, it implies that meeting people's basic needs should be the first priority of justice. I find this to be a very plausible view. But I am also convinced that the insertion of such a principle will imply further changes in Rawls theory, some of which I cannot investigate here. Given the moral significance of needs, and the changes that a needs principle would seem to imply for the rest of Rawls's project, one could wish that he had said more about it.

3. Formulating a Needs Principle

Generation neutrality

What form might a lexically prior needs principle take? I will urge that such a principle should be *generation neutral*. That is, it should not give special weight to the needs of the members of any particular generation, including the present generation. If future needs are less predictable or less certain than present needs, this will give us some reason to discount the needs of future people when we might otherwise serve the more certain and predictable needs of present people. But other things being equal, a needs principle should not discount the needs of future persons simply because they are future. This form of neutrality is sometimes controversial, since economic models typically include a temporal or generational discount rate. But there are few defenses (and no good ones) of pure time discounting, which is widely regarded to be morally unjustifiable. The view under consideration would not prohibit discounting for uncertainty, and discounting for the rate of interest will still be justifiable and appropriate in many contexts where resources are growing over time. This form of generation neutrality is thus consistent with the defensible uses of discounting in economic theory, though specifically inconsistent with 'felicity discounting,' which has few contemporary defenders in any case.[15]

Maximin v min-deprivation

I will consider two alternative formulations of a generation neutral needs principle. The *Maximin Formulation* [MM] would require satisfaction of the needs of the worst-off members of society first, and would permit satisfaction of the needs of those who are not worst off only after the needs of those who are worst offs have been met. An alternative formulation which we might call *Min-Deprivation* [MD] would require minimizing deprivation with respect to basic needs.

The *Maximin Formulation* may have appeal for Rawlsians, since it captures the spirit of the difference principle. Some of the same arguments used to motivate the difference principle might be adduced to motivate a needs principle with this form. But this formulation is subject to what is sometimes called the 'black hole' problem: the principle affording strict priority for those who are

---

[15] Some economic models assume a felicity discount rate (sometimes called a 'pure time discount rate') without argument. Since 'defence' requires argument, I do not include those who merely *assume* that we may permissibly engage in felicity discounting among those who *defend* the practice. Harrod (1948) and Ramsey (1928) famously argued that discounting is irrational and morally wrong. Arrow (1999) asserts his acceptance of pure time discounting, but acknowledges that he provides no argument in defence of the practice. Sen (1982) and Lind (1982b) both provide nuanced discussions of discounting that effectively distinguish among different currencies of discount and alternative reasons one might have for discounting. Excellent discussions of the economic and philosophical aspects of discounting the future can be found in Lind (1982a) and in Portney and Weyant (1999). Broome (1992) and Parfit (1982) offer decisive practical and moral arguments against felicity discounting.

worst off may come in sharp conflict with the objective to minimize unmet needs.[16] Under some circumstances, it might take all of our resources to create only a marginal improvement in the situation of the worst-off person in society, while those resources might otherwise make a large difference in the lives of many other people who are very badly off, but who aren't quite in the worst-off class. In such circumstances, the principle of priority for the worst off would hold society hostage to the predicament of the very worst-off member. Within the 'official' reading of Rawls's view, the obligation to promote the needs of the worst-off members of society is moderated by the *Equal Liberty* and *Open Offices* principles, but if a needs a principle is made the first priority of justice, the 'black hole' problem becomes even more pressing.

This problem militates strongly in favor of formulating a needs principle as a requirement to minimize deprivation with respect to basic needs [MD] instead of giving priority to the worst off [MM]. In extreme circumstances where not all needs can be met, MD will permit or require a form of *triage,* in which the needs of the very worst off are left unmet since meeting those needs would make it impossible to address other urgent needs. Where minimization of deprivation is best accomplished by addressing the needs of those who are not in the very worst-off class, MD will recommend that we minimize deprivation anyway. The maximin formulation MM would instead require that we address the needs of the worst off-individual even if that individual would glean few benefits if all our resources were directed to her benefit, and where those resources might otherwise have been used to provide great benefits for other seriously needy people. MD will not hold us hostage to the predicament of the worst-off members of society, but will instead require that we structure institutions so that as few people as possible will suffer from unmet needs.

Min-deprivation and liberal anti-consequentialism

MD is an essentially consequentialist principle: it focuses our attention on the needs-indexed welfare consequences of alternative choices we might make. In considering whether a negative welfarist principle like MD can be included within an acceptable liberal theory of justice, however, we need to consider whether it violates the spirit of liberalism to give lexical priority to a consequentialist principle like MD. An express aim of Rawls and many liberal theorists was to develop an alternative to utilitarian and consequentialist conceptions of

---

[16] Allen Buchanan called this the 'black hole' problem in his lectures in political philosophy at the University of Arizona in 1991–92.

justice. By re-inserting a consequentialist principle as a first priority of justice, have we sacrificed the essential element of a liberal conception of justice?

In response, note that needs-consequentialism, and especially a *negative* needs consequentialism like that embodied in MD, will not be subject to the objections that led Rawls and other liberal theorists to reject consequentialist accounts of justice. Positive consequentialist principles require that we max-imize good consequences, while negative principles require minimization of bad consequences. The objective to minimize deprivation with respect to basic needs will not justify the oppression of the needy few in order to promote the happiness of the majority. And unlike positive consequentialist views, negative consequentialist theories are satiable. They cease to generate requirements once the relevant bad consequences (in this case, deprivation) have been eliminated. Positive consequentialist views are *in*satiable. They imply a *prima facie* obliga-tion to increase the goodness of consequences without limit: more goodness is always better.[17] MD is thus significantly less demanding than conventional consequentialism, and would focus our attention on people whose predicament is very plausibly regarded as a first priority of justice.[18]

Finally, note that MD may be essentially bound to the rights many regard as the defining characteristic of liberalism: liberal theorists, Rawls included, often argue that certain rights are so fundamental that they must be included among the basic needs. Those who are concerned that rights might be violated in the effort to minimize deprivation must argue for the importance of the rights in question. But any argument capable of showing that certain rights should have such a high priority will also be an argument in favour of including those rights on any plausible list of fundamental needs. Thus, while a needs principle like MD may be consequentialist in an important sense, it is unlikely to come in conflict with the most fundamental liberal rights, and is still a plausible principle for a liberal theory of justice.

Which needs?

But this response raises another concern: which are the basic needs? And among the basic needs, how should we prioritize when we face opportunities to address *different* needs. In formulating a needs principle, it will be crucial to specify which needs are basic. It will also be valuable to specify priorities among needs, since we may often be faced with alternatives that address different needs,

---

[17] See Wolf (2004) for a discussion of these issues.

[18] For further discussion of positive and negative consequentialist views, see Wolf (1997) and Wolf (2004). For a defence of a negative consequentialism as a component of a larger theory of justice, see Wolf (1999).

each of which may be fundamental. While some items on the list of 'basic needs' may be relatively uncontroversial, others at the margin between 'basic' and 'non-basic' may be essentially contestable. Some conceptions of need, like that specified by the *Human Development Index,* are exceptionally spare. Others, like that offered by David Braybrooke (1987), or the complex lists of functional capabilities developed by Nussbaum (2000) and by Sen (1993) are far more generous.[19] All proposed lists of basic needs are controversial, but if a needs principle is made a first priority of justice, there is good reason for such controversy. Because of the priority of the needs principle, arguments from need will support claims to entitlement. This gives us good reason not to adopt too expansive a list of basic needs, since doing so risks expanding the set of entitlements, and thus the burdens on others. But we also have good reason to insure that all needs that are truly basic should be covered. A more expansive list of basic needs will make the needs principle much harder to meet, while a more constrained list will render its satisfaction less significant.

Instead of specifying the set of basic needs in a list, we might identify them with a membership criterion like the one suggested in the discussion above: on this view, the basic needs include just those things that are necessary 'for citizens to understand and to be able fruitfully to exercise [their] rights and liberties.'[20] This criterion gives focus to the question which needs are basic, and what needs to be shown in order to argue that some specific need should be on the list. We may be able to prioritize among needs by considering the extent to which they are necessary for the values emphasized in this membership criterion. For the balance of my discussion here, I will assume that the set of basic needs can be identified as those that satisfy this criterion.

4. Intergenerational Saving and Intertemporal Distributive Justice

Intergenerational saving and accumulation under the difference principle

Rawls specifies a two-stage process for intergenerational saving, requiring that earlier generations should save until just institutions can be put in place. After that point, capital stocks simply need to be maintained to insure that justice can

---

[19] For a brief discussion that places the human development index in the context of other lists of basic needs, see also Wolf (1998).
[20] Rawls (1993) p. 7.

be maintained. But it has sometimes been objected that this process requires those who are worse off (the earlier generations who do not have sufficient resources) to make sacrifices for those who are better off (the later generations who are wealthy enough to implement just institutions). Such sacrifices run contrary to the spirit of justice that animates the difference principle, but Rawls was convinced that they were necessary to make economic growth possible. This is his expressed reason for abandoning the difference principle in his account of intergenerational distributive justice. He writes:

> [W]hen the difference principle is applied to the question of savings over generations, it entails either no savings at all or not enough savings to improve social circumstances sufficiently so that all the equal liberties can be effectively exercised.[21]

Rawls was convinced that the difference principle would make it impossible, under some adverse circumstances, ever to implement just institutions. The implementation of just institutions typically requires saving and accumulation during early stages of development. So the poorer early generations must simply bear the cost for the sake of the wealthier generations that follow. This ordering of priorities is quite consistent with Rawls's project, since the protection of rights and liberties, in his view, is prior to the distributional requirements of the difference principle. Where the difference principle comes in conflict with the protection of fundamental rights and liberties, or the institutions that protect them, the difference principle must give way.

But the idea that those who are poor should not be required to make sacrifices for those who are wealthy still holds considerable force, and one might regard Rawls's solution as unfair where it violates this principle. Rawls sees this as a dilemma. If the economic growth described in the first stage is justified, then we must abandon the principle that those who are poor should not be required to make sacrifices for those who are better off. But if we cannot sanction sacrifices made by the relatively poor for the sake of the relatively wealthy, then we must abandon the first 'accumulation stage' of Rawls's account. The dilemma can be avoided entirely if intergenerational economic growth, in the sense of real capital accumulation, can be accomplished without burdening the badly-off first generations. Rawls may simply have been wrong to assume that an intergenerational application of the difference principle would make economic growth and accumulation impossible. Intergenerational accumulation cannot be ruled out *a priori* by the difference principle, because

---

[21] Rawls (1999a) p. 254. See also Arrow (1973) p. 325 and Dasgupta (1994) p. 105. For a more thorough treatment of this problem, see Wolf (forthcoming). Wall (2003) also points out the tension between the difference principle and Rawls's remarks on intergenerational justice, and argues that we should replace the difference principle with a less egalitarian principle for distributive justice.

the possibility for growth depends on the rate at which capital resources grow from one generation to the next, as well as on the rate of consumption.

To see that this must be so, consider a Plentiful World in which capital resources grow independently, like plants, but at a rate far faster than they can be used or consumed. This might be the case either where the growth rate is very high, or where consumption rates are very low. In this world no one must experience deprivation with respect to physical needs: everyone's material needs are fully satisfied, and material goods are so oversupplied that they are free. In such a world, economic growth would not conflict with the difference principle because well-being (including the well-being of those who are worse off) would not depend on the distribution of scarce physical goods, but on the non-material primary goods. One might urge that inhabitants of the Plentiful World are not in the Circumstances of Justice, since 'moderate scarcity' is usually included among the conditions that make justice necessary and injustice possible. But the argument here seeks only to show that capital growth is sometimes consistent with the requirement that the relatively poor earlier generations should not be required to make sacrifices for the sake of the relatively wealthy. And one might argue (against both Rawls and Hume) that justice is an important virtue even in circumstances of unmanageable resource abundance. Even in the Plentiful World fundamental rights and liberties and democratic liberties will require protection, and inappropriately described property rights might leave some people's needs unmet. And some needs are not material: Rawls lists such things as 'the social bases of self-respect' among the primary goods. Thus the difference principle would still have work to do in a Plentiful World, but its operation would not stand in the way of spontaneous material accumulation.

Obviously, we don't live in a Plentiful World. But consider another possible world that may be closer to our own: in this Sufficient World basic well-being is very cheap, and it is quite inexpensive to meet people's needs. The rate of economic growth is not astronomically high, but it is quite high enough to keep pace with people's needs and to keep the price of necessities low. Once material needs are met, personal well-being in this world is a function of such things as community engagement, public equality, and the existence of worthwhile creative outlets. In the Sufficient World, economic growth is the result of free, creative, voluntary, and mutually advantageous interactions among people who find their efforts intrinsically fulfilling and rewarding. In this world, it would violate the difference principle to *prevent* economic growth and capital accumulation. Since there are possible worlds in which capital accumulation will not violate an intergenerational difference principle, Rawls was wrong to rule out such a principle *a priori*.

In the Sufficient World, economic growth *need* not come at cost to the worst off. Evidently, we don't live in the Sufficient World either. But what about the Actual World? Perhaps Rawls was right to think that economic growth must come at cost to the worst off in the Actual World, though this would then be a contingent feature of our world. To judge whether our world is like this, we would need to consider the rate and causes of economic growth, and the rate of per capita consumption. We would also need to factor in the rate of population growth and resultant increase (or decrease) in consumption over time. In considering whether economic growth must violate the difference principle in the Actual World, it will be important to notice some of the differences between the Actual World and the Sufficient World. In the Actual World, there are many people who are poor and destitute and whose fundamental needs are not met. Much of what passes for economic accumulation in the Actual World results from our extraction and consumption of nonrenewable resources. Apparent economic growth resulting from this process may not really be 'accumulation' at all, since the process may deprive future generations of resources without replacing them with anything of enduring value. In the Actual World, a significant proportion of measured economic growth is the result of exploitation and oppression, in which the wealthy and powerful appropriate the goods of others, or squeeze wealth out of the labour of those who lack the power to resist. One need only consider the process of production within repressive authoritarian regimes to find examples of such exploitation. Like the extraction and insufficiently productive consumption of resources, economic 'growth' due to exploitation is only apparent growth, not real accumulation. Such exploitation is simply a form of coercive redistribution from the weak to the powerful.

But as in the Sufficient World, in the Actual World we have more than enough *stuff* to meet the basic needs of everyone, and needs provision is shockingly inexpensive. In the actual world, the rate of measured economic growth has been quite high enough to keep pace with human needs, though those who are in need may have no institutional entitlement to the things they need.[22] As in the Sufficient World, quite a significant amount of economic growth is the result of spontaneous creativity and mutually advantageous cooperation that is costly to no one. Perhaps we could expect the rate of spontaneously productive activity to increase if fewer people were exploited and oppressed, struggling to meet their basic needs. The difference between

---

[22] One would need, of course, to subtract that portion of economic growth that is only *apparent* growth, like the varieties discussed in the paragraph above.

the Actual World and the Sufficient World may simply be that the Actual World contains so much injustice.

Rawls abandoned the difference principle as an intergenerational principle of distributive justice because he was convinced that it would prohibit the economic growth that he believed to be necessary for the implementation of just institutions. Alternately, one might be tempted to abandon Rawls's two-stage account of intergenerational justice and accumulation in order to accommodate an intergenerational difference principle. But if mutually advantageous growth is possible, as argued above, then both of these moves are precipitous. Rawls was too quick to abandon the intergenerational difference principle as a principle for intergenerational distributive justice, and he did so for the wrong reasons. While this does not constitute an argument in *favour* of an intergenerational difference principle, it would imply that the difference principle should be reconsidered as a principle of intergenerational justice. In reconstructing Rawls's theory below, I will include an intergenerational version of the difference principle that requires maximal advantage for the worst-off person, regardless of what generation or at what time that person will live. However, the addition of a lexically prior needs principle will have additional implications for the problem of saving and accumulation necessary for the implementation of just institutions.

Intergenerational saving and accumulation under the needs principle

Principle MD requires minimization of deprivation with respect to basic needs. It should also be given a generation-neutral interpretation, since the importance of needs provision does not depend on the generation in which a needy person may live. MD implies that saving and capital accumulation will be required by justice whenever they are a necessary and an effective means to minimize deprivation and unmet needs. Since the needs principle is prior, saving will be required, in such circumstances, even when the only feasible saving plan would violate the difference principle. This is the other side of the 'black hole' problem described above: while negative welfarism will not always hold us hostage to the predicament of the very worst off, it will sometimes permit or require 'triage'. If saving and sacrifice are necessary in the early stage of institutional development for the creation of just institutions capable of meeting needs and satisfying the other requirements of justice, then that is what the principle requires.

This implication forges a link between Rawls's two-stage account of intergenerational justice, and his remarks concerning the lexically prior require-ment to meet basic needs. For Rawls also believed (wrongly, as I have argued) that such accumulation would necessarily come at cost to the worst-off earlier generations. Rawls took himself to be abandoning, in the intergenerational case, the principle that worse-off people should not be required to make sacrifices for the sake of others who will be better off. Still, he was willing to make an exception to the difference principle in this special case, where difference-principle-violating growth was necessary for the implementation of just institutions. Perhaps Rawls's reasoning reflects his conviction that just institutions are necessary to meet people's basic needs, and his willingness to make other priorities of justice subsequent to the prior requirement that basic needs must be met. Rawls was willing to make an exception to the difference principle in the context of intergenerational distributive justice, and he was willing to do so because he believed that intergenerational saving is sometimes necessary for the implementation of just institutions. This constitutes some support for the claim that Rawls really did accept a lexically prior need principle.

5. A Generation-neutral Theory of Justice

In the discussion above, I have considered some of the implications of taking seriously Rawls's passing suggestion that meeting basic needs might be prior to other priorities of justice. The resultant theory of justice can now be stated, specified by three basic principles and a priority rule:

Needs Principle [NP]: The first priority for just institutions is to minimize deprivation with respect to fundamental needs.

Equal Liberty Principle [ELP]: Each person has an equal right to the most extensive total system of equal basic liberties compatible with a similar system for all.

Principle of Tolerable Inequalities [TI]: (two parts)

Open Offices Principle [OOP]: Social and economic inequalities are to be attached to offices and positions open to all under conditions of fair equality of opportunity.

Difference Principle [DP]: Social and economic inequalities are to be arranged so that they are both to the greatest benefit of the least advantaged, regardless of the generation in which the least advantaged exist.

Priority Rule: The needs principle, suitably constrained, is prior to the equal liberty principle, which is in turn prior to the principle of tolerable inequalities. The open offices principle is prior to the difference principle.[23]

---

[23] See Rawls (1971), Ch 2, Section 11, pp. 60–5. Casal (2007) offers powerful arguments against narrowly sufficientarian theories of justice that do not incorporate additional distributive requirements. But if I understand her arguments properly, they do not constitute an objection to a view such as this one, which gives special *priority* to sufficiency, but which includes further requirements as well.

The changes between this view and the standard or 'official' version of the Rawlsian view include the addition of a negative welfarist needs principle, and the removal of the generational restriction on the difference principle.

Although I have given a generation-neutral interpretation of the difference principle, I have otherwise left its structure intact. Still, I would like to mention three reservations about that principle both in the generation-neutral form given above, and as it exists in Rawls's own works. First, as mentioned in section 2 above, the addition of a needs principle calls into question Rawls's claim that the original position choice meets the conditions for the rationality of maximin reasoning. The addition of this principle diminishes the 'downside risk' associated with the choice of alternate principles, undermining what many have taken to be Rawls's primary argument for the difference principle. Second, one might reasonably urge that the importance of inequality will diminish as the worst-off members become increasingly better off, and that a more satisfactory principle would recognize and accommodate this inverse relation. In particular, the importance of inequality will be quite different when the worst-off members are *well* off than when they are *badly* off, and may even diminish to insignificance within communities where everyone is extravagantly well off. If so, then the principle governing tolerable inequalities should be variable, sensitive to the absolute position of those who are worst off. But third and finally, there are reasons why inequalities among contemporaries may be problematic for reasons that simply will not apply intergenerationally. For example, material inequalities among contemporaries can often undermine democratic equality, since those who have more may be able to use their resources unfairly to influence the democratic process. But it is not at all clear that material inequalities between generations will undermine democratic equality. While I am not able to articulate a succinct principle that accommodates these complex considerations, it seems quite clear that Rawls's difference principle is not able to take them into account.[24]

One further reservation should be mentioned, concerning the problem of conflict among principles. Rawls himself is very quick to resolve such conflicts by assigning lexical priority rules. I follow Rawls here, in giving principles their role in a lexically ordered hierarchy. But there are alternatives to lexical priority that should be considered: we might instead assign principles varying weight, or define a function that would assign different proportional weight to different principles depending on context. There are reasons why priority rules, or some comparably simple arrangement, might be especially appropriate

---

[24] But see Casal (2007) for powerful arguments against the view that distributive justice may be restricted to considerations of sufficiency or needs provision.

in the context of institutional justice, even if ideal principles would be more complicated and sensitive to the circumstances in which they are applied: these principles are intended to define the structure of society's basic institutions. But where such principles are very complex, the institutions whose structure they define may themselves be more complex and less transparent. Since it is important not only that public institutions conform to the relevant conception of justice, but that these institutions must be seen and known to conform to the requirements of justice, it is crucial that institutions be as transparent as possible.

For the balance of my discussion here, I will set aside these reservations for two practical reasons: The difference principle will not play a central role in the discussion that follows, so it is not necessary to adjust that principle here. Further, there are a number of other independent arguments that may be used to motivate and justify the difference principle. Some of them provide strong alternative grounds for the difference principle, and they must be taken into account in any attempt to develop an alternative principle to govern tolerable inequalities.

Ironing out the kinks in a theory of value?

Sufficientarian theories of justice have other features that will be regarded as counterintuitive to some people: they imply a value theory that has 'kinks' instead of being continuous. An example makes this clear. Suppose Alph is just below the threshold at which his needs would be met, while there are millions of people who are just at the threshold. We can either help Alph by improving his situation marginally so that his needs will be met (just barely!), or we could benefit the millions of other people tremendously. Sufficientarianism implies that we should forego the tremendous benefits we might provide for the many, and that we should instead bring Alph to the threshold. In this respect, sufficientarianism is still subject to a version of the 'black hole' objection discussed above.[25] This is indeed an implication of the view I have been describing here, and of its near relatives.

Those who find the objection compelling might soften the priority rules that provide guidance when principles conflict. Lexical priority rules imply strict trade-offs with sharply kinked indifference curves, but a similar alternative might soften the kinks to permit some marginal tradeoffs. On the other hand,

---

[25] I am grateful to Lukas Meyer for pressing me with this important objection. For further discussion, see Vallentyne (2000), Arneson (2000), Crisp (2003), and Roemer (2004). Roemer usefully distinguishes alternative principles, including one like the sufficientarian principle recommended here, and discusses their formal implications. The sufficiency principle discussed above is closer to Roemer's 'universal decency' principle (p. 274) than to his 'sufficientarian axiom' (p. 278).

the argument for the priority of NP over ELP is strong, since the value of the liberties protected by ELP depends on prior satisfaction of NP. Where a theory of justice incorporates plural values, and where the importance of some values essentially depends on the satisfaction of others, we should expect the resultant theory to have kinks. It may be less surprising to find such kinks in a theory of justice, which must be complex and must be part of an overlapping consensus among many (permissible) conceptions of the good. Those who reject a 'kinky' conception of the good might still be able to accept a sufficientarian priority rule as a component of the theory of justice.

Needs sufficientarianism, intergenerational justice, and sustainability

The articulation of a needs principle with lexical priority over the other principles of justice has especially important implications for Rawls's discussion of intergenerational justice. In particular, such a principle implies a strict limit on the kinds of intergenerational trade-offs justice will permit when the interests of present and future persons are in conflict. If needs have priority over other human interests, then it must be impermissible to promote the less basic interests of some at the expense of the needs of others. A generation-neutral needs principle would prohibit such trade-offs between generations as well as among contemporaries. Thus it will be impermissible to promote the less basic interests of members of the present generation if this would compromise the needs of future generations. This is a natural way to apply the needs principle to the intergenerational case, and would commit Rawls to the view that institutions must be intergenerationally sustainable in what has become a standard sense: while we should strive to meet the needs of the present generation, we should do so in a way that does not compromise the ability of future generations to meet their needs. This conception of sustainability is usually associated with the so-called Brundtland Report, issued by the World Commission on Economic Development in 1987, and has become a centrepiece in the literature on institutional sustainability and economic development.[26] On the interpretation I have developed here, the Brundtland Report's conception of sustainability is simply a special case of a more general first principle of justice. As I will urge, this special case has important practical implications in the context of policies designed to mitigate greenhouse gas (GHG) emissions and to address the problem of global climate change.

---

[26] World Commission on Economic Development (1987), p. 43.

6. Climate Change and Climate Politics

Global environmental change and climate policy

The problem of global environmental change, and climate change in particular, is an obvious context for the application of a theory of intergenerational justice. Our present actions will influence the lives of future generations for good or for ill, and we need to decide whether we are prepared, or obliged to bear burdens or endure costs for their sake. A sufficientarian account of intergenerational justice has important implications concerning climate change and climate policy. In particular, the sufficientarian theory sketched here will prohibit us from satisfying our own relatively trivial needs at cost to future people's ability to satisfy basic needs. Rawls's two-stage account of saving and sustainability also has a direct corollary in the context of climate policies designed to reduce or mitigate greenhouse gas emissions. But the application of Rawls's theory to the problem of climate change will make it clear that the theory is limited and that it incorporates several important but unjustified assumptions. The theory will need to be expanded and generalized before it can be used to choose among alternative policies we might adopt.

Intergenerational cosmopolitanism

One limitation of Rawls's theory must be briefly addressed from the start: Rawls's theory was designed to apply within a nation, but the problems of climate and environmental change are global and international. No single nation can unilaterally regulate global GHG emissions. Still, we need standards to judge and select among alternative policies and international treaties the world community might adopt. Rawls's account of international justice in the *Law of Peoples* (1994) offers little help in this regard, since in that work Rawls is primarily concerned to show limitations on the theory of justice as it might be used to regulate international relations among reasonably just regimes. Rawls's work on the law of peoples offers no resources at all for evaluating international treaties or policies—but among policy choices that will influence the lives of future generations, many of the most important involve international agreements. Clearly we need to be able to apply an account of intergenerational justice more broadly, for guidance in the practical realm of policy choice.

In my discussion here, I will simply assume that it makes sense to ask whether international agreements and global policies may be unjust because of their likely effects on the lives of members of distant future generations. I employ considerations of justice in the evaluation of policies and international agreements designed to address the problem of climate and global environmental change. This is, I believe, a plausible but risky extension for a theory of liberal justice. It is plausible because so many of the same terms and political values that we use to evaluate domestic policies can be used to judge international agreements, and because many of the arguments we might use in defense of a theory of domestic justice seem quite general and unrestricted in their implications. In both domestic and international contexts we may reasonably consider whether policies are exploitative, whether they disproportionately distribute benefits to the wealthy and powerful at the expense of the poor and weak, whether they effectively protect rights and liberties, and whether they appropriately respond to people's basic needs. These are paradigmatically considerations of justice. We can also consider whether our international policies or treaties unjustifiably sacrifice the fundamental needs of future generations for the sake of less central interests or mere 'wants' of present generations. As I have urged above, this is a central concern for a theory of intergenerational justice.

But applying norms of justice internationally is risky. In international and intercultural judgments, people often mistake their own parochial norms for universal standards. The risk of arrogant ethnocentrism should be a conscious consideration whenever we consider the international application of evaluative norms. But if the values employed in the account of justice under consideration are not narrowly parochial in the relevant sense, then it seems quite appropriate for an account of justice to apply internationally. I hope, though I do not take for granted, that this risk of ethnocentric application of parochial norms will not present a problem in my discussion here.

GHG emission reduction as a saving problem

The most obvious way to mitigate the effects of climate change would be to implement policies that reduce the rate of GHG emissions. This might be done via a tax on emissions, or by determining in advance the acceptable rate of total global emissions and distributing them (cap and trade) or by auctioning them off on an open market. The Kyoto agreement was specifically designed to limit GHG emissions through a 'cap and trade' system.[27] The

---

[27] While this was the main intent of the Kyoto agreement, there are many good reasons to doubt that the agreement accomplished its aim. The emission allowances granted by Kyoto were, in some cases, unreasonably generous, permitting some nations (Russia, for example) far more than they need. And the 'flexibility mechanisms' included in the Kyoto agreement may actually increase GHG emissions, by promoting the export of carbon-intensive technologies to developing countries. For reasons I cannot explain here, I would argue that there are good reasons to prefer an open auction over a cap-and-trade system.

idea behind such a policy is simple. There is a more or less fixed rate at which the global environment can digest and eliminate such emissions. If net global emissions are greater than this level, then our activities are *degrading* the resource by making the problem of global warming worse. In the long run, it is extremely risky to degrade a global resource on which we depend, and long-term degradation of environmental systems necessary for human welfare implies correlate degradation of human welfare.[28]

If global emissions could be reduced so that they were no greater than the level at which the atmosphere and global environment can process and rid itself of them, then our activities would be *sustainable* in an important sense: they could then be continued over time without exacerbating the problem. In the long run, reducing emissions to this state would result in our passing on to later generations a climate resource that would be in no worse shape than it is presently. But we are already in trouble. The earth's atmosphere has already been exploited at an unsustainable rate by the present and immediately past human generations. In order to avoid progressive degradation and to avert the risk of future harm and misery, it would now be necessary to reduce GHG below the sustainable level until the atmosphere can recover from the assaults that it has already suffered. Many GHGs like CO_2 have a long life in the earth's atmosphere, so this recovery period may be centuries long. While existing climate agreements like the Kyoto Protocol aim to mitigate the effects of global warming by reducing the level of GHG emissions, it is unlikely that the emission reductions they propose are near the sustainable emissions level, let alone a level that would allow the atmosphere to recover from existing emissions.[29] In this sense, we should understand existing policies as pursuing the aim to reduce the rate at which we are presently imposing harms and costs on future generations, not as an effort to provide benefits. Since existing international agreements are not sufficient to protect future generations from serious harm, and since many existing emissions are unnecessary for satisfaction of present needs, justice requires much stricter limitations.

Global climate change and human interests

Our failure to implement an appropriate climate policy places the basic interests of future generations in serious peril. Global climate change and consequent changes in ecosystems around the world have put at risk the environmental

[28] The fact that climate policy can be modelled in this way shows that the problem of emission reduction is closely related to the problem of just saving discussed in Arrow (1973), Solow (1974), Dasgupta (1974a, b), Gosseries (2001), and Wolf (forthcoming).

[29] Gardiner (2004) includes a sober assessment of the Kyoto Protocol and argues that it is unlikely to have any significant effect at all on greenhouse emissions.

systems on which people depend for life and well-being. In environmentally sensitive parts of the world, people are already experiencing serious hardships because the rate of global warming has been so unexpectedly swift. Risks associated with climate change include consequent loss of biodiversity, a dramatically increased risk of violent weather events, and increased incidence of drought and famine in many parts of the world. Many of the most serious of these risks fall on poor people in the global 'South', but no one is immune. Since climate and global environmental change implicate the needs of future generations, and the prospect that they may live in reasonably favorable circumstances under just institutions, climate policy should be a paradigmatic context for the application of a theory of intergenerational justice.

Climate sustainability: a two-stage strategy

In order to recover a sustainable relationship between human communities and the earth's atmosphere, it would be necessary to implement a long-term plan for the reduction of GHG emissions. The simplest such plan would involve a two-stage strategy similar to the two-stage saving program described by Rawls. During the first stage, the 'austerity' stage, we would need to respond to the fact that past and immediately present anthropogenic GHG emissions have been unsustainable, and would need to adopt policies to reduce emissions so that the atmosphere could recover to a relatively stable 'equilibrium'.[30] This would involve net emissions reduction below the rate that would otherwise have been sustainable, if historical atmospheric emissions had not taken place. The austerity stage could end once the atmosphere and climate ceased to degrade as a result of past emissions. At that point, we could enter a second stage, the 'sustainable' stage, at which point emissions could resume at a sustainable level—that is, emissions would be capped at a level consistent with maintenance of stable levels of atmospheric GHGs over time.

Within the first stage, emission reductions might be eased gradually. There is concern that mandated emission caps could impose a shock to the global economy, and that an inappropriately designed policy might impose more

[30] The description given here is a simplification in several important respects. In particular, the description of climate stability as an ecological 'equilibrium' may trade on an excessively simple account of climate and atmosphere as an environmental system. There is a clear sense in which environmental systems are not naturally in equilibrium in the long run, and some regard the notion of an ecological equilibrium as a discredited scientific paradigm. (See Tarlock (1994).) A more accurate and economically viable model of climate sustainability may be somewhat more complex than the two-stage strategy described here, but will have many of the same properties. For the present purposes, I will adopt simplifying assumptions and will regard the atmosphere's ability to absorb emissions as described above: a system that would need time to recover before the earth's human population could achieve a sustainable relationship with the atmosphere.

hardship than it would eventually prevent. Thus a policy to reduce emissions might begin more modestly, by reducing the rate at which present emissions are *increasing* over time. Then further restrictions might be gradually implemented, balancing the risk to the economy against the prospective benefits to be achieved by reducing emissions. We may hope that there is a feasible development path along which emissions can be reduced swiftly enough to move toward a dynamic environmental equilibrium, but along which emission restrictions are not so sudden or so severe that they cause serious economic hardship in the short term. It cannot be assumed *a priori* that there is a possible development path that meets these competing requirements.[31]

Turning a moving freighter

In spite of the obvious similarity between the two-stage strategy described above and Rawls's two-stage model for saving and development, there is also an important difference: climate change is already underway, and the processes involved have a momentum of their own. A number of different physical processes lie behind this momentum: Global warming is expected to cause an enormous increase in the release of methane, a powerful greenhouse gas, as northern permafrost melts. Reduced ice cover in polar seas reduces their reflectivity and increases the rate at which they collect and preserve the heat of the sun, which in turn increases the rate at which ice floes melt. As a result of these and related processes, events caused by global warming are expected to increase the rate of global warming. Because these processes are already well underway, even the most aggressive present efforts to implement an appropriate climate policy cannot be expected to reverse the current trend for many years. Like the pilot of a barge or freighter, we can turn the wheel now by implementing policies to reduce GHG reduction, but there will be a significant lag time before these policies have any perceivable effect on the system. Our present efforts to turn back the process of damaging environmental change may reduce the rate of destruction, but even on the most optimistic projections it will be decades or even centuries before the global climate and the environmental systems of the earth will begin to recover.

---

[31] I would like to thank an anonymous reviewer who made this suggestion. This reviewer writes 'Stabilizing greenhouse gas concentrations at (say) twice the pre-industrial norm would require carbon dioxide emissions reductions of 60–80%. Achieving this goal, however, is consistent with a time path in which emissions rise slightly in the short-term (10–20 years) with continuing reductions in the more distant future. The idea is to phase in policies over time to avoid imposing a sharp shock on the economy.' As noted, we may hope that such a policy is feasible, but it cannot be assumed. Another reviewer, Axel Gosseries, has similarly suggested that one might consider a one-stage approach with decreasing levels of investment toward the achievement of sustainability.

Rawls's account of intergenerational saving is not designed for a world where things are getting worse as a result of a process with its own momentum. But like other plausible liberal theories of justice between generations, Rawls's view will not permit the present generation to compromise the needs of later generations merely to satisfy present adventitious needs. Present investment to mitigate climate change does not aim to make later generations better off than earlier ones. Instead, it aims to protect later generations from risks that might make them much *worse* off than earlier ones. Climate policy is a present investment to protect future generations from serious harms including those suffered when people are unable to meet their basic needs.

7. Conclusion: Climate Policy and Priorities of Intergenerational Justice

Since protection from harm is a matter of basic need, and since significant climate mitigation can be accomplished without compromising the needs of present persons, climate policy is an urgent priority of justice. Unless our efforts to mitigate the effects of climate change will cause more misery and deprivation than they will relieve, we have an obligation of justice to undertake them. Considerations of justice cannot by themselves tell us which practical alternative will best satisfy the needs principle. But where our present activities are not necessary for satisfaction of present fundamental needs, and put at risk the basic needs of future generations, then they are unjust. The first priority for a just climate agreement should be to prevent activities that involve this kind of regressive trade-off between present and future persons.

References

ARNESON, R. (2000), 'Perfectionism and Politics', *Ethics*, 111: 37–63.

ARROW, K. (1973), 'Rawls' Principle of Just Savings', *Swedish Journal of Economics*, 75: 232–35.

——(1999), 'Discounting, Morality, and Gaming', in Portney and Wyeant (eds.), 13–21.

BAER, P. (2002), 'Equity, Greenhouse Gas Emissions, and Global Common Resources', in S. H. Schneider, A. Rosencranz, and J. Niles (eds.), *Climate Change Policy* (Washington DC: Island Press).

BRAYBROOKE, D. (1987), *Meeting Needs* (Princeton: Princeton University Press).

BROOME, J. (1992), *Counting the Cost of Global Warming* (Cambridge: White Horse Press).

CASAL, P. (2007), 'Why Sufficiency is Not Enough', *Ethics*, 117: 296–326.

CRISP, R. (2003), 'Equality, Priority, and Compassion', *Ethics*, 113: 745–63.

DASGUPTA, P. (1994), 'Savings and Fertility: Ethical Issues', *Philosophy and Public Affairs*, 23: 99–127.

——(1974a), 'On Some Alternative Criteria for Justice Between Generations', *Journal of Public Economics* 3: 405–23.

——(1974b), 'On Some Problems Arising from Professor Rawls' Conception of Distributive Justice', *Theory and Decision*, 4: 325–44.

GARDINER, S. (2004), 'Ethics and Global Climate Change', *Ethics*, 114: 555–600.

GOSSERIES, A. (2001), 'What do We Owe the Next Generation(s)?' *Loyola of Los Angeles Law Review*, 35: 293–355.

——(2005), 'The Egalitarian Case Against Brundtland's Sustainability', *Gaia- Ecologicla Perspectives for Science and Society*, 13/5: 300–5.

——(2007), 'Cosmopolitan Luck Egalitarianism and the Greenhouse Effect' *Canadian J. of Phil.*, Suppl. Vol. 31: 279–309.

HARROD, R. (1948), *Towards a Dynamic Economy*, (London: MacMillan).

INTERGOVERNMENTAL PANEL ON CLIMATE CHANGE (IPCC), *Climate Change 2001: Impacts, Adaptation, and Vulnerability* (Cambridge: Cambridge University Press, 2001).

——*Climate Change 2007: Climate Change Impacts, Adaptation, and Vulnerability* (2007), available at <http://www.ipcc.ch/ipccreports/ar4-wg2.htm> (accessed October 2008).

LIND, R. (ed.) (1982a), *Discounting for Time and Risk in Energy Policy* (Baltimore MD: Resources for the Future.

——(1982b) 'A Primer on the Major Issues Relating to the Discount Rate for Evaluating National Energy Options', in Lind (1982a), 21–94.

MASLIN, M. (2004), *Global Warming*. (New York: Oxford University Press).

MEYER, L. (2003), 'Intergenerational Justice', in Edward N. Zalta (ed.), *The Stanford Encyclopedia of Philosophy*, available at <http://plato.stanford.edu/archives/sum2003/entries/justice-intergenerational/> (accessed June 2007).

MILLENIUM ECOSYSTEM ASSESSMENT (2005a), *Ecosystems and Human Well Being*. (Washington DC: Island Press,).

——(2005b), *Living Beyond our Means: Natural Resources and Human Well-Being* (United Nations Environment Program).

NORTON, B. (2003), *Searching for Sustainability*, (New York: Cambridge University Press).

——(2005), *Sustainability: A Philosophy of Adaptive Management* (Chicago: University of Chicago Press).

NOZICK, R. (1974), *Anarchy, State, and Utopia* (New York: Basic Books).

NUSSBAUM, M. (2000), *Women and Human Development* (New York: Cambridge University Press).

PARFIT, D. (1982), *Reasons and Persons*, (Oxford: Clarendon Press).

PORTNEY, P., and WEYANT, J. (1999), *Discounting and Intergenerational Equity* (Washington DC: Resources for the Future).

RAMSEY, F. (1928), 'A Mathematical Theory of Savings', *Economic Journal*, 38: 543–59.

RAWLS, J. (1971), *A Theory of Justice*, (Cambridge: Harvard University Press).

——(1993), *Political Liberalism*, (New York: Columbia University Press).

——(1999a), *A Theory of Justice*, revised edition (Cambridge: Harvard University Press).

——(1999b), *The Law of Peoples* (Cambridge: Harvard University Press).

——(2001), *Justice as Fairness* (Cambridge: Harvard University Press).

ROEMER, J. (2004), 'Eclectic Distributional Ethics', *Politics, Philosophy, and Economics*, 3:267–81.

SEN, A. (1982), 'Approaches to the Choice of Discount Rates for Social Benefit-Cost Analysis', in R. Lind (ed.) (1982), *Discounting for Time and Risk in Energy Policy* (Baltimore MD: Resources for the Future), 325–53.

——(1994), 'Population: Delusion and Reality', *New York Review of Books* 41(15): 62–71.

SHUE, H. (1993), 'Subsistence Emissions and Luxury Emissions', *Law and Policy*, 15/1: 39–59.

——(1999), 'Bequeathing Hazards: Security Rights and Property Rights of Future Humans', in M. Dore and T. Mount (eds.), *Global Environmental Economics: Equity and the Limits of Markets*, (Oxford: Blackwell Publishers).

——(2001), 'Climate,', in D. Jamieson (ed.), *Blackwell Companion to Environmental Philosophy* (Cambridge: Blackwell Publishers), 449–59.

SINNOT-ARMSTRONG, W., and HOWARTH, R. (2005), *Perspectives on Climate Change: Science, Economics, Politics, Ethics* (New York: Elsevier).

SOLOW, R. (1974), 'Intergenerational Equity and Exhaustible Resources', *Review of Economic Studies,* Symposium Issue, 29–45.

TARLOCK, A. D. (1994), 'The Non-Equilibrium Paradigm in Ecology and the Partial Unraveling of Environmental Law', *Loyola of Los Angeles Law Review*, 27: 1121–44.

TRAXLER, M. (2002), 'Fair Chore Division for Climate Change', *Social Theory and Practice*, 28: 101–34.

VALLENTYNE, P. (2000), 'Equality, Efficiency, and the Priority of the Worse-Off', *Economics and Philosophy*, 16: 1–19.

WALL, S. (2002), 'Just Savings and the Difference Principle', *Philosophical Studies*, 116: 79–102.

WOLF, C. (1995) 'Contemporary Property Rights, Lockean Provisos, and the Interests of Future Generations.' *Ethics*, vol 105 no. 4: 791–818.

——(1996), 'Markets, Justice, and the Interests of Future Generations', *Ethics and the Environment*, 1/2: 153–75.

——(1997), 'Person-Affecting Utilitarianism and Population or, Sissy Jupe's Theory of Social Choice', in J. Heller and N. Fotion (eds.), *Contingent Future Persons* (Dordrecht: Kluwer), 99–122.

WOLF, C. (1998), 'Theories of Justice: Human Needs', in P. Singer, R. Chadwick, and D. Callahan (eds.), *Encyclopedia of Applied Ethics, Vol. 4* (Burlington MA: Academic Press), 335–45.

——(1999), 'Health Care Access, Population Ageing, and Intergenerational Justice', in H. Lesser (ed.), *Ageing, Autonomy, and Resources* (New York: Ashgate Publishers), 212–45.

——(2000), 'The Moral Commitments of Political Liberalism', in V. Davion and C. Wolf (eds.) *The Idea of a Political Liberalism* (New York: Rowman and Littlefield), 102–26.

——(2003), 'Intergenerational Justice', in C. Wellman and R. Frey (eds.), *Blackwell Companion to Applied Ethics* (Cambridge: Blackwell Publishers).

——(2004), 'O Repugnance, Where is thy Sting?', in H. Ryberg and T. Tannsjo (eds.), *The Repugnant Conclusion: Essays on Population Ethics* (Dordrecht: Kluwer), 61–80.

——(forthcoming), 'Intergenerational Justice and Saving', in J. Lamont, G. Gaus, and K. Favor, (eds.), *Values, Justice, and Economics* (Amsterdam: Rodopoi).

WORLD COMMISSION ON ENVIRONMENT AND DEVELOPMENT (WCED) (1987), *Our Common Future* (New York: Oxford University Press).

14

The Problem of a Perpetual Constitution

VÍCTOR M. MUÑIZ-FRATICELLI

Is it unjust to future generations for those presently living to adopt a constitution that binds both present and future members of a political society? I shall refer to this question as the *problem of a perpetual constitution*. Put more formally, are there good reasons to think that fundamental laws have normative authority extending beyond the generation responsible for their enactment or, to the contrary, is this presumption of perpetuity an unjust curtailment of the liberty of future persons to choose their own political arrangements?

Let us think of a *perpetual constitution* as one which aims to settle the political structure of a society and secure the rights of its citizens, not for a fixed and finite period of time, or subject to regular and periodic reconsideration in conventions or referenda, but rather indefinitely.[1] A perpetual constitution has no 'sunset clause', no date of expiration; it may contemplate for its amendment and even specify a procedure for its modification, but it does not consider its own abolition. When adopted, it is intended to govern a society for as long as that society exists, and to be accepted by the present and future members of that society as a valid charter of political association.[2] Moreover,

Thanks to Loren Goldman, Mara Marin, Lukas Meyer, Emily Nacol, Deva Woodly, the participants in the University of Chicago Political Theory Workshop, and three anonymous reviewers for comments on previous drafts. A special debt of gratitude is due to Axel Gosseries, who commented extensively on every version. A fellowship from the Institute for Humane Studies helped support my research. My first thoughts on this subject came about in a seminar with the late Iris Marion Young; we had several conversations—and many disagreements—about the content of this chapter, and I miss her kind encouragement and sharp critique.

[1] The term 'perpetual constitution' I take from Thomas Jefferson, although he intends it as a mark of disapproval (Jefferson 1975: 449).

[2] Whether a constitution can bind future generations is both a normative question and a question of fact. As a question of fact, people in any generation may disregard the laws passed by their predecessors or replace them with new ones; no legislative act can prevent a people determined to cast off their

as a *constitution*, it is distinguished from ordinary legislation by its rigidity and subject matter.[3] As a rule, the norms of a constitution are difficult to change, either because the process of amendment is expressly designed to be especially onerous, or because the political culture of a society regards certain norms as fundamental—'sacred' even—and would rebuff attempts at their repeal or substantial revision.[4] In this regard, constitutions are different from ordinary laws, which can usually be rescinded or modified by subsequent legislatures. Constitutions are usually different from ordinary laws also in that they proclaim the defining features of the state (such as its name, type of regime, founding principles and national symbols), determine the structure of government and regulate the manner in which ordinary laws are made, and recognize the rights and liberties of the citizenry. In a *perpetual* constitution, the norms governing these matters are assumed to be valid and binding without needing to be reenacted or ratified periodically with the appearance of each new generation.[5]

Now, perpetual constitutions are common features of our political culture; most, if not all, of the world's current constitutions are of this sort. Moreover, the members of most democratic societies do not seem to perceive the inherited

---

form of government from doing so. The issue here, however, is whether later generations should feel normatively bound to the constitution passed by their predecessors, i.e. whether they have a (*prima facie*) political obligation to abide by that constitution. This obligation involves, at least, the presumptions that the existing constitution is valid and applicable to the present generation, that it is wrong for a member of the political community to violate an existing constitutional provision, and that the constitution should not be overhauled but for normatively weighty reasons.

[3] The meaning and form of 'a constitution' is contested, and I will not bother with definitions here. The complexity of the question is well addressed by Grey (1979).

[4] Common requirements are of a parliamentarian or popular supermajority, concurrent majorities of different houses of the legislature or concurrence of different branches of government or successive votes of the legislature after a general election has intervened. A combination of these is also possible, as in the United States Constitution, which combines a supermajority in each house of the legislature with the concurrence of both houses and the further concurrence of a supermajority of the electorates of the federated states (*Constitution of the United States*, Art. V). Barriers to constitutional change, however, do not need to take an explicit, positive form. Sometimes political conventions or longstanding practices establish a sufficient distinction between ordinary law and constitutional provisions, so that it may be said with some confidence that the repeal of at least some elements of the constitution is highly unlikely. This is arguably the case in the British constitution which, although unwritten, is identifiable through these conventions and traditions (see n 26 below).

[5] As Brian Barry observes, '"[g]enerations" are an abstraction from a continuous process of population replenishment' (Barry 1977: 268) and thus any boundary drawn between one generation and another is, from a general perspective, arbitrary. It may, nonetheless, be informative in a narrower context. Throughout this chapter, I define (in the words of an anonymous reviewer) 'the border between the current and the next generation [as] that which separates those who were of voting age at the time of the constitutional vote from those who were not of voting age then, either because they were less than that age or not yet born.'

origin of their constitutions as a threat to their moral and political legitimacy. For a constitution to be successful—to organize a political society and guarantee the freedom of its citizens and their participation in the process of government, in short, to secure liberal democracy as such—it needs to last through many generations.[6] Yet perpetual constitutions seem to subvert one of the foundational principles of liberal democracy, namely that political legitimacy rests on the consent of the governed and that 'the people' are the source of all political authority. But those born under a perpetual constitution are expected to acquiesce to the foundational norms approved by their predecessors with neither their consent nor their participation. If a constitution is discussed, negotiated, and approved by citizens who are, necessarily, contemporaries, what normatively binding force does it retain for future generations who took no part in its discussion, negotiation, or approval? This is the heart of the quarrel, and the subject of this chapter.

In the first and second parts of this chapter I lay out Thomas Jefferson's and Michael Otsuka's voluntarist arguments against a perpetual constitution. In the third part I reply to Jefferson and develop an instrumental argument in favor of an enduring foundational law. In the fourth part, in response to Otsuka, I examine the merits of the mechanisms of tacit and hypothetical consent in constitutionalism, and defend the use of the latter. In part five, I make a general argument against voluntarism, on the grounds that it does not possess an adequate political ontology. In the sixth part, I discuss the place of interpretation, amendment, and reconstitution in a theory of perpetual constitutionalism. I conclude that a perpetual constitution, rather than subverting the obligations of justice between generations, creates the conditions for the exercise of these obligations by incorporating enduring institutions of popular participation in government, enshrining basic rights owed to all citizens, and prescribing an orderly process of interpretation and revision of the political charter that nonetheless preserves the historical continuity of the body politic through the succession of generations.

---

[6] I will assume throughout that some form of democracy is a cardinal component of political justice. This assumption has an external and an internal implication. Externally, it means that the democratic people is not subject to the political authority of an agent external to the people; that is what is meant by the people being sovereign. Internally, it means that 'all citizens ... have an equal right to take part in, and determine the outcome of constitutional processes that establish the laws with which they are to comply' (Rawls 1999a: 194, quoted in Cohen 2003: 92). Whether and how this demand for democracy may be reconciled with a perpetual constitution in the context of generational succession is the problem at hand.

1. The Earth Belongs to the Living: Thomas Jefferson's Objection to a Perpetual Constitution

Thomas Jefferson's letter to James Madison of 6 September 1789 is the classic articulation of the democratic objection to perpetual laws and constitutions. 'I set out on this ground,' he declares, 'which I suppose to be self evident, "*that the earth belongs in usufruct to the living*": that the dead have neither powers nor rights over it' (Jefferson 1975: 445). Jefferson concludes that the constitution and all the laws should expire automatically when the generation that enacted them is no longer the majority of the population—that is, when the majority of the population is composed of people who were not of voting age when those laws were originally approved.[7] His argument proceeds in three stages: first, he denies that an individual has any authority under natural law to ordain the disposition of his assets after his death; second, he extends that injunction to the whole of society; third, he expands on the injunction to dismiss the legitimacy not only of the *post-mortem* disposition of property, but of all perpetual laws and constitutions.

The claims that an individual has to his property under the natural law, Jefferson argues, cease upon his death, and he can neither profit nor enjoin his survivors to do or refrain from doing anything with the goods he leaves behind. These 'revert to the society,' that is, they revert to their original condition as commonly owned things of which anyone may take private possession in accordance with the laws of nature.[8] Elsewhere, Jefferson states more clearly that, in the state of nature, the only property right that may be privately claimed is mere possession; consequently, once a person dies, possession is necessarily relinquished and with it are extinguished all *natural* claims to property (see, for example, Jefferson 1975: 529). The only valid surviving claims are those instituted by positive law. Jefferson does not deny the validity of wills or of laws in the transmission of inheritance, but he does deny that the power of a man to determine the disposition of his estate after his death, or of his heirs to take possession of it, is founded on natural right. Rather, he says, such transmission is carried out 'by a law of the society of which they are members, and to which they are subject' (Jefferson 1975: 445).

The second stage of Jefferson's argument questions the limits of the societal prerogative to positively legislate the transmission of property and obligations.

---

[7] I will refer to this period of time as a 'generational cycle'.

[8] Jefferson invokes the right of first occupancy to suggest that the family of the deceased will most likely have the strongest claim to his estate, as they are most likely to arrive at it before others (1975: 445).

Society does not have any more rights than its component members: as none of them can legitimately incur a debt the payment of which will fall on his heirs, except as allowed by the positive laws of his society, neither can all of them burden a future generation with the obligations that they collectively acquire. But here Jefferson's distinction between natural and municipal (that is, positive) law is determinative. An individual is subject to municipal legislation, as he is a member of and subject to his society. But generations themselves are not part of a common entity, and there is over them no mutual sovereign that could bind past and future persons to a municipal law. Only the natural law obtains in their mutual relations, and that, Jefferson has already argued, allows no claims to property to survive the death of the owner.

[W]hen a whole generation, that is, the whole society dies, as in the case we have supposed, and another generation or society succeeds, this forms a whole, and there is no superior who can give their territory to a third society, who may have lent money to their predecessors beyond their faculties of paying. (Jefferson 1975: 446)[9]

The third stage of Jefferson's argument moves beyond the objection to trans-generational laws regulating property and inheritance, and applies that injunction to all laws, including constitutions. From his discussion of the intransmissibility of collective debt, Jefferson concludes that each generation is sovereign in its own time, and cannot bind another through the laws that it enacts: 'by the law of nature, one generation is to another as one independent nation to another' (Jefferson 1975: 448). The content of the sovereign will is to be determined by the majority of each generation, uncontrolled by the laws of its predecessors.[10]

---

[9] Jefferson was meticulous in calculating when a generation could be reckoned 'dead': it stood at nineteen years in his day. I will not consider these calculations here. For one, they are outdated, as Michael Otsuka has pointed out (Otsuka 2003: 137). But they also add little to the normative discussion.

[10] A persistent problem, however, is how to interpret Jefferson's majoritarian language. The problem is that by 'majority' Jefferson may mean that the majority of citizens were able to cast a vote on the constitution, or he may mean that the majority of citizens voted affirmatively for it. The first alternative refers to the drawing of the boundary between those who are within and those who are outside the democratic assembly; the second refers to the procedure for determining the assembly's will. This distinction between boundary and decisional concerns was suggested by Axel Gosseries.

The answer is not altogether clear. In an 1816 letter to Samuel Kercheval, Jefferson explains that '[t]his corporeal globe, and everything upon it, belong to its present corporeal inhabitants during their generation. They alone have a right to direct what is the concern of themselves alone, and to declare the law of that direction; and this declaration can only be made by their majority' (1975: 560). On the most plausible construction, Jefferson's concern is that later generations have been totally excluded from the assembly that enacts the constitution. If so, Jefferson limits the assembly to 'present corporeal inhabitants', and sets the point at which the constitution and laws ought to expire at the time when the majority of the population would have been born after the original enactment. At this point, all presently-living persons would be called upon to pass new legislation; the decision procedure at this moment would be majoritarian.

On similar ground it may be proved that no society can make a perpetual constitution, or even a perpetual law ... [The living generations] are masters too of their own persons, and consequently may govern them as they please. But persons and property make the sum of the objects of government. The constitution and the laws of their predecessors extinguished then in their natural course with those who gave them being. This could preserve that being till it ceased to be itself, and no longer ... If it be enforced longer, it is an act of force, and not of right. (Jefferson 1975: 449)

What happens, then, to the laws of a previous generation? Do they lose their force automatically after a specified period, or do they remain presumptively valid until a future generation repeals them?[11] In a sober concession to the difficulties of democratic politics, Jefferson prefers the first alternative. '[T]he power of repeal' he writes, 'is not an equivalent [of the automatic lapse of legislation]' because of the susceptibility of representative assemblies (which Jefferson assumes to be the organs of legislation) to factionalism, bribery, and personal interest (Jefferson 1975: 449–50). Thus, to prevent future generations from having to endure the legislative acts of their departed forebears, all legislation should include a clause mandating its expiration after a period corresponding to the time when the previous generation is no longer a majority of the people.

There are important problems with Jefferson's proposal, most of them prefigured by James Madison in his 4 February 1790 reply to Jefferson's letter (Madison 1986: 70–1). These fall into two categories: those pertaining to the consequences of adopting a system of expiring legislation, and those internal to the theory itself. I will discuss the practical objections at length later in this chapter, as they are the most substantial; here I will only point out an important theoretical difficulty first noted by Madison.

The constitution and laws, for Jefferson, lose their authority at the moment when the enacting generation is no longer the majority of the adult population. But, in the meantime, persons who reach the voting age shortly after a constitutional vote have to wait a full generational cycle before being included in the franchise. How can the constitution bind these 'disenfranchised young' during this time? The problem arises because Jefferson insists on obtaining the express consent of the people to their constitution. But, as Madison also points out, carried to its logical conclusion, this insistence exempts the older members of the new generation from any obligation under the constitution and laws, perhaps for nearly two decades. To resolve this under Jefferson's plan 'either a

---

[11] An alternative way of phrasing the question would be to ask whether new generations must 'opt in' to their forebears' constitution if it is to retain its authority, or whether the new generations remain under the constitution until and unless they decide to 'opt out' by repealing it. I owe this alternative formulation to Axel Gosseries.

unanimous repetition of every law would be necessary on the accession of new members, or an express assent must be obtained from these to the rule by which the voice of the Majority is made the voice of the whole' (Madison 1986: 71).[12] Both alternatives are unattractive, not only because they are impractical but because, in exempting a whole class of citizens from political and legal obligation, they add uncertainty and instability to what (as I will explain later) is an already precarious system.

2. Constitutions and Consent: Michael Otsuka's Objection to a Perpetual Constitution

Michael Otsuka has recently attempted to improve upon Jefferson's case against perpetual constitutionalism. Otsuka believes that the Jeffersonian provision for periodic re-enactment of the constitution and laws would be an improvement on the present condition in which perpetual laws and constitutions are allowed to hold their illegitimate sway over many succeeding generations (Otsuka 2003: 139–41). But periodic re-enactment is not enough. The permanent presence of a class of disenfranchised young compromises the legitimacy of Jefferson's proposal and, as Otsuka rightly indicates, presents a problem to the political voluntarist.

Otsuka defines political voluntarism as the thesis, derived from John Locke, that '[a]n individual is subject to the legitimate political authority of a government if and only if, and by virtue of the fact that, he has given his free, rational, and informed consent to this subjection' (Otsuka 2003: 90).[13] The constitution and laws of a political society, on this account, are binding on the living only because they have actually consented to them; their validity can therefore not be transferred to future generations unless those generations consent to these directives anew. But the disenfranchised young have two decades to wait before being able to express their express consent. The solution to their predicament, Otsuka argues, is also found in Locke, through the mechanism of tacit consent, the assertion that 'every Man, that hath any Possession, or Enjoyment, of any part of the Dominions of any Government, doth thereby give his *tacit Consent*, and is as far forth obliged to Obedience to the Laws of that Government, during such Enjoyment, as anyone under it' (Locke 1988: 348, and §§117–122 of the *Second Treatise* generally; Otsuka

---

[12] Madison's alternative is the mechanism of tacit consent, which is also adopted by Michael Otsuka; I discuss tacit consent more fully in section four, below.

[13] Thomas Jefferson's democratic theory also fits this definition of voluntarism.

2003: 148f).[14] The disenfranchised young, by voluntarily remaining in society, tacitly consent to abide by its rules, at least until the next generational cycle comes around.[15]

Otsuka's understanding of tacit consent, however, is thicker than Locke's. Whereas for Locke mere presence or possession of property in a commonwealth signifies consent to be bound by the laws there in place—and, by extension, the continued presence of a person in a country after reaching maturity is tantamount to submission to the authority of laws passed by her predecessors—, Otsuka argues that tacit consent can be presumed only when an individual both (1) has a realistic and not too onerous opportunity to exit her political society, which implies that she has the resources to exercise her exit rights, and (2) has access to a variety of diverse but equivalent communities in which to settle (Otsuka 2003: 95−105).[16] Such an arrangement guarantees that every person, of whatever generation, who is living in a political society, is considered a to be consenting member of it.[17]

[I]n order to ensure that tacit consent by residence is morally binding some fairly radical steps involving the egalitarian redistribution of worldly resources and the

---

[14] Otsuka credits James Madison for first invoking the mechanism of tacit consent to bridge the gap of consent between generational cycles. In a personal communication, Nathan Tarcov adds that, for Locke, tacit consent binds all persons (even passer-bys) to obey the law, but only express consent makes a person a member of civil society; members, as opposed to passer-bys, have a voice in passing future legislation.

[15] A different way to bridge the gap of consent between generations is the complete-life view of justice between age groups. On this view, 'as long as people receive the same amount of a good over their whole life, justice will be met' (Gosseries 2003: 474). Thus, the fact that some citizens are excluded from the constitutional assembly because of their age is not unjust if they can reasonably expect to take part in such a vote eventually. Over their whole life, they will have had a roughly equal chance to shape their form of government.

It may be argued, however, that the complete-life view does not remove the injustice because people are not, in Jefferson's scheme, treated equally across their whole life; someone lucky enough to come of age immediately before the end of a generational cycle has almost twenty more years of political participation than someone who comes of age immediately after the next cycle begins, although they are, by any reasonable account, at the same stage of life. But a similar complaint would hold against any system of fixed elections: a day's difference in age may result in one person choosing who governs over another for whatever the duration of the electoral mandate. Even so, there is a difference, which should not be ignored, between choosing a government and settling on a constitution, and also between conferring a mandate for a few tears and settling fundamental law for nearly two decades. Other alternatives, beside the complete-life view, exist but they are not advanced by Jefferson, and for reasons of space I cannot discuss them here; Gosseries (2003) gives an overview of them, and discusses their application to political rights generally.

[16] There is an alternative, namely 'the option of withdrawing into a self-governed plot of land to which one would be entitled by the Lockean principle of justice in acquisition' (Otsuka 2003: 103).

[17] The very young (children under the age of eighteen, say) are, of course, unable to exit such a society, having no means of independent support or capacity to acquire or employ such means. But it is not clear that they have a valid complaint of injustice while under their parents' care—if paternalistic reasons ever apply, it is in such a case.

decentralization and pluralizing of political societies must be taken to ensure that such consent is freely given in circumstances of genuine equality. (Otsuka 2003: 149)

Interestingly, the mechanism of tacit consent not only complements, but also supplants the Jeffersonian proposal. The political arrangements that can be justified with respect to the disenfranchised young can be justified in the same way with respect to any person of whatever generation. Perhaps periodic reenactment, Otsuka suggests, would retain the merit of signaling the formal recognition that the laws are the expression of the will of the living, but it would not be necessary for political legitimacy (Otsuka 2003: 146, 150).

We have, then, two challenges to the idea of a perpetual constitution. Jefferson's argument is that a perpetual constitution has no authority over subsequent generations because the latter have not had the opportunity to express their consent to the constitution through a democratic procedure; such an opportunity, offered when the younger generation becomes more numerous than its predecessor, is sufficient to resolve this injustice. Otsuka's argument is that a perpetual constitution has no authority for the same reason that Jefferson explains, but that the younger generations can be presumed to give their tacit consent to their predecessors' laws by continuing to reside in their society; as long as the social conditions necessary to presume tacit consent obtain, it is not even necessary to reenact the constitution at periodic intervals.[18] I do not believe that either of these arguments works. I will discuss my specific objections to each—to Jefferson on instrumental grounds and to Otsuka on the mechanics of consent—and follow with an argument against voluntarism in general grounded on the political ontology of a constitutional people.

3. Against Jefferson's Voluntarism: Constitutionalism as an Enabling Condition

I mentioned above that the most significant objection to a self-expiring constitution, such as that proposed by Jefferson and endorsed by Otsuka, is the practical consequence of its adoption. It is not that such a system 'is very nice

---

[18] Axel Gosseries observes that Jefferson's and Otsuka's arguments correspond, respectively, to Albert Hirschman's alternatives of 'voice'—the expression of dissatisfaction while remaining within an organization—and 'exit'—the abandonment of the organization (Hirschman 2006). For Jefferson, an individual voices her opinion about the laws of a previous generation in each constitutional vote; for Otsuka, this form of expression is not necessarily excluded (e.g. in liberal polities), but is not required of any given polity, provided that individuals may leave it for another.

in theory but … would never work in practice.'[19] Rather, the kinds of social practices engendered by the institution of automatically expiring legislation are objectionable because they overlook legitimate public and private interests of the members of a political society, including their interests in liberty and justice.

A self-expiring constitution raises an overwhelming hurdle to the establishment of a prosperous and stable social system. The hurdle is not insurmountable—both Jefferson and Otsuka allow for the periodic reenactment of laws at every generational cycle—but it is formidable for political, economic, and psychological reasons.[20] For one, many important projects in a political society cannot be completed in the span of a single generation, and therefore demand for their conclusion a legal framework that will remain in place over the span of many years. Often plans are laid out—frequently (though not only) for the benefit of posterity—that necessitate the assumption of long-term obligations. The most obvious example, which Madison brings up, is a debt incurred for the defense of the nation in a time of war, which benefits present and future generations. As Madison notes, '[d]ebts may even be incurred principally for the benefit of posterity' (Madison 1986: 70); to allow default on state debt at the end of a generational cycle would be a powerful deterrent to potential creditors, and make the business of defending the nation all that more difficult. There are many other public projects that would also give greater returns to

[19] Michael Otsuka thus characterizes what he calls a consequentialist objection to Jefferson's proposal (Otsuka 2003: 139). The term 'consequentialist' is somewhat misleading, suggesting perhaps a utilitarian inclination that is not evident in Madison's writing, and is absent from my argument in this chapter. 'Pragmatic' is similarly burdened with philosophical baggage. 'Instrumental' seems the most neutral choice, and I will use it henceforth.

[20] The distinction may be framed as one between *de facto* and *de jure* perpetuity: Jefferson and Otsuka can accept the former, but not the latter; it is the latter, however, that perpetual constitutionalism mandates. (I thank an anonymous reviewer for pointing out this distinction.) Now, even under a *de jure*-perpetual constitution, there are few guarantees that the laws that undergird a just and stable political society will persist as long as the legal (or extra-legal) power to amend or repeal the constitution remains (of which I say more in section six).

Still, two arguments favor *de jure*- over *de facto*-perpetuity: Instrumentally, *de jure*-perpetuity is likely to shape political, economic, and psychological interests in view of continuity, not of renegotiation, and thus to create institutional bulwarks that would make repeal less likely. Whether these bulwarks are themselves acceptable from a moral point of view is debatable, and surely depends in part on the substance of the laws in question. But a general democratic-majoritarian argument is not enough to dismiss such entrenchment because the political, economic, and psychological interests protected by a constitution are often individual interests to be opposed even (or especially) to the majority. Normatively, *de jure*-perpetuity is attractive if there is a moral duty to enter into a certain kind of civil relation with others, such as that established by a common constitution, and also a prohibition on renouncing this relation once it obtains. Kant's version of this argument, in the *Doctrine of Right*, depends on an idealistic conception of freedom (Kant 1996: 408–08 [*Ak.* 6: 255–56]; see also Pippin 2006). But it is surely possible to construct less idealistic or metaphysically-grounded versions of a similar line of reasoning.

the generations that follow than to those who presently labour in them. In barring the assumption of long-term projects—even if they are accompanied by long-term, but manageable, debt—Jefferson precludes general social endeavours that would render, to the very generations that he seeks to protect, benefits that far outweigh the burden that they are asked to assume. This dissuasive effect might be especially pernicious to developing societies, as the United States was at the close of the eighteenth century. Jefferson might be right in condemning the decadence of self-indulgent generations, who would have their descendants pay for their excesses, but this is by no means the general case.

From a rationale focused exclusively on generalized social benefit, the very project of democratic self-government is arguably a greater boon to future citizens than to the founding generation. Stephen Holmes interprets this as the crucial message in Madison's retort to Jefferson. A binding commitment to a constitutional form of government, reinforced by restrictions on the power of amendment, such as concurrent and super-majorities, Holmes explains, should not be conceived as an unwelcome limitation on democratic rule, but rather as the enabling condition that allows both present and future generations to fruitfully engage in self-government. The establishment of a constitution accomplishes this by liberating future generations from the unwieldy burden of renegotiating the conditions of civil association at every generational turn, a course of action that can be paralyzing to a nation. It also secures the conditions of freedom in the present and the future by constraining the power of the majority of the moment to curtail the liberties of its contemporaries (a danger in every generation), and of the generation of today or tomorrow to disenfranchise the ones that will come still later in time.

A preceding generation cannot use legal entrenchment to prevent a succeeding generation from saying: 'No more freedom!' No constitutional arrangement, however well-designed, can protect against a 'violent popular paroxysm.' But this factual incapacity does not imply that predecessors have no right or reason to design institutions with an eye to inhibiting the future destruction of electorally accountable government... To grant power to all future majorities, of course, a constitution must limit the power of any given majority. (Holmes 1995: 162; internal references omitted)

If a generation wishes to change the norms of its political society, moreover, it will be better placed to do so—and to make sure the change is an improvement—if it already has institutions in place to organize its deliberation and direct its energy to a fruitful effort.

Yet sparing future generations of the burden of renegotiation is not the only instrumental rationale that favors a perpetual constitution. Individual endeavours also suffer from automatic expiration. Private projects require investment in time and capital, and no such investment would be made unless there was a reasonable certainty of reaping its reward. Institutions may enhance this reasonable certainty—assuring, for instance, the performance of contracts and securing the rights to property—or undermine it. A system in which the constitution and laws are self-expiring increases uncertainty about the future and undercuts many, if not most, long-term projects.[21] This institutional effect has normative consequences. As Lukas Meyer has suggested, we owe respect to the *future-oriented* practices of past persons, and to the ongoing interest of present and future people to continue these practices.[22] Many practices, Meyer explains, are future-oriented in the sense that the value of the practice depends, at least in part, on the possibility that it will continue to be realized. For some projects, the benefit or continued involvement of future people in the project is constitutive of its value for the past- or presently-living people who undertake them. Some of these strongly future-oriented projects in fact require intergenerational cooperation. It is important for contemporaries to expect that there will be people in the future who will understand, appreciate and continue the project in which they are presently engaged. This requires a certain kind of society, Meyer indicates—one that is *open to the future*. Such a society is valuable both to those presently living, who thereby know that their strongly future-oriented projects will retain their value, and to future persons, who thereby have the option of participating in or benefiting from future-oriented projects undertaken by their predecessors (Meyer 1997: 141–44). 'We are under a general duty' Meyer states, 'not to destroy the conditions of living in a society that is open to the future' (Meyer 1997: 150).

These conditions, I would add, include enduring constitutional arrangements, permanent protections of civil and political rights, as well as legal institutions of property and contract. In their absence, it would be very difficult to sustain projects that can be continued across many years. There would be no possibility of dedicating present property to a certain future use, as is routinely done now by philanthropists and charitable foundations. Dissenters and innovators would be wary of establishing unpopular associations, even if permitted by the current law, or invest their time and effort in building social

---

[21] As explained in the previous note, mere *de facto*-perpetuity is not likely to provide a reasonable degree of certainty. Even if a constitution has been re-enacted once, or many times, the uncertainty of its future ratification will shape interests and expectations with a view towards the short term.

[22] This respect 'is simply an instance of the respect that we generally owe to people's highly valuable activities and the conditions that are constitutive of them, that is, the social practices in which these activities are embedded and on whose existence the possibility of pursuing these activities depends' (Meyer 1997 :148).

movements, for fear that present protections would be allowed to lapse. On a more mundane level, there would be little incentive to make productive improvements on one's property, or even to preserve it in a minimally decent state, if one is not sure of the permanence of the laws that guarantee one's ownership or enable one to transfer it to others. Without perpetual laws there could be no mortgage loans, market investments, or pension benefit plans. Nor would there be an incentive to extend a loan beyond a Jeffersonian generational cycle if the laws that obligate debtors to pay these loans will expire upon the cycle's end.[23]

A fear of anarchy, or of political turmoil well short of anarchy, can also provide a rationale for perpetuity. Indeed, the very anticipation of the end of a cycle is bound to set loose the most intense political passions. Madison predicted that:

Unless such laws should be kept in force by new acts regularly anticipating the end of the term, all the rights depending on positive laws, that is, most of the rights of property would become absolutely defunct; and the most violent struggles be generated between those interested in reviving and those interested in new-modelling the former State of property. (Madison 1986: 70)

Michael Otsuka contests Madison's fear of anarchy. Otsuka recognizes that to recklessly allow the constitution and laws to lapse at the end of each generational cycle may have a destabilizing effect on society. Nonetheless, he trusts that citizens and their representatives will consider this fact and act on the presumption that the constitution should be reenacted, absent very weighty reasons to the contrary. Otsuka also trusts that, as present legislatures are held back from repealing ordinary laws by 'strong informal barriers,' so also citizens of a voluntarist polity would be hesitant to allow the lapse of previous legislation, or to experiment with frequent constitutional change (Otsuka 2003: 140).

This trust, I fear, is misplaced. Citizens and their representatives do not think with one mind or speak with one voice. They have heterogeneous interests, which are often antagonistic and not always noble.[24] The partial or

---

[23] The virtue of a perpetual constitution is partly about predictability, but in some cases perpetuity is also constitutive of certain projects. An endowment to found a university, for instance, must account for a long process of maturation and institutional development, which requires that the resources donated be employed in the intended purpose for an extended period of time. That the production and transmission of knowledge which is the work of a university are an ongoing, never-ending task also tells in favour of perpetuity. Those who found universities do not intend for them to be task-forces to produce a report on the state of the disciplines and disband at the end of a decade.

[24] Otsuka's trust may be attributable to his desire to remain at the level of ideal theory which, by assuming full compliance with public normative principles, avoids the problem of the insincere, reckless,

short-term interests of a citizen whose goals are hindered by the established constitution may oppose the long-term institutional needs of the society at large. Regardless of their reasons or motivations, we should not presume that most citizens would regularly favour lasting institutional effects over more immediate particular benefits.[25] But even if we attribute the best motives to them, we should not be too quick to conclude that substantial disagreements over the shape and course of government will be easily resolved. The ensuing conflict over the political structure of a society and the rights of its citizens will surely be heated, and perhaps explosive—there would simply be too much at stake—injuring private interests and damaging present and future prospects of self-government.

As for the restraint exhibited by present-day legislatures, it is doubtfully the product only of considered prudence, but likely dependent, to a great degree, on the effect of perpetual laws and constitutions. In countries in which constitutional provisions may be changed by ordinary acts of the legislature (as in the UK), restraint is often nurtured by entrenched traditions—the 'prejudices of antiquity', which Madison fears will be eroded if laws are vulnerable to periodic expiration.[26] In the case of most other countries, in

---

or corrupt citizen. But ideal theory does not resolve the problem of constitutional disagreement. Ideal theory implies a body of norms to comply with; if the end of every generational cycle calls those norms into question, compliance with them is meaningless (Otsuka 2003: 40, and also Rawls 1999a: 8).

[25] Assume, for instance, that at the end of a generational cycle some citizens call for the laws mandating the payment of interest on loans to be allowed to lapse. Some may be motivated by a genuine compassion for the plight of the destitute, but others by an irresponsible desire to default on their financial obligations. Regardless on their motivation, however, their successful effort would have the effect of depriving lenders of the compensation that they had legitimately expected to receive and, by creating such a precedent, would make future loans less likely to be expended. The short-term, partial interest of present debtors would undermine a viable, long-term lending system.

[26] The British 'unwritten' constitution is an exception to standard constitutional practice, as it relies more on constitutional conventions than formal constraints of Parliamentary authority. This does not mean that the British constitution does not aspire to *de jure*-perpetuity, only that the legal character of these constraints must go beyond a positivist definition of law, and into natural-law criteria (an argument made by Coke and others, but to which I am less than sympathetic). Even if the British constitution is only *de facto*-perpetual, it is unclear if its longevity explains its stability, or if the causal arrow runs in the other direction. In any case, my argument does not deny the possibility that constitutional conventions could limit Parliamentary fiat enough to make a constitution sufficiently perpetual, but this is not the ideal case.

Moreover, British integration into the European Union has already set some constitutional principles apart from ordinary law (e.g. through the Human Rights Act of 1998), although it is unclear whether the sovereignty of Parliament has been legally constrained (Jenkins 2003: 864f, 922–4). In some quarters, this ambiguity has spurred the call for a full-fledged written constitution, e.g. 'It is longstanding Liberal Democrat policy to enshrine the rights of the British people and the responsibilities of Government in a written constitution against which all new legislation should be measured. The constitution should also set out the powers of Parliament, Ministers, Judges, the Head of State and the national assemblies' (*Policy Briefing* 11, January 2005).

which constitutional provisions are more difficult to change than ordinary laws, the barriers are formal, which has the effect of placing those who would ignore the extraordinary but codified process of amendment to define themselves as unconstitutional actors or as revolutionaries, and thus reduces the force of their appeals. In situations of extreme injustice, this may be undesirable, but in most circumstances it allows political change to occur at a more deliberate and well-considered pace.

It is not too alarmist to warn that expiring constitutions are a recipe for perpetual revolution. Jefferson may not have found this distasteful—he famously recommends a revolution every twenty years, about the length of a generational cycle.[27] But whatever the theoretical advantages of Jefferson's proposal, it is morally irresponsible to purchase them at the cost of national and personal ruin. The very possibility of democratic government, and of preserving the conditions that made public and private justice bearable, seems to rest on having a perpetual constitution.

4. Against Otsuka's Voluntarism: the Bases of Liberal Legitimacy

Whether Otsuka's reconstruction of the voluntarist case against a perpetual constitution succeeds depends on his treatment of the mechanics of consent. But the concept of consent is complicated—consent can be either actual or hypothetical; actual consent can be either express or tacit. Express consent is unequivocal: it is the open and explicit acceptance of an obligation, such that, when given, it leaves nothing to be presumed. This is the sort of consent that Jefferson demands of the people, and it justifies his call for periodic reenactment of the constitution and laws. Yet express consent is notoriously difficult to obtain or to prove in most circumstances, and is thus usually not relied upon as a guide to political obligation. Tacit consent and hypothetical consent are left as the alternatives. Tacit consent is also actually given, but not explicitly; it is deduced from some other action, such as holding property in a municipality, which implies that the proprietor consents to be made subject to its real-estate

---

[27] The statement is from a 1787 letter to William Stephens Smith, in which Jefferson expresses admiration for Shay's Rebellion, an uprising of Massachusetts farmers. The farmers were admittedly burdened by unjust taxes, harsh penalties for defaulting on loans, and intolerable indifference from the state. In response to the horror of the American elites at the uprising, Jefferson exclaimed 'God forbid we should ever be twenty years without such a rebellion.' But he goes further and asks, '[w]hat signify a few lives lost in a century or two? The tree of liberty must be refreshed from time to time with the blood of patriots & tyrants. It is its natural manure' (Jefferson 1905).

laws (see Simmons 2001: 165ff, for a fuller account). Hypothetical consent, by contrast, does not purport to be actually given consent, whether overt or tacit, but is rather the normative supposition that an individual, if reasonable, *ought* to consent to a certain arrangement because of certain morally salient characteristics of the choice situation (see Rawls 1999b: 400−1, especially the accompanying footnotes, and Larmore 2003: 369−71).

Otsuka falls back on tacit consent because he takes as a premise that state authority can only be legitimate if political society is a voluntary association.[28] But when the detail of Otsuka's political society is laid out, it is difficult to justify his reliance on tacit consent, or indeed of any variant of actual consent, to secure legitimacy. Otsuka's political society requires pluralism, equality, and order: First, individuals must 'have a diverse range of choices of political societies which occupy the full range of political, cultural, and urban-to-rural possibilities to which people tend to be attracted'. They must also 'possess the material resources to flourish in any of a range of these societies and to easily relocate from one to another' (Otsuka 2003: 104).[29] If they do not have such plurality available, it becomes more difficult to infer that they have tacitly consented to be bound by the rules of the polity in which they reside. Finally, the relations between these autonomous political societies must be regulated by 'an interpolitical government body' which is non-consensual yet democratic: non-consensual because it is indispensable to prevent 'disorder and chaos'; democratic 'on the grounds that, other things being equal, the more democratic the means, the more closely such a body would approximate one that is based on unanimous consent' (Otsuka 2003: 108 n. 46).

In Locke, the conditions of tacit consent are satisfied so long as the government to be consented to is not tyrannical, and the potential subject has minimal contact with it; but the defining condition for presuming consent is always the action of the subject, however negligible.[30] In Otsuka, consent can be inferred only in a highly specified political, cultural, and economic context; as a practical matter, it is this context and not the abstract appeal to consent that legitimately binds the subject to a political society. Legitimacy obtains not by the actual consent of these future persons, but by the conditions which make the inference of consent possible.

---

[28] In this, his foil is John Rawls, who famously denies this premise (Rawls 2001: 4). I return to Rawls's position later in this chapter.

[29] If none of the available polities satisfy an individual's preferences, she should have the resources necessary to constitute a 'monity', or community of one (Otsuka 2003: 100).

[30] For this reason, Lockean tacit consent has been criticized as too easy to obtain (see Pitkin 1965: 994−7, for the interpretation of Locke, and Simmons 1979: 83−95, for a reply). See also n 14, above.

A recent reply to critics by Otsuka validates this conclusion. He explains why actual consent is required of political societies, but not of the interpolitical governing body that secures the conditions of plurality, equality, and order by arguing that:

[s]omething like an interpolitical governing body must exist in order to ensure the appropriate background circumstances of equality for legitimate political associations to arise by unanimous consent and the means of settling disputes among these societies. ... When such conditions are in place, there would be no compelling justification for the overriding of our right to be governed only with our own consent, as we could no longer point to the impracticality of respecting such a right. But since, in the absence of an interpolitical governing body, we would not have the conditions in place in which the rise of legitimate unanimous consensual governance is feasible, it would be unreasonable to insist that such a governing body arise only by unanimous consent if at all. (Otsuka 2006: 333–4)

Otsuka perceives the conditions secured by the interpolitical governing body as minimal, 'more like a United Nations with teeth than the modern-day state' (Otsuka 2006: 332). But the line is difficult to draw. Empirically, it is not hard to imagine that the demands of plurality, equality, and order may extend the size and competence of the interpolitical governing body until it comes close to those of the modern nation-state. Theoretically, it is not hard to find arguments for the state itself that circumscribe it to a few barebones functions.[31] The mechanics of the case remain the same: whatever is required to obtain the conditions of legitimacy cannot be held hostage to unanimity.

While rhetorically grounded on actual (if tacit) consent, Otsuka's argument in fact mimics the mechanics of hypothetical consent. *If* future generations come of age in a political society that has a sufficient variety of polities, guarantees to each person the resources to settle in her community of preference, and secures order among these polities through a democratic interpolitical government body; *then* we can safely presume that all have consented to the polity in which they eventually settle. This is the voluntarist principle of legitimacy. But for a society to retain its legitimacy for future generations, it must maintain the conditions of pluralism, equality, and order. It is then difficult to understand why Otsuka finds a perpetual constitution objectionable. While it is likely that a suitably diverse plurality of communities will emerge spontaneously as an effect of differences in human preferences, the authority and structure of the interpolitical government body and the redistributive mechanism that will ensure a sufficiency of resources to each individual necessarily depend on something like a constitution, or some similar legal set of norms, that is intended to endure.

---

[31] Nozick's (1977) is, of course, the most famous.

By contrast, a hypothetical (not tacit) account of consent underlies Rawls's 'liberal principle of legitimacy,' which holds that:

our exercise of political power is fully proper only when it is exercised in accordance with a constitution the essentials of which all citizens as free and equal may reasonably be expected to endorse in the light of principles and ideals acceptable to their common human reason. (Rawls 1993: 137)[32]

This liberal principle is preferable to the voluntarist one, in part, because it is more transparent: it does not presume that the legitimacy of a constitution is dependent on the fiction of consent, and avoids the difficulty of determining whether consent has actually been given.[33] Consent, in this context, is a fiction on both moral and factual grounds: morally, because constitutional essentials are required to secure legitimacy (which is a demand of justice) and, as explained above, even the assumption of tacit consent to the laws of a polity can hardly proceed in their absence;[34] factually, because membership in a political society is *not* a matter of actual consent (except rarely, e.g. for naturalized citizens), but rather of birth, socialization, and personal ties.[35]

The liberal principle is also preferable because it intends to secure the conditions of political legitimacy in perpetuity, and thus inter-generationally. A perpetual constitution to which all reasonable persons should agree is a

---

[32] See also the first paragraph of this section, and accompanying references.

[33] Axel Gosseries points out that hypothetical consent shifts the problem from the question of whether consent was *actually* given, to whether it would be *reasonable* for someone to confer it. This is entirely right, and is a problem for Rawlsian liberal. But the problem does not show hypothetical consent in a worse light than Otsuka's tacit alternative, as Otsuka must likewise determine whether the conditions of plurality, equality, and order have been sufficiently met so that tacit consent can be safely presumed.

[34] Rawls's constitutional essentials are not equivalent to Otsuka's conditions for inferring tacit consent, but there are significant similarities in their operation. As constitutional essentials, Rawls mentions basic rights such as liberty of conscience and freedom of association, freedom of movement and free choice of occupation, and 'a social minimum providing for the basic needs of all citizens' (Rawls 1993: 228). Otsuka would allow particular polities to circumscribe liberty of conscience and association, but would allow a rather robust right to exit and a substantial social minimum to facilitate emigration (Otsuka 2003: 116ff, 126–7). Conversely, although Rawls holds that political society should adhere to liberal principles, he does allow significant latitude to illiberal associations within the liberal framework (Rawls 2001: 163–4). See also n 17, above, on the substitution of exit for voice.

[35] Rawls reiterates this at various times. 'No society can, of course, be a scheme of cooperation which men enter voluntarily in a literal sense; each person finds himself placed at birth in some particular position in some particular society, and the nature of this position materially affects his life prospects' (Rawls 1999a: 12); '[a]gain, political society is not, and cannot be, an association. We do not enter it voluntarily. Rather, we simply find ourselves in a particular society at a certain moment of historical time' (2001: 4).

Rawls's position is not that society is not a voluntary association because the conditions of voluntariness have not obtained, but rather that, as a matter of sociological fact, the voluntary paradigm misunderstands what it meant to be in society. The most we can do is to approach the ideal of voluntariness hypothetically, as an exercise in moral justification.

means of securing the minimal conditions of pluralism, equality, and order (or some other suitable set of values) for present and future persons, and of institutionally fixing the principles that would make obligations normatively binding between people succeeding each other in time. Such institutional guarantees are required in order to ensure access to important political values, values that all citizens are owed as a matter of justice. It is difficult to determine which institutions would be acceptable over several decades, even centuries; social conditions will change, and institutions with them. But the general (or at least initial) parameters of a political society may be laid out by considering the institutions that members of every generation could reasonably consent to, that is, institutions that would secure basic rights and liberties for each individual, allow each generation to arrive at collective decisions in an orderly and representative fashion, and prevent one generation from unjustly disadvantaging another.[36] A perpetual constitution, so conceived, would not be an infringement on the political rights of future persons. Present generations would, in fact, have a duty with regards to their successors to establish and sustain a perpetual constitution that secured the conditions of political legitimacy. Within the structure created by a constitution, citizens could then frame their mutual obligations of political justice.

5. Against Voluntarism in General: the Political Ontology of Constitutionalism

In replying to Jefferson and Otsuka, I have offered two arguments in defence of a perpetual constitution: an instrumental argument (against Jefferson) that a perpetual constitution is vital in undertaking valuable public and private endeavours; and a normative argument (against Otsuka) that a perpetual constitution is necessary to maintain the morally obligatory conditions of political legitimacy across generations, conditions that are better discerned through the mechanism of hypothetical consent than that of actual consent.

But a perpetual constitution may also be defended against voluntarism in general through an ontological argument about the nature of political society. If we adopt the voluntarist conception of political society, the idea of constitutional democracy is paradoxical. *Democracy* usually presumes that the people are free and sovereign, and that their will is the ultimate and unassailable authority

---

[36] An example of a principle for preventing such disadvantages is Rawls's principle of just savings (1999a: 120–1, 251–8).

in politics. *Constitutional government*, by contrast, usually presumes that certain rules (indeed, those most foundational to the political community) ought to remain beyond the reach of the sovereign (popular or otherwise). On this account, a constitution does no more than constrain the will of the democratic sovereign. A constitutional democracy is less democratic the more entrenched its constitution becomes, and less constitutional the more democratic it is.[37]

The paradox is only augmented when generational succession is taken into account. Voluntarism, because it has an aggregative conception of political society, must accept a break in the ontological continuity of the democratic sovereign when later generations succeed previous ones and different individuals come to bear political authority. There are two parts to the paradox. The first is a question of priority—is the democratic sovereign prior to the constitution, that is, is the constitution a product of its will and freely altered by that will; or is the democratic sovereign itself constituted by the constitution? The second is a question of identity—does the democratic sovereign retain its identity through time; do 'the people' continue to be, in some normatively relevant sense, the same people through the succession of different generations? I will argue that the democratic sovereign is a creation of the fundamental charter, and that only though the perpetuity of this charter does it retain its identity over the years.

5.1. Historical precedents

The difficulty of justifying the maintenance of constitutional democracy through the succession of generations is not exclusive to the era of popular government, but is a mere extension of older arguments over sovereign authority and temporal continuity that raged through the sixteenth and seventeenth centuries. Two positions emerge from that debate: on one side stands the medieval conception of the sovereign as a juridical, not only natural person, inherently limited by custom, royal charters and natural law, and having an identity that persists through time; on the other stands the emergent absolutist conception of sovereignty as the unencumbered exercise of the sovereign's will, a will that stands above customs and charters, and is only nominally bound by legal constraints or by the actions of its predecessors in office.

Medieval constitutionalism accepts that, in his governing or administrative capacity, a king has no superior, no judge but God to limit his authority; but the normative source of that authority is the law itself. In laying down the conditions by which a monarch gains legitimacy, the law is *constitutive* of

---

[37] For the paradox of constitutional democracy, see Schochet (1979: 12) and Michelman (2005: 5ff).

kingship, both in the sense of creating the office of the monarch and of defining (and thus restricting) its authority. If a king cannot overstep the legal bounds of his authority without undermining his own legitimacy, it is because the source of these limits is the same as the source of his authority: the sovereign is a creature of the law—that is, of the 'ancient constitution'—not the law an act of sovereign will (McIlwain 1947: 74–87; Kantorowicz 1957: 148ff; Black 1992: 152–5). By the same token, the law makes it possible to differentiate between the office of the sovereign (the Crown) and the individual (the King) who occupies it. The King is an ordinary, human, mortal person, but the Crown—the 'body politic'—is artificial, mystical, and immortal.[38] Thus, because of this political capacity, the actions of previous monarchs are binding on the present one. Though the individual monarch be succeeded by a future generation, the identity of the sovereign remains the same, and the actions of earlier tenants of the office—in the granting of charters, or the tolerance of custom, say—can be imputed to later ones.

From the late seventeenth century, the proponents of royal absolutism challenge the medieval account of both the question of priority between the sovereign and the law, and the question of continuity of the sovereign's identity through time. James VI and I foreswears the obligations of custom, the authority of the Common Law, and even the binding force of the promises and charters of his predecessors. The prerogative of the king, he argues, is absolutely free; he is bound to the law only through his good will, but not because the law sets enforceable limits on his authority.[39] While the king takes an oath at his coronation to maintain the constitution of the realm—an oath which James acknowledges as 'the clearest, ciuill, and fundamentall Law, whereby the Kings office is properly defined' (James VI and I 1994: 81)[40]—this oath is not enforceable, as the king is bound neither by the fundamental law nor by the promises of previous monarchs.[41] Thomas Hobbes echoes James's

---

[38] 'It is true,' writes Sir Edward Coke in *Calvin's* case, 'that the King hath two capacities in him: one a natural body, being descended of the blood royal of the Realm; and that this body is the creation of Almighty God, and is subject to death, infirmity, and such like; the other is a politic, body or capacity, so called, because it is framed by the policy of man ... and in this capacity the King is esteemed to be immortal, invisible, not subject to death, infirmity, infancy, nonage, &c.' (Coke 2003: 189; see also Kantorowicz 1957: 302–13, and Berman 2003: 238ff).

[39] Thus the title of James's work: 'The Trew Law of *Free* Monarchies' (James VI and I 1994: 75; italics mine).

[40] In the oath, the king promised 'to maintaine the Religion presently professed within their countrie ... to maintaine all the lowable and good Lawes made by their predecessours ... to maintaine the whole countrey, and euery state therein, in all their ancient Priuiledges and Liberties, as well against all forreine enemies, as among themselues' (James VI and I 1994: 65).

[41] Other absolutist theorists share this opinion: Thomas Hobbes argues that custom does not derive its authority from the passage of time, but rather from 'the will of the sovereign signified by his

conception of sovereignty, as does Robert Filmer. Although Hobbes insists that the sovereign is the agent of the corporate person of the Commonwealth, he refuses to make the sovereign bound to the legal or constitutional acts of his predecessors in office, or to prevalent custom (Hobbes 1994: 174). Even the norms of succession to the office of sovereign are dependent on and alterable by the sovereign's will (Hobbes 1994: 124–7). Filmer's summation is more direct: there were kings before there were laws, he writes; the law originated entirely from the king and did not constitute his office or prescribe the proper extent of his rule (Filmer 1991: 32ff, 57–8).

In the aftermath of the Glorious Revolution of 1688, the locus of sovereignty decisively moves from king to Parliament. But, although the parliamentarians frame their cause in medievalist language, the conception of sovereignty they embrace is decidedly absolutist. The prerogative to be free from the constraints of prior charters and laws, even the Common Law, is in time claimed by Parliament itself.[42] By the end of the seventeenth century, Parliament is 'a body absolute and arbitrary in its sovereignty; the creator and interpreter, not the subject, of law; the superior and master of all other rights and powers within the state' (Bailyn 1992: 201). This is the conception of sovereignty that the American colonists inherit, and in which Thomas Jefferson frames the modern indictment of the perpetual constitution as unjust to future generations (Bailyn 1992: 201).[43]

Jefferson's replaces the figure of the absolutist king with that of the democratic people. His political ontology takes 'the people' to be an aggregate, not an entity; there is no 'society' except in the flesh-and-blood men and women who share contemporaneous existence.[44] The popular sovereign is the product of an actual agreement among particular, presently-living, individuals.

---

silence, (for silence is sometimes an argument of consent)' (Hobbes 1994: 174). Robert Filmer reiterates that there were kings before there were laws; the law originated entirely from the king and did not constitute his office or prescribe the proper sphere of his authority (Filmer 1991: 32ff, 57–8).

[42] The shift to Parliamentary supremacy was not automatic, but a decisive change had occurred in 1689 which resulted in the sovereign being reconstituted as King-in-Parliament, with effective control being on the second part of the formula (Bogdanor 1997: 2–8; but see pp. 9ff for the complications that followed in the eighteenth century).

[43] To be sure, 'ancient constitutionalism' was not absent from American revolutionary discourse. Benjamin Franklin, examined before the British Parliament in 1766, opposed the Stamp Act in the name of '[t]he common rights of Englishmen, as declared by Magna Charta, and the Petition of Right' (House of Commons, 1766: 15), and James Otis appealed to 'the first principles of law and justice, and the great barriers of a free state, and of the British constitution in particular ... [that] no man or body of men, not excepting the parliament, justly, equitably and consistently with their own rights and the constitution, can take away' (Otis, 1764: 52, 55).

[44] An 1813 letter to John Wayles Eppes has Jefferson speak of generations as corporations, but he considers each generation to be a corporation unto itself, which ceases to exist upon the death of its members Jefferson (1905).

When they die, the sovereign dies with them, unless the agreement is expressly renewed by other living individuals. Likewise, Jefferson shares the absolutist notion that law, including constitutional law, is an expression of a prior sovereign will, and not a constitutive condition for that will to exist. Each generation is free in the same manner in which King James thought himself free from the pronouncements of his own royal forebears, and it is absolved of prior obligations like James thought himself absolved from obedience to the Common Law and the duties of Magna Charta.[45]

5.2. A constitutionalist alternative

The central elements of democratic constitutionalism are anticipated in the medieval conception of sovereignty: the political community is a juridical person distinct from the individuals that take part in it, and this juridical person retains its identity through time, even as citizens enter and leave the community through birth, death, and migration. But, in the context of a liberal democracy, the medieval conception has important limitations. For one, it is essentially *descriptive* of the constitutional order, and does not purport to provide a normative justification of the order itself. Secondly, it is fundamentally *static*, and does not allow for a process of participation in shaping one's constitutional government; the possibility of criticizing, discussing, interpreting, and amending the charter—which is essential to democratic self-government—is foreclosed.

A conception of sovereignty that is both constitutionalist and democratic should reflect the political self-understanding of most citizens of present-day liberal democracies. Citizens commonly speak of their country in the past, present, and future tense, as existing and acting before they were born and continuing its agency after their demise. They believe that they conduct their political lives under fundamental legal norms and institutions that are at least presumptively valid, even if they themselves did not expressly enact them, and that there is genuine value in maintaining constitutional continuity over time. Contemporary governments also seem to depend on this self-understanding in order to own and administer public land, enter into international treaties, and take part in legal proceedings.[46] I do not think

---

[45] In a letter to Edmund Randolph, Jefferson states unequivocally of '[t]he law being law because it is the will of the nation' (1975: 481). Later in life, in a letter to Judge Spencer Roane of Virginia, he writes that '[i]t should be remembered, as an axiom of eternal truth in politics, that whatever power in any government is independent, is absolute also ... Independence can be trusted nowhere but with the people in mass. They are inherently independent of all but moral law' (1975: 563).

[46] To give some examples, states regularly own property in the name of the state itself, not as the sum of fractional holdings of each citizen. To say that a certain parcel of land is public property is not

that these beliefs are a product of bad-faith or self-delusion. Rather, they reflect a distinctly constitutionalist conception of popular sovereignty, one in which citizens govern themselves through their ongoing participation in the deliberative procedures of a sovereign body: the constitutional democratic state. That body, however, cannot be reduced to the aggregate of citizens. The act of enacting a constitution, when successful, produces an ontological transformation in the body politic; in effect, it *constitutes* the sovereign.[47] With the adoption of a constitution, an enduring juridical entity comes into existence, one which persists through time and brings the continuous exercise of self-government by past, present, and future persons under a single political identity. It is not reconstituted every time a citizen is born or dies (much like a corporation is not reconstituted every time a stockholder buys or sells stock, or a believer joins or leaves a church) but rather it retains its identity through time.[48]

Jed Rubenfeld gives a compelling account of what is involved in the adoption of such a constitution. He makes the case that the eighteenth-century drafters of written constitutions were committed not only to a constitutional form, but also to a democratic ideal, and synthesized the two in the impulse 'to

equivalent to saying that each citizen is entitled to an equal portion of the land or of its value. The same parcel of land can also remain in public hands for decades, even centuries, even through the succession of many governments, without necessitating a transfer of ownership. An international treaty, likewise, does not bind the citizens individually, but the state as a separate agent. Also, when a state is called as a party in a legal proceeding, it may be asked to perform (or abstain from performing) a certain action, or pay (or collect) a certain sum. To say that the state owes compensation to a citizen, say, is not equivalent to saying that every other citizen owes an equivalent portion of that compensation to the aggrieved party.

[47] The words 'constitution' and 'constitute' both derive from the Latin *constituere*, 'to set up, post, establish, appoint, ordain'. Constitutions were originally imperial or ecclesiastical decrees. The modern sense of '[t]he system or body of fundamental principles according to which a nation, state, or body politic is constituted and governed' enters the English language with the Glorious Revolution, in 1689 (*Oxford English Dictionary*, 2nd edn.).

[48] Contrast this to Lukas Meyer's proposal that presently-living people may attempt to repair the injustices committed by a former generation in the name of the political society common to both, and that they may be morally bound to make such an attempt, because those presently-living people 'understand themselves to be persons committed to support the just claims of those who have been injured and to be persons prepared to contribute to the establishment and maintenance of a just political society' (Meyer 2004: 180). I agree that this is a valid moral obligation. Presently-living people may see themselves bound by the actions of their predecessors and compelled to make reparations for these actions because their membership in a common political community between them and their predecessors is part of their identity. They thus take upon themselves to repair their forebears' unjust actions. But I would claim something stronger. The actions of the former and presently-living generations, if both are part of the same political community, are not the actions of distinct agents, but of the same ongoing agent—the political community itself—which persists through time. The later generation is not making reparations for the injustices of the former, but for its own injustices, that is, for the actions of the political community which is ontologically indistinct in its past and present manifestation.

make a democratic constitution democratically' (Rubenfeld 2001: 166). This mode of constitutionalism he observes especially in the American founding.

> American written constitutionalism holds that a people achieves self-government not by conforming governance to authoritative democratic will at any given time, but by laying down and holding itself to its own democratically authored foundational commitments over time. That was and is the revolutionary meaning of the Constitution's writtenness. (Rubenfeld 2001: 168)

Democratic constitutionalism is the self-government of a people under the terms of a constitution that the people enact upon themselves. But how this enactment should be understood is the interesting question. Rubenfeld makes the provocative claim that a people properly comes into existence as a singular collective entity only through 'the reach of a certain political-legal order' (Rubenfeld 2001: 153).[49] The self that is the product of this order is the subject of self-government. It is a self that is temporarily as well as geographically extended—'a *generation-spanning* political entity'—and is therefore not limited to an assembly of contemporaries (Rubenfeld 2001: 254). Consequently, the work of democratic constitutionalism cannot be undertaken except through time, in the historical experience of self-government in which many generations participate. 'The citizens here and now ought to regard themselves not as the bearer of the sovereign voice of self-government, but as participating in a temporally extended people whose commitments deserve respect regardless of present political will' (Rubenfeld 2001: 176–7).

Another way to understand the emergence of the distinct 'self' of the political community is through a transcendental argument.[50] As sovereignty is more than the mere exercise of force, it must be the case that there exists a norm that recognizes legitimate authority in the sovereign. Sovereignty presupposes such a norm; otherwise it is merely the exercise of power without justification. Now, popular sovereignty is the sovereignty of 'the people'; it is not the imposition of the will of the majority of individuals in a certain territory, but the exercise of sovereignty by the people as a whole, as a collective entity.

---

[49] The collective equivalent of personality, Rubenfeld calls *popularity*, which designates 'the status or condition of being a people' (2001: 145).

[50] In characterizing the argument as transcendental, I follow Eva Schaper's definition. 'I take transcendental arguments in general to be arguments which establish the logical presuppositions of something being the case, and of our being able to say, truly or falsely, that it is the case. They exhibit the necessary presuppositions without which something we say, or want to be able to say, cannot be said at all. Such arguments, therefore, include, but need not be restricted to, arguments eliciting the preconditions of conceptualizing experience in the way in which it is conceptualized by us, i.e. the necessary presuppositions of empirical inquiry as we know it' (Schaper 1972: 101; see also Illies 2003: 46).

Therefore, for popular government to be intelligible there must exist a norm that grants legitimate authority to this collective agent. While it is true that the norm must have an origin, the sovereign people itself cannot be the source of it; before the norm there is no 'people', but only an individual or group of individuals exercising arbitrary power. In conferring legitimacy to 'the people', the legitimating norm and the democratic sovereign come into being at once. The norm that entitles the sovereign to exercise legitimate authority must also constitute it.[51]

Michael Otsuka objects to the appeal to a collective self to justify the continuity of political obligations across generations. He argues, first, that the power of past generations over future ones is not symmetrical, since the laws enacted by past generations bind future ones, but not vice versa; the resulting condition is unjust—'a throwback to the abuses of colonialism' (Otsuka 2003: 142)—and can only be remedied by exempting future generations from the obligations incurred by their forebears. Secondly, he argues that voluntarism provides an account of how political communities may be geographically extended, namely through the agreement of contemporaries; but no such account is available in cases of temporal extension, as present persons cannot obligate future ones to the terms of a collective sovereign self.

Otsuka's concerns are best answered through the integration of the instrumental and hypothetical consent arguments proposed in sections three and four, above, with the ontological claims advanced here. The emphasis on the asymmetry of power between past and future generations gets the benefits of a perpetual constitution wrong. Overwhelmingly, future generations are the beneficiaries, not the victims, of a constitution enacted by their predecessors. A constitution makes possible a multitude of private and public projects that would be unrealizable in its absence; foremost among these is the project of self-government, which requires the juridical creation of a people through a constitutive act. The second claim, on the impossibility of justifying the

---

[51] This argument gives rise to an admittedly unorthodox interpretation of the constitutional identity of a people. The people of the United States of America, I would argue, did not exist *as such* until the constitutional document containing the words 'We the People of the United States...' was drafted, adopted, and ratified. Now, there were surely individuals engaged in various enterprises of self-government across the former thirteen colonies, and many of these may have even thought themselves as part of an American people. The American people may have been a sociological reality, but it was not a normative political reality. The legal person of the United States did not exist until the ratification of the constitution. Moreover, its continued existence as a juridical entity—as a legitimate sovereign—depends on the continued existence of the instrument that created it. But as long as it exists under that constitution, the collective self will retain its identity through time. This identity, as I mentioned, is distinct from that of its citizens. The popular sovereign, as a distinct self, is the bearer of its own rights and obligations, and these do not change because of a change in the makeup of the citizenry.

temporal projection of political obligations, is just as solidly founded on the substantive rights, liberties and procedures guaranteed by a constitution that meets the standard of liberal legitimacy, as by a voluntarist account that requires similar institutions to presume the tacit bestowal of consent.[52]

6. Interpretation, Amendment, and Reconstitution

After a constitution has been adopted, the exercise of collective self-government over the span of many generations—what Rubenfeld calls the continuing 'authorship' of the constitution—is realized primarily through two mechanisms: interpretation and amendment. I will not propose a full theory of intergenerational constitutional interpretation here, but only suggest some considerations that should bear on constitutional exegesis.

Take, as an example, the clause of the Eighth Amendment of the Constitution of the United States, which forbids the infliction of 'cruel and unusual punishments'. How should we read this clause in a way that demonstrates respect for the constitutional commitments of generations past and also recognizes our own participation in the constitutional endeavor? Historical, philosophical, and social scientific analysis may enter into our constitutional deliberation about the proper meaning of the clause, but none settles the question conclusively. All three inform what should be our ultimate question: Are we, as inheritors of a people's history but also as rational individuals, able to affirm our commitment to past or current practices of punishment? If not, we may recognize a change in popular opinion by interpreting the terms 'cruel

---

[52] I must note that Jed Rubenfeld objects to Rawls's model of hypothetical consent, because he regards it as a version of voluntarism: instead of the will of the present, Rawls substitutes the predicted will of a future people (Rubenfeld 2001: 65–67). This has the effect of denying that constitutional self-government is a temporally extended enterprise in which past and future generations are both authors; the future trumps the past. But I believe that Rubenfeld's interpretation of hypothetical consent is mistaken. From the standpoint of hypothetical consent, we can ask if, as participants in a perpetual constitutional enterprise, our fellow citizens situated in the future are well served by our present institutions; we can recommend that, in the spirit of the constitutional tradition in which we are placed, certain amendments be made to our legal and constitutional structure, or call for the constitutional text to be interpreted in ways that do not unjustly disadvantage our future fellow citizens. Rawls's self-assessment of his theory of justice directly engages it in this sort of perpetual constitutional enterprise: 'Our predecessors' he writes, 'in achieving certain things leave it up to us to pursue them further; their accomplishments affect our choice of endeavors and define a wider background against which our aims can be understood. To say that man is a historical being is to say that the realizations of the powers of human individuals living at any one time takes the cooperation of many generations (or even societies) over a long period of time. It also implies that this cooperation is guided at any moment by an understanding of what has been done in the past as it is interpreted by social tradition' (Rawls 1999a: 459–60).

and unusual' in a new way, or by amending to the constitution's text. But we ought not do this in abstraction of the history of the clause and the way that it has shaped our society, but rather in full awareness that we are full participants in that history. We may not always believe that we have arrived at a better truth about punishment, but rather to have evolved as a people.

Another way in which the distinctiveness of the project of a perpetual constitution can be appreciated is in the institution of constitutional amendment. The manner in which different generations can participate in the project of self-government while maintaining the collective identity of their political society through time is through the orderly evaluation and revision of their foundational charter within the terms and in accordance with the spirit of that charter. Through the power of amendment the conditions of justice between generations are preserved both by continuity and change: the just conditions of participation presuppose the permanence of the constitution itself, and participation in crafting those conditions—which is a necessary condition of self-government—is effected by the provisions for amending it. 'The very principle that gives the Constitution legitimate authority—the principle of self-government over time—requires that a nation be able to reject any part of a constitution whose commitments are no longer the people's own' (Rubenfeld 2001: 174).

The power of amendment is no argument against the perpetuity of a constitution, as long as it is contemplated in the instrument itself.[53] And it should be so contemplated, since it would be at best inconvenient, and at worst unjust, to make it impossible for a political society to make adjustments to its charter in response to changing circumstances. The power of amendment assures the ontological continuity of a political society by allowing it to change within the very set of norms that constitute its identity. But a valid question is whether, through change, that identity could be so dramatically altered as to cause a break in the society. In a constitution, there are limits to the manner by which change is effected and to the subject matter that is changed. On the one hand, a constitution is not respected if the mode of amendment is ignored; the formal guarantees of proceduralism are one of the ligaments that bind the ongoing identity of the political body: that we accept this constitution as constitutive means that we reject extra-constitutional means of amendment or repeal.

---

[53] Otsuka does grant that, in a self-expiring constitution, the clause that provides for periodic re-enactment would itself have to be approved again in every cycle (Otsuka 2003: 138n13). But does this clause reflect a demand of justice, or (a more stringent) one of legitimacy? And if the latter, why is it not counted among the conditions of legitimacy that are exempt from the requirement of consent? See the discussion in section four, above.

But there are also other provisions that may be essential to the identity of a legally constituted political community, and these will vary in each case. Rubenfeld states that, in a constitution of the kind he endorses, there cannot be 'a single permanently entrenched provision' (Rubenfeld 2001: 174). Yet many constitutions have just such entrenched clauses, and they perform an important function.[54] There are other provisions still that, while not formally sheltered from alteration or repeal, can nonetheless be historically understood as essential to the identity of a political society.[55] Certain political arrangements may also be so identified with a constitutional scheme as to require—not formally, but politically—the enactment of a new constitution in order to alter them.[56] It is not that a constitution cannot have unamendable provisions; that is factually and theoretically untrue. What we may conclude is that, if those provisions are changed, we no longer have an amended constitution, but an altogether different one.

Throughout this section, I have emphasized certain normatively important elements in the constitutional condition. But there are moral principles beyond it, and they may come into conflict with the project of a perpetual constitution.

[54] The definition of the United States as a federation of semi-sovereign states is so central to its constitution that the power of amendment is limited so 'that no State, without its Consent, shall be deprived of its equal Suffrage in the Senate' (*Const. of the United States*, Art. V). The German Basic Law removes from the scope of the power of amendment 'the division of the Federation into Länder, their participation in principle in the legislative process,' as well as the principles protecting human dignity (Art. 1) and the maintenance of constitutional order (Art. 20) (*Basic Law of the Federal Republic of Germany*, Art. 49). The Constitution of France prohibits any amendment that would subvert 'the republican form of government' (*Const. of the French Republic*, Art. 89). The Turkish constitution famously prohibits the repeal of the clauses 'establishing the form of the state as a Republic,' declaring that it is 'a democratic, secular and social state governed by the rule of law; bearing in mind the concepts of public peace, national solidarity and justice; respecting human rights; loyal to the nationalism of Atatürk, and based on the fundamental tenets set forth in the Preamble', and affirming the inviolability of its territory, the national language and the elements of its flag (*Const. of the Republic of Turkey*, Arts. 1–4).

These provisions of the Turkish constitution have been criticized, especially because the current constitution was imposed in 1982, under conditions of military rule. But the controversial provision on secularism was present in Turkish constitutions as early as 1928, and that on indivisibility of the state since 1961 (Jenkins 2001: 43). It is small comfort to note that there are undemocratic periods in most nations' histories, and the constitutional principles developed in these periods are often accepted once a transition to democracy is in effect.

[55] The First Amendment, although not originally part of the Constitution of the United States, or expressly protected from alteration or repeal, has presumably attained this status (Rawls 1993: 237–9; Fleming 1994: 371–3).

[56] Presumably, the change from the parliamentary democracy of the Fourth French Republic (inherited from the Third Republic) to the presidential system of the Fifth Republic was significant enough to require not just amendment of the old constitution, but a new fundamental charter (Thomson 1969: 255–8, 259–74). Nonetheless, the Constitution of the Fifth Republic incorporates, by reference, the Preamble of the 1946 Constitution (of the Fourth Republic), as well as the Declaration of the Rights of Man and Citizen of 1789, thus claiming (justifiably) some constitutional continuity with the original Republic.

It may be that the framework established by a constitution is no longer workable, has caused ever increasing instability, or has deep moral faults that cannot be remedied within the present structure. In that case, it may be necessary to make a break and reconstitute the political society along new lines. This prospect should be squarely faced. When the American colonists declared their independence it was not for the exclusive purpose of giving themselves a modern constitution, even if the prospect was in the minds of many. Their immediate reason was to extricate themselves from the constitution of Britain, which they deemed irreparably broken. Amendment was impossible under those circumstances; the polity had to begin anew. Similarly, after the Second World War, it was impossible for Germany to simply amend the laws of the Third Reich, or even to return to the Weimar constitution. The military defeat was incidental; what was crucial was that a moral transformation should occur, and that could only take place by negating continuity with the previous political society. In both cases, the continuity of the constitutional project was trumped by other moral considerations, and in both cases discontinuity was the right option. The political obligations which all generations commit themselves to respect, through their participation in a perpetual constitutional project, are important, but not absolute. It is also the responsibility of a constitutional people to know if and when—when justice demands it—to reconstitute itself.

7. Conclusion

A perpetual constitution aims to settle the political structure of a society and secure the rights of its citizens for an indefinite period of time, binding both present and future generations. Objections to the legitimacy of a perpetual constitution have been based on its supposed injustice to future generations, who would have had no part in enacting the constitution and would thus be precluded from choosing their own form of government. Thomas Jefferson argues that each generation is entirely sovereign unto itself, as no one has a natural right to bind his successors without their consent; a constitution, therefore, should lapse once a generation has passed from the world, and require reenactment by subsequent generations. Michael Otsuka improves on Jefferson's account by arguing that, given certain specified political conditions—pluralism, equality and order—members of a generations can be inferred to have actually, if only tacitly, consented to a constitutional structure; absent these conditions, however, a perpetual constitution is illegitimate, as consent to it cannot be inferred.

I have argued in this chapter in favor of the legitimacy of a perpetual constitution on three grounds: instrumental, normative, and ontological. On the first ground, a perpetual constitution is necessary to the pursuit of valuable public and personal endeavours. This argument is prefigured by James Madison, who predicts that a constitution that needs to be ratified at set periods will lead to political and economic instability. Yet a perpetual constitution not only prevents instability, but creates the conditions that enable individuals to engage in self-government and pursue what Lukas Meyer calls future-oriented projects. As such, a constitution should be understood not as a limit, but as what Stephen Holmes refers to as an enabling condition of democratic society.

On the second ground, a perpetual constitution can secure what John Rawls identifies as the bases of liberal legitimacy, the constitutional essentials that all reasonable citizens are expected to endorse. The defense of a perpetual constitution need not resort to the fiction of tacit consent to set up an enduring framework for democratic self-government, but has recourse to the mechanism of hypothetical consent, whereby the generation that enacts the constitution—and later ones called to interpret or amend it—ought to establish an institutional framework that ensures, to the greatest degree possible, that succeeding generations will be able to exercise popular sovereignty, that each will be capable of participating in the enterprise of collective self-government. These institutions, and the perpetual constitution that enshrines them, are not unjustly imposed on future generations; rather, they establish an institutional framework that secures the conditions of legitimate collective self-government.[57]

On the third ground, a perpetual constitution creates a collective agent—a people—from an aggregate of separate selves, each acting in their individual capacity. Where the normative argument looks to the relation between the sovereign and the individual, the ontological argument looks to the nature of the sovereign itself, explaining how the sovereign is a juristic person distinct from the individuals who exercise sovereignty. The medieval tradition of constitutionalism understood this, while the defenders of royal absolutism—of whom Jefferson is a reluctant heir—denied it. As Jed Rubenfeld maintains, collective self-government depends on the notion of a temporarily

---

[57] Now, that something is due to someone as a matter of justice does not mean that it may be imposed against the person's consent. An anonymous reviewer brings up military intervention intended to provoke the collapse of an unjust regime as a case in point. It seems true that the injustice of a regime is not sufficient to justify intervention. But we may think that there is a difference between an unjust regime and an illegitimate one, where the latter would not be able to object to intervention on consensual grounds, even if other reasons (e.g. harm to civilians) would advise against military action (cf. n 20 above).

extended people, in which past, present and future generations successively participate in the exercise of sovereignty. Constitutionalism makes the idea of a people intelligible. This argument can also be understood transcendentally: a constitution is a necessary precondition of sovereignty, and must therefore be presumed by any reference to the exercise of self-government by a collective agent.

Finally, it must be recognized that a perpetual constitution is not immutable. It calls for interpretation and may require amendment; in both cases, a people should be mindful of the historical development of their collective identity, and not succumb either to blind deference to the past, or to atemporal abstraction. Sometimes, however, practical or moral conditions may require a rupture in the constitutional identity of a people. But this is not to be taken lightly. Under ordinary circumstances, all generations who take up the task of self-government through time have a duty to respect the project of constitutionalism itself, which involves obligations of justice—for instance, in improving the institutions that secure popular sovereignty—and also a certain historical sensibility that understands the need to maintain and continue the constitutional endeavour.

References

BAILYN, B. (1992), *The Ideological Origins of the American Revolution* (Enlarged edn) (Cambridge, Mass.: Belknap Press).

BARRY, B. (1977), 'Justice Between Generations' in P. M. S. Hacker and J. Raz (eds.), *Law, Morality and Society: Essays in Honour of H.L.A. Hart* (Oxford: Clarendon Press), 268–84.

BERMAN, H. J. (2003), *Law and Revolution, II: The Impact of the Protestant Reformations on the Western Legal Tradition* (Cambridge, Mass.: Belknap Press).

BLACK, A. (1992), *Political Thought in Europe, 1250–1450* (Cambridge: Cambridge University Press).

BOGDANOR, V. (1997), *The Monarchy and the Constitution* (Oxford: Oxford University Press).

COHEN, J. (2003), 'For a Democratic Society', in S. Freeman (ed.), *The Cambridge Companion to Rawls* (Cambridge: Cambridge University Press), 86–138.

COKE, E. (2003), *The Selected Writings of Sir Edward Coke*, ed. S. Sheppard (Indianapolis: Liberty Fund).

FILMER, R. (1991), *Patriarcha*, ed. J. P. Sommerville (Cambridge: Cambridge University Press).

FLEMING, J. E. (1994), 'We the Exceptional American People', *Constitutional Commentary*, 11/2: 355–78.

GOSSERIES, A. (2003), 'Intergenerational Justice', in H. La Follette (ed.), *The Oxford Handbook of Practical Ethics* (Oxford: Oxford University Press), 459–84.

GREY, T. C. (1979), 'Constitutionalism: an analytic framework', in J. R. Pennock and J. W. Chapman (eds.), *Constitutionalism (NOMOS XX)* (New York: New York University Press), 189–209.

HIRSCHMAN, A. O. (2006), *Exit, Voice and Loyalty: Responses to Decline in Firms, Organizations, and States* (Cambridge, Mass.: Harvard University Press).

HOBBES, T. (1994), *Leviathan*, ed. E. Curley (Indianapolis: Hackett).

HOLMES, S. (1995), *Passions and Constraint: On the Theory of Liberal Democracy* (Chicago: University of Chicago Press).

HOUSE OF COMMONS (1766), *The Examination of Doctor Benjamin Franklin, before an August Assembly, Relating to the Stamp Act, &c.* Available at <http://galenet.galegroup.com/servlet/ECCO>.

ILLIES, C. F. R. (2003), *The Grounds of Ethical Judgement: New Transcendental Arguments in Moral Philosophy* (Oxford: Clarendon Press).

JAMES VI & I (1994), *Political Writings*, ed. J. P. Sommerville (Cambridge: Cambridge University Press).

JEFFERSON, T. (1905), *The Works of Thomas Jefferson*, Vol. 11, ed. Paul L. Ford (New York and London: G. P. Putnam's Sons). Available at <http://oll.libertyfund.org/ToC/0054-11.php>.

——(1975), *The Portable Thomas Jefferson*, ed. M. D. Peterson (New York: Penguin Books).

JENKINS, D. (2003), 'From Unwritten to Written: Transformation in the British Common-Law Constitution', *Vanderbilt Journal of Transnational Law* 36/3: 863–960.

JENKINS, G. (2001). *Context and Circumstance: The Turkish Military and Politics*. Adelphi Paper No. 337 (Oxford: Oxford University Press).

KANT, I. (1996), *Practical Philosophy*, ed. M. J. Gregor (Cambridge: Cambridge University Press).

KANTOROWICZ, E. H. (1957), *The King's Two Bodies: A Study in Mediaeval Political Theology* (Princeton: Princeton University Press).

LARMORE, C. (2003), 'Public Reason' in S. Freeman (ed.), *The Cambridge Companion to Rawls* (Cambridge: Cambridge University Press), 368–93.

LIBERAL DEMOCRATS (2005), *Liberal Democrats Policy Briefing 11*.

LOCKE, J. (1988), *Two Treatises of Government*, ed. P. Laslett (Cambridge: Cambridge University Press).

MADISON, J. (1986), 'Letter to Thomas Jefferson' (4 February 1790), in P. B. Kurland and R. Lerner (eds.), *The Founders' Constitution* (Chicago: University of Chicago Press), 70–71.

MEYER, L. (2004), 'Surviving Duties and Symbolic Compensation', in Lukas H. Meyer (ed.), *Justice in Time: Responding to Historic Injustice* (Baden-Baden: Nomos Verlagsgesellschaft), 173–83.

——(1997), 'More than they have a right to: future people and our future-oriented projects', in N. Fotion and J. C. Heller (eds.), *Contingent Future Persons: On the*

Ethics of Deciding Who Will Live, or Not, in the Future (London: Kluwer Academic Publishers), 137–56.

MᶜILWAIN, C. H. (1947), *Constitutionalism, Ancient and Modern* (Ithaca: Cornell University Press).

MICHELMAN, F. (2005), *Brennan and Democracy* (Princeton: Princeton University Press).

NOZICK, R. (1977), *Anarchy, State and Utopia* (New York: Basic Books).

OTIS, J. (1764), *The Rights of the British Colonies Asserted and Proved*. Available at <http://galenet.galegroup.com/servlet/ECCO>.

OTSUKA, M. (2003), *Libertarianism without Inequality* (Oxford: Oxford University Press).

—— (2006), 'Replies', *Iyyun* 55(July): 325–36.

PIPPIN, R. (2006), 'Mine and Thine? The Kantian state', in Paul Guyer (ed.), *The Cambridge Companion to Kant and Modern Philosophy* (New York: Cambridge University Press), 416–46.

PITKIN, H. (1965), 'Obligations and Consent—I', *American Political Science Review* 59/4: 990–9.

RAWLS, J. (1993), *Political Liberalism* (New York: Columbia University Press).

—— (1999a), *A Theory of Justice: Revised Edition* (Cambridge, Mass.: Harvard University Press).

—— (1999b), *Collected Papers* (Cambridge, Mass.: Harvard University Press).

—— (2001), *Justice as Fairness: A Restatement*, ed. E. Kelly (Cambridge: Cambridge University Press).

RUBENFELD, J. (2001), *Freedom and Time: A Theory of Constitutional Self-Government* (New Haven: Yale University Press).

SCHAPER, E. (1972), 'Arguing Transcendentally', *Kant-Studien*, 63/1: 101–16.

SIMMONS, A. J. (1979), *Moral Principles and Political Obligations*. Princeton: Princeton University Press.

—— (2001), *Justification and Legitimacy: Essays on Rights and Obligations* (Cambridge: Cambridge University Press).

SCHOCHET, G. J. (1979), 'Introduction: Constitutionalism, Liberalism, and the Study of Politics', in J. R. Pennock and J. W. Chapman (eds.), *Constitutionalism (NOMOS XX)* (New York: New York University Press), 1–15.

THOMSON, D. (1969), *Democracy in France since 1870* (5th edn., London: Oxford University Press).

Index*

* The editors warmly thank Keith Bustos (University of Bern) for having edited, revised, and finalised the Index.